D1569477

ALEXANDER P. DE SEVERSKY
AND THE QUEST FOR AIR POWER

# Alexander P. de Seversky

*and the* QUEST *for* AIR POWER

JAMES K. LIBBEY

*Potomac Books*
*Washington, D.C.*

© 2013 by the Board of Regents of
the University of Nebraska
All rights reserved
Potomac Books is an imprint of the
University of Nebraska Press.

Excerpts from Alexander P. de Seversky
Papers courtesy of Joshua Stoff, Curator,
Cradle of Aviation Museum;
Excerpts from "The Making of a War Hero"
by James K. Libbey in *Aviation History*
courtesy of Carl von Wodtke, Editor;
Excerpts from "Remember Billy
Mitchell!" by Alexander P. de Seversky
in *Air Power Historian* courtesy of Jim
Vertenten, Executive Director, Air
Force Historical Foundation; and
Excerpts from Elmer Sperry Papers courtesy
of Lynn Catanese, Manuscript & Archives
Department, Hagley Museum & Library.

Printed in the United States of
America on acid-free paper that meets
the American National Standards
Institute z39-48 Standard.

First Edition
10 9 8 7 6 5 4 3 2 1

Library of Congress Cataloging-
in-Publication Data
Libbey, James K.
Alexander P. de Seversky and the quest for
air power / James K. Libbey. — First edition.
pages cm
Includes bibliographical refer-
ences and index.
ISBN 978-1-61234-179-8 (hardcover:
alk. paper) — ISBN 978-1-61234-180-4
(electronic) 1. De Seversky, Alexander
P. (Alexander Procofieff), 1894–1974.
2. Aeronautical engineers—United
States—Biography. 3. Air power—United
States—History—20th century. 4.
Aeronautics, Military—United States—
History—20th century. I. Title.
TL540.D363L53 2013
623.74'6092—dc23
[B]
2013008387

Potomac Books
22841 Quicksilver Drive
Dulles, Virginia 20166

*To Joyce's friend*
*Diane M. A. Procofieff de Seversky*

Alexander P. de Seversky. *Courtesy of the Cradle of Aviation Museum*

# Contents

# Acknowledgments

Alexander P. de Seversky lived such a long and event-filled life that a reasonably complete biography can emerge only with the help of numerous individuals and organizations. In terms of the latter, the starting point for research began with support from Embry-Riddle Aeronautical University and a grant from the Kennan Institute of the Woodrow Wilson International Center for Scholars. Naturally, it is the archivists and librarians who open and make available the documents and literature held by their institutions. The centerpiece, of course, for the study of aviation history and aviators is the Smithsonian's National Air and Space Museum, now divided between Washington, D.C., and the Udvar-Hazy Center at Dulles International Airport. Until recently, both its library and photo archive were located in the nation's capital. The author's visit was arranged and materials were secured for him by Brian Nikles, Philip Edwards, Kate Igoe, and Mark Taylor. On the other hand, the largest collection of de Seversky documents is held by the Cradle of Aviation Museum on Long Island. While museum associate Julia L. Blum assisted with photos, curator Joshua Stoff and museum associate Glenn Appel made the author and his wife feel right at home during two lengthy visits to run through more than forty boxes of materials. The latter were large storage containers, not the elegant gray cartons employed by the Manuscript Reading Room of the Library of Congress. Regardless, the Library of Congress holds a number of de Seversky documents but also a bountiful collection of important collateral papers. Over a period of time, Jeff Flannery, Patrick Kerwin, Joseph Jackson, Bruce Kirby, Ernie

Emrich, and Jennifer Brathovde rendered their kind assistance. Because of de Seversky's lengthy association with the air force and its predecessors, a tremendous amount of information was acquired via the U.S. Air Force Historical Research Agency at Maxwell Air Force Base near Montgomery, Alabama. M. Sgt. Daniel Wheaton arranged the author's visit and archivist technician Sylvester Jackson secured numerous requested papers and rolls of microfilm.

Beyond the four significant collections listed previously, the author visited, received documents, or secured vital pieces of data from the following individuals: Victoria R. Aspinwall, director, Long Island Studies Institute, Hofstra University; Christine Yanette, publications assistant, *Signal Magazine*, Armed Forces Communications and Electronics Association; Marjorie McNinch, reference archivist, Manuscripts and Archives Department, Hagley Museum and Library; Valerii Matveevich Shishkin, director, Russian Central State Historical Archive, St. Petersburg; Emma Hochgesang, U.S. Air Force records officer; Lynn Steward, archivist, Washington National Records; David Giordano, archivist, National Archives and Records Administration; Abby L. Boggs, FOIA analyst, Wright-Patterson Air Force Base; John Espinal, ICIOD analyst, U.S. Air Force, Pentagon; Leslie Miller, customer service representative, *Dayton Daily News*; Karen M. Cook, base records manager, Wright-Patterson Air Force Base; V. M. Shabanov, department head, Document Information and Publication, Russian State War History Archives, Moscow; V. S. Sobolev, director, Russian State Archive War-Naval Fleet, St. Petersburg; Thomas W. Branigar, archivist, Dwight D. Eisenhower Presidential Library; Bruce Turner, head, Archives and Special Collections, University of Louisiana–Lafayette; Krista Strider, curator, U.S. Air Force Museum.

The author benefited from an outstanding collection of aviation-related, secondary sources located in the Jack Hunt Library at Embry-Riddle Aeronautical University. For books and articles not available in that library, needed materials were acquired promptly with the expert assistance of the interlibrary loan section staffed by Sue Burkhart, Ann Cash, Elizabeth Davis, and Doreen Winters. Suzanne Eichler responded to general library questions and Ed Murphy assisted with digital images. Additionally, Michael Gallen, director of Library Services, Proctor Library, Flagler College, made available helpful electronic databases. Finally, Annette Marotta, technician,

Billy Rose Theatre Division, New York Public Library, clarified information related to de Seversky's wife, Evelyn, and her career as a dancer.

The author is extremely grateful for the professional help and wise assistance of a number of well-qualified readers who viewed individual chapters. Because of technical details, some chapters received the attention of more than one specialist. The following list identifies each reader with the position held at the time the chapter was critiqued: David Schimmelpenninck van der Oye, chair, Department of History, Brock University; Terry Savery, former pilot, U.S. Air Force; Bruce W. Menning, professor of strategy, Department of Joint and Multinational Operations, U.S. Army Command and General Staff College, Fort Leavenworth; Stephen L. McFarland, vice provost for academic affairs, University of North Carolina–Wilmington; Rex Wade, professor, Department of History, George Mason University; Stephen G. Craft, associate chair, Department of Humanities/Social Sciences, Embry-Riddle Aeronautical University; Melville R. Byington Jr., professor emeritus of aeronautical science, Embry-Riddle Aeronautical University; Robert P. Cly, colonel, U.S. Air Force (retired); Bert Frandsen, associate professor, Air Command and Staff College, Maxwell Air Force Base; Peter Rounseville, chair, Department of Aeronautical Science, Embry-Riddle Aeronautical University; Ronald P. Bobroff, senior lecturer, Department of History, Wake Forest University; Walter J. Boyne, author and colonel, U.S. Air Force (retired); Douglas G. Culy, aircraft engine development engineer; Doris L. Rich, author; Dik Alan Daso, curator, National Air and Space Museum; Russell E. Lee, curator, National Air and Space Museum; Michael S. Sherry, R. W. Leopold Professor of History, Northwestern University; George C. Herring, history professor emeritus, University of Kentucky; Stephen Budiansky, author; Richard P. Hallion, curator, National Air and Space Museum; Tom D. Crouch, senior curator, National Air and Space Museum; Glenn J. Dorn, professor, Department of Humanities/Social Sciences, Embry-Riddle Aeronautical University; Anthony Reynolds, associate professor, Department of Physical Sciences, Embry-Riddle Aeronautical University.

Six individuals deserve special thanks. First and foremost, my wife, Joyce, served as the alpha editor to critique most chapters. Before that, she was the navigator for our many road trips to various archives. She often took notes or helped make copies of documents used as sources for the narrative.

Moreover, as a certified public accountant and certified internal auditor, she could decipher and interpret the economic data associated with de Seversky's several companies. Second, Dmitry Avdeev, a friend and native of St. Petersburg who had helped me gain entry to archival materials during one of my trips to Russia, also assisted me in securing key documents on de Seversky's early life. Meanwhile, Dudley A. Baringer, M.D., was kind enough to give his professional diagnosis of de Seversky's health during the Russian-American's declining years. While I have had the pleasure of talking with several people who remembered de Seversky, two knew him extremely well and were willing to share with me their detailed knowledge of the subject of this biography. Michail S. Ryl became a trusted employee in de Seversky's last corporation and was also close to Alexander's brother, George. Nicholas A. Pishvanov, who spent the summers of his youth in the de Seversky household and was treated like a son by the de Severskys, provided significant personal and background information. The author enjoyed and benefited from hours of conversation with Pishvanov. He also became a frequent correspondent who shared pages and pages of his reminiscences with me. Lastly, the book is dedicated to Joyce's friend, Diane M. A. Procofieff de Seversky. Diane's love for her father has turned her home into a shrine dedicated to his memory. She supplied me with a folio full of documents that might otherwise not be available. Among the unique items she gave me were rare recordings of Russian songs sung by de Seversky's brother, George, and father, Nicholas. In other cases, she saved me time by providing copies of documents, such as her father's death certificate, that are available to the public but only after a time-consuming request process. Finally, it would be impossible for me to keep the French side of the Procofieff/Seversky family straight without Diane's personal attachment, visits, and correspondence with that branch of Russian émigrés.

ALEXANDER P. DE SEVERSKY
AND THE QUEST FOR AIR POWER

# 1

## Introduction: The Russian in the Russian Context

Alexander P. de Seversky was born Aleksandr Nikolaevich Prokof'ev-Severskii. An obscure bureaucrat in the Russian Ministry of Foreign Affairs thought he would do a favor for the twenty-three-year-old Aleksandr (Alexander) when he applied for a passport to travel to the United States. Recognizing that the young naval air officer had earned acclaim across the empire as a war hero and had been fathered by a member of the upper class, the bureaucrat dropped from Alexander's passport his patronymic Nikolaevich (Nikolayevich), shifted half of his last name Prokof'ev (Procofieff) to the middle, and replaced the hyphen with a "de." The intended effect of this gesture is a bit subtle for most residents of the twenty-first century. Though soon replaced by English, the French language still served in 1917 as the medium of diplomacy. All those individuals who held responsible positions within the international realm would quickly recognize that the "de" often served as a mark of high status.[1]

The naval air officer accepted this alteration to his name and later explained his reasons to a writer for *The New Yorker* when the magazine decided to interview him in 1940. In the first place, the Russian government bowed to the reality of the times by issuing passports and other documents in the French language and forgoing the Cyrillic alphabet. Additionally, the hyphen in his last name conveyed a meaning similar to the French "de," which translates as "of" or "from." Since "sever" is Russian for "north," his original last name can be presented as "Procofieff of the North." Finally, between the time he applied for his travel documents and actually arrived in the United States, the revolution in Russia had brought a Soviet government to power, one that had no sympathy for the upper classes. Thus the Soviets were unlikely at any time to correct his documents. Indeed, the young man was fortunate to escape Soviet Russia with his life.[2]

His survival enabled the naval air officer to accept and use his altered name, one that served him well until his death in 1974. Alexander was born to Nikolai (Nicholas) and Vera in the city of Tiflis in the Caucasus Mountain region of the Russian Empire on June 7, 1894. His nativity occurred in the surroundings of the extended family and in what is T'bilisi today, the capital of the troubled Republic of Georgia. Eventually, the family would make the empire's capital city of St. Petersburg their home. Mother, father, and their newborn were with Nicholas's father Georgii (George) when Vera gave birth to the first of her two sons. The new grandfather served as a *polkovnik* (colonel) in the Imperial Russian Army Engineers. He distinguished himself by his participation in designing and supervising the construction of the Georgian Military Road through the Caucasus Mountains. And this brings us to an interesting feature at the start of Seversky's life. For centuries, Russia continued and even strengthened the medieval tradition of equating nobility with military leadership. The line of blue-blooded military officers who preceded Alexander as his ancestors guaranteed his birthright as a member of the aristocracy.[3]

### Like Father, Like Son

One exception broke this tradition and affected the course of Alexander's life. He inherited more from his father than simply brown hair, gray eyes, a pleasant face, and a short stature. Nicholas G. Seversky (his actual stage name) proved to be a free spirit and initially a great disappointment to the family and its conventions. Certainly, he briefly attended military school; however, he chose not to pursue an army career but instead to nurture his talents as a writer and singer. Eventually, his vocal talents gained for him widespread fame. Just as importantly, he availed himself of family resources and applied them to the Catherine Theater, where he became an impresario, producing popular music shows for the capital's citizens. His son Alexander managed to adhere to the older tradition by attending military schools and, later, by serving as a captain (junior grade; equivalent to the U.S. Navy's lieutenant commander) in the Russian navy and then, still later, a major in the U.S. Army Air Corps (U.S.A.A.C.). On the other hand, he also gained international fame as a writer who enjoyed singing and composing songs for fun.[4]

Alexander's father proved crucial to the course of his son's life in another way. Those who have written about Nicholas often describe him as a sportsman. Among the sporty activities earning him the sobriquet, he bought in 1909 and 1910 two French-designed aircraft, a Farman Model IV and a Bleriot Model XI. Before this purchase, Alexander and his younger brother, George, had become juvenile aviation buffs. They built numerous toy airplanes powered by rubber bands. Even at this early stage, Alexander's inventive streak emerged as he developed contra-rotating propellers to neutralize the torque produced by one set of whirling blades. In addition, he made a pendulum device linked to control surfaces to create stability in flight, a primitive precursor to the modern autopilot.[5]

One can imagine the great thrill these young aviation enthusiasts experienced when their father acquired the airplanes. Nicholas flew them frequently when weather permitted. In the natural course of events, Alexander and his younger brother became intimately familiar with both flight and these two distinctive flying machines. Nicholas and his friends had selected the aircraft because of their international reputations. Indeed, the Bleriot lookalike and Farman were well known among associates of the Imperial All-Russian Aero Club that licensed Russian aviators on behalf of the Fédération Aéronautique Internationale (FAI). Members included Nicholas Seversky as well as another aviator who would gain fame in Russia and America, Igor I. Sikorsky.[6]

Besides their familiarity among aero club members, the planes represented an important ingredient in the education of Alexander because of their significant differences in design as well as in the methods applied to control the craft in flight. The Farman, which had won prizes in 1909 for distance and duration during the world's first international air meet at Reims, France, was a biplane. This double-wing configuration remained standard in the construction of many aircraft built before 1930. By comparison, the original Bleriot Model XI, which was the first airplane to fly across the English Channel in 1909, possessed a single wing. In addition, these aircraft employed alternative ways for changing the attitude of the machines in flight.[7]

Both aircraft used elevators and rudders as control surfaces to alter pitch (up-down) and yaw (side-to-side) movements, respectively. The Wright brothers, Orville and Wilbur, are credited with placing the first movable elevators and rudders on successful aircraft in their glider of 1902 and their powered Wright Flyer of 1903. There is, however, a third way to change the attitude of an aircraft in atmospheric flight. This involves rotating the machine around its longitudinal axis or, succinctly, the roll function. When roll and yaw are combined, the airplane turns. The Wrights accomplished lateral control by twisting the tips of the wings in a technique called wing-warping. The designer Louis Bleriot, impressed by Wilbur Wright's demonstration flights in France in August 1908, borrowed the technique when he built the Model XI.[8]

By contrast, Henry Farman used ailerons (French for little wings) that were first installed on a 1904 glider built by another Frenchman, Robert Esnault-Pelterie. Wing-warping, though, soon went out of fashion. World War I accelerated technical advances as wartime manufacturers and military procurers sought stronger and faster aircraft with stable wings that could handle higher speeds and bear heavier loads. By the 1930s, when Alexander de Seversky developed one of America's first modern fighter aircraft, the P-35, the torsional flexing of wings for lateral control was not even a distant option. In fact, at that point, wings of high-performance aircraft were, and still are, cantilevered, meaning they possess such internal strength that external bracing of wires and struts is totally unnecessary.[9]

Despite aviation technology's speedy abandonment of wing-warping, the Bleriot replica turned out to be important to Nicholas and his son for symbolic and practical reasons. In addition to sponsoring the empire's first flight magazine, *Aeronautics*, the Imperial All-Russian Aero Club arranged for the serial manufacture of the Model XI. Nicholas Seversky and other club members formed the First Russian Aerostatics Company, which was housed in the Shchetinin Works of St. Petersburg. The latter enjoyed the status as Russia's first aircraft factory. Photographs of the Model XI from a correspondent in France enabled engineer Nicholas V. Rebikov to design and construct a Bleriot look-alike, christened the *Russia*, in 1910.[10]

Outwardly, the airplane matched the French original except for a skid that replaced the swivel tail-wheel. In reality, the craft did not measure up to the Model XI. From photographs, Rebikov could only hazard an educated guess at, for example, the length of Bleriot's fuselage. A three-cylinder, air-cooled engine powered *Russia*. Designed by an Italian, Alessandro Anzani, who made motorcycle engines, the aero motor achieved a horsepower rating of only twenty-five. The small, underpowered engine could barely get the plane airborne. And Nicholas Seversky was that first pilot to own the empire's first production aircraft. It is impossible not to conclude that Alexander's father served as a symbol of Russia's aviation pioneers.[11]

*Russia* worked well for Alexander's father for two years. After that, it became what is called in the trade a grass cutter, a powered but unflyable aircraft. By 1912 the damp Baltic weather increased the weight of the wood and fabric plane and the small Anzani motor lost power owing to wear. Nevertheless, the craft continued to serve a practical purpose. It and similar machines in various countries, including the United States, served as primary trainers. In those early days before computers and sophisticated simulators, flight students familiarized themselves with the movements, sounds, and controls of an airplane on the ground before engaging in actual flight. Even though the *Russia* no longer flew, Alexander de Seversky gained additional knowledge about flying machines through his intimate acquaintance with the grass cutter. Access to the Bleriot and rides in the Farman explain why several years later he required only six minutes and twenty-eight seconds of dual instruction before successfully completing his first solo flight as a military aviator.[12]

### The Declining Empire Strikes Back

In 1904, when he was ten years old, Alexander P. de Seversky entered a military school, fulfilling one of the traditions held by his aristocratic family. This notably auspicious start to Alexander's military career occurred at a decidedly unfavorable moment for the Russian Empire. It engaged Japan in war in 1904 and suffered during that conflict the Revolution of 1905. Collapse of the social order forced Tsar Nicholas II to make two decisions that violated his deepest convictions. First, he admitted defeat in the Russo-Japanese War by ratifying the Treaty of Portsmouth. Second, in the face of a massive general strike that shut down transportation, industry, and the government itself, he issued the October (1905) Manifesto. This was one of the very few concessions to public opinion in his reign. And it worked. The tsar promised to revise the Fundamental Laws, expand civil rights, and provide a legislative assembly, or Duma. Even though the latter was unrepresentative and unsubstantial, the manifesto effectively split the opposition. Most members of the upper and professional classes found hope in the manifesto, while many workers and peasants and their radical leaders despaired. This split, along with peace with Japan, enabled returning military units loyal to the tsar to join other security forces in reasserting central authority over industrial districts and the countryside.[13]

There is no information about how Alexander responded to these momentous events. What is known is that his attention was drawn to the difficulties between his parents, who divorced. His father subsequently remarried, Barbe (Barbara) Grigorievna Chonikin, who gave birth to Alexander's half sister, Nika, in 1906. Thus it would be an unbelievable stretch even to suggest that the preteen possessed anything more than a vague appreciation of the troubled Russian world he inhabited. On the other hand, the crises that erupted during the first two years of his formal education would profoundly affect the future of the young man whom friends and family called "Sasha." The tsar's manifesto managed to delay the successful revolution until 1917. And the tenuous control exercised by the tsarist administration, coupled with military defeat and a flawed industrial base, indirectly explains both the empire's quick participation and poor performance in the war that began in 1914. Serbia connects the dots of these issues. The tiny Balkan country was composed of Slavic speakers who also shared Russia's dominant Orthodox religion and Cyrillic alphabet. Most importantly, it had gained its independence from the Turks in the nineteenth century because of Russian victories over the Ottoman Empire. It is not too far-fetched to claim that the empire served as one of the founders of modern Serbia. This Russo-Serbian bond was tested by a serious critical situation in 1908, when the Austro-Hungarian Empire annexed the former Turkish province of Bosnia-Herzegovina, which had a substantial Serbian population. Belgrade had hoped to merge with the province to fulfill its dream of creating Greater Serbia. War nearly erupted as angry Serbian and Austrian troops confronted each other along their common border.[14]

After Germany sent Russia a threatening note, the Russians swallowed their pride and disappointed the Serbs by acknowledging Austria's annexation. Taxed by Japan's victory and weakened by internal strife, Tsar Nicholas II and his advisors had no choice; the use of military force to support Serbia was not an option. However, the tsarist government decided it could not fail its godchild a second time. In 1914 Austria declared war on Serbia following the assassination of the heir to the Austrian throne by a Serbian nationalist in June. The Russian Empire struck back by mobilizing its military against Austria and then Austria's German ally. At the beginning of August,

Germany moved against Russia and its partner, France. To accomplish the latter, the Germans invaded Belgium. Furious with Germany's assault on its small continental neighbor, wary of German hegemony on the continent and true to its entente with Russia and France, Great Britain and its empire entered the fray in opposition to Berlin and Vienna.[15]

## War and a Young Russian Naval Officer

By August 4, 1914, when the United States officially announced its neutrality, the conflict had already engulfed much of Europe, and it eventually ensnared Brazil, Bulgaria, China, Greece, Italy, Japan, Liberia, the Ottoman Empire, Portugal, Romania, Siam, and even the United States, which traded its neutral status for belligerency on April 6, 1917. The conflict, filled with a measure of honor and an abundance of horror, disrupted the lives of millions, including the Seversky family. Alexander's father enlisted in the Imperial Russian Air Service and became a flight instructor. By 1916 the Russian military operated twelve flight-training schools, but the oldest and largest were in Sevastopol, located on the Crimean Peninsula, and Gatchina, sited outside the capital (renamed the more Slavic-sounding Petrograd when war broke out). Nicholas was stationed at Gatchina, not far from home. His youngest son, George, joined him there and also served as a military flight instructor; his eldest son was already in the military before war began.[16]

Alexander had studied engineering and graduated in the fall of 1914 from the Imperial Russian Naval Academy and later earned the rank of *michman*. The term is correctly translated as warrant officer but is comparable to an ensign or second lieutenant in the U.S. military. When war began in August, he was placed in an accelerated program that assigned him as a cadet to complete his studies through active duty on board the torpedo boat *Beaver* in the Baltic Sea. The *Beaver*, hence de Seversky, participated with a flotilla of approximately one hundred warships in a grand defensive strategy designed to protect Russia's principal Baltic ports and the capital from German naval attack. The Russian navy accomplished its goal until 1917, when German land forces occupied Riga on September 3. Subsequently, the German navy successfully attacked Ösel, Dago, Worm, and Moon Islands—the gateway to the Gulf of Riga.[17]

The *Beaver* and its numerous sister boats along with destroyers and a dozen capital ships, cruisers, and dreadnoughts took up positions in the central Baltic Sea. The Imperial Russian Navy surprised the Germans by executing a mine-laying offensive. In the late summer and fall of 1914, Russian vessels placed thousands of mines in the central Baltic and then 1,164 mines along the German coast from Kolberg (today, Kolobrzeg) to Memel (today, Klaipeda). Six German ships, including a cruiser, fell victim to what the Russians considered the first line of defense for their leading ports. Over time, key islands were fitted out with large guns. Great attention was also paid to aircraft. For example, hangars were built to house flying boats (aircraft with hulls like ships) on several islands. Two of the more important naval air stations were located at Kilkond (today, Kihelkonna) and at Zerel (today, Sêäre) on Ösel (today, Saaremaa) Island commanding the entrance to the Gulf of Riga.[18]

The excellent strategy employed by the Baltic Fleet was attributable to its visionary commander, Adm. Nicholas Otto von Essen. Along with the effective mine-laying operation, he enjoyed a triumph in intelligence-gathering when he seized German naval codes from the grounded cruiser *Magdeburg*. Before his early death in 1915, Admiral Essen promoted aviation and integrated it into combined-arms operations, relying on aircraft for long-range reconnaissance of German naval activity. Ultimately, the Russian naval air arm in the Baltic expected to operate two air brigades composed of a total of six air divisions, each with three detachments or flights of six aircraft. The contemplated number of operational aircraft totaled 108, but when war began the Baltic Fleet possessed a mere eight pilots.[19]

## The Making of a Russian Naval Aviator

De Seversky was part of the solution to the scant number of aviators assigned to the Baltic Fleet. Responding to a naval plea for personnel interested in flying, the young sea officer submitted a successful transfer request. He could indicate on the form his intimate knowledge of flying machines. His father took him up in the Farman as early as 1910. And during his studies at the naval academy in St. Petersburg, de Seversky spent much of his free time at the Korpusnoi Aerodrome, where his father's friend, Sikorsky, tested a number of airplanes he designed, including the behemoth *Il'ia Muromets*, the world's first four-engine, reconnaissance-bomber. Not only did de Seversky fly in Igor's larger craft, but he gained an appreciation for the science of design and the importance of flight-testing new airframes.[20]

Over the winter of 1914–1915, de Seversky took a four-month course at the School of Theoretical Aviation in Moscow. It functioned as a type of ground school for aviators, but it also included elements of design taught by the school's founder and Russia's most famous aerodynamicist, Nikolai E. Zhukovskii. Coupled with his engineering studies at the naval academy, the instruction at the school gave de Seversky several of the basic skills needed for designing an airplane. Zhukovskii, for example, had calculated the lifting capacity of various wing forms, a key ingredient in creating flyable, heavier-than-air, craft. After his studies in Moscow, the young naval officer was ordered in March to continue his basic aviation training at the army's largest flight center in Gatchina.[21]

Twenty-seven miles south of Petrograd, Gatchina had been a nondescript village until 1766, when Empress Catherine the Great engaged Italian architect Antonio Rinaldi to plan and build a summer palace there. The location was removed from the unhealthy marshland upon which the capital and her winter residence, the Hermitage, were erected. By the time de Seversky arrived in March 1915, the Gatchina Palace had become more art museum than Romanov summer home. During the interim, the Imperial Russian Army Air Service had converted vacant lands adjacent to the palace into a large and well-equipped training center for pilots, pilot-observers, and engine mechanics. All three categories of personnel learned from flying or working on the Farman Model IV.[22]

Farman quickly emerged as Russia's ubiquitous aircraft for primary flight instruction for civilians and the military in the years immediately before and after World War I began. Alexander's father was partly responsible for this phenomenon. The Imperial All-Russian Aero Club encouraged a member, Vladimir A. Lebedev, to travel in 1909 to France, then the aviation center of the world. Lebedev attended a flight school sponsored by the internationally renowned pioneer Henry Farman. The Russian also purchased and returned to St. Petersburg with a Farman Model III airplane. Shortly thereafter, he gave rides and flight instruction to aero club members, including Nicholas Seversky. Added to the fact that most of Russia's pioneering aviators learned how to fly on the machine, a Moscow-based firm, the Dukh Company, converted from motorcycle to aircraft production and manufactured in 1910 the first six of hundreds of Farmans built in Russia under license.[23]

The early Dukh-built aircraft carried the designation Model IV, which differed from the previous mark by the shortened length of the wooden skids. Attached near the two sets of the double-wheeled landing gear, the skids prevented the craft from nosing over during a rough landing. Powered by a Gnome or similar rotary engine rated at fifty horsepower, the Farman's key advantage as a trainer was that, unlike the single-seat Bleriot discussed previously, the Model IV possessed enough capacity to carry two people at the exceptionally tame speed of thirty-five miles per hour. In one sense, the Model IV resembled the earliest pusher biplanes associated with such American pioneers as the Wright brothers and Glenn H. Curtiss. For instance, similar to the Wright Model A, the pilot sat on the leading edge of the lower wing. By contrast, the Farman's controls anticipated more modern aircraft. A single stick moved ailerons and elevators and a pivoting crossbar operated by the pilot's feet manipulated the rudder to the left or right.[24]

While Alexander and his brother George played from time to time with the Bleriot look-alike, *Russia*, they learned to fly airplanes by sitting with their father during flights of his Farman Model IV. It is this youthful experience that explains the unusually short flight training course reserved exclusively for Alexander when he arrived at Gatchina in the early spring of 1915. He could dispense with the normal training program. It required student pilots to begin their lessons by spending several sessions handling and steering the Model IV on the ground in order to gain a feel for the sights, sounds, and controls of the plane. The "groundlings" performed their orientation tasks for a number of days on a lengthy strip. It bordered railroad tracks on one side and a stand of tall trees on the other, which separated the isolated strip from the main airfield that the Russians (and English) called an aerodrome.[25]

In lieu of this preliminary activity, George took his older brother up for a short reorientation flight that lasted less than seven minutes. It had to be an "interesting" moment in their lives since the pair had jointly gulped down a major swig of sibling rivalry years earlier. At Gatchina, the Farman was set up with a small, slatted wooden seat for the student who sat immediately behind the pilot instructor during the dual instruction phase of the training program. Despite the seating arrangement, the brothers could share the tall stick that controlled pitch and roll. While Alexander knew the aircraft well, he needed this flight opportunity to remind his brain and muscle memory about the peculiarities of the Model IV. Later in the war, the Russians employed for training purposes an advanced and safer Farman equipped with an enclosed fuselage, a pilot cockpit, a passenger seat, and an eighty horsepower engine. Meanwhile, it was only too easy to mishandle and suffer mishap in the earlier version flown by the Severskys.[26]

Besides the Gnome rotary taking a vacation at inopportune moments, the engine barely produced enough power for the task. Alexander also appreciated the fact that in this airplane he was never very far from a stall. The latter occurs when lift is suddenly lost from the breakdown of airflow over the wings. As a result, the elder Seversky brother knew the benefits of beginning a shallow descent to pick up speed before attempting to turn; otherwise, the wings' angle of attack to the relative airflow would reach a critical point as lift disappeared and the Farman would be converted abruptly from a flying machine to a falling rock. And landing the Model IV often proved hazardous to plane and pilot alike.[27]

The rotary engines used at the time lacked carburetors and operated only at full power. To regulate speed, the pilot had to flip the ignition switch back and forth between the "on" and "off" positions. When the engine was "off," the powerplant and propeller blades continued to rotate around the crankshaft as the aircraft glided through the air. The engine's constant rotation allowed it to resume full power the moment the pilot flipped the ignition switch back to the "on" position. In more advanced rotary-powered aircraft, a pilot would perform deadstick landings by turning off the engine during the landing approach. By contrast, the Farman Model IV possessed an eccentric characteristic. Cutting the engine caused the tail to drop. The pilot who prematurely turned off the ignition while approaching a landing strip would be lucky to destroy only the plane's landing gear and suffer serious bruises. As George and Alexander returned to the Gatchina Aerodrome from the brief flight, they had to bring the craft down in a powered, shallow glide, switching off the engine and leveling the plane just before the wheels touched down.[28]

After several circles around the Gatchina Aerodrome and with just a few minutes of official flying time, Alexander was prepared to take his first solo flight as a military aviator. His rapid completion of the preliminary flight training program near the Petrograd capital resulted in his immediate transfer south in the early spring of 1915. He traveled by train to the Imperial Russian Army's Military School of Aeronautics near Sevastopol. The city also served as the home port to the Imperial Russian Navy's Black Sea Fleet, then fully engaged in wartime activity against both Turkish and German vessels. At the army school, de Seversky studied military tactics and the interrelationship of the air service with those tactics. He subsequently took advanced courses from the navy that focused on naval aviation and structural mechanics. The latter sharpened his skills as a promising aeronautical engineer.[29]

Meanwhile, de Seversky undertook advanced flight training on the French-designed Voisin III. A product of the company founded by the brothers Charles and Gabriel Voisin, the first version, or Model L, appeared in 1913. It was an engaging pusher biplane with a cruciform tail and an open, two-seat cockpit forward of the engine and propeller. The landing gear consisted of four wheels spaced like those of an automobile, or, more accurately, like those of a shopping cart since the front wheels were closer together. The early series that de Seversky flew in April and May 1915 had 60 percent more power and twice the speed of the Farman. Later editions, Model LA and Model LAS, had bigger engines. Neither as fast nor as maneuverable as contemporary warplanes, the Voisin III and successors IV–XI were remarkably adaptable, ranging from bombers to trainers, and hence stayed in production for war's duration.[30]

The fact that Voisin had performance issues and never quite measured up to comparable German machines partly explains why France willingly supplied its Russian ally with a large number of these aircraft. And, of course, Russia always acquired last year's model. Regardless, on May 14, 1915, de Seversky received his naval aviator wings, a circular pilot's badge made from oxidized silver and showing a winged Imperial Russian crest surmounted by an anchor. It was worn on the left breast pocket of the uniform. The navy also promoted him to *mladshii leitenant*, the equivalent of lieutenant junior grade in the U.S. Navy or first lieutenant in the U.S. Army. In June, after completing both army and navy courses and just days after his twenty-first birthday, de Seversky received orders to return to the northern theater of war from which he had come. Now, however, instead of one of many and often anonymous naval officers, he returned to duty on the Baltic Sea as a member of an elite and often romanticized group of military pilots serving Imperial Russia at its moment of greatest trial.[31]

## Reflections

Experience has taught the author that the subject of a biography inevitably conducts guerrilla warfare against current or future life writers. If still alive, the subject tends to forget his/her questionable actions and negative attributes in an interview; if deceased, the subject has culled personal papers and removed most documents that might be unflattering. Alexander P. de Seversky is certainly no different. Moreover, two other problems make it difficult to re-create his life story. First, and beyond the fact that his contemporaries are deceased, de Seversky did not realize until later in life that he was a person of consequence who should save materials to validate his accomplishments. Second, he was among the vanquished, rather than the victors, of the Russian Revolution. As a result, his family and home were torn apart, and he was forced to flee the country of his birth or forfeit his life. Thus the normal panoply of heirlooms, pictures, official documents, diaries, and correspondence that a member of the Russian upper class would possess in the period before World War I vaporized in the flames of political and social chaos that occurred in 1917–1918.

Despite these severe limitations, there is sufficient evidence to make several basic observations about de Seversky during the first twenty-one years of his life. He relished his aristocratic heritage and confirmed his social status by attending military schools and graduating from the Imperial Russian Naval Academy. In addition to membership in Russia's exclusive society, de Seversky's father gave him two lifelong loves: music and airplanes. It is important to keep in mind that the elder Seversky was not only a professional musician but also a genuine aviation pioneer who owned and operated two quite different aircraft. Seversky's first-born son gained intimate knowledge of these planes. In addition, he became familiar with a variety of other aircraft owned or built by members of the Imperial All-Russian Aero Club, including those designed by a lifelong acquaintance, Sikorsky. Finally, through study in military schools, de Seversky not only gained an appreciation for the tactics and strategies required for successful warfare; he also developed engineering skills that merged this appreciation with his growing knowledge of the structures and qualities of airplanes. Coupled with his childhood experiences as an innovator in building model airplanes, the adult engineer soon demonstrated an inventive streak in advancing technologies to improve the effectiveness of military aircraft. It is a trait that will color and characterize de Seversky's life for the next quarter century.

# 2

# The Russian Ace in
# the Great War

When Alexander P. de Seversky arrived at the Imperial Russian Navy air station at Revel (today, Tallinn) at the start of July 1915, he was one of only a handful of qualified pilots then available to the Baltic Fleet. He spent a couple days at Revel flying and becoming acquainted with the common piece of equipment on hand at the time, the Franco-British Aviation Company's FBA flying boat. Designed by Russia's wartime allies in the west, the hulled craft was built in Russia by Vladimir A. Lebedev, the same individual sent to France in 1909 by the Imperial All-Russian Aero Club to study flight under the direction of the great aviation pioneer, Henry Farman. The FBA was configured as a sesquiplane, a biplane with a smaller lower wing that mounted a balancing float at each tip. When loaded with two crew members and four small bombs, its single Clerget rotary engine of 130 hp swinging a backward-facing propeller could barely push the craft through the air faster than a mile a minute.[1]

Thus the FBA failed to match even the poor performance of the Voisin, which de Seversky had flown at Sevastopol. Despite this, his brief flights at Revel earned him his military pilot rating, Certificate No. 337. Immediately, the naval air arm transferred him to the Second Bombing-Reconnaissance Squadron, a hydroaeroplane unit headquartered at Kilkond on Ösel Island. Along with three smaller islands, Ösel served as a gateway to the entrance of the Gulf of Riga. These islands represented the Imperial Russian Navy's last line of defense to protect Riga, one of the empire's most important cities, against German attack from the sea. Once de Seversky arrived at the island base, Squadron Leader Vladimir Litvinov assigned the freshly minted naval pilot to his billet, his FBA, and his mechanic-observer, Anatolii Blinov. He repaired the FBA and serviced its engine. Before a mission, Blinov also installed, after removing the detonation cap guards, small bombs, two each on racks located immediately next to both sides of the cockpit. Stored upright, the business end of each bomb was on top to prevent an enemy bullet from striking the detonation cap. One feature of the FBA merits mention. The craft had a range (flight distance) of approximately 180 miles, or a practical combat range, a round-trip that also accounts for time over target of eighty miles. Kilkond was around 175 miles from Memel, the closest German city. De Seversky's squadron, however, regularly bombed and reconnoitered German forces, one of many indicators suggesting the war had gone horribly wrong for Russia by the summer of 1915.[2]

## How the War Came to Kilkond and de Seversky

This was not the case in the earliest phases of the conflict. The empire shocked both Germans and Austrians by the relative speed with which it mobilized its armies. Military commanders in Berlin and Vienna had assumed that Russia's backward nature and limited railroad capacity would require the Russians to take six or more weeks to organize forces and supplies before conducting a major military operation. To the contrary, Petrograd sent two northern armies into German East Prussia and additional vast forces in the south into Austro-Hungarian Galicia all within the war's opening month of August 1914. From the standpoint of the Allies, the good news was the Russian initiatives seriously challenged the military agendas of both Germany and Austria-Hungary, the nucleus of the Central Powers. Russian troops in East Prussia forced German commanders to send reinforcements eastward, which aided the French and British in stalling the German attack in the west during the Battle of the Marne. Meanwhile, the Austrians frantically focused their military energies on defending their territory against the Russians. As a result, the Austro-Hungarian Empire failed to conduct a decisive offensive against Serbia. Thus the tiny country responsible for involving Russia and firing the war's first shot managed to retain its autonomy until October–November 1915.[3]

Over the winter of 1914–1915, battles raged between Germans and Russians over territory that today belongs to Poland. Both sides enjoyed victory and suffered defeat, but the same could not be said for the southern portion of the eastern front. There the Austro-Hungarian units took such a beating that the Germans feared one more Russian offensive in the spring of 1915 might cause the army of their Viennese ally to disintegrate. To end the ponderous and painful progress of the war in the north and avoid outright defeat for Austria-Hungary, Germany took an extraordinary step. It transferred eight seasoned and well-equipped divisions from the stalemated western front in order to gain an advantage on the eastern front. Organized as the Eleventh Army, it began on May 2, 1915, a four-hour bombardment that served as a frightful lesson of what artillery can do against a semi-exposed enemy. Russians perished by the thousands. Through an elephantine gap that soon reached twenty-eight miles poured German and Austrian troops. The breakthrough was so wide and deep that the Russians could not close it off. In a relatively short time, the eastern front from the Baltic to Romania crumbled and then mutated into the Great Retreat, which drove the empire's soldiers deep within Imperial Russia.[4]

Before the German offensive began, a related plan emerged in April 1915, one that soon impacted the naval air station at Kilkond and shortly thereafter its newest pilot, Lt. de Seversky. Late in April, Gen. Erich Ludendorff, one of the Second Reich's principal commanders in the east, set in motion a strong cavalry and infantry force that invaded Russia north and east along the Baltic coast in Courland (today, the country of Latvia). Though much of the territory lacked strategic value, a successful foray could and would carry German forces to the edge of Riga. A major port and metropolitan center, Riga was the terminus for a direct rail line to the Petrograd capital. Any threat to this center would evoke an aggressive Russian response. And this was the whole point to Ludendorff's exercise. It cleverly drew Russian reserve forces away from the German attack in Galicia. The Russians did indeed comb their reserves and eventually thrust sixteen divisions against the enemy, checking but not overcoming the German incursion. During the interim, the lightly defended area quickly fell to the Germans. For example, their army and navy conducted a combined operation halfway up the Courland coast. On May 7 and 8, 1915, the fortress and port of Libau (today, Liepāja) was captured, enabling the German Fleet to convert the city into a forward naval and air base. It was aimed at the Irben Straits between Courland and Ösel Island, which led into the Gulf of Riga. By June 28, two German cruisers, *Beowulf* and *Augsburg*, accompanied by destroyers and aircraft, shelled the town of Windau (today, Ventspils) about forty miles from the southern tip of Ösel.[5]

## The Lieutenant's First Mission

On July 18, 1915, shortly after Alexander P. de Seversky's first mission, the Germans occupied Windau. Hence, just as the young naval aviator arrived at his post, the German military nearly completed their conquest of Courland and already probed with ships and aircraft Russian defenses around and in the Irben Straits. Personnel at the naval air stations at Zerel and Kilkond found themselves in a state of continuous alert and activity, performing reconnaissance and bombing targets of opportunity against the German enemy. It was no surprise, then, on the evening of July 15, when Squadron Commander Litvinov carried news of the enemy to his pilots in the Officers' Club. The men were playing cards, listening to phonograph disks, and telling their favorite war stories. Litvinov interrupted their relaxation long enough to brief them about a couple of German gunboats that had been spotted in a nearby cove. Since most Russian warships engaged the Germans farther south, the single remaining destroyer had to stay in Kilkond Bay. He asked for a volunteer to join him in startling the craft by dropping a few bombs. Damage from ordnance that weighed somewhere between thirty and forty pounds would be minimal, but the shock of being attacked as well as exposed would likely force the gunboats to cast off and sail away.[6]

"I was a tough-muscled youngster with a daredevil streak . . .," de Seversky later recalled, "[and] jumped to my feet faster than anyone else." Litvinov had his volunteer and de Seversky had his first combat mission as a pilot. Before long, the two armed FBAs glided away from the air station and took off from Kilkond Bay. Despite the late hour, the "season of white nights" produced a glimmer of light and gave the crews some visibility. The challenge, though, proved to be flying as much as seeing. Windy and cloudy conditions forced the flying boats to split apart out of formation. De Seversky, his aircraft some distance from his commander's and in dim light, failed to see Litvinov's frantic hand signals indicating his intent to turn around and head back to the Kilkond Naval Air Station. Hence Lieutenant de Seversky and Sergeant Blinov approached the cove that held German war vessels without support.[7]

The Germans were caught off guard and, most likely, very unhappy that the Russians had uncovered their cozy anchorage. But well before de Seversky and Blinov dropped any bombs, the sailors heard the loud clatter of the Clerget rotary engine as the FBA approached the vessels. The Russians managed to release all but one of their bombs. A bright flash from the deck of a gunboat marked a successful strike. The hope, however, of a massive ship-sinking explosion could be fulfilled only if a small bomb struck mines or other ordnance stored on the top deck of the enemy ship. Meanwhile, as the bombs fell, the Germans peppered the sky with antiaircraft and small arms fire. Bullets notched and splintered the FBA's wooden hull, but a shell fragment from a larger gun tore a hole in one of the control surfaces of the machine.[8]

Immediately, de Seversky broke off the attack and counted his blessings that the flying boat still flew. The Russians headed back to Kilkond, but the FBA proved hard to handle and lost altitude with each passing kilometer. Fortunately, the craft descended to the water just as it entered Kilkond Bay and within sight of the naval base. As the FBA splashed down with a jolt, de Seversky caught out of the corner of his eye Blinov trying desperately to replace the detonation cap guard on the last bomb. Suddenly, the device exploded, killing the mechanic-observer, pulverizing the starboard side of the craft, and hurling the pilot into the water. Dazed, de Seversky briefly sank but the cold water revived him enough that he struggled to the surface, coughing out salt water and gasping for air. A port-side lower wing with a balancing float at the tip also managed to survive to give the young man a small island of safety as a defense against fainting and then drowning.[9]

As might be expected, intelligence of nearby German war vessels prompted the Russians to have the air base destroyer patrolling the waters in and around Kilkond Bay. Officers and men on the Russian ship observed the flash of the FBA's bomb and steamed quickly to the site to investigate. Amazingly, as the destroyer approached, de Seversky remained conscious. In excruciating pain, he explored his body. Nearly thirty years later, he could state matter-of-factly that when he reached his lower right leg, "I found warm and mushy nothingness." Through his sharp pain, he viewed a "newsreel" of his earlier life when he fenced, skated, skied, flew, played football (soccer), and danced with attractive young ladies in St. Petersburg/Petrograd. "And above it all, pounding through every aching nerve, was the incredible, the impossible thought that I was crippled forever and ever; that I could never fly again; that even if I were saved, life was ended now that my physique was broken."[10]

The destroyer raced the injured combat pilot to the spanking new base clinic. Not only did everything shine in the facility, but the doctor and nurses all smiled and behaved in almost a festive mood. As de Seversky later discovered, he inaugurated the facility as its first combat casualty, one who offered interesting complications to the health care personnel. His weakened condition prevented the use of anesthetics. He had to sit on the operating table, his leg injected with morphine, and sip brandy as he watched the surgeon amputating his leg below the knee. After the procedure, another war vessel transferred him to the larger hospital at the main destroyer base at Revel. His father, Nicholas, met him there after flying to Revel from what was then his combat duty station as a pilot with the Squadron of Flying Ships, or EVK, which operated Igor Sikorsky's four-engine reconnaissance-bomber, the *Il'ia Muromets*.[11]

## From Recovery to Reassignment

Together, father and son warded off the doctors' recommendations that Alexander undergo a radical leg amputation at the hip. Medical specialists feared the onset of deadly gangrene should the traumatized stump remain. De Seversky, who briefly contemplated suicide while still in the waters of Kilkond Bay, now took heart and hope in preserving every centimeter of flesh and bone. More leg meant a better chance he could fly again. Anything less, in his opinion, would be death regardless. And de Seversky had to continue this battle to save his stump with two more sets of doctors. Because the naval base at Revel might come under Zeppelin attack, the young pilot was transferred to the naval hospital at Kronstadt, a key port on Kotlin Island at the eastern end of the Gulf of Finland within twenty miles of Petrograd. Finally, the injured flyer completed his recuperation in the capital city at a luxurious clinic under the control of Adm. Ivan Grigorovich, minister of the Imperial Russian Navy.[12]

Precisely because he ended up in Petrograd near family and friends and with the best medical care then available, his months of convalescence were not totally unpleasant. To be sure, there were moments of pain and discomfort when doctors felt compelled to whittle away a small portion of his stump. But once the crisis passed and his strength returned, de Seversky could appreciate the "sympathy and human understanding" that surrounded him and the joy of being "pulled back from the brink of extinction." Indeed, there were flirtations with nurses and comradeships with patients plus other distractions to make hospital life more than tolerable. De Seversky even acquired from his half sister, Nika, a stuffed toy monkey, Iasha, which became his good luck charm for the remainder of the war. Over time, he mastered the use of crutches and applied his inventive streak to designing artificial limbs that would enable him to take to the sky.[13]

The young man possessed a consuming desire to return to a combat squadron as a pilot. Regrettably for him, everyone else from medical personnel to military officers assumed he would never fly again and issued certificates and judgments that converted this assumption to the status of military fiat. So, in March 1916, after his full recovery but before he had been fitted for a wooden prosthesis, the navy reassigned him to the duty of chief naval aircraft inspector for the Petrograd District. The title was a bit more glorious than the task. De Seversky examined aircraft and reviewed flight tests of planes destined for war service. Considering the number of aircraft factories in the capital, the assignment might have been overwhelming, except for the fact that the navy's immediate, though not exclusive, concern focused on flying boats.[14]

These had been built by Vladimir A. Lebedev's factory but increasingly the navy turned to the Shchetinin Aircraft Company, Russia's first airplane manufacturer. It built the "M" series of flying boats ("M" for *morskoi*, or naval) conceived by Dimitrii Pavlovich Grigorovich. De Seversky worked with Grigorovich on what turned out to be the first Russian-designed naval aircraft to go into major production during the war, the M-9. The young pilot's brief combat experience allowed him to encourage the Shchetinin designer to include a forward, rotating machine gun for the craft and some armor for the crew. Indeed, Grigorovich used thicker planking and extra frames for the hull to provide a sturdy flying boat, one impervious to small arms fire and strong enough to carry forty-pound bombs or heavier weapons.[15]

As de Seversky worked and conversed with Grigorovich, Lebedev, Sikorsky, and other airplane architects, he gained an appreciation for how an aircraft design is translated from the drawing board to the finished product through a multistaged manufacturing process. The young, one-legged naval officer absorbed the techniques for creating serially built aircraft and applied them later in life when he held contracts to produce military aircraft for the U.S. Army Air Corps, grandfather to the modern air force. By his own admission, de Seversky originally viewed flight as sport. Now his time in factories and talks with engineers gave him fresh insights into the problems of aerodynamics and, in the case of flying boats, hydrodynamics. His simpler notions metamorphosed into a more sophisticated understanding that science, rather than daring, is the chief component to flight.[16]

In the midst of his inspections, de Seversky was fitted with a wooden prosthesis from the knee down. At first, he thought, "I should never be able to manage it. I seemed to be dragging a thousand tons through life; it was hopelessly painful." But over time and with daily use, the artificial limb became an accepted extension to his body. Muscles around his lower abdomen, pelvis, hips, and thighs adjusted to the weight and slowly he shifted from dragging the wooden device to lifting it and using it much as he had when his right lower leg was flesh and bone. Meanwhile, as his navy assignment took him to air stations and aerodromes, sympathetic pilots allowed him to fly as an observer. And on the basis of ground-testing the controls, he spent hours in the cockpits of aircraft purchased by the navy. In reality, he tested his ability to manipulate the floor-located rudder bar with his real and artificial limbs.[17]

De Seversky's interaction with pilots who were either coming from or going to war zones only sharpened his desire to return to the air and combat. In fact, he flew surreptitiously. His secret could not be kept from several lower level officers, but no one in authority wanted to make a decision that might lead to the destruction of government property whether pilot or plane. So the brash young man plotted a public display of his ability to fly, one that would force the issue. In May 1916 de Seversky and a team of mechanics and pilots traveled by train from Petrograd to Sevastopol, accompanied by several dismantled M-9 flying boats. They were going to be shown to the military brass of both the Baltic and Black Sea Fleets. De Seversky supervised the reassembly of the aircraft and readied the M-9s for the demonstration flights.[18]

"On the morning of the big show," de Seversky remembered, "one of the airplanes gave the damnedest exhibition of stunting that the gold-braided dignitaries down below had ever seen." The M-9 climbed, dove, rolled, looped, and performed a chandelle in which the craft ascended and turned to change flight direction and gain altitude at the same time. The thrilling display of aerobatics was capped by absolute shock when it was discovered the craft had been piloted by the one-legged de Seversky. Capt. M. Shcherbachov, the young lieutenant's superior officer, was furious and had the unauthorized pilot arrested for insubordination. Many of the high-ranking officers, however, were more amazed than annoyed. Some, in fact, were downright pleased by the expert skill and bold spirit demonstrated by the amputee. Clearly, de Seversky, even minus a limb, had to be counted among the best pilots in the Imperial Russian Navy.[19]

One witness, Rear Adm. Adrian I. Nepenin, sent a report of the incident to Mogilev, General Headquarters, or Stavka, of the Russian military after the great German offensive of 1915. At the time, Nepenin commanded naval aviation for the Baltic Fleet. A few weeks after this event, he replaced Rear Adm. Vasilii Kanin as commander-in-chief of the Imperial Russian Navy in the Baltic theater. Nepenin's report focused on the courage and flying talent of de Seversky and raised the question whether permission should be granted to allow the young lieutenant to return to combat flight duty. At Stavka, the admiral's interesting report made the rounds until it ended up in the hands of Tsar Nicholas II. The autocrat of all the Russias returned the report with a handwritten note: "Read. Admire. Let Fly. Nikolai."[20]

## The Making of an Ace Pilot

Hence Alexander P. de Seversky did not have to face a court-martial. In fact, he traveled north to the Baltic as a Russian folk hero since his audacious act received the blessing of the tsar and attracted exposure in the press. The amputee returned to duty early in July 1916 as a naval pilot rather than as an inspector of naval aircraft. He participated in the navy's first experiment to have the M-9 and later models of the flying boat flown directly from the factory in Petrograd to the naval facility at Revel, which had become the primary base of operation to save Riga and the Bay of Riga from falling into German hands. Powered by a Salmson liquid-cooled engine, de Seversky's M-9 took three and a half hours to cover the 225 miles. Not very fast, but still the ferry process saved enormous amounts of time and labor. Earlier, the craft had to be disassembled in Petrograd, placed in trucks, taken to trains, railed to Revel, carried by trucks to the naval air station, and reassembled before distribution to Russia's naval outposts in harm's way.[21]

De Seversky ferried a second M-9 from Petrograd to Revel before mid-July 1916, when he received orders to rejoin the Second Bombing-Reconnaissance Squadron on Ösel Island, but this time at the naval air station at Zerel (today, Seare). The station was located at the tip of Sworbe (today, Sorve) Peninsula, which pierces the heart of the Irben Straits. The squadron had recently developed an auxiliary base on tiny Runo (today, Ruhnu) Island, about forty-five miles east-southeast of Zerel near the middle of the Gulf of Riga. It was perfectly situated to launch flying boats that could spot German submarines when they slipped unnoticed by Russian warships into the gulf. During one of de Seversky's first reconnaissance flights from Runo, he engaged and shot down a German Albatros C.Ia that had been converted from a land to a seaplane by replacing wheels with floats.[22]

The Russians, comparing the graceful appearance of their flying boats with that of the Germans', marked the Albatros as a bastardized contraption by giving it the unflattering sobriquet, *zhuk* (beetle). Bug-like or not, the debut of enemy aircraft over the midsections of the Gulf of Riga confirmed the nearby presence of a fully equipped seaplane base. The only serious danger threatening the flying boats came from any "beetles" that might approach and attack the reconnoitering Russians. In truth, during the last portion of July and the first part of August, de Seversky and his comrades engaged in frequent aerial combat. Most of these encounters proved to be more exciting than deadly, but they revealed the grave, ongoing threat posed by the operations of a German seaplane base. Finally, an M-9 spotted an Albatros C.Ia taking off from Lake Angern (today, Engures). The lake parallels for ten miles the western shore of the Gulf of Riga. From the German standpoint, the lake was an ideal location precisely because it was less than a mile into the interior. Virtually on the gulf, the base nonetheless was absolutely invisible to Russian warships.[23]

On August 12, 1916, the navy decided to send a small squadron of three M-9s from Runo Island to Lake Angern to do as much damage as possible to the German seaplane base. Selected for the perilous honor were pilots Lieutenant Dideriks, Lieutenant Steklov, and Lieutenant de Seversky. Each officer was accompanied by a sergeant mechanic-observer who manned the single machine gun mounted on a rotating arm on the right side of the two-person cockpit. The M-9, also known as the "Grigorovich" after its designer, carried several bombs installed, like FBAs, on each side of the hull next to the pilot and mechanic-observer. The uneventful flight from Runo became lively once the M-9s crossed the shoreline adjacent to Lake Angern. If nothing else, the three noisy Salmson engines prevented the Russians from completely surprising the enemy. Nevertheless, the craft made a beeline for several station sheds and dropped their ordnance on target. "The naval air base," de Seversky boasted later, "looked as if a cyclone had struck it."[24]

The pilots and crews focused on their objectives and ignored temporarily the ground fire, small arms, and at least one antiaircraft cannon, erupting as the M-9s reached the enemy's facilities. By the time the flying boats completed their successful pass over target, all of the craft had acquired one or more holes that did not exist just a few moments earlier. Fortunately, the burst of slugs and shell fragments failed to penetrate flesh as the crews were cocooned in armor and a thick planked hull. Lieutenant Steklov, though, soon broke away from the squadron and turned north and then northeast away from the combat zone. His comrades could see why. Steam poured from a shell-pocked radiator. Fortunately, the M-9 carried two smaller elongated radiators, one on each side of the liquid-cooled engine. The second, intact radiator bought a few minutes of precious time before the overheated engine froze. Steklov used those minutes to gain altitude and return to the gulf. Once his Grigorovich lost power over water, he was able to glide far enough from the German-controlled shore to be picked up safely by a Russian gunboat.[25]

Meanwhile, for de Seversky and Dideriks, their combat mission had just begun. The two remaining crews had directed their attentions so completely to the bomb run and Steklov's radiator that they missed the additional activity on Lake Angern. By the time they circled back to play their guns on German aircraft in the water, several seaplanes that had warmed up for patrol duty took off to confront the M-9s. Shortly thereafter, several more beetles joined their airborne compatriots in forming a flight of seven planes seeking payback for the mess caused by the Russians. Thus began an epic air battle that lasted over an hour. It was a fascinating engagement because of the machine gun setup on the opposing craft. The Russians could aim at targets on the sides and front of the Grigorovich. By contrast, the observers in the rear cockpits of the beetles could only shoot at objects on the sides and rear of the Albatros.[26]

The pivotal factor of the battle centered on position and maneuver. At the wrong end of the odds, seriously outgunned and in slightly slower aircraft, the Russians did what they could to keep the Germans behind them. Cleverly, de Seversky and Dideriks began an aerobatic dance in the sky. Their planes synchronously wove in and out with tight crossovers, creating a series of loops or an imaginary chain that was difficult for the enemy to penetrate. Without the benefit of radio communication of a later age, the German attack lacked coordination. Enemy planes willy-nilly moved forward and back, exchanging gunfire with the Russians. De Seversky's plane took thirty hits in the running gun battle, but fortunately control surfaces of the M-9 continued to function and the hull and armor preserved the crews.[27]

By comparison, the wooden veneer that covered the fuselage of the German craft left the crew vulnerable. As a result, the odds for the Russians improved during the battle when the Germans lost two planes. Concurrently, the Russians constructed their aerobatic chain in a manner to move the duel slowly away from the region of the German base, into the gulf, and toward Runo Island. The favorable direction of the battle was abruptly upset when Dideriks's gun jammed. As an Albatros moved forward to finish off the defenseless Grigorovich, de Seversky deftly and fearlessly changed heading to place his craft on a collision course with the approaching beetle. Rather than ram the enemy, the Russian machine gun opened fire at deadly range into the fore and aft cockpits, killing the crew and sending the seaplane nose down into the gulf. Such audacious action and the sudden appearance of several M-9s from Runo—"the most beautiful sight I have ever seen," de Seversky later recalled—encouraged the Germans to decide they were low on fuel and needed to return to Lake Angern.[28]

In October 1918 American journalist Chloe Arnold interviewed de Seversky for a feature article in The (New York) Sun. The Russian aviator recalled that not long after this heroic engagement,

> my father was in a restaurant when the newspaper telling of our fight was brought in. He said to his friends when he learned that Dideriks and I had been engaged by seven Germans: 'Read it, I can't; I know my son is killed.' They told me that I hadn't been killed, and he snatched the paper from them and read it aloud himself.[29]

Not only was Nicholas cheered, proud, and pleased at his son's survival, courage, and combat success but so were millions of Russians who heard or read about this extraordinary air battle. The military could only add luster to the incredible story of the one-legged aviator by promoting him to *starshii leitenant* (senior lieutenant). The commander-in-chief of Imperial Russia's forces, Tsar Nicholas II, personally awarded him for valor the Gold Sword and Knight of the Order of Saint George, often equated with the U.S. Congressional Medal of Honor. De Seversky more than lived up to the fame accorded to him by this single engagement. Over time, he became a legend who earned ace status with thirteen kills (some not confirmed) in fifty-seven combat missions. His additional awards eventually included the Order of

Saint Vladimir, Fourth Degree; Order of Saint Ann, Fourth, Third, and Second Degrees; and Order of Saint Stanislas, Third and Second Degrees.[30]

De Seversky continued, at least briefly, flying combat missions in the Gulf of Riga. Full of confidence, he joked with his comrades-in-arms that his artificial leg was a distinct advantage. "Look here," he would say to his fellow pilots, "I'm exactly 25 per cent less vulnerable than you are." And, indeed at one point during the war when he flew land-based pursuit aircraft, an enemy slug shattered his wooden prosthesis. Meanwhile, the military credited him with four confirmed kills in the M-9, a performance unmatched by any other naval aviator. As described earlier, the M-9 was a slow-flying boat designed to serve as an observation plane and an occasional bomber. It was never intended to be a fighter aircraft, yet de Seversky nearly achieved ace status (five kills) in this unlikely plane. The remainder of his air victories were accomplished in a Nieuport.[31]

## Revel and Adventures of a Different Kind

The following month, September 1916, the navy reassigned de Seversky to the air station at Revel. By then, the military had become extremely concerned by the frequent presence of German submarines. By laying mine fields, U-boats threatened Russian surface vessels not only in the Gulf of Riga but along what is today the Estonian coast north of Riga. Even more worrisome, submarines penetrated the Gulf of Finland. The latter provided anchorage at Helsingfors (today, Helsinki, Finland) and Kronstadt for Russia's capital ships and functioned as the water highway to the empire's capital city of Petrograd. De Seversky now began to fly strictly reconnaissance flights, sometimes in FBAs, to search and pinpoint enemy U-boats for Russian destroyers. As summer became fall, the weather transformed the Baltic phase of the war. Reconnaissance missions grew shorter as temperatures dropped from cool to cold. Flights hugged the shoreline once the Baltic Sea chilled to the point where a pilot in water could suffer hypothermia and death in a matter of minutes. And, as soon as ice formed, ships of both Germany and Russia headed for winter ports to await spring thaws and the resumption of conflict. With more and more time on his hands and with ample tools, materials, and craftsmen from the naval air station, de Seversky embarked on the adventure of invention.[32]

His creative mind focused on five areas that would result in a more effective war plane. As might be expected, de Seversky spent time and energy on rebalancing control surfaces and adjusting the linkage of those surfaces with the control column and rudder bar in the cockpit. The improvements made it easier, especially for one-legged pilots, to maneuver aircraft during missions. Second, his reconnaissance flights targeted U-boats prompting him to design a very visible, droppable buoy that would alert nearby Russian warships to the location of an observed German submarine. Third, he worked on developing an automatic bombsight. It was extremely difficult for an individual in a flying vehicle to drop a bomb on a given target. Aircraft, ordnance, ambient air, and even the target (e.g., a ship) may be moving at different speeds and directions. De Seversky would eventually design a workable, automatic device and then receive a small fortune for his invention from the U.S. government but, obviously, after the naval aviator had left Russia.[33]

Fourth, the stunning defeat suffered by Russia at the hands of Germany and Austria in the spring and summer of 1915 not only pushed Russians deep within their own territory but added distance between their naval aircraft and potential German targets. This troublesome fact inspired de Seversky to devise a method for refueling M-9s in the air. It would extend their bombing range to encompass distant enemy naval facilities such as those at Memel and Königsberg (today, Kaliningrad). Despite a successful demonstration of the process, the Imperial Russian Navy, narrowly defined as a tactical adjunct to the army, chose not to pursue de Seversky's initiative. He brought the concept, like the bombsight, with him to the United States. Actually encouraged by officers of the U.S. Army Air Service (U.S.A.A.S.), one of the precursors to the U.S. Air Force (USAF), de Seversky submitted an application in 1921 and later secured the U.S. patent for refueling aircraft during flight.[34]

Finally, de Seversky developed skis for flying boats to give them all-weather capabilities that would enable the aircraft to operate off snow or ice as well as water. The idea of attaching skis to aircraft certainly did not originate with the young naval air officer. However, de Seversky did invent a universal mounting device that quickly converted flying boats for winter operations. Such a compelling concept earned him the Imperial Russian Naval Prize for the most meritorious invention of 1916. The navy transferred the prize winner early in 1917 to Petrograd, where he served as a technical adviser to the Shchetinin Aircraft Company. He worked alongside designer Dimitrii Grigorovich in mounting the new ski apparatus on the M-11. It was a single-seat aircraft with a fixed, forward-firing machine gun and armor plating for both pilot and engine. In the M-11, Grigorovich and de Seversky created an all-weather flying boat, reputedly the fastest in the world, which served the role of pursuit or fighter aircraft.[35]

## Reflections

"The devil is in the details" is a common expression in the repertoire of athletics coaches, among others. Unfortunately, in a couple of rare instances, details failed the author entirely. At this point, it is pertinent to note that several modern philosophers of history and life writing have argued that historians and biographers must possess a few of the attributes of a police detective. Confronted with a mystery concerning who committed a crime, the detective conducts an investigation, gathers evidence, interviews people, takes notes, ponders data, and draws conclusions to solve the mystery. Historians must sometimes follow similar steps. For example, solid sources, including a document signed by de Seversky's commanding officer, indicate the young naval aviator briefly ferried M-9s from Petrograd directly to a naval air station in the combat area. Unfortunately, the sources fail to mention the station's location. On the other hand, the documents do specify that the flight took three and a half hours. Since the M-9 flew at 65 mph, it covered about 225 miles. The only naval air station in harm's way at that distance was Revel. The mystery of this detail was solved. Hence the narrative, without hesitation, presents the "fact" that de Seversky ferried M-9s from Petrograd to Revel.

Continuing with the subject of details, the key one presented in this chapter centers on the loss of de Seversky's lower right leg. The missing body part emerged as the governing emblem of his life. And, rather than being a true disability, it simply posed a series of obstacles to be hurdled. The young man nurtured discipline and perseverance in adjusting to the prosthesis. Moreover, each new activity from dancing and ice-skating to motorcycle and horseback riding represented interesting problems and special victories that bolstered his confidence, strengthened his character, and won him plaudits from contemporaries. Flying proved difficult, so he spent more time in the air than his comrades, volunteered for more combat missions, and took greater pride in excelling as a pilot. By reason of his lost leg, de Seversky's combat flights in Russia and record flights in the United

States earned him an unusual amount of newsprint and glory. Lastly, the stump heightened de Seversky's awareness of aerodynamic phenomena. It made him sensitive to issues of how to alter airplanes so as to make them more effective and easier to fly. His special condition goes a long way to explain why by 1938 he held dozens of patents that enhanced the technology of flight.

# 3

## Revolutionary Changes

Early in March 1917, Alexander P. de Seversky received appointment as squadron leader of the Second Pursuit Squadron being established on Ösel Island and employing the new M-11 flying boat. Unfortunately, on one of his Petrograd trips between the Shchetinin Aircraft factory and the Admiralty building, headquarters of the Imperial Russian Navy, the young aviator suffered a bad accident. Freezing weather and reckless driving explain why a truck skidded into de Seversky's motorcycle. It left him with bruises and injuries, including multiple fractures of his good leg along with absolute destruction of his wooden one. He stayed in the hospital not only until his injuries were all healed but until he was completely rehabilitated and refitted with a new prosthesis. The hospital did not release him until May 21.[1]

### Russian Revolution

As a result, de Seversky missed both his combat assignment and the first phase of the Russian Revolution. Bread and fuel shortages in Petrograd ignited on March 8, 1917, a popular uprising in opposition of the regime of Tsar Nicholas II. Four days later, some members of the dismissed Duma—the unrepresentative assembly with limited powers—met in the Tauride Palace and appointed themselves and other public figures to the Provisional Government. Overly sensitive of their temporary status, the new ministers deferred many decisions, including such pressing issues as land reform and the status of minorities. Elected delegates representing the capital's workers as well as soldiers, who generally came from the peasant masses, occupied another hall in the same Tauride Palace on March 12, to establish a popular council, or soviet. Dominated by socialist parties and soon to be imitated in most Russian towns and cities, the Petrograd Soviet exercised real power because of its electoral base in the larger population. When de Seversky left the hospital in May, he certainly understood that dramatic events had taken place. He was not a Slavic version of an awakened and clueless Rip Van Winkle. While recuperating from his injuries, he read newspapers and journals and heard stories and rumors from patients, nurses, and visitors. Nevertheless, he reentered a world turned upside down. He had pledged his life and loyalty to a tsar and government that had collapsed. Moreover, the military system he had known no longer existed. The Petrograd Soviet had issued Order Number One on March 15, 1917. It established a system of soldier and sailor committees that undermined officers' authority. Over the next several months, discipline seeped away from the Russian army as peasant soldiers walked out of the war, especially in midsummer, to participate in removing land from the gentry during the greatest confiscation of property in the history of the planet.[2]

When committees mandated by Order Number One asserted power over officers, de Seversky found his privileged status in both nobility and military transformed into a liability. Indeed, the greatest potential threat to him and other naval officers came from the lower ranks. Often sharing a proletarian heritage with the Marxist-oriented working class and often receiving harsh treatment from arrogant officers, sailors quickly resorted to violence once the opportunity arrived. As March riots in the capital unleashed turmoil, seamen in the Baltic Fleet sought revenge for real or imagined grievances by murdering seventy-six officers, including the commander-in-chief of the Baltic Fleet, Adm. Adrian I. Nepenin. Later, many of these same sailors from the Baltic theater served as the armed guardians upholding and protecting the second, or Bolshevik, phase of the Russian Revolution.[3]

While traditional command and harsh discipline gave way to an increasingly ill-disciplined and hard-to-command military force, exceptions existed. Two of them influenced de Seversky's life for the remainder of the war. One departure centered on the Gulf of Riga. Naval officers and men who had served together on dangerous missions possessed a bond missing for those in ships anchored months on end in ports outside of the combat area. This bond allowed officers to command ships as they had in the past but now under loose protocol and with the endorsement of sailor committees. Another deviation occurred at military aerodromes. True, mechanics now wanted better food, housing, and pay for their services, while some lower ranks that had provided muscle, maintenance, and security drifted away from their posts. Nevertheless, even under lax conditions and growing shortages, aerodromes continued to function because most pilots persisted in their willingness to fight an enemy that occupied Russian soil.[4]

### Nieuport Pursuit Planes

The ability of military airfields to remain active serves as background for the Admiralty's orders at the end of May, sending de Seversky to the Moscow Aviation School at Khodinskoi Aerodrome. Operated by the army, the school instructed the young naval aviator and gave him flight time in the land-based pursuit aircraft, Nieuport 17. This may seem odd since the navy showed a strong preference for developing and using flying boats for most of the war. On the other hand, circumstances and technologies in the Baltic theater and specifically the contest for the Gulf of Riga had changed. The Germans not only occupied the gulf's western shore but were building a major naval air station at Windau. These facilities were constructed to house and launch more advanced seaplanes such as the Albatros W.4, which went into production in the summer of 1916.[5]

The Russian navy recognized over the winter of 1916–1917 that its air arm would soon confront enemy seaplanes with two forward-firing machine guns and more speed and maneuverability than the typical flying boat. Unfortunately, the M-11 developed by Dimitrii P. Grigorovich and modified for quick conversion to skis by de Seversky was underpowered. Hence the new flying boat failed to match the latest enemy aircraft. German planes, then, could threaten not only M-9s and M-11s but also endanger shore batteries, supply depots, air stations, security units, and even war vessels because of German air superiority. In the spring of 1917, between the revolution and the reopening of conflict in the Baltic, the navy decided to retrain pilots and acquire land-based aircraft that could outperform German seaplanes.[6]

Obviously, de Seversky and his new assignment illustrated at the individual level the first part of the navy's strategy to meet the German challenge in the air. The other element in the navy's response began when it conducted negotiations to purchase advanced planes from Russia's largest aircraft manufacturer, the Moscow-based Dukh Company. On April 5, 1917, it signed a navy contract to build seventy-five Nieuports, including fifteen dual-control trainers, fifteen two-seat reconnaissance craft, and forty-five single-seat pursuit aircraft labeled by the Russians as destroyers. Model 17s and their variant, Model 21s, constituted the bulk of the pursuit planes. The Nieuport 17 was so advanced by contemporary standards that it entered the air forces of most Allied countries, including the U.S. Army Air Service. The craft was built with a wooden airframe and covered by fabric. It carried a machine gun mounted in front of the pilot and fired synchronously through the propeller disc. In terms of performance, the Model 17 reached 112 mph when powered by a 130 hp Clerget rotary engine. By today's standards, the airplane was extremely slow, but it still flew faster and could outmaneuver the German seaplanes faced by Russian pilots in the Baltic theater.[7]

Trained and certified after a high pilotage examination on the Nieuport 17, de Seversky more often flew the Nieuport 21 variant. It had a less powerful engine but larger control surfaces, making the plane both slower and more maneuverable. The latter was a key benefit during a dogfight. Regardless, in the second half of June, de Seversky completed his course at the Moscow Aviation School. Near the same time as his "graduation," disaster struck the naval air station at Zerel on Ösel Island, fulfilling the navy's worst fears about the loss of air superiority over Russian defensive positions in the Gulf of Riga. German aircraft bombed large sheds at the air station, destroying two flying boats and damaging four others. Surviving Russian aircraft were too slow and could neither defend the air station nor pursue German machines once their bomb run was over.[8]

It may seem surprising that de Seversky was not commanded to return immediately to the Baltic. One reason for the delay in his transfer centered on the fact that naval Nieuports were still in production. Another focused on the navy's logical decision about the rotation of personnel. Once de Seversky completed his army training on the Model 17, he stayed at the school to guide fellow naval officers in learning to fly the same equipment. Still a third reason that prevented his timely return to the war zone emerged when the Admiralty asked him to perform special duty in the capital city near the end of his flight instructor assignment. At this point in the revolution, the Provisional Government tottered under the weight of a failing offensive it had ordered (June 1917) against the Central Powers. The floundering effort highlighted the impotence of the undisciplined Russian army as it energized soldiers, sailors, and workers in Petrograd to protest the war and demonstrate in opposition of the Provisional Government.[9]

During the summer and fall of 1917, Russia's industrial situation deteriorated rapidly, affecting war production. Shortages of raw materials, transport problems, and growing conflict between workers and management led to work stoppages at numerous factories, including ones producing military hardware. One of these was the Shchetinin Aircraft Company. Put simply, work stoppage at Shchetinin ruined the Admiralty's plans to address German air power over the Gulf of Riga. Not only did the factory build flying boats, which continued their bombing and reconnaissance roles, but the shop also finished putting together Nieuports from sectional parts supplied by the Dukh factory in Moscow. Nearly apoplectic at this turn of events, the Admiralty hastily sent a telegram to de Seversky at the aviation school in July. The message asked the naval pilot to come immediately by train to the capital city.[10]

De Seversky arrived at Petrograd's Nicholas (today, Moscow) Station, which was several blocks away from the Admiralty building via Nevsky Prospect. The navy's headquarters stood next to the Winter Palace, which housed the Provisional Government. At the Admiralty, the architects of naval air strategy greeted de Seversky—Capt. Boris Dudorov (Doudoroff), chief of the Naval Aviation Department of the Russian Naval General Staff, and his aide Cdr. Alexander A. Tuchkov (Toochkoff). In the very near future, both officers would be promoted as Captain Toochkoff replaced Rear Admiral Doudoroff, who became deputy minister to the minister of the Russian Navy in the Provisional Government. The pair asked their newly arrived visitor to go to the Shchetinin factory and try to convince the workers to return to their work stations so the navy could acquire desperately needed aircraft.[11]

Doudoroff and Toochkoff selected the best person for a task both delicate and dangerous. They understood de Seversky had a natural connection with many Shchetinin workers who knew him as an inspector of aircraft in 1916 and more recently as a designer of aviation skis. Moreover, the naval aviator was an admired war hero who had put his life on the line for the Russian cause. Finally, even though he would face an audience that potentially contained armed and hostile men, de Seversky possessed an abundance of courage. He later admitted, however, that his confidence came from "the impetuousness of youth" rather than some form of experience or training in delivering a speech that persuades. Taken by car from the Admiralty to the factory, de Seversky entered the shop and gave height to his five-foot, seven-inch frame by climbing awkwardly on top of an empty fuselage crate. Idle workers, curious by the appearance of the famous one-legged pilot slowly gathered around him. The senior lieutenant dismissed the politically tainted and overly used term "comrades" to address the workers as citizens, at least as he remembered the talk many years later.[12]

[Citizens]:

We men on the front are doing our best to prevent the invasion of our territory by the enemy. We cannot perform that duty diligently and efficiently unless we are confident that the political situation at home will be taken care of in the same manner.

We soldiers know nothing of politics and trust that you, the working class, who continually drive for the attainment of personal liberty and recognition of your labor, are more important to the country at this hour than any of us.

If you will not continue with your important work, millions of men in the army and navy will be subjected to slaughter and annilihation [sic]. The enemy will occupy our land and you will never in this world have the chance to liberate yourselves, recognize the government and thus receive the proper recognition for your class.

We are not leaving our positions and dropping our arms, and running to the rear to participate in all this political upheavals [sic]. We still fight and a number of us have sacrificed [our] lives in order to hold off the foreign invasion and give you people a chance to reorganize our government. We trust in your ability and know that you will do the right thing by the people of Russia. We trust you implicitly. We feel that we deserve the same consideration. So, go ahead! Build up a new government or bring the house in order, but give us the ammunition which means our strength to hold off the enemy until the house is put in order. Then, when the new government is organized which will be representative of your ideas, that government can decide the question of peace or war. Until then, let every one of us, whether man on the front against the enemy, or man in the rear on the front against political enemy, do our duty and support each other to the fullest extent.[13]

De Seversky's speech had the desired effect. The workers cheered the aviator at the end of his pep talk and carried him to his waiting car. More significantly, work resumed in the plant and the navy had its order for airplanes fulfilled: Presumably his talk had contributed to the resolution of the problems that had caused the stoppage. Small wonder the Admiralty gave the senior lieutenant the chance to fill his earlier assignment as commander of the Second Pursuit Squadron at Zerel on Ösel Island. By the time the squadron leader settled into his post near the end of July, his unit was reequipped with four Nieuport 17s, one Nieuport 21, one Grigorovich M-9, and six Grigorovich M-15 flying boats. The M-15 was simply a slightly smaller and, powered by a Hispano-Suiza V8 engine, somewhat faster variant of the M-9.[14]

## The Battle of Riga

Soon augmented by a few additional Nieuports, these airplanes and their pilots were among the most active of the war despite the fact that the eastern front remained generally silent during 1917. In that fateful year of revolution, and precisely because of revolution, there were only three serious military engagements between Russians and Germans: the disastrous Russian offensive in July, the successful German counteroffensive in Galicia, and the Battle of Riga. Thus de Seversky and his squadron ended up in the center of the last major clash of Russian arms in World War I. Over the next nine weeks, the unit leader would fly dozens of combat sorties and, in the unfolding contest over air space, would shoot down an average of one enemy plane each week. All this activity supported the squadron's military orders. Its prime objective centered on protecting the battery of four 12-inch guns on Ösel that prevented German surface vessels from entering unchallenged the Bay of Riga via the Irben Straits.[15]

Strangely enough, the first threat to the squadron's task came from German minesweepers. In August they regularly appeared off the Courland coast and in the Irben Straits below Zerel to rid Russian mines from the entrance to Riga Bay. German success in eliminating explosive charges would allow the approach of dreadnoughts that could bombard Russian batteries. After clearing Russian land and sea ordnance, German warships could then enter the bay and join land forces in an assault on the city of Riga. Hence every day, weather permitting, de Seversky sent M-15 flying boats over the straits to intercept minesweepers and harass them by dropping small bombs. "As soon as they tried to sweep the mines," the squadron leader later remembered, "we attacked them, and they dropped their gear and beat it." Russian ascendancy over minesweepers prompted the Germans to send seaplanes on patrols over the straits. This, in turn, forced de Seversky to assign himself and other Nieuport pilots to fly their planes as escorts for the protection of the slower M-15s. This disposition of aircraft anticipated tactics used in World War II, when pursuit aircraft accompanied bombers to shield them from enemy fighters during a bomb run.[16]

De Seversky and his squadron, along with a sister detachment on Ösel's southern coast at Arensburg (today, Kuressaare), enjoyed, in the short term, a favorable outcome in their campaign to prevent the Germans from clearing mines from the entrance to Riga Bay. Nevertheless, Russia suffered a backdoor defeat. Its army, progressively smaller and undisciplined, withdrew from Riga and moved south and east of the Dvina River. On September 3, 1917, German forces occupied Riga and, soon after, the Dünamünde (today, Daugavgriva) fortress. The Germans quickly transformed the port into a base for minelaying submarines such as the UC-57 and UC-78. Russians discovered the tables had been turned against them as Germans laid mines to interrupt Russia's supply as well as warship protection of Ösel, Moon, and Dago Islands where Russian troops continued to man guns that posed a danger to German ships.[17]

Meanwhile, Ösel Island received frequent visits from German planes. Throughout September, de Seversky and the other Nieuport pilots successfully intercepted the enemy, occasionally shooting down German machines and forcing others to retreat to their main base at Windau. Under frequent attack, the Second Pursuit Squadron could not maintain a perfect record. During a raid at the end of September, one German aircraft managed to drop a bomb on the munitions depot near the Zerel battery. The bomb detonated loaded shells, resulting in a devastating explosion that killed seventy-four garrison soldiers and wounded many more. Russian guns, however, survived intact and continued to pose a serious obstacle to the free navigation of German ships below the Sworbe Peninsula of Ösel. On the other hand, the streaming level of German attention by sea and air foretold that even greater action could be expected. In fact, on September 18, 1917, German General Headquarters decided to rectify the Irben Straits problem as well as eliminate Russian control of Moon Island and Moon Sound between the island and the Estonian coast. It ordered Operation Albion to crush Russian air, sea, and land forces and open Riga Bay to German ships. The ultimate goal was to be able to use the port of Riga as the main supply base for the German army as it prepared an assault on Russia's capital city. Once Petrograd fell to German arms, the Second Reich hoped the war would formally end, allowing the military to redirect most of its resources to a victorious campaign against the Allies on the western front.[18]

Anticipating the start of Operation Albion, larger numbers of German aircraft conducted hit-and-run reconnaissance and bomb runs against various island positions held by the Russians. During one of these attacks on October 10, de Seversky intercepted a squadron of enemy planes. Another lengthy air battle ensued resulting in the squadron leader adding two more victories, one bomber and one pursuit plane, to his tally of downed German machines. It proved to be one of the last triumphs of Russian arms in the war and reconfirmed the pilot's status as a major war hero with the largest number of confirmed kills of any naval aviator. Two days later, a German armada of three hundred ships with minesweepers in front approached the northwestern shore of Ösel Island and entered Tagga (today, Targa) Bay.[19]

Commanded by Rear Adm. Ehrhardt Schmidt in his flagship, the battle-cruiser *Moltke*, the fleet contained ten dreadnoughts, nine cruisers, fifty-five destroyers, and an assortment of minesweepers, torpedo boats, and supply ships. Nineteen transport vessels carried a contingent of 24,000 troops composed largely of soldiers from the 42nd Infantry Division and the Second Bicycle Brigade. Six dirigibles and 109 aircraft protected the sky above the flotilla and projected its power across the island even before troops landed. The odds overwhelmingly favored the Germans since the Russians could field only 12,000 infantry and approximately thirty airplanes, two ancient dreadnoughts, three light cruisers, eight destroyers, and a small collection of gunboats, minesweepers, minelayers, and supply ships. These forces fell under the command of Rear Adm. Mikhail K. Bakhirev, former chief of mine defense who, fortunately, had a clear idea where his ships could safely navigate around the islands and entrance to Riga Bay.[20]

On October 12, 1917, German capital ships opened fire and silenced by 0600 hours the two Russian batteries guarding Tagga Bay. German troops via motor launches soon disembarked from their ships and landed on shore virtually without contest from the Russian garrison. Just as some Russian sailors decided their ships would not participate in this last battle, neutralizing some twenty destroyers, most Russian infantry chose to surrender or run rather than engage the enemy in a deadly firefight. As a consequence, German infantry confronted few obstacles in completing their mission to cut Ösel Island in half by moving southeast to capture the town of Arensburg, including its garrison, battery, and naval air station. When German troops occupied the northwestern shore of Tagga Bay, a "cloud" of Fokker and Albatros aircraft descended on Zerel and the Second Pursuit Squadron. While most personnel survived the fire of machine guns and the explosion of small bombs, the assault damaged sheds and aircraft and started an uncontrollable fire in the officers' barracks. Except for Lt. Mikhail I. Safonov and two Nieuports, de Seversky transferred flyable aircraft and their pilots thirty-five kilometers up the coast to Arensburg. By the time the aircraft arrived, the navy understood Germany's invasion of Ösel endangered their air stations. To save as many aircraft as possible, the navy quickly closed its facilities at Arensburg, Kilkond, and Zerel and ordered surviving planes to fly to Kuivast (today, Kuivastu) on the east side of Moon Island. Fortuitously, the naval base there was located a short distance by water from the Russian-controlled Estonian mainland. De Seversky and his friend Safonov had volunteered to stay behind and conduct reconnaissance flights. This was made possible by the fact that the army garrison, at least for the time being, stood by their guns. That meant food, fuel, ordnance, personnel, and even a wireless were available to the island's only remaining Russian airmen.[21]

On October 12 and 13, de Seversky and Safonov courageously flew multiple reconnaissance missions in the Irben Straits before storms and rain arrived late in the afternoon of the thirteenth. Approached by small enemy patrols, the pair fought brief air battles but did not long continue an engagement for fear of being overwhelmed by additional German seaplanes. More than once their faster land planes saved them to fly another sortie. After several hours of nonstop action their faces were blackened from the soot and castor oil of their Nieuports' Gnome rotary engines. And a nervous tick distorted Safonov's face though he and de Seversky managed to bolster their spirits by keeping up a brave and merry banter between flights. Despite the good news of their continued survival, their reconnoiters were not encouraging. De Seversky had to inform Admiral Bakhirev's staff that a fleet of German minesweepers had gathered to the southwest along the Courland coast out of range of the Zerel battery.[22]

It appeared likely that the minesweepers would take advantage of the miserable weather and the cover of darkness to clear a mine-free channel during the night of October 13–14. The narrow passage would permit German warships to draw near the straits and bombard Russian positions. Once the guns of Zerel were silenced, other ships could enter Riga Bay and attack the Baltic islands from the south, literally placing the Russian navy in the middle of a closing vise. And, with some modifications, this scenario matched reality. In the afternoon of October 14, the dreadnoughts *Friedrich der Grosse*, *König Albert*, and *Kaiserin* approached the tip of Sworbe Peninsula and opened fire. As the ships' guns thundered with the first volley of deadly ordnance, de Seversky and Safonov had no choice but to flee. To the north, German infantry had already reached Arensburg, occupying most of Ösel Island in the process. Only the Sworbe Peninsula remained in Russian hands, but the garrison there was cut off from associate forces except for a precarious, mine-free sea lane. With the enemy navy blasting Zerel, and with its army poised to sweep down the peninsula, the only way de Seversky and Safonov could assuredly save themselves and their Nieuports from capture or destruction was to follow their original orders by flying to Kuivast on Moon Island. Hence the airmen clambered into their cockpits and flipped on their ignition switches as ground-crew soldiers turned over their propellers to start the engines. Luckily, the pair rolled singly down the field between damaged sheds and burned-out barracks and bounced into an ugly and drizzly sky without becoming victims of the dreadnoughts' guns.[23]

Safonov landed at Kuivast and spent the night in officers' quarters. He was separated during the flight from de Seversky, who failed to land at the temporary haven on Moon Island. Shortly after takeoff, the senior officer's rotary engine, a delicate piece of technology often equated with a watch, sputtered to a stop. In a cold mist and under a gloomy sky, de Seversky had to make an emergency landing in a peasant's field in the middle of German-occupied Ösel. The date October 14, 1917, would forever be etched in de Seversky's mind as his second worst day in wartime service. After an injury-free landing, the naval pilot busied himself by removing the Vickers 7.7 mm machine gun from in front of the cockpit. Then, unscrewing the fuel tank's filler cap, he dipped a rope-twisted rag into the liquid and used it to start a fire in the protected forward section of the cockpit. By the time he limped a safe distance from the plane, the fuel tank erupted in a blast of light and flames. While de Seversky accomplished his goal of demolishing the aircraft and denying its use by the enemy, he also succeeded in raising an alarm among the occupants of a nearby village. The good news was the fact that villagers, not Germans, soon surrounded the pilot; the bad news was the fact that the villagers were Estonians who generally had no love for Russians.[24]

To some villagers, the sight presented by de Seversky must have been ominous at best. His eyes were enlarged white circles that had been protected by goggles, and the rest of his face was dotted with dark splashes of engine oil. On his head sat a textured helmet with flaps that fell on his shoulders and bulged around his ears where extra fabric protected him from frostbite. Peeping out of his leather jacket was the head of an unmoving and plush monkey, his talisman, Iasha. And for a walking stick, the pilot carried a ponderous metal tube. The strange apparition might have come from the underworld rather than the sky. Fortunately, one of the Estonians recognized in de Seversky's limp and aviation attire that here in the flesh was the famous "Peg-leg Ace of the Baltic." The enlightened villager convinced his neighbors that they should help the apparition rather than turn him over to the Germans.[25]

Thus began a painful and arduous two-night journey across thirty versts (twenty miles) of the island. The nocturnal hikes over rugged and less-traveled paths allowed de Seversky to avoid detection by German patrols. Estonians passed him from one village to the next in an operation resembling the Underground Railroad that helped American slaves escape the antebellum South. Well before sunrise on October 16, de Seversky reached the outskirts of Orissarskii (today, Orissare), a port on the channel between Ösel and Moon Islands. Despite being shot at from shore by German soldiers, he rowed safely across the waterway to the security of his own lines. The ordeal left the tired amputee with a sore stump and a deteriorated prosthesis that had to be replaced.[26]

De Seversky reached Moon Island just in time. With Ösel in the hands of the Germans, there were no Russian batteries or aircraft to stop enemy minesweepers from clearing explosive charges out of the Irben Straits. Indeed, through that watercourse now steamed a substantial flotilla of twenty-eight German war vessels headed by the dreadnoughts *König* and *Kronprinz*. By the evening of October 16, as an exhausted de Seversky lay recovering in a naval infirmary in Kuivast, German ships anchored in the Arensburg harbor. The next morning, seventeen of the flotilla's vessels approached Moon Island from the south. At 0600 hours, a furious gun battle commenced between Russian land batteries and sea forces and their naval adversary. Over time, the superior number of German warships pounded Russian batteries, damaged the *Grazhdanin* (*Citizen*) and an armored cruiser *Baian* (*Accordian*), and battered the *Slava* (*Glory*), which had to be scuttled. At 1030 hours, Admiral Bakhirev, on board the *Baian*, ordered the withdrawal of Russian forces. Over the next twenty-four hours, the admiral's ships evacuated most army and navy personnel from Moon, Dägo, and Worm Islands—soon to be occupied by Germany. The Russian fleet then retreated northeast into the Gulf of Finland, leaving a protective trail of mines behind the ships.[27]

One of the retreating destroyers carried de Seversky to Petrograd. Precisely because Russia had lost its three-year battle to hold the Baltic islands, the naval aviator was welcomed as a hero. He was one of the few bright lights in an otherwise dark tragedy. He had stayed, along with Safonov, who was promoted to senior lieutenant, and flew against the Germans while surrounded by enemy land, sea, and air forces. Then the amputee had courageously limped his way across enemy-infested Ösel Island to escape capture. For these exploits, de Seversky's status as an exemplary paladin jumped to the stratosphere. Despite the ongoing, chaotic revolution and Russia's tumble toward the radical, organizations lined up to bestow tributes to the one-legged ace pilot, a role model for the dwindling few who wanted to continue the war. The Admiralty promoted the twenty-three-year-old to lieutenant commander and placed him in charge of all pursuit aviation in the Baltic theater. At the same time, members of the All-Russian Aero Club elected him to be their honorary governor. And the Provisional Government, already on its deathbed, acknowledged his heroism. Alexander Toochkoff, who formed and led the Russian Naval Aviation Mission to the United States, appointed him vice chairman of the group. "I felt," Toochkoff later stated in explaining his choice of de Seversky, "that his experience in combat, his inventive talents, and the technical contributions that he had already made, would be of great service not only to my mission, but also the American government."[28]

The Admiralty, however, asked de Seversky to delay his departure to America because of the fear of an imminent German operation against Russian bases in the Gulf of Finland. In fact, the threat of Petrograd's occupation by the enemy caused a near panic as people, goods, and organizations began moving to the former (and future) capital city of Moscow. These fears and threats prompted de Seversky to reconstruct at the end of October several naval air squadrons from units that recently fled the Baltic islands. The new chief of pursuit aviation revived, among others, his old Second Pursuit Squadron and placed his comrade-in-arms, Lieutenant Safonov, in charge of the unit early in November. The Baltic units, now on the mainland, certainly found occasion to engage the enemy. Safonov, for one, achieved ace status by shooting down his fourth and fifth German aircraft before the December Armistice was signed.[29]

## Bolshevik Revolution

Despite the continued air war, the Germans did not follow up their Baltic victory with immediate preparations for an assault on Petrograd. Instead, they consolidated their gains in the Baltic while making plans and transferring troops for a major spring offensive along the western front. For the German High Command, the revolutionary anarchy in Russia and the utter collapse of Provisional Government authority failed to inspire a quest for a military end to the Great War in the east. If its land forces occupied Petrograd, with whom could German representatives negotiate an official peace? As the German military pondered this question, the coup de grâce was delivered to the Provisional Government. On the evening of November 7–8, 1917, Red Guards and Baltic sailors surrounded the Winter Palace and arrested government ministers. Power fell to a congress of soviets then opening its deliberations in the Smolny Institute, a former girls' school that also served as the headquarters for the Bolshevik Party. Through its central executive committee, the congress formed the first Soviet government, the Council of People's Commissars chaired by V. I. Lenin. One of the first actions of the new government was the "Decree on Peace," calling for immediate general peace negotiations.[30]

The Soviet takeover caused two very difficult problems for de Seversky. First, the new government's official position seeking peace put the naval commander in, at best, an awkward position. Except for the Baltic, the war on the eastern front had virtually ended months earlier; yet, because of the recent battle around Riga Bay, German naval aircraft remained active reconnoitering and even bombing Russian positions on the Estonian mainland. As a result, de Seversky's three pursuit squadrons had to be maintained with good pilots and various supplies at a time when both military personnel and goods were scarce. Moreover, despite the government's hope for an official and timely end to the war, the uncertain peace process meant de Seversky also had to plan for a continuation of at least some form of the air war. As a result, he divided his time between his squadrons and the Moscow Aviation School, where he trained pilots to become combat-ready and tested a new, French-designed pursuit plane produced in Russia by Dukh—the SPAD Model VII.[31]

Second, the new government adhered to a Marxian ideology that expected the upper classes to be eliminated. In one sense, de Seversky's heroic status and leadership position over naval aviation neutralized the fact that as heir to wealth and nobility, he should be persona non grata in Soviet Russia. Regardless, he still had to be careful how, when, and where he interacted with society. Gangs of soldiers and sailors plagued the empire with criminal behavior. They often pummeled or shot officers who, like de Seversky, had pledged their lives and loyalty to the tsar. The tenuous security enjoyed by the commander explains why his mother, Vera, came to live with him after the December Armistice. Revolution had broken the rest of the family apart and taken its property. Alexander's father, Nicholas, and his brother, George, ended up serving with officers opposed to the Soviet regime. Later, his father and his second wife and daughter escaped through north Russia while George and his Polish bride, Elizaveta, bolted the country via Constantinople. As their homeland lapsed into horrific civil war, this segment of the family reunited and joined the large Russian émigré community in France.[32]

Meanwhile, Commissar of Foreign Affairs Lev Trotskii formed and sent on December 2 a Soviet delegation to German-occupied Brest-Litovsk (today, Brest). The group negotiated an armistice with Central Powers representatives led by Maj. Gen. Max Hoffmann, German chief of staff for the eastern front. Unfortunately for the Russians, the peace talks proved disappointing. Long before the Bolshevik electoral victories for the November All-Russian Congress of Soviets, the councils had argued for a peace without "annexations or indemnities." It soon became clear, however, that the Germans expected Soviet Russia to pay millions of gold rubles and surrender parts or all of Finland, the Baltic, Poland, Ukraine, Kars, Batum, Ardagan, and White Russia. Such outlandish terms prompted Trotskii to respond in kind with his unorthodox "no peace, no war" formula before abruptly walking out of the Brest-Litovsk negotiations on February 10,

1918. The Soviet refusal to sign a treaty or fight a war stunned the Germans only temporarily. On February 18, they initiated their last and uncontested offensive on the eastern front.[33]

Accompanying these extraordinary events were decisions that compelled de Seversky to move in a new direction. On February 11, 1918, the Council of People's Commissars demobilized the Russian navy and laid the groundwork for the eventual establishment of the Red Fleet. The decree implementing these decisions left the young naval air commander and his military position in limbo. As de Seversky pondered his future and how best to protect his mother against the vicissitudes of revolutionary Russia, the German offensive supplied the answer. Resumption of the one-sided war caused a crisis among Soviet leaders. Some, like Lenin, bowed to the reality of a nonexistent army and called for signing a draconian German peace treaty. Others, as the capital moved out of harm's way from Petrograd to Moscow, argued for taking the government farther eastward into Siberia and cobbling together armed units to continue the war.[34]

If the Soviet government adopted the latter option, it had to have immediate and massive amounts of war materiel from Allied countries that, until February 10, had ranked Soviet Russians somewhere below the level of pariahs. This partly explains a whole series of steps taken by Lenin and Trotskii to reestablish ties with the Allies. For example, Trotskii approved the landing of British troops in the northern port of Murmansk. British forces could safeguard unused Allied supplies still stored there. In addition, they could prevent the Germans from occupying the port and turning it into a submarine base. By the same token, although his motives may be questioned, Lenin sent a message to U.S. President T. Woodrow Wilson presenting a series of interrogatories to find out the kind of help Soviet Russia could expect from America should Russia reenter the war.[35]

The pseudo lovefest with the Allies promoted by Soviet leaders helped resolve de Seversky's future. At the end of February 1918, the ace naval pilot secured official permission to travel to the United States in order to obtain a better prosthesis and to join his colleagues on the Russian Naval Aviation Mission. With a government pass signed by Trotskii in hand, Alexander and his mother boarded a train in Petrograd early in March. Because of frequent stops, it would take several weeks to travel 6,117 miles on the Trans-Siberian rail line to Vladivostok on the Pacific coast. Mother and son occupied a coach that also carried Japanese diplomats toward home after their embassy in

Petrograd shut down. And the pair carried hard (i.e., transferable) currency, including some U.S. dollars that were cached in the amputee's prosthesis.[36]

Ample money, the official diplomatic character of the car, and de Seversky's official pass from the Soviet government made the pair feel reasonably secure. Still, Vera asked her son to remove the insignia of rank from his uniform. Regrettably, his military jacket showed marks where, for example, the officer stripes had appeared on the lower sleeves. The precaution failed. A group of armed sailors boarded the train at a stop on the third day out from Petrograd. Immediately, they spotted de Seversky and recognized the cut of his naval officer uniform and even his rank from the imprint left by the removed insignia. They took no interest in his documents. Instead, to Vera's horror, the sailors grabbed de Seversky and yanked him off the coach with the intention of putting him before a firing squad:

> It looked like curtains, but the squad leader noticed his wooden leg. "Aren't you the Aviator de Seversky?" he inquired. De Seversky admitted his identity. "Well, sir, I'm the Sailor Krutchnov of the destroyer *Cossack*," said the leader. "You saved our lives once by downing a German plane that was about to bomb us. You fought for the Russian people. We're not looking for officers like you!" And they let him go![37]

Days later, at a stop shortly before crossing into the Chinese province of Manchuria, two soldiers entered the coach. They had never seen a Trotskii pass before and so ordered de Seversky to follow them off the train to be interrogated by their awaiting comrades in the station. Two thoughts raced through the pilot's mind. Either the soldiers would murder him or hold him long after the train departed, leaving his abandoned mother to an uncertain fate. As the three men reached the narrow door and stairs of the coach, de Seversky acted out of total desperation. He seized an overhead support and swung his body into the nearest man who then fell into the second soldier. Both men yelled and cursed as they tumbled out of the car onto the platform. The ruckus prompted three other soldiers to rush out of the station, firing their weapons. The shots panicked the engineer who applied full steam to the engine. Fortunately for de Seversky, the soldiers who discharged their weapons assumed somebody was trying to escape from the train. As a result, they fired in the direction of the tumbling bodies of men, who, in turn, let out bloodcurdling screams of "Nyet, Nyet!" By the time the soldiers attended to their wounded comrades and cleared up what had happened, the train had departed at a fast clip toward Harbin, China.[38]

From Harbin, Vera and her Sasha rode to the terminus of the Trans-Siberian Railroad at Vladivostok, where the pair bought passage on a ship to Tokyo. Once in Japan's capital city, de Seversky spent time with members of the Russian community and especially with his superior officer and former chief of naval aviation, Adm. Boris Doudoroff, then the attaché to the Russian Embassy. On March 30, 1918, Doudoroff prepared and signed an official document highlighting and certifying the combat pilot's military record as an ace pilot and aviation inventor. On several occasions, this certificate served well as a favorable introduction of de Seversky to American military aviators who could be impressed only by the Russian's inventive and courageous activities during the Great War. Finally, the lieutenant commander and his mother embarked on a transoceanic vessel in Tokyo for the two-week voyage to San Francisco, arriving on April 21, 1918. At the time he stepped off the gangplank and planted his real foot on American soil, de Seversky would not have believed that the United States would become his permanent home and, indeed, that he would never again see the land of his birth.[39]

### Reflections

One episode that requires further exploration centers on de Seversky's escape from German-occupied Ösel Island. Several sources deal with this event; three of them are based on interviews with the aviator. Unfortunately, the published accounts vary significantly. This may be because the interviewer had a hard time with de Seversky's heavy Russian accent, which he continued to display as long as he lived. The interviewer may also have focused on what would otherwise be toss-away comments; by the same token, the interviewee may have forgotten details, or inadvertently added material, or purposefully created stories to make the event more entertaining. Regardless, the tales varied and caused the author grief in his effort to produce a reasonably truthful biography.

For example, one account indicates that de Seversky took off from Riga (then controlled by Germans!) and crashed on Ösel. Another story had de Seversky land on Ösel, where he talked (interesting for someone who admitted that he did not know the Estonian language!) locals into helping him cover his aircraft with hay. And a third tale has Estonians helping him repair the airplane and even starting the engine (one poor Estonian lost his arm turning over the propeller and engine, but with no hard feelings!) before de Seversky flew to safety. What to do with all these stories? There is an official, brief summary of what happened. German naval bombardment caused de Seversky to flee, and he was soon forced to land, burned his airplane, walked across German-held Ösel, rowed to Moon Island, and all the while he carried his aircraft's machine gun. The author employed the official outline of de Seversky's adventures to form an authentic, verifiable narrative that was then embellished with plausible elements from the three different interviews.

While episodes in this and earlier chapters require sources to be analyzed critically, the revolutionary theme of chapter 3 is above reproach. The two-phased Russian Revolution moved from changing government to changing society. A radically new Russia witnessed the born-special and privileged few brought low by a torrent of new forces and ideas. The most important force to surface in the tumultuous year of 1917 was the soviets. By staking out a position as leaders of the most radical wing of the Petrograd Soviet, Lenin and the Bolsheviks were able to capitalize on the mistakes of moderates and direct the soviets in seizing power. Skill and luck combined to make the new government. Meanwhile, flying fragments from society's disintegration destroyed the de Seversky fortune and family as they also ended Russia's participation in the war. The main temporary exception was the Baltic theater. Alexander P. de Seversky's brave response to the German offensive in the Battle of Riga sealed his military reputation at a level far above most contemporaries and granted him extraordinary awards and honors, including membership on a mission to America. The latter, of course, proved to be the most revolutionary change he would ever experience in his life.

# 4

# The Russian Test Pilot and Consultant in America

For nearly three years, Alexander P. de Seversky kept one eye on Russia in hopes a Communist collapse would allow him to go home and the other eye on the sky in hopes he could find an aviation position that would reward him financially and release his inventive talents. By the time he and his mother, Vera, reached the Palace Hotel in San Francisco in April 1918, he already knew that the Russian Naval Aviation Mission had been disbanded. More than likely, this unhappy piece of news had been given to him in Tokyo by Attaché Doudoroff, who regularly communicated with the Russian Embassy in Washington, D.C. Russian diplomats in both capitals shared the challenging problem of representing a government that no longer existed. Regardless, the mission's demise is easy to understand. During Sasha and Vera's hazardous journey across Siberia, on the evening of March 15, 1918, a Congress of Soviets ratified the harsh Treaty of Brest-Litovsk.[1]

### From the Russian Embassy to the War Department

A minor fallout from the treaty left the Naval Aviation Mission dangling without a purpose. Like many Russian officers who were also members of the nobility, de Seversky rejected the treaty and continued to support the war. Thus, when he was interviewed in San Francisco on April 21, he speculated that he might find a wartime role in the United States by joining a squadron, training pilots, or inspecting aircraft. The interview made clear that when Sasha and Vera left San Francisco by train for Washington, de Seversky hoped the nation's capital would be a good starting point to find

49

a useful aviation post. He would not be disappointed. Ambassador Boris Bakhmetev and the Russian Embassy assisted the lieutenant commander in his transition to war service for the United States. He received appointment as deputy naval attaché for aviation. It was clear, however, that embassy resources were limited and his appointment was temporary.[2]

The attaché post, however, automatically gave de Seversky entrée to American military circles in the U.S. War Department (now, Department of Defense). He took several additional steps to improve his opportunities for employment outside the embassy. Later that spring, he joined the Voluntary Association of Russian Army and Navy Officers. The association provided "[m]utual moral and material self-support among its members"; its purpose was to help "Russia in her great struggle against the coalition of the Central Empires and against Bolshevism in all its forms." Naturally, most members served with the U.S. military or worked as consultants or engineers for war-related industries. In anticipation of interviewing with Americans, de Seversky received advice from association members early in the summer and prepared translated, notarized copies of official documents that certified his military career in Russia as an ace pilot, aircraft inspector, and aeronautical inventor.[3]

During the summer, de Seversky established contacts with staff members of the U.S. Army Air Service, great-grandfather to the current air force. He reached a point where he could submit documents and a formal request for a military appointment to Brig. Gen. William L. Kenly, director of the Division of Military Aeronautics, who reported directly to Secretary of War Newton D. Baker. Someone on Kenly's staff actually reviewed de Seversky's paperwork carefully. Although they rejected the Russian's initial request for combat flight duty, staff members recognized that de Seversky could make an important contribution to America's war effort as an inspector, consulting engineer, and test pilot for U.S.-manufactured war planes. General Kenly approved the naval attaché for assignment to the War Department's Bureau of Aircraft Production at the Buffalo District Office, New York.[4]

In midsummer 1918 de Seversky and his mother moved to Buffalo, where he joined a small, intrepid group of test pilots. Much of de Seversky's time was centered on the Curtiss Aeroplane and Motor Company. The North Elmwood Plant of that war-driven, expanded company worked to fulfill a contract to build a thousand Scout Experimental 5s. By the time the German Armistice was signed, ending the war on November 11, 5,125 S.E. 5s had been built among five companies in the United Kingdom and France. Curtiss Aeroplane and Motor Company added only one more to the total, although the company did build fifty-six S.E. 5s from parts imported from England. Regrettably, the prototype S.E. 5 sent to Curtiss arrived with incomplete drawings that mixed two variants with engines of different sizes. As a result, the fuselage and center of gravity had to be reengineered. Then, when de Seversky began flight-testing the craft for acceptance by the military, he discovered multiple problems with the engine and radiator system. Once the bugs were worked out, the war ended and so did the contract. De Seversky received kind letters of recommendation from both the War Department and Curtiss. But the rapid cancellation of military contracts left the Russian without employment on December 1, 1918.[5]

## Hannevig Aircraft

Despite being out of a job, de Seversky had enjoyed a great experience. Coupled with the fact that he also flew with the Allied Aerobatic Team to promote the sale of Liberty Bonds, his government employment gave him valuable contacts with the military, various aviators, and representatives of industry. If nothing else, he caught the favorable attention of the Information (Intelligence) Section of the U.S. Army Air Service, which kept track of the Russian because of the interesting gifts and skills he possessed as an aviator and inventor. Meanwhile, he and his mother moved to an apartment at 71 West 109th Street near the north end of Central Park on Manhattan Island, New York. The city attracted de Seversky because it served as home to many Russian émigrés and as headquarters for the Voluntary Association of Russian Army and Navy Officers. Through his ethnic and aviation connections, he soon found a position with Hannevig Aircraft.[6]

Unlike most aviation enterprises that failed or suffered severe cutbacks at war's end with the abrupt termination of military business, Hannevig Aircraft was a specialty firm indirectly connected to the war. Norwegian-American shipping magnate, Christoffer Hannevig, presided over a ship brokerage that carried his name and offered marine finance and insurance. He also owned three other businesses: Pusey and James Shipbuilding Company, Pennsylvania Shipbuilding Company, and New Jersey Shipbuilding Company. Together, these marine facilities built thirty-four merchant vessels for the U.S. Shipping Board, a federal agency that purchased and operated supply ships during the Great War. Hannevig recycled profits from wartime contracts into two projects. One supplied $100,000 to the National Portrait Gallery to buy paintings of contemporary U.S. leaders beginning with President Wilson and Secretary of War Baker.[7]

The other project led to Hannevig Aircraft, a design bureau created to fulfill the dream of flying a seaplane across the Atlantic Ocean. As a consultant and backup test pilot, de Seversky joined in midstream a small team of draftsmen headed by Swedish engineer and pioneer pilot Hugo Sundstedt. The team detailed a blueprint of the *Sunrise*, an airplane given three-dimensional life by subcontractor Witteman-Lewis Aircraft Company of Teterboro, New Jersey. Two Hall-Scott pusher motors each rated at 220 hp powered the sesquiplane built of ash and spruce. The fifty-foot fuselage sat on top of two large floats constructed of linen-covered balsa. When time came for Sundstedt, accompanied by de Seversky, to flight-test *Sunrise* in February 1919, the floats failed, causing irreparable damage to the aircraft. Fortunately for the Russian, whatever blame existed for the plane's shortcomings fell to the head engineer and subcontractor. De Seversky, in fact, ended up working for two years in Hannevig's brokerage office at 139 Broadway.[8]

A little over a month after the seaplane's demise, an old acquaintance of the family arrived in New York on March 30, 1919. Igor I. Sikorsky fled Russia a few days before de Seversky; however, he immigrated not to the United States but to France, where he designed a multiengine bomber for the French Aerial Division, advancing the work he had performed for the defunct Russian Empire. As it had in the United States, aircraft production collapsed in France after the Armistice. Unemployed, Sikorsky decided to join his numerous compatriots in America, "the land of opportunity." Through mutual friends in New York's Russian community, Sikorsky and de Seversky found each other. The latter introduced Igor to Christoffer Hannevig and his brother, Finn, and rekindled the dream of building a large transoceanic airplane. On May 27, 1919, Hannevig Aircraft was reorganized formally as the Hannevig-Sikorsky Aircraft Corporation under the laws of the state of New York. A point of encouragement for the revived company may have come from hotelier Raymond Orteig, who five days earlier offered a $25,000 prize for the first airplane to fly nonstop from New York to Paris, or vice versa.[9]

With $20,000 invested in the new enterprise by Finn Hannevig, another design bureau reemerged headed by Sikorsky. Because de Seversky had better language skills—he took English lessons from a young lady who danced for Florenz Ziegfeld in his annual follies—the test pilot also served as the bureau's manager. He could communicate the bureau's progress to the Hannevig family. The company could no longer be the first to fly across the Atlantic. The U.S. Navy's NC-4 flying boat accomplished that goal when it flew from Newfoundland to the Azores shortly before the new corporation was registered in Albany, New York. More significant for the project, the Hannevig empire may have faced a cash-flow problem because the U.S. Shipping Board delayed payment on a bill for ships manufactured during the war. Undoubtedly for multiple reasons, Finn Hannevig and his brother decided not to fund construction of the airplane designed by Sikorsky.[10]

After the design bureau disbanded in the fall of 1919, Sikorsky secured a temporary position with the Engineering Division of the U.S. Army Air Service at McCook Field in Dayton, Ohio. He would not have the resources to form his own Sikorsky Aero Engineering Corporation until March 1923. The mystery, however, is why de Seversky continued working for the ship brokerage firm. True, he had graduated from the Imperial Russian Naval Academy. Much of his wartime experience, though, had focused not on leasing or financing ships but on how to use aircraft to damage or destroy them. A rumor may solve the mystery. Christoffer Hannevig had a third brother, Edvard or Edward, who remained in Norway. Edward Hannevig led a syndicate that negotiated a concession with Soviet Russia to build a rail line between the Ob and Northern Dvina Rivers, with additional tracks connecting this Great Northern Railroad to lines running to Murmansk and Petrograd.[11]

The concession would be subsidized and garner a profit via 2.6 million acres of timberland that could be harvested for wood products, including pulpwood used in the manufacture of paper. Concessionaires received Soviet permission to bring ships and improve harbors to carry timber goods to American and European ports. Rumors circulated in New York that Edward secured the financial backing of his brothers in America. Logically, Christoffer and Finn would want to invest in their brother's project and not simply because of blood ties. The U.S. brokerage firm stood to gain solid earnings by leasing and insuring vessels employed in the concession's international trade. If true, the rumors may be the best explanation for why the American Hannevigs stopped their support for the airplane project and yet kept de Seversky on the payroll. The former naval officer did know something about Russian navigation and ports; he could also assist the Hannevigs in translating and understanding Soviet documents related to the concession.[12]

## Christmas *Bullet* and *Aeromarine 75*

Regardless, de Seversky had a small office with Christoffer Hannevig, Inc., where he worked at least part-time until March 1921. The Russian devoted his free days to flying and performing the duties of a test pilot. Although records for this period are skimpy, they reveal two interesting personalities and their companies that engaged de Seversky to inspect and flight-check aircraft. One of them was Dr. William Whitney Christmas, a trained medical doctor who gave up his practice to design and build airplanes. He hired de Seversky to test his latest aircraft, the *Bullet*. Located at Copiague near the south shore of Long Island, the Cantilever Aero Company built the *Bullet* in 1918. It was originally intended to be a pursuit plane for the military. A single-bay, single-engine sesquiplane, the *Bullet* possessed a dramatically different profile from other biplanes since the wings lacked external bracing, hence the name Cantilever for the doctor's latest company.[13]

Tragically, structural failure led to the crash and obliteration of the first *Bullet* on December 30, 1918. De Seversky took on the task of testing the second version in April 1919. On the positive side, the Russian noted that Dr. Christmas employed a veneer-clad fuselage for the *Bullet*, which reduced skin-friction drag and improved the plane's performance. On the other hand, the test pilot observed that the wings were remarkably thin and flat. In fact, the larger upper wing was designed to be flexible, bending upward to a dihedral position as the plane left the ground in flight. Physically a small man but with the build of an athlete, the Russian possessed unequalled courage. Despite fitness and fearlessness, de Seversky had no intention of committing suicide. He viewed the wings as unstable and weak and a serious danger to the life of anyone piloting the plane.[14]

In 1919 de Seversky celebrated his tenth anniversary of flying in, or piloting, airplanes. Arguably, he had more hours in the air and had flown more types of aircraft than any contemporary American. Moreover, he was a trained engineer and an experienced inspector who had taken aeronautical courses and had witnessed the methods and tests employed in manufacturing flyable aircraft. He simply knew the *Bullet*'s wings exhibited deadly deficiencies. Given the construction materials available at the time, wings that bent back and forth regularly would break unexpectedly. The most obvious flaw, though, was the fact that cantilevered wings could succeed only if internal bracing replaced external supports. The *Bullet*'s thin wings did not contain the robust longitudinal struts joined with cross-pieces or ribs to give them the strength necessary to carry into the air the load of engine, pilot, and fuselage. And Dr. Christmas failed to recognize that the flat wing represented a technology long out of season. Even the Wright brothers used a wind tunnel to get the appropriate curvature on the leading edge of the wings of their 1902 glider. Lower pressure above the curvature produces higher pressure below the wing, adding lift to a glider or an airplane in flight.[15]

Once de Seversky finished his ground rolls and brief hops at Lufbery Aviation Field outside Seaford, Long Island, he told Dr. Christmas he could not conduct a complete program of test flights until he secured a parachute. His remaining tests would have to include sharp turns, dives, spins, and loops that would increase exponentially the weight carried by the wings. Those who knew the Russian would be surprised by his reaction. He hated parachutes and never deployed one despite close calls and crashes over a lifetime of flying. Forty years later, he explained why in an interview with an old acquaintance, Brig. Gen. George W. Goddard, a pioneer and genius in the field of aerial photography. De Seversky had nightmares about a para-chute landing that splintered his wooden prosthesis and drove the remnant into the trunk of his body. Meanwhile, he informed Dr. Christmas that he would finish testing the *Bullet* after leasing a parachute. The first packed parachute small enough to be worn by a pilot in a pursuit plane had been developed the previous year by Lawrence B. Sperry, the aviation-minded son of the Brooklyn gyroscope manufacturer, Elmer A. Sperry.[16]

As de Seversky headed to New York on April 27, 1919, via the south shore branch of the Long Island Railroad, Dr. Christmas did something despicable, if not criminal. He asked a young military aviator who had just returned from France to flight-test the *Bullet*. Why the rush? Kerr Steamship Company agreed several days earlier to use a fleet of *Bullets* to fly delayed consignment papers to ships a day out of port (New York, Boston, Philadelphia, New Orleans, Galveston, and others) to save time and hence money. The notion of getting a substantial contract from Kerr and putting the *Bullet* into serial production evaporated whatever patience and common sense had been endowed to the former physician. Despite the clear misgivings of his hired and experienced test pilot, Dr. Christmas sent Lt. Allington Jolly into the air and to his death. Not far from Lufbery Aviation Field, the wings of the *Bullet* collapsed in midair. By the time de Seversky reached New York, Lieutenant Jolly's broken body was at the Mary Southard Mortuary.[17]

A more pleasant and productive relationship formed between de Seversky and Inglis M. Uppercu. The Manhattan Cadillac dealer hired the Russian as an engineering consultant and test pilot for occasional work in 1919 and 1920. During the Great War, not only did Uppercu serve on the Liberty Loan Committee of the Automobile Trades, he formed the Aeromarine Plane and Motor Company to build large flying boats as a subcontractor for the U.S. Navy. After the Armistice, Uppercu ended up with ten war surplus F-5-Ls, a jointly developed, multiengine, Anglo-American flying boat. By the summer of 1919, he used the craft to give flying tours of New York City and carry U.S. mail and messages of welcome to incoming troop ships at sea. As Uppercu began employing the craft for commercial purposes, he discovered the warplane's limitations. Gun emplacements were certainly superfluous, and any passengers had to sit in two open and uncomfortable cockpits behind the pilot.[18]

De Seversky, then, helped Uppercu remodel and test the F-5-L during its transformation from warplane to commercial aircraft. In the course of conversion, it was renamed *Aeromarine 75*. The dorsal cockpits were capped and the gun emplacements removed. Craftsmen altered the interior to seat up to ten passengers in a closed cabin lighted in the daytime by six circular windows. Both the process and the result required de Seversky's expertise. The remodeling of the interior could not violate the integrity of the fuselage and especially the hull, which, in essence, was a cross-braced box girder. Not only could de Seversky provide guidance on remodeling, he flew the refurbished plane to make certain the plane's center of gravity had not been abused and that the craft could remain stable in flight despite changes in load or configuration of passengers and freight.

On November 1, 1919, Uppercu's Aeromarine West Indies Airways began service by taking passengers and freight between Key West, Florida, and Havana, Cuba; it was the first bona fide commercial airline in the United States.[19]

## William (Billy) Mitchell

Despite his occasional work as test pilot, de Seversky's "day job" continued at Hannevig until early March 1921, when Maj. Horace Hickam dropped by his office. Fourteen years later, Hickam would perish tragically in an airplane accident. Contemporary opinion of his military leadership can be measured by the fact that Hickam Field, Hawaii (today, Hickam Air Force Base), was named in his honor. In 1921 he headed the Information Section of the U.S. Army Air Service. De Seversky and the major knew each other socially, but this visit fell under the category of official government business. Brig. Gen. Billy Mitchell, assistant chief of the U.S.A.A.S., requested de Seversky's presence in Washington at his earliest convenience. De Seversky later recalled that he had "met General Mitchell, informally, in 1919, right after the War, at several social and military functions. We were friends from the start. We spoke the same airmen's language." As a result, de Seversky was eager to respond to the general's invitation in a timely fashion. As soon as he packed a grip and informed his mother, he and Major Hickam boarded a train for the nation's capital and soon participated in several sessions with Mitchell. Along with the Soviet victory in the Russian Civil War, these conversations proved to be a life-altering experience as they resulted ultimately in giving de Seversky an American career and prompted him to become a citizen.[20]

Like most pilots and many Americans, de Seversky was in awe of the handsome and bold general and considered him a hero of military aviation. A month before the U.S. Congress declared war on Germany, Mitchell went to Europe as a military aviation observer of the western front. After American entrance in the conflict and after U.S. forces had arrived in France in sufficient numbers to conduct major operations, Colonel Mitchell served as chief of air service for the First Army of the American Expeditionary Force (AEF) led by Gen. John J. (Black Jack) Pershing. As the AEF prepared to go on the offensive against the German-held St. Mihiel salient in September 1918, Mitchell cobbled together 1,481 aircraft from French and U.S. squadrons. He divided these assets into two basic divisions, both tactical in nature: one group of squadrons directly supported American doughboys on the ground by attacking enemy trenches and intercepting enemy airplanes; the other group flew seven to fourteen miles behind German lines to bomb and strafe supply dumps, railroad depots, rolling stock, and reserve columns of troops.

Promoted from colonel to the temporary rank of brigadier general, Mitchell repeated on a lesser scale the strategy during the second U.S. offensive in the Meuse-Argonne sector. The obvious contributions rendered by the air service to the success of both offensives drew high praise from General Pershing.[21]

Mitchell returned home in 1919 convinced that future conflicts would be decided by the new technology of the air rather than the archaic infantry on the ground. In his mind, the airplane represented the future, quintessential weapon for both defense and offense. Not only could it wreak havoc on enemy troops, it could destroy an enemy's industrial and transportation infrastructures, turning armies in the field into defenseless mobs. Over time, Mitchell's writings, press interviews, and testimony before the U.S. Congress in 1919 and 1920 bore a repetitive element, though the mode of expression varied. Funds, he stated, were needed to strengthen America's air defense and produce in quantity advanced and reliable aircraft; army and navy pilots and their equipment should compose a single air force under a unified department of defense with subheads or assistant secretaries for air, army, and navy. Mitchell soon bolstered his assertions for modern aircraft and a strong, independent air force through comments on the vulnerabilities of warships when confronted by warplanes.[22]

### Warplanes versus Warships

It was a clever approach. In the years before World War I, the U.S. Navy fared well in competition with the army for limited funds from Congress. As a result, the United States possessed one of the largest and most modern navies in the world, and for a logical reason. Given weak or friendly neighbors north and south, and mammoth oceans east and west, the potential threat to American security could come only from an enemy with a strong navy. Mitchell, however, claimed that naval vessels, especially battleships, were expensive, slow, and now open to destruction by aircraft. Moreover, this new technology cost but a small fraction of the funds invested in a warship. One of many implications of Mitchell's observation was that an air force would be a more effective and less expensive way to protect coastal America. Meanwhile, when the United States received ships from defeated Germany as war booty, it had agreed with its wartime Allies to destroy them. Thus, as Mitchell repeated his challenge in testimony in January 1921 that dreadnoughts were a dead technology that could be sunk by aircraft, Congress responded. Enough members, supporters and skeptics alike, were intrigued by the provocative claim to pass a resolution urging the navy to provide target vessels for U.S.A.A.S. bombers. Even before the end of 1920, the Operations Division had worked out a plan of attack for the bombardment of a warship. In addition, Mitchell had several aces up his sleeve. Two of these were the newly produced Martin MB-2, twin-engine bomber that could carry a recently designed 2,000-pound blockbuster bomb. Alexander P. de Seversky represented the third ace for the current project but also two trump cards for future tests that might pit aircraft against moving warships on the high seas.[23]

Major Hickam took de Seversky to General Mitchell's Washington office for the first of several interviews. At the time of the first meeting, plans were under way to set up target ships for aerial attack by the beginning of summer. The vessels were to be located some seventy miles east of Cape Charles or about one hundred miles from Langley Field near Hampton, Virginia. The latter served as headquarters for the First Provisional Air Brigade created especially for the tests. Naturally, Mitchell focused most of his energies on gathering the best personnel, aircraft, and ordnance for the upcoming experiments, which he viewed as crucial for the future of American military aviation. Despite his crowded schedule and administrative duties, Mitchell saved time for de Seversky. The general eagerly probed the mind of the Russian who, after all, had witnessed and engaged in many bombing assaults on naval ships during the recent war. Mitchell totally missed such an experience in his otherwise well-seasoned military career.[24]

Just as importantly, Mitchell expressed great interest in two of de Seversky's inventions, in-flight refueling and a sophisticated bombsight, begun though not perfected when he flew for the Imperial Russian Navy. The upcoming tests required army planes to fly some two hundred miles round-trip over water. Heavy bomb loads reduced further the limited ranges of such aircraft as the DH-4 and MB-2, leaving little spare fuel for flying time over the target area. This limitation could not be addressed in 1921, but Mitchell focused frequently on the future. Neither the military nor the U.S. Congress would assign aircraft a serious role in coastal defense unless the combat range of aircraft could be extended. In-flight refueling promised a quick solution to the problem. By the same token, the U.S.A.A.S. lacked a good bombsight. Dropping ordnance on ships dead in the water posed a challenge; bombing a radio-controlled vessel running at full steam in the water seemed impossible without a highly accurate bombsight. Mitchell understood that, if not in 1921 then sometime, the air service would be called upon to demonstrate an airplane attack on a moving ship.[25]

## The Patented Consultant

Based on his interviews with de Seversky, Mitchell took several steps over the next few months to draw thoroughly upon the Russian's expertise. He secured through the office of Secretary of War John W. Weeks an appointment for de Seversky as a paid engineering consultant to the U.S.A.A.S. branch of the War Department. In addition, Mitchell ordered Major Hickam to take the Russian to the War Department's Patent Section under the direction of Col. Robert Young and his lawyer assistant, Lt. Ernest E. Harmon. Together, the four men completed, and subsequently filed on June 13, 1921, applications for patents. To his great credit, Mitchell insisted that de Seversky pay the filing fees out of his own pocket so there would never be any question over who actually held the patents. Finally, General Mitchell took his new consultant to Langley Field and gave him a personal guided tour, including an up-close, hands-on look at each of the several aircraft and the ordnance and fuses the U.S.A.A.S. would employ during the bombing exercise against naval ships. As it turned out, Mitchell's care in cultivating a collaborative relationship with de Seversky paid big dividends. Initially, after navy air units had sunk the U-117 submarine on June 21, 1921, the First Provisional Air Brigade successfully demolished the German destroyer G-102 on July 13 and the cruiser *Frankfurt* on July 18. Moreover, army aircraft located in two hours on the high seas the radio-controlled U.S. battleship *Iowa* in a 25,600 square mile area. The latter proved Mitchell's claim that it was easier for aircraft to spot an enemy at sea than on land. More troubling, however, was the fact that a navy air unit dropped on the moving ship eighty small water bombs, scoring only two hits and confirming the need for a good bombsight.[26]

Naturally, the focal point of the bombing program centered on the *Ostfriesland*. The whole plane versus ship exercise, after all, had been set in motion by Mitchell's contention that aircraft could sink battleships. While several admirals agreed that sooner or later aircraft would make large vessels obsolete, most naval officers firmly believed the battleship could survive an air attack even if undefended. Germany had built the *Ostfriesland* in 1911. It was a huge ship stretching almost 550 feet in length; it was also watertight to the point that telephone lines did not pierce internal bulkheads. On July 20, the first of two days of bombing, ordnance dropped by both naval and army air units failed to compromise the hull and caused only minor surface damage. This disturbed Mitchell because, while the navy employed smaller 250-pound bombs that often proved to be duds, the U.S.A.A.S. had released a cascade of perfectly functioning, 600-pound bombs. Thus the assistant air chief asked Major Hickam to call de Seversky in New York about this before the next day's last run, when plans called for six MB-2 and two Handley Page bombers to attack the ship with bombs weighing 2,000 pounds each.[27]

As the major and Russian conversed, de Seversky related the following incident in the Baltic during the Great War:

> My bombing squadron had been sent to an advance position on Runo, a little island in the Gulf of Riga. Our air activities were so intense that we ran out of gas, food and ammunition. As a result, we were grounded and at the mercy of German bombers. Finally, a large transport came with supplies. After unloading, it left the bay for the open Gulf. Almost immediately the vessel was attacked by a German plane. We chuckled with relief as we saw the string of eight light bombs miss their target and fall into the water alongside the ship. In a few minutes, however, our glee turned to anxiety. An SOS signal (flag) was raised on the ship's mast, and our radioman came running from the radio tower shouting that the transport was in distress. Those small bombs, exploding under water near the ship, had produced enough pressure to open the steel plates![28]

As he described to Hickam what is commonly referred to now as the water-hammer effect, de Seversky noted another potential benefit of dropping bombs alongside, rather than on, the *Ostfriesland*. In addition to his tour of Langley Field, de Seversky spent time at the Aberdeen Proving Grounds, Maryland, to watch tests of the new 2,000-pound bomb. The tests revealed a potential problem in creating an explosion through the entire mass of TNT because of the use of multiple fuses. In the fraction of a second after a bomb hit an armored deck, the bomb's casing might actually start to fall to pieces before the several fuses kicked in, reducing the effect of a half ton of TNT exploding in a single blast. A streamlined bomb, though, hitting water would preserve the casing's integrity and allow the fuses to detonate the explosive material in a mass of destructive energy. Major Hickam promptly relayed de Seversky's information to Mitchell, who instructed his pilots to target the water next to the battleship.[29]

The next day, July 21, at about 1215 hours local time, a line of six MB-2 and one Handley Page aircraft (one failed to reach target) flying nearly 3,000 feet overhead dropped their one-ton bombs. Four of these hit water in rapid succession next to the *Ostfriesland*, which rose ten feet from the underwater blast. Naval personnel on witness ships felt the water concussion more than a mile away. Immediately after the explosions, the battleship began listing to port and in minutes completely rolled over. From his observation post in a DH-4 that flew over the foundering vessel, General Mitchell observed that the port plates of the ship's bottom had been separated aft of amidships. Slightly more than twenty minutes after the start of the bomb run, the *Ostfriesland* disappeared from the ocean's surface. Mitchell and his pilots were jubilant in their victory over the battleship. And de Seversky shared in the celebration because of his contribution to the historic occasion, which also sealed his relationship with the general.[30]

While the air-minded around the world marked the *Ostfriesland*'s demise as a portent to air power's supremacy over large warships, America's naval brass began disparaging the results of the test before the bombers had a chance to return to Langley Field. An anchored and crewless ship, they argued and offered unrealistic competition to military aircraft. And some pro-navy politicians suggested that the limited range of its equipment meant the U.S.A.A.S. might help guard coastal marsh but the U.S. Navy must continue to protect America on the high seas. So it was not a shock that a joint army-navy board under the leadership of Gen. John J. Pershing concluded in September 1921 that the battleship remained the centerpiece of the fleet and a key to the nation's defense. At the time Pershing issued this verdict, de Seversky was busy designing and constructing two inventions with the potential to turn the board's conclusion into an archaic curiosity.[31]

### Reflections

Both primary source documents and secondary source publications related to de Seversky and available for the 1918–1921 period are scanty in number and contradictory in content. Thus it may be a surprise that the author ignored a juicy piece of testimony. In the early 1930s de Seversky took a speech class to build his confidence and skill in making a public address. He wrote out his class presentations, which are now preserved in his papers in the Cradle of Aviation Museum. The speech in question recounts his birthday celebration as a young adult; it centered on spending a night on the town with several friends. There is nothing terribly revealing in this episode except that he conformed to the ubiquitous Russian custom of drinking vodka. Other than the implication that the event occurred years earlier, de Seversky failed to inform his audience which birthday he celebrated. It is possible to hazard a guess of June 7, 1919, because he makes reference to neither a "speakeasy" nor Prohibition, which went into effect in January 1920, one year after the ratification in 1919 of the Eighteenth Amendment to the Constitution.

The only reason to mention the speech now is to confirm that the young man and his mother enjoyed a reasonably stable existence. In the talk, the birthday celebration began when de Seversky left his and Vera's apartment and ended when he returned home. This belies a secondary source article hinting that the Russian suffered dire poverty after he left government service and spent many nights sleeping on a park bench. The same article ignores completely the fate of his mother during this time of "hardship." Moreover, there is one piece of de Seversky correspondence with American Express in this period that clearly indicates Sasha and Vera lived in an apartment in Manhattan. In a recorded interview and in a publication written by de Seversky (both, of course, potentially self-serving), he paints a different picture. De Seversky states that he flew planes as a test pilot, had an office, and worked for two years as a broker of merchant vessels. Frankly, the latter seems unlikely or at best like puffery. This is why the chapter narrative contains speculation that his employment with Christoffer Hannevig, Inc., may have focused on investments in a Soviet Russian concession. Because de Seversky had little to say about this era in his life, his job with Hannevig may have been both occasional and unsavory, at least for a member of the Russian nobility.

# 5

## The Russian Inventor

On March 22, 1921, Alexander P. de Seversky arrived at McCook Field, Dayton, Ohio, home to the U.S. Army Air Service Engineering Division, carrying with him letters of introduction. They revealed to Maj. Thurman H. Bane, division chief, a strong desire on the part of General Mitchell to have de Seversky fashion for the air service, first, an effective bombsight, but also the technology for transferring fuel from one airplane to another during flight. The Russian joined a group of civilians employed by the division that conducted research and development for all aspects of military aircraft, including design, construction materials, airframes, engines, propellers, parachutes, cameras, radio navigation, fuel systems, superchargers, and instruments of all types. After the U.S. Congress passed legislation reorganizing the air service as the U.S. Army Air Corps in 1926, the unit became the Materiel Division and moved to nearby Wright Field, later renamed the Wright-Patterson Air Force Base (AFB).[1]

### The Engineering Division

Meanwhile, Maj. L. W. McIntosh, assistant chief of the Engineering Division, took de Seversky on a tour of McCook Field. Besides aircraft sheds, the field sported laboratories to test propellers, airspeed devices, and wings or airframes; it also possessed a dynamometer laboratory plus several workshops, including one for designing and developing mechanisms such as bombsights. As part of the tour, the Russian met and conversed with three figures with whom he would collaborate occasionally over the next eighteen months: Maj. Eddie L. Hoffman, in charge of the Equipment Branch; Capt. Harold Harris, who headed the Flight Test Branch;

and Henry B. Inglis, former captain turned civilian who now focused his mechanical engineering skills on assisting the Russian with the bombsight. And de Seversky needed the help of an engineer as well as an instrument manufacturer because his bombsight was far more complex than those employed during the Great War.[2]

Once pilots or bombardiers in World War I discovered guesswork or intuition failed to let them know when to release a bomb, they turned to physics. The prime ingredients requiring analysis centered on the altitude and speed of the bomber, the wind direction, and the measure of both inertia and gravity on a free-falling bomb dropped from a moving airplane. A device that attempted to account for most of these factors was adopted by the U.S.A.A.S. from the work of Lt. Cdr. Harry E. Wimperis of Great Britain's Royal Naval Air Service. The early Wimperis employed two rifle-type sights adjusted for speed, altitude, and the ballistics of the bomb. To avoid the impact of wind drift on falling ordnance, pilots flew directly into or away from the wind and released bombs when the front and rear sights lined up on the target. The Wimperis had a chance to work but only at a low altitude and in a perfect scenario in which the plane's heading remained absolutely straight and level.[3]

Unfortunately, reality intruded on this scenario. At 10,000 feet, the Wimperis had "circular error probable" over a target of more than 600 feet. But why? The answer resides in part in the fact that an airplane in flight is a floating object in a gaseous fluid; it simply oscillates as a matter of course. A virtually unnoticeable change in pitch up or down of only one degree would cause a bomb to miss its target completely. De Seversky had a solution to this problem. As an officer trained in the Imperial Russian Navy, he was familiar with another vehicle that oscillated in a different kind of fluid: the warship in water. Similar to a serious bombardier in an airplane, a battleship's gunner had to consider the pitch of his craft. Major war vessels constructed or reequipped shortly before or after 1914 often contained gyroscopes to provide the stability necessary so gunners could accurately fire a salvo against enemy ships.[4]

During the recent global conflict, de Seversky began experimenting with the notion of merging a ship's gyroscope with an airplane's bombsight. He also started to develop a calculator, a primitive computer that would quickly synchronize the numbers of an airplane's altitude and speed with the vector of a falling bomb to know the precise moment when to release ordnance that actually had a chance to hit the target. De Seversky, good at math and engineering, understood his limitations as a craftsman. He knew what kinds of instruments were needed and their operation but not how to build them. Moreover, the Russian had no thought of forming a company to manufacture the bombsight. He simply lacked the capital resources necessary to buy the sophisticated and expensive machine tools needed to build such intricate devices.[5]

Instead, he would be happy to receive a regular paycheck from the army along with the hope of a royalty for each bombsight the government purchased from a manufacturer who built the device under his patent. Thus the first activity shared by de Seversky and Inglis found the pair riding the rails to Chicago, Philadelphia, and New York on a mission to find a company capable of translating the Russian's concept into a workable apparatus. Despite stops on their way to Brooklyn, it was all but a foregone conclusion that the Sperry Gyroscope Company would end up with a contract. In fact, by the time de Seversky and Inglis entered Elmer Ambrose Sperry's office on April 9, 1921, the company president had already been in telephone contact with General Mitchell. The general discussed with Sperry the subject of gyroscopically controlled bombsights and his firm's ability to produce such equipment in timely fashion.[6]

## Sperry Gyroscope Company

One reason Mitchell expected de Seversky to select the Brooklyn firm is because by 1921 the Sperry name was synonymous with the term "gyroscope." Born in Cortland, New York, in 1860, Elmer Sperry attended Cornell University, where he studied electricity. A skilled mechanic and an inventive genius, he applied his Cornell education to improving or developing dynamos, arc lights, electric locomotives, mining machines, trolley cars, electric automobiles, storage batteries, and the electrochemistry used in plating metal. By the 1890s he began studying and building gyroscopes, which he first applied to the stabilization of naval vessels. While functional, gyro stabilizers for ships proved expensive, heavy, and hard to maintain. By contrast, Sperry invented a gyroscopic compass that overcame the shortcomings of the magnetic compass on board ships now constructed of metal rather than wood. Small wonder Mitchell automatically considered the Sperry Gyroscope Company the best firm for manufacturing de Seversky's bombsight.[7]

In fact, Sperry would build several bombsights for the army in the 1920s and early 1930s. Besides de Seversky, a Swiss immigrant, Georges Estoppey, also worked for the Engineering/Materiel Division and designed Sperry-built bombsights. And, because Henry B. Inglis assisted both de Seversky and Estoppey, the former army captain tried his hand at designing bombsights as well. He spent so much time with de Seversky and Estoppey in Brooklyn that in 1928 he left the Materiel Division for a position with Sperry. From the viewpoint of Sperry and the army, the years of effort and money spent on bombsights ended in a cruel and expensive joke. The device installed in American bombers in World War II was designed and manufactured not by Sperry but by a former Sperry employee, Carl Lukas Norden. The Dutch immigrant secured support and a contract from the army's competitor in sports and congressional funding, the U.S. Navy.[8]

### De Seversky's Original Bombsight

But back at the beginning, Sperry sent Engineering Division chief Bane a lengthy letter on April 13, 1921. He detailed his telephone conversations with General Mitchell as well as his interview with de Seversky and Inglis. While the company president admitted the "device that Mr. Seversky had in mind seemed to us to be very complex," he was confident that his firm either had or could manufacture all the needed parts and in a relatively short period of time. In separate communications to Inglis at McCook Field, Sperry actually listed for the knowledgeable engineer several elements of de Seversky's bombsight that were already available. This is not to suggest that the company executive promised quick off-the-shelf technology. He recognized that weight and space constraints on aircraft required downsizing many parts and encasing major components in aluminum rather than steel.[9]

As correspondence and telegrams between McCook Field and Brooklyn became a daily occurrence, Sperry made a request of Major Bane just a week after his first letter to the Engineering Division chief. "Inasmuch as the interconnections and factors of the (bombsight) system are so clearly in mind of Mr. Seversky, it might be wise for you to consider having the work done under his supervision." Appreciating the logic of the situation, Bane endorsed Sperry's recommendation. Soon, de Seversky became a semipermanent fixture at the Sperry headquarters, where he had his own office and worked alongside company engineers and technicians. As a result, the Russian inventor eventually moved his mother, Vera, and his residence to Brooklyn at 7 East 42nd Street. Located near Flatbush Avenue, his new home gave him an easy commute to the Manhattan Bridge Plaza and the Sperry Company.[10]

Once established at Sperry's, de Seversky worked in concert with company technicians to outline major components and identify subassemblies required to build the main structures. The seminar-like group brainstormed the functions and how to accomplish the functions of the bombsight system conceived by de Seversky. By May 18, 1921, de Seversky and his collaborators described six unitary structures: a gyroscope, an observer's or bombardier's station with telescope, a gyroscopic compass, a wind-driven generator, and two reading indicators. These six primary mechanisms required at least fifty-five subassemblies; others were added later. On this basis, Sperry requested and received a development contract from the air service for the sum of $6,600. Even though the amount at that time could buy a brand new military pursuit plane, the expense of creating the complex device far exceeded the funds sought by Sperry, who intended to recoup his costs through a generous profit margin on the sale of the finished and serially manufactured bombsight.[11]

Early in June, the army contract arrived at Sperry's and thus began, in some cases quite literally, the nuts and bolts work of building the de Seversky apparatus. Much of the next twelve months was devoted not so much to inventing new devices as to reducing the size and weight of existing mechanisms for use in aircraft and then putting these components together in new ways to create what would be, at least for the moment, the most accurate bombsight in the world. During the course of these labors, de Seversky served in the roles of supervisor, inspector, and tester of the various components as they emerged from the hands and machine tools of Sperry craftsmen. Accompanying these necessary though often mundane tasks were three interesting problems that also engaged the attention of de Seversky. The first of these involved the question of how many men would be required to operate the bombsight.[12]

De Seversky's original plan called for three manned stations: telescope, compass, and central. Engineering Division officers quickly concluded the weight penalty of a three-man crew to be excessive and required an adjustment to eliminate one of the manned stations. After attending a Society of Automotive Engineers convention in the Midwest, Elmer Sperry visited Inglis at McCook Field on May 21, 1921. Together they tried, but failed, to find a logical way to reduce the number of manned stations. Subsequently, Sperry wrote,

> Here the matter rested until my arrival in New York when I summoned Mr. Seversky and told him what . . . [the] Division wished to accomplish. He immediately set to work on this with excellent cooperation and, as a result, I am happy to state that a system completely practical and considerably simpler than the one that Captain Inglis and I had in mind in Dayton has been settled upon.

De Seversky had found an easy way to link the compass to the telescope station eliminating one crew member.[13]

Another important issue appeared in the form of a question about how to place a device that weighed two hundred pounds and took up three cubic feet of space in the MB-2. The twin-engine craft that served as the principal U.S.A.A.S. bomber would have to be altered. De Seversky, noted for his humor and prized for his appealing personality, joked that he would have to take a saw and hatchet to carve out enough space in the nose of the plane to house both bombsight and bombardier. Actually, engineers and craftsmen at McCook Field carefully redesigned the MB-2. Space, however, remained at a premium. During later tests, de Seversky, who naturally took the role of bombardier, found the elbow room of the airplane's nose so limited he removed his right leg to fit his body around his invention during flights. When de Seversky informed General Mitchell about his unusual solution to the space problem, the general, also known for his sense of humor, smiled devilishly and said, "Don't let that bother you. If the bombsight goes into service we can remedy that very easily. The right leg of all bombardiers will be amputated!"[14]

With the assistance of the War Department's Patent Office and specifically its patent attorney, Lt. Ernest E. Harmon, de Seversky officially "abandoned" his 1921 application and submitted a successful document for a bombsight patent on April 10, 1922. Hence the third and most striking issue connected with the apparatus was that neither de Seversky nor Sperry considered the task complete despite the fact that the inventor finished designing in April and the company would shortly finish constructing the original device. As early as January 1922, de Seversky convinced Sperry that another major component should be added to the system, a calculator to merge bomb ballistics with the speed, altitude, and direction of the airplane. Potentially, the coordination of data from system components would create the option of employing one person, a bombardier, to operate the sight.[15]

Despite warnings from Capt. Robert H. Fleet, contracting officer, that the Engineering Division had not authorized the design of a calculator, Sperry chose in the spring to make available to de Seversky a small amount of company research funds for a preliminary investigation into a calculator that both men considered to be a crucial concept for the success of the sighting device. In the meantime, the Russian inventor accompanied components of the original bombsight on a trip to McCook Field for initial testing. Lt. Donald L. Bruner, revered today for his development in 1922–1923 of night-flying equipment for the military, conducted tests in the first two weeks of July 1922. The de Seversky bombsight showed great promise. Even when dropped from an altitude of 8,000 feet, a few dummy bombs landed as close as forty feet to a marked line. With the promise that a calculator would improve accuracy even more, the Engineering Division awarded the Sperry Gyroscope Company another development contract for a second, now data-coordinated, de Seversky bombsight.[16]

While Lieutenant Bruner traveled to Brooklyn on July 17, 1922, to personally hand the results of the preliminary bombsight tests to the Sperry Gyroscope Company, de Seversky stayed behind at McCook Field. Technically finished with the bombsight project, he worked as engineering consultant on several other projects with Maj. Eddie Hoffman of the Equipment Branch. One project that later resulted in another patent application focused on aircraft landing gear. De Seversky devised a refined method of employing hydraulics to cushion the shock to aircraft and pilot when an airplane came in for a landing. In no sense can the Russian be credited with inventing the oleo struts that connected and buffered the wheels to the fuselage. The invention is generally assigned to French pioneers Robert Esnault-Pelterie in 1908 or Louis Bréguet in 1910. De Seversky improved the concept, which in the 1920s gradually replaced the standard vee-braced struts that softened aircraft landings via rubber cords or metal springs.[17]

### In-Flight Refueling

De Seversky now shared specific designs for another technology, in-flight refueling, with Hoffman. It will be recalled from the previous chapter that Mitchell recognized the great potential refueling could have for military aviation. Moreover, he insisted the Russian apply quickly for a patent. On the surface, the in-flight refueling principle is simple. A supply aircraft with an extra fuel tank drops a hose from the tank to a receiving aircraft during flight and, through gravity or pump, transfers fuel to extend the flying time and range of the receiving airplane. There are, however, a few noteworthy elements that make the process a bit more complicated. These include using a method (for de Seversky, a collapsible mechanism) to guide the hose to the receiving aircraft, linking the hose to a special receptacle built to rotate to permit a degree of motion between distributing and receiving craft, and building a device at the receptacle end of the hose that would quickly and effectively cut off flowing fuel should the hose be removed accidentally.[18]

While de Seversky had discussed in general terms in-flight refueling with Major Hoffman in the spring of 1921, he now disclosed detailed plans and technical specifications for the device along with its tactical applications. To be sure, de Seversky presented several arguments in his patent application for why in-flight refueling could prove to be valuable, including the benefit of extending the range of commercial aircraft. Fascinatingly, in his list of potential applications, his first line of reasoning was as follows:

> It is well known that dirigibles and large bombing planes are almost completely at the mercy of the small, easily maneuverable, pursuit planes, and that it is almost essential that in every bombing expedition the dirigible or large bombing plane must be accompanied by an escort of pursuit planes for purposes of defense. However, the small weight carrying capacity of these small fast planes permits them to carry only two or three hours fuel and thus limits their range of operation to such a considerable degree that it is impossible to conduct a bombing expedition any great distance into the enemy territory.[19]

De Seversky's first point in his patent clearly reflects his personal wartime experience, one shared by aviators on both the eastern and western fronts of the 1914–1918 conflict. What is troubling is that U.S. military pilots "unlearned" this lesson. With the notable exception of Claire L. Chennault and a handful of others, most members of the U.S. Army Air Corps adopted the notion in the 1930s that bombers were virtually invincible. Boeing's magnificent B-17 reinforced this belief in the second half of the decade. The Flying Fortress carried multiple ports for machine guns to give the bomber defensive protection. And it could fly faster than America's top pursuit plane, the P-26, when the four-engine aircraft was first tested in 1935. Thus the tragedy of 1943 resulted. The United States temporarily lost the air war over Germany in World War II as American bombers without cover from pursuit planes fell victim to German fighters. De Seversky had stated the solution in the 1921 patent. Near the end of 1943, the U.S. Army Air Forces found a way to add fuel and hence range to pursuit planes, which enabled them to accompany and protect American bombers on long-distance runs over German targets.[20]

Over the winter of 1922–1923, the Equipment Branch prepared, tested, and then sent the components of de Seversky's in-flight refueling process out West to a U.S.A.A.S. tactical unit. The first practical demonstration of his invention took place on June 27, 1923, in a pair of DH-4 biplanes flying above Rockwell Field, San Diego. Lt. Virgil Hine piloted the tanker while Lt. Frank Seifert occupied the aft cockpit and took care of unwinding the hose. Capt. Lowell Smith flew the receiving DH-4 and Lt. John Richter inserted the hose with its special shutoff valve into the flexible receptacle. After this favorable trial, multiple refuelings of an airplane were accomplished in succeeding days. The capstone to these early tests occurred on August 27 and 28, when, after fourteen refuelings, Smith and Richter set the world's endurance record for airplanes by flying 3,293 miles nonstop over a measured course. This demonstration, however, did not lead to a permanent role for in-flight refueling with the U.S.A.A.C. Rapid improvements in aircraft engineering in the 1920s and 1930s made planes of all types not only safer, faster, and stronger but also gave them much better range. Only with the advent of the Cold War and the emergence of the Strategic Air Command (SAC) did the U.S. Air Force establish the first aerial refueling units. On June 30, 1948, the 43rd and 509th Air Refueling Squadrons were created to service B-50 and, later, B-52 bombers. Near that date, de Seversky "celebrated" with mixed feelings the first anniversary after his patent had expired and become public property.[21]

Meanwhile, in July 1922, he could celebrate unequivocally his good fortune. The bombsight he had worked on for a year showed promise of meeting air service requirements for accuracy and the Sperry Gyroscope Company received a government contract expressly devoted to developing de Seversky's calculator. The new addition to the original bombsight would no longer depend on the largess of the company president. Moreover, a little over two months after the Russian inventor returned to Brooklyn and his office at Sperry, the circumstances of his employment changed in a way that propelled him in a new, exciting direction. On October 13, 1922, the acting chief of the Engineering Division at McCook Field, Maj. A. H. Hobley, sent de Seversky a formal, third-person letter for the record confirming the major's telephonic conversations with Sperry and the Russian concerning the latter's employment status.[22]

## Seversky Aero Corporation

A frugal U.S. Congress had cut the military budget. The U.S.A.A.S. responded by looking for ways to save funds for military personnel and equipment. Hence the air service chose to separate civilians from government employment. The U.S. Civil Service regulations, though, forced the Engineering Division to reduce expenditures by eliminating only those individuals hired, like de Seversky, on temporary status. Sperry Gyroscope Company, then, was asked to agree to a change order in the contract for the calculator. "The effect," Hobley concluded, "of the arrangement, therefore, is to transfer the cost of Mr. Seversky's service from the payroll of the Engineering Division, which must be decreased, to the cost of the automat[ic] calculator which is being built by the Sperry Company. The rights of both the government and Mr. Seversky with respect to the calculator will remain unchanged."[23]

The last point was a key. Maj. Gen. Mason M. Patrick, chief of the U.S. Army Air Service, had adamantly refused to pay royalties for items designed by civilians on government payroll. So now de Seversky could sign a contract that ensured him a share of the proceeds should the calculator go into Sperry production for army purchase. Regrettably, the document seems not to have survived; however, de Seversky's bombsight rival, Georges Estoppey, received a similar, if not identical, contract that promised him a 7.5 percent royalty on the sale price of any device he designed after leaving the employ of the U.S.A.A.S. Since de Seversky now earned a regular paycheck from Sperry and secured the potential for augmenting his income via royalties, he took the next logical step. With the help of his friend and former naval commander in Russia, Alexander A. Toochkoff, the inventor established under the laws in Delaware the Seversky Aero Corporation in the fall of 1922.[24]

The organization was beyond modest. Officially headquartered in de

Seversky's Brooklyn residence on 42nd Street, the head of the household served as president, general manager, director, and founder of the corporation. His friend Toochkoff assumed the lofty post of treasurer. The corporation produced absolutely nothing; it was a patent-holding, royalty-collecting entity pure and simple. Within six years of its establishment, the corporation oversaw twenty-two patents in seven countries. While a couple of these patents stood alone, such as an anchor attachment for seaplanes and a testing device for aircraft floats, most centered on some aspect of landing gear, in-flight refueling, or bombsights. In 1935 the company ceased to exist, and these early patents along with dozens of new ones (over time de Seversky applied for more than a hundred patents) folded into the Seversky Aircraft Corporation, a manufacturing firm that actually made something.[25]

Over the winter of 1922–1923, de Seversky worked assiduously on the calculator. The effort proved intense because the device turned out to be extremely intricate. Not only did it coordinate the ballistics of the bomb with the other bombsight instruments to let the bombardier know the exact moment when to release a bomb, it mechanically transferred information to the pilot that enabled him to fly the aircraft accurately above the observed target. In the spring of 1923, the Russian accompanied the completed bombsight to McCook Field. With the help of the Equipment Branch, he set up an indoor testing facility. A remote-controlled model battleship maneuvered at different speeds and directions on the floor. Above the battleship stood a movable platform-airplane on which was mounted the bombsight and small missiles to be released at the time indicated by the inventor's analog computer.[26]

Once he had successfully completed several trials of the bombing simulator, de Seversky contacted Major Hickam, who arranged for General Mitchell to fly to McCook Field for a demonstration. As the inventor later recalled,

> I have never seen anyone so boyishly excited, so enthusiastic. He climbed onto the platform and acted the role of bombardier; then General Mitchell was the pilot; then he was on the floor manoeuvering the "battleship" to test the bombsight under every conceivable condition—all the while giving me valuable pointers for its future installation and operational use. When "hits" were scored, as they were every time, he shouted with exuberant joy. "That's the stuff, Seversky!"[27]

## Warplanes versus Warships: Round Two

Congressional legislation heightened Mitchell's excitement during the simulations. The U.S. Congress authorized $50,000 in an army appropriations act to continue airplane bombing tests against obsolete U.S. Navy warships. This measure helped America comply with tonnage limitations of capital ships agreed upon by the Great Powers during the Washington Naval Disarmament Conference of 1921–1922. A portion of the authorized funds paid for the de Seversky bombsight and calculator as well as for the work of Dr. Sanford A. Moss, who developed the supercharger. The latter supplied compressed air to the cylinders of an internal combustion engine to maintain sea-level conditions at altitude. Thus, after his sojourn with de Seversky, Mitchell informed the navy about the new bombsight and indicated that he favored tests that mimicked battle conditions by having target ships carry live ammunition and operate under full power with radio-controlled movement. The navy chose to avoid "battle conditions" that might prove the superiority of air power. Instead, the sea service challenged, and the general accepted, the air service to drop some bombs from 10,000 feet—1,500 feet higher than the normal service ceiling of the MB-2/NBS-1 bomber and 2,000 feet higher than the normal testing altitude for bombsights.[28]

After General Mitchell left for Washington, D.C., de Seversky collaborated with the Equipment Branch to modify an NBS-1 bomber and install the latest bombsight. Once finished, the inventor entrained for New York to put the finishing touches on his patent application for the calculator and get ready for a lengthy stay at Langley Field. As de Seversky traveled south to Virginia, Lt. John F. Whiteley of the Flight Test Branch flew the NBS-1 bomber from McCook to Langley. Between June 18 and September 1, 1923, Whiteley and de Seversky worked as a team, pilot and bombardier, to perfect the settings and operations of the C-1 bombsight under actual flying conditions. They dropped live and dummy ordnance on stationary targets. In addition, de Seversky came up with a unique way to practice hitting objects in motion. He asked that on sunny days an army airship accompany the NBS-1 in flying over safe ground and water ranges. De Seversky then practiced dropping bombs on airship shadows to imitate an attack against a moving ship.[29]

Despite all the energy devoted to testing, followed by C-1 training for a couple pilots and bombardiers, de Seversky still had room in his schedule for an active social life at Langley. He spent much of his free time at the officers' club, where he met men with whom he would cross paths in the future. At the club, he loved being entertained and being entertaining; the amputee absolutely refused to allow his wooden leg to dampen his, or anyone else's, fun. Not only did he go swimming nearby, he cut an expert figure on the club's dance floor. His partners, wives of officers, marveled at his agility. And he played the piano and sang with gusto Russian songs from a happier era. The officers especially noted de Seversky's playful jests. They were one of the reasons Whiteley enjoyed the Russian's company. Although they saw each other only occasionally after 1923, the pair remained friends for life.[30]

At the beginning of September, when air service attention shifted south from Langley to a temporary field on the sandy dunes by Cape Hatteras, de Seversky returned to Brooklyn and the Sperry Gyroscope Company. As the inventor developed a final piece of technology—a speed drive for his calculator—his bombsight received its final test. On September 5, 1923, a special tactical squadron of seventeen bombers, formed and trained by General Mitchell, dropped explosives on the dreadnoughts *Virginia* and *New Jersey*. Both launched in 1906, the sister ships each weighed 15,000 tons and measured 441 feet in length. Three hundred witnesses watched the demonstration from the transport vessel, the *St. Mihiel*, and included the U.S. Army chief, Gen. John J. Pershing; Assistant Secretary of War Dwight F. Davis; U.S. Army Air Service chief, Maj. Gen. Patrick M. Mason; naval war plans director, Rear Adm. William R. Shoemaker; a number of army and navy officers; an assortment of senators and representatives from the U.S. Congress; and twenty journalists representing the fourth estate.[31]

Unlike in 1921, when bombs fell alongside the *Ostfriesland* to separate the hull's plates, both army and navy wanted ordnance to strike, or try to strike, the ships. The main point was to note how accurate aircraft at different altitudes could be in releasing live bombs. Naturally, there was also great interest by all parties in how much damage would be caused by different-sized bombs falling on the vessels. Three surprises awaited observers on board the *St. Mihiel*, unexpected shocks that alarmed the navy. First, the two-day exercise lasted only one day because the targets no longer existed. Second, a bomber equipped with de Seversky's C-1 sighting device actually hit the *New Jersey* with lighter bombs from nearly two miles above the battleship. It was indeed "a revelation in bombing accuracy." Subsequently, the *New*

76

*Jersey* sank after several aerial attacks at lower altitudes with heavier shells, including one-ton bombs dropped at 3,000 feet.[32]

Third, seven planes at 3,000 feet dropped bombs each weighing 1,100 pounds on the battleship *Virginia*. Most of the devices were slightly off target and caused little visible damage. One bomb, though, landed aft of the superstructure and penetrated the top deck before exploding in flame and smoke like a belching volcano. When the air and debris cleared, witnesses on the *St. Mihiel* were astounded by the sight. The blast demolished *Virginia's* superstructure as masts and funnels rolled up in a tangled mess over the forward turret of guns. In a matter of minutes, the battleship succumbed to the inevitable and disappeared from the ocean's surface. The naval officers were initially dumbfounded and distraught by the apparently quick, devastating work of a single, medium-sized bomb. Once the officers regained their composures, they excitedly talked among themselves about how to deal with the situation that turned out to be the worst-case scenario for the U.S. Navy.[33]

Salvation came during the preparation of the official press release to be issued in the name of General Pershing. The U.S. Army chief of staff did the right thing in seeking approvals of General Patrick and Admiral Shoemaker. When Shoemaker read the statement, he was overheard to say it was completely accurate, but it would "ruin" the U.S. Navy. He and naval aides went to work and blue-penciled the draft. Consequently, the final statement emphasized that the demonstration focused on bombing from different altitudes, not on destroying ships; the ships lost their integrity by the prior removal of some watertight doors; and the *New Jersey* withstood prolonged and multiple aerial attacks. And General Pershing was made to say, "These tests against these obsolete ships will not, I hope, be considered any conclusive evidence that similar bombs would sink modern types of battleships, particularly when manned, defended, and able to take protective measures (i.e., movement and smoke screens) against the effects of damage by bombs."[34]

While de Seversky in Brooklyn could take satisfaction in reading Pershing's comments about the success of the "new sighting device," Billy Mitchell was furious. The navy virtually closed the avenue of communication for *St. Mihiel* journalists as it sent the heavily edited Pershing statement out by wireless. The net effect guaranteed that early editions of next-day newspapers contained only the navy's interpretation of the bombing demonstration. Mitchell's frustration over this and related incidents augmented his exasperation and heightened over time the level of his criticism of the military and political leadership in the nation's capital. This, in turn, led to his court-martial in the fall of 1925 for insubordination and defiance of civilian authority. Sentenced to five years' suspension at reduced pay, Mitchell elected to resign from the army and devote much of his remaining years to writing about air power. His publications found an avid reader in the person of de Seversky. As the Russian-American moved from inventing aviation components to designing and manufacturing aircraft, he sought Mitchell's counsel. The quest for guidance revived and strengthened the collaborative relationship the two men enjoyed between 1921 and 1923.[35]

## Reflections

There are over fifty boxes and folders of Alexander P. de Seversky papers spread among a variety of libraries and archives. Thus, coupled with his numerous publications, there is ample information to outline his major activities as well as detail his views on military aviation. On the other hand, personal letters are few in number in the aforementioned collections and only occasionally does de Seversky offer a private observation in what might be termed his official correspondence. As a result, the common elements of his daily life can only be divined. We will never know, for example, whether he hated brassy blondes, tall people, train rides, and asparagus. Someone culled the bulk of personal letters from his papers.

The process eliminated the possibility of a future biographer exploring the full range of the Russian-American's ideas or opinions. Proof that someone tossed his personal papers is the complete lack of correspondence from France. That country held his family—aunts, uncles, cousins, father Nicholas, stepmother Barbara, half sister Nika, and his brother George; yet documents clearly prove George served as European agent for Alexander's patents. What happened to George's business letters to his brother in America when de Seversky kept at the same time a large number of totally innocuous business correspondence? Did George's missives bring up embarrassing moments or characteristics about his brother? Did his brother discuss scandals about the Procofieff (Seversky) clan in France? Or did someone decide to dump all letters written in a foreign language precisely because he or she did not know the language and hence was afraid of what the letters might reveal?

All of the previous "reflections" express the author's enormous frustration over the lack of information about de Seversky's mother, Vera—information likely to be found in private family letters. She is mentioned in passing by her son in several publications and in interviews as well as in articles by individuals who visited the de Seversky apartment in the early 1920s; otherwise, she is only a cipher. We have no idea what she looked like, the content of her character, and, most sadly, the level of love and support she may have given her son. Moreover, like Alexander, we will never know whether she hated brassy blondes, tall people, train rides, and asparagus.

# 6

# The Russian Inventor Becomes
# an American Designer

At first, Alexander P. de Seversky's life in the early fall of 1923 appeared to be no more than an extension of his previous activities. He returned to his office at Sperry Gyroscope Company and finished a variable speed drive mechanism for his calculator, filing an application with the U.S. Patent Office on November 23. On some weekends, he drove his car from Brooklyn to Mitchel Field to see his friend Lt. John F. Whiteley, who had been assigned after the bombing experiments to a tactical unit of the U.S. Army Air Service on Long Island. On one of these weekend visits, the pair flew the short distance to Roosevelt Field, where Igor I. Sikorsky completed building his first (but #29 overall) American airplane, a twin-engine transport, out in the open. "We landed close by," the lieutenant remembered five decades later, "and taxied up to the spot. The two were good friends and had quite a conversation before we returned. Seversky evidently wanted to tell Sikorsky what he was doing and how he was getting along."[1]

On another weekend, Whiteley spent a day and evening at the de Seversky apartment off Flatbush Avenue. He noted that Alexander's mother, Vera, was a gracious hostess who knew very little English. In fact, Whiteley heard a great deal of Russian during his brief stay. Moreover, he described the interior of the residence as resembling what he imagined the decor of a prerevolutionary Moscow apartment must have looked like. Fascinatingly, he noticed a picture of Vera's former husband, Nicholas, hanging on the wall. Whiteley had the impression that Nicholas was some type of entertainer, which was correct, and deceased, which was incorrect. Nicholas would die in the Paris suburb of Asnières in 1941 and be buried in the Russian Orthodox

Courbevoie Cemetery near the French capital. Why is this so interesting? It seems that eighteen years after Vera and Nicholas had divorced, both mother and son preferred to consider their husband/father to be dead.[2]

## The Hiatus

Later that fall, de Seversky went to Washington, D.C., to submit a patent application and discuss his future with staff members in the office of Gen. Mason M. Patrick, chief of the U.S.A.A.S. In essence, the Russian had completed his assignment on the bombsight and would soon be unemployed. In fact, to enhance his future opportunities, he had recently applied for, and would soon be granted, a professional engineering license from the University of the State of New York. Moreover, as the head of Seversky Aero Corporation, he now negotiated a sum of money from the U.S. War Department. Technically, because he worked for the government when he designed the original bombsight, the only rights he could "sell" were those assigned to his corporation for the calculator. Along with a nice letter from General Patrick on November 26, he received a check, probably in the range of $10,000, that would enable him to live comfortably and travel widely during the next year.[3]

When the Russian failed to receive the $50,000 he apparently hoped for, he decided to implement "Plan B," which began as a bargaining chip to secure more funds from the army. That plan would take him to Europe to deposit patent applications and enter negotiations with various militaries in the quest for additional financial compensation for his inventions. The U.S. Army, however, found its own bargaining chip and negotiated a compromise. It discovered that de Seversky had an interest in becoming a citizen of the United States. In return for help in securing citizenship through the Immigration and Naturalization Service, then housed in the Labor Department, de Seversky promised to limit his bombsight discussions to the British. Hence, Secretary of War John W. Weeks sent Secretary of Labor James J. Davis a letter requesting favorable and timely consideration of de Seversky's application for citizenship.[4]

The secretary went on to explain,

The War Department is peculiarly interested in this proceeding due to the fact that the applicant has been employed by and associated with the War Department for a period of more than five years, has rendered highly valuable technical service to this Department, has invented a bomb sighting device of peculiar interest to this Department, which is of such military value that negotiations are now being conducted looking towards the purchase from him of the exclusive and confidential rights therein having in mind the possibility of preventing other powers from acquiring the necessary knowledge that would enable them to use it as an offensive weapon against the United States. For these reasons it is regarded as desirable that Mr. Seversky should become a full-fledged citizen of the United States and thereby subject to the laws of war that would apply to citizens of this country.[5]

The inventor went back to Brooklyn in December 1923, not entirely empty-handed to be sure but hopeful of additional monetary rewards. True, he filled out preliminary papers for citizenship, though he delayed completing his final application until 1925. The explanation for the postponement centers on his activities in 1924. Along with Vera, he took two lengthy trips to Europe, one in the spring and the other in the fall. In view of the large Russian émigré community in France, including Procofieff-Seversky family members ranging from cousins to siblings, de Seversky must have pondered over where he belonged. However, the experience of his brother, George, did not encourage him to stay in Europe and specifically in France. A flight instructor and master pilot in Russia, George could not find a position in aviation. He first drove a taxi in Paris before adopting his father's profession by becoming a singer and entertainer in a Parisian nightclub, the Caucasian Château. Complicating the issue was the resolve of Alexander's mother not to return to the United States. Nevertheless, at the close of his second European sojourn when de Seversky left Cherbourg, France, on the RMS *Homeric* and returned alone to his Brooklyn apartment on November 20, 1924, he had made up his mind to stay in America.[6]

His brother's experience and the limited success of his efforts in Europe helped him reach that decision. De Seversky applied for in-flight refueling patents in France, Great Britain, Italy, and Spain. But without lawyers and agents to oversee his proprietary rights in these countries, the possibility of generating revenue from the patents bordered on zero. He also submitted secret patent applications in Great Britain for the principal components of his bombsight. De Seversky's preliminary talks with George Granville, the Fifth Duke of Sutherland who served as undersecretary of state for air under

British prime minister Stanley Baldwin, turned into a three-way conversation. It included an American representative, John Doran, operating out of the London branch of the Sperry Gyroscope Company. The British apparently acknowledged de Seversky's rights through some type of payment, but their real interest was to see some of the Sperry-built hardware. At the end of December, the Duke of Sutherland and the Sperry representative were on board the RMS *Aquitania* heading to New York.[7]

## A Life of Change

As the British developed an interest in de Seversky's Sperry-built C-1, the U.S.A.A.S. decided to hold off awarding the Sperry Company a contract for quantity production. After extensive bombing tests in 1924, the air service confirmed the C-1's accuracy but also noted that it was heavy, bulky, complex, and fragile. The coup de grâce arrived on December 29, 1924, when Elmer A. Sperry sent General Patrick a telegram informing the chief of the unhappy news that the price of the C-1 bombsight would be $625,000 for a production run of fifty or a unit price of $12,500. By contrast, de Seversky's competitor, Georges Estoppey, developed a lighter, smaller, simpler, and sturdier bombsight, the D-1, which cost an average of only $600. Little wonder that Patrick asked the Engineering/Materiel Division to contract Estoppey and Sperry in 1925 to design and build an improved version of the D-1 bombsight, one that might come close to matching the performance of the C-1 but without the unfortunate characteristics of de Seversky's bombsight.[8]

As might be expected, de Seversky was very disappointed. He knew, or felt he knew, that the bombsight was the most accurate in the world. Moreover, he possessed complete confidence that he could redesign and transform the C-1 so it would overcome its limitations. Fortunately, the U.S.A.A.S. Engineering/Materiel Division shared his confidence and awarded him a development contract. The president of Seversky Aero Corporation then spent the next two years creating the C-2 bombsight. His first step addressed a ubiquitous problem that plagued all bombsights. At altitude it is difficult for a pilot to estimate the lateral drift of an airplane owing to crosswinds or the lateral movement of an object such as a train or ship at ground or sea level. During the first half of 1925, de Seversky conceived, engineered, diagrammed, and described what is generically called a "drift control" mechanism.[9]

While his life as an independent agent took on the focus and discipline he demonstrated as an employee, first of the government and then of Sperry, the Russian inventor also had time for activities of quite a different nature. Emptied of his mother, his apartment home failed to provide the love, companionship, and conversation that abounded before 1924. He had dated young ladies in the past. In fact, he may have been engaged in Russia, but war and revolution interrupted marriage plans; in America, he dated intermittently several dancers from Florenz Ziegfeld's Follies. When, however, he returned home from France, he had reached the mature age of thirty and seemed ready for a serious and permanent relationship with someone who would fill his otherwise lonely life and apartment. An air service friend, Lt. (later, Col.) Phillips Melville, arranged to take de Seversky to a nightclub on a blind date with Evelyn Olliphant.[10]

Born in 1902 in New Orleans, Evelyn was still a toddler when she moved with her parents, Evelyn Kennedy and Samuel Rutherford Olliphant, M.D., to New York. Her father, a noted dermatologist, received a faculty appointment at the New York Post Graduate Hospital. Although the daughter returned to Louisiana to visit relatives and attend classes at Southwestern Louisiana Institute, she had loved singing and dancing since childhood. As a result, she studied dance with Russian choreographer Michel Fokine, whose studio on Riverside Drive made him a neighbor of the Olliphants. Evelyn was fortunate to have such an internationally recognized dance instructor who is often credited with creating modern ballet. Her polished and practiced talent earned her brief appearances in Broadway and off-Broadway shows such as Irving Berlin's *Music Box Review*.[11]

As the threesome settled in their nightclub table near the dance floor, the Russian admitted he found the tall, attractive young lady with dimpled chin and patrician features to be more than interesting. He discovered, however, that Evelyn focused her attentions on the young lieutenant. As de Seversky later wrote in an article for *Ladies' Home Journal*:

> Finally I asked her for a dance. As we walked to the floor I told her timidly not to hesitate to drop me if I were awkward as a dancer, because—well, I had an artificial leg. I knew well enough that the beautiful and tender-hearted girl would rather die on her feet, after that, than admit that I was anything less than a genius as a dancer. I had her to myself for hours and proceeded to "sell" myself, apparently with some success.[12]

Indeed, they were married on June 23, 1925, in a Methodist church in Biloxi,

Mississippi, near the home of Evelyn's grandmother, Mrs. E. R. Kennedy. Unfortunately, Dr. Olliphant had passed away before his daughter had met de Seversky. Thus her uncle gave away the bride. After a honeymoon trip to Europe, where Evelyn met her mother-in-law, the couple returned to New York and moved into a new apartment at 104 Sackville Road, Garden City, Long Island. The Russian kept his old apartment in Brooklyn as his work-space and headquarters for his corporation. De Seversky not only acquired a bride and lifelong companion who shared completely his enthusiasm for aviation, he gained an in-law who was wonderfully supportive. When his mother, Vera, passed away later that same year in Europe, Evelyn Kennedy Olliphant turned over a plot at Woodlawn Cemetery in the Bronx where Vera could be interred. On a happier note, Evelyn Kennedy kept a diary of stock and bond investments. It shows that de Seversky and his mother-in-law formed an investment partnership that proved to be remarkably successful and financially rewarding in the halcyon days of the stock market before the October 1929 crash. The diary makes clear that de Seversky contacted his broker to buy and sell, but both members of the partnership made decisions about what stocks and bonds to trade. As might be expected, de Seversky invested heavily in aviation stocks, especially Curtiss Aeroplane and Motor Company directed by Clement Keys, whose holding company, North American Aviation, also held majority interest in numerous compa-nies, including Sperry Gyroscope.[13]

Two additional and related changes in de Seversky's life were accomplished or initiated the same year of 1927. On June 3, he applied for an American pilot's license. Because of his aeronautical courses and military flight training in Russia during the Great War, de Seversky had been awarded an aviator's certificate from the internationally recognized Fédération Aéronautique Internationale, headquartered in France since 1905. Like other countries, however, the United States decided to create its own licensing agency. In 1926 Congress passed the Air Commerce Act. It not only established the U.S. Army Air Corps, it also created the Aeronautics Branch within the U.S. Commerce Department. The latter now had responsibility for certifying aircraft, regulating air traffic, providing navigational aids, and licensing pilots. The branch began accepting license applications for three distinct categories of pilot: private, industrial, and transport. The transport license held the highest rank and prestige because it demanded the most experience and gave the holder an automatic license for the other two pilot classifications.[14]

De Seversky applied for the transport license. He could document hundreds of hours of flight time in all types of aircraft and, in the first half of 1927, averaged flying fifteen hours a month. The only reason for the slight delay in his receipt of Transport Pilot Certificate No. 1769 was his failure to secure his U.S. Certificate of Naturalization until November 26. Since his official application for citizenship was submitted only two years earlier, he barely met the minimum time required in the 1906 congressional legislation. His application came under the "special" category and cleared all hurdles because of the intervention of the U.S. War Department. Its quest to control de Seversky and prevent him from transferring sensitive technology to foreign powers received a commanding boost when, in 1928, the U.S. Army Air Corps commissioned him a major in the reserves. It is the equivalent to a naval lieutenant commander, the highest rank earned by the Russian-American in World War I. Despite completing his five-year reserve stint in the air corps in 1933, de Seversky clung to the title of major and used it as a point of honor, if not a trademark, for the rest of his life.[15]

Meanwhile, de Seversky completed his redesign of the C-1 bombsight so that the C-2 was less bulky and simpler to operate. And the U.S.A.A.C. Materiel Division actually signed a contract with the inventor for his automatic drift control mechanism. The contract provided him with an initial cash payment of $10,000 plus a royalty on each bombsight manufactured with the attachment of his device. An option allowed the air corps to purchase outright exclusive rights to the invention for $50,000. Patrick, who would retire as air corps chief on December 12, 1927, refused to sign off on the contract because he felt it was excessively generous. De Seversky's setback over the failed contract was accompanied by other bad news. Despite his success in altering the C-1, the Georges Estoppey–designed D-1 bombsight had metamorphosed into improved versions, such as the D-4, which went into production by Sperry Gyroscope Company in 1926 and became by 1927 the standard bombing aid in the inventory of the U.S.A.A.C.[16]

### De Seversky's Final Bombsight

These negatives were dramatically erased by events that occurred in December 1927. The state of North Carolina donated a reinforced concrete bridge across the Pee Dee River to the U.S. War Department for target practice by land and air forces. Located some ten miles east of Albemarle, the government seat for Stanly County, the relatively new bridge had become superfluous. It would soon be flooded over by a lake formed by a dam downstream. The First Provisional Bombardment Squadron, composed of twin-engine LB-5 bombers built by Keystone Aircraft Corporation, flew from Langley to Pope Field (today, Pope Air Force Base). Pope served as the staging area for bombing attacks against the Pee Dee Bridge. In beautiful weather, clear and windless, the squadron flew twenty missions a day for five days from altitudes ranging between 6,000 and 8,000 feet. True, after five days and one hundred missions, the central span of four hundred feet collapsed. The massive effort, though, witnessed numerous bombs missing the bridge entirely or failing to hit the targeted central span. Almost inadvertently, the exercise exposed the fact that the air corps had equipped its planes with an inferior bombsight.[17]

At the time of the December bombings of the Pee Dee Bridge, Maj. Gen. James E. Fechet replaced Patrick as U.S.A.A.C. chief. Shortly after Fechet reviewed the results of the target practice in North Carolina at the start of the new year, he sent on January 6, 1928, a lengthy memo requesting a summary of bombsight development from Brig. Gen. William E. Gillmore, Materiel Division chief at Wright Field. Fechet expressed in measured prose his extreme disappointment with the current equipment. "I cannot too strongly emphasize," the chief continued, "the importance of a bomb sight of precision, since the ability of bombardment aviation to perform its mission of destruction is almost entirely dependent upon an accurate and practical bomb sight." Not only did Fechet want a résumé of all the work in this area from the Materiel Division, he wanted information about the U.S. Navy's latest bombsight. The latter project was so secretive that the air corps chief did not know that he was referring to Carl L. Norden's Mark XI, the device that after many refinements and many squabbles with the navy finally became in the 1930s the army's choice of bombsight.[18]

The U.S. Navy's tightfisted, tight-lipped control over the Mark XI forced General Fechet to proceed separately with the army's project. Without waiting for Gillmore's response, Fechet sent Wright Field a letter advising the Bombardment Board, then convening at Wright, to discuss in detail the bombsight development and procurement process and submit a report and recommendation. The air corps chief strongly urged (in essence, mandated) the parallel development of two or more devices to ensure the availability of a highly accurate bombsight in the near future. The board completed its review and wrote up a report with specific guidance shortly after the end of the first week in February. It advised that a contract be executed to develop and procure six L-1 bombsights developed by Henry B. Inglis, then employed in the Materiel Division's Armament Branch. The board also recommended a contract with de Seversky for twenty-five sights, specifying that the contract must have a built-in mechanism for refining and improving the C model bombsights as they were being constructed.[19]

The combination of the Bombardment Board's recommendation and the army's view that even the older C-1 was still the most accurate bombsight available prompted telephonic negotiations with the Russian-American. De Seversky indicated that he expected, no matter what, the original $10,000 he requested for the drift control device. In addition, he wanted a minimum of $10,000 to prepare new drawings for the redesign of the first three bombsights, $20,000 for supervising and testing construction of the devices, and a royalty of $8,000 for the package of twenty-five bombsights with his drift control invention. As early as February 21, 1928, the air corps made multiyear budgetary plans to set aside nearly $50,000 to meet the inventor's requirements. Once this preliminary part of the project had been settled, the chief of the Materiel Division's Experimental Engineering Section, Maj. Leslie MacDill, initiated contract negotiations through a memorandum on March 16. MacDill pointed out that a final agreement would occur only after de Seversky's interview with General Fechet in Washington.[20]

De Seversky learned he would have only one chance to get the budget right. Thus he first met with the Bombardment Board in Washington on April 20 to make certain he understood the board's expectations for the proposed C-3 bombsight. Moreover, since Sperry Gyroscope would again build de Seversky's bombsight, the Russian-American went over the budget, line by line, with Sperry representative John Doran. The first three experimental sights would cost the air corps $86,250. Admittedly expensive, these devices were the ones that required significant amounts of engineering and a development time of two to three years. The cost also ballooned because of the front-loading of de Seversky's requirement of $10,000 to merge his drift control with the C-3. Twenty-two additional sights were each priced at $9,660. The latter figure was broken down to reflect such things as the cost for labor, materials, overhead, tools, and, among others, engineering supervision. Sperry expected to earn $1,260 for each bombsight, which was the standard 15 percent profit allowed on military contracts.[21]

A week after de Seversky met with the Bombardment Board, he had his successful contract interview with Air Corps chief Fechet. Between July 1, 1928, and January 1, 1930, de Seversky would commute from Garden City to his Brooklyn office near Flatbush Avenue and spend most of his workaday time at his drafting table when not conferring with Sperry technicians at the Manhattan Bridge Plaza. After completing his redesigns of the C-1/C-2 and until July 1, 1931, the Russian-American served as an occasional consultant to the company and especially with Inglis, who left his civilian job at Wright Field for a full-time position with Sperry on November 16, 1928. Unfortunately for the mechanical engineer, his L-1 bombsight could not match the accuracy of the C model and so the L-1 never went into production. On the other hand, Inglis collaborated with the Russian-American to merge a few elements of the L-1 into the experimental C-3s to form the C-4, which became the standard for the package of bombsights produced by Sperry and installed in air corps bombers during the middle third of the 1930s. By 1935, however, when the navy permitted the army to test the improved Norden Mark XV, the army chose the latter to be its future bombsight. Nevertheless, it took the remainder of the 1930s and time-consuming negotiations with the rival naval service before the army secured enough Nordens to equip frontline bombers.[22]

## To Dance in the Sky

As indicated previously, de Seversky received major funds from the government for his work on the experimental bombsights. The monies were dispensed over several fiscal years and capped by royalties on the production run of the C-4. The net result placed him among the fortunate few who enjoyed a strong infusion of cash during the opening years of the otherwise devastating Great Depression. And the economy's severe downturn, leading to a nationwide unemployment rate approaching 30 percent, only enhanced the value of his income. By the time the Gold Reserve Act of 1934 went into effect and President Franklin D. Roosevelt attempted to reverse deflation by setting the price of gold at $35 an ounce, de Seversky's income was no longer based on decisions made in 1928. In the meantime, as the Russian-American's fortune improved, it had a direct and interesting impact on his lifestyle.[23]

In his early years in New York, he often borrowed and occasionally rented aircraft to fly, but now he could purchase a new airplane. Moreover, he had attended numerous air shows in the past, but now he became a participant. His new hobby had two serious advantages. First, it kept him a member of the close-knit family of well-known aviators, both military and civilian, such as Jimmy Doolittle, Amelia Earhart, Zanford Granville, Emil Laird, Charles Lindbergh, Clyde Pangborne, Louise Thaden, Roscoe Turner, and, later, Jackie Cochran. Second, even when he flew for charity as often happened in the darkest hours of economic depression, air meet organizers paid noteworthy participants their expenses and victory in contest-supplied prize money that turned into pure income. De Seversky's first event took place on October 19, 1929, at Hicksville Field, not far from his and Evelyn's Garden City home. The Long Island Aviation Country Club, to which the de Severskys belonged, sponsored the air meet consisting of races, stunts, and deadstick (power off) landings. De Seversky took first place in a contest to see which pilot could land closest to a mark on the field.[24]

In later air shows, de Seversky's repertoire of stunt flying expanded because of his purchase of a new Brunner-Winkle *Bird* airplane for $3,895 in 1930. Originally housed at Roosevelt Field, the firm continued to piece together airframes at that location after moving its headquarters to Glendale in Brooklyn. Designed by Russian émigré Mikhail Gregor, the stagger-wing sesquiplane featured two open cockpits that could carry a pilot and two passengers. Welded steel tubing framed the fuselage as wooden spars and ribs outlined the wings. The entire airframe was covered with tightly stitched cotton cloth that received several coats of varnish-like material to strengthen the skin and reduce wind drag. The light but sturdy plane was a joy to fly. It won the 1929 Guggenheim Safe Airplane Contest, which explains why the world's most famous pilot bought a *Bird* for his wife, Anne Morrow Lindbergh.[25]

De Seversky, however, acquired the *Bird* because of its flight characteristics, which were perfect for the kind of stunts he wanted to perform. Its Kinner air-cooled radial engine was enormously reliable. Minus passengers, the small K-5 powerplant could pull the plane through the envelope of air at a remarkable 120 mph. Just as importantly, the craft was fully controllable at speeds as low as 40 mph. Indeed, it could land on the proverbial dime and needed only one hundred feet of runway to take off. Finally, its handling characteristics were amazing. The *Bird*'s controls and control surfaces endowed a pilot with the ability to climb, dive, turn, roll, loop, and spin with the grace of a ballerina. In fact, the Russian-American gained fame in the air show circuit by dancing in the sky. During the National Air Races at Cleveland, Ohio, on September 4, 1931, he used a radio receiver to put on a spectacular show for a crowd of 10,000. "Spectators," reported the *Cleveland Plain Dealer*, "who thought they had seen planes do everything that it is possible for airplanes to do watched in amazement as the Russian danced in the sky in perfect time to the strains of 'The Skater's Waltz' by [Émile] Waldteufel, which was played in front of the grand stand by Maurice Spitalny's National Air Race Orchestra."[26]

Next month, de Seversky was one of the featured stars in an extravaganza of four air shows in the New York area sponsored by the Aeronautical Chamber of Commerce to raise money for the unemployed. And the following month, on November 22 and 23, he appeared in the Eastern Championship Races and Contests at Glenn Curtiss Field at North Beach in Queens (today, LaGuardia Airport). Two newspapers, the *New York Evening Journal* and *New York American*, publicized and underwrote the event to raise money for their Christmas and Relief Fund. In these five air shows, de Seversky not only demonstrated his now-famous airborne waltz, he also flew a different kind of dance in the sky that also proved to be a crowd pleaser. After gaining altitude over the spectators, he turned off the *Bird*'s engine and performed a noiseless program that began with a loop and then proceeded to a slow roll, inverted glide, another loop, several wingovers, and finished with a precision landing.[27]

And Alexander was not the only family member who danced in the sky. Evelyn enjoyed flying with her husband so much that she decided to surprise him by secretly taking flight lessons. She began training on June 4, 1930, through the facilities offered by the Long Island Aviation Country Club at Hicksville Field. Her secret soon failed as too many of their mutual friends saw what she was doing; as a result, her husband quickly learned her secret and happily became her co-instructor. Evelyn first soloed on July 13 and shortly thereafter tested for and secured her pilot's license. Before the couple flew to the National Air Races in September, she had the honor of carrying Jimmy Doolittle as a passenger. One of America's best-known and best-educated pilots, he reached the highest level of heroism when he led a squadron of B-25 bombers on a morale-boosting raid against Tokyo during America's worst moment in World War II. Doolittle took a ten-year vacation from the U.S. Army Air Corps starting in 1930. He then worked for

Shell Petroleum Corporation, where he coordinated the company's Aviation Department. Because he kept Shell in public view through his participation in air shows, he was closely acquainted with, and often a houseguest of, the de Severskys. On one occasion, a last-minute appointment prompted him to ask Evelyn to fly him from Islip, Long Island, to New York.[28]

Despite the distinction of serving as Doolittle's pilot, Evelyn experienced a rocky moment in her early training as revealed by her husband during a 1938 interview on New York's WJZ radio station. He participated in the popular evening program, *If I Had a Chance*. When asked, "What was the most dangerous experience you ever had?" de Seversky immediately retorted, "When I got married!" After a hearty laugh, the host repeated the question but emphasized he wanted the "actual" dangerous moment. The Russian-American paused and then began his response by referring to his role as a combat pilot during the Great War:

> Every battle I went into was equally dangerous and roughly speaking, there were thirty such battles during the four years of war. But it took my wife, Evelyn, to really frighten me. She is a pilot in her own right and has had many hundreds of flying hours since I taught her to fly. In order to give her courage and prove to her that she was capable of flying an airplane alone, I decided to go with her, as a passenger, and threw out the control stick that was in my cockpit. When we were only fifty feet off the ground, the engine stopped and the plane nosed down, headed into the hangar. I feverishly worked the imaginary controls instinctively, but although I was panicky I learned that my contention was right and that she could fly. She headed towards the adjoining field and made a perfect landing—upside down. However, this was not her fault since a bad ditch in the field turned the plane over.[29]

## Origins of the Seversky Aircraft Corporation

The incident proved to be an anomaly. She later enjoyed many hours of accident-free flight. Additionally, she joined her husband as participant, rather than spectator, at air shows; she also became a member of the women's aviation organization, the Ninety-Nines, cofounded by, among others, Amelia Earhart. Moreover, like her husband, Evelyn enjoyed flying the *Bird*. She actually began recommending the airplane to her friends in the Long

Island Aviation Country Club. When President William E. Winkle of the Brunner-Winkle Aircraft Company realized that Evelyn was responsible for several sales of the *Bird*, he gave her a commission for each airplane sold because of her endorsement. Shortly thereafter, Winkle awarded Evelyn a letter contract that conferred on her a "ten percent commission on any *Bird* airplane" bought by a club member with or without Evelyn's obvious encouragement. The de Seversky family connection with Winkle-Brunner played a small part in the new company Alexander incorporated early in 1931.[30]

Meanwhile, the remarkable parallel in the aviation path followed by husband and wife stretched even further. Finished with his active work on the C-3 bombsight, de Seversky signed a contract on January 27, 1930, to demonstrate and sell aircraft for the Sikorsky Aviation Corporation, successor to Sikorsky Aero Engineering. Not long after Sikorsky had established his first American company at Roosevelt Field, Sikorsky and de Seversky had become neighbors on Long Island. During the middle third of the 1920s, Sikorsky built and sold nine different airplanes, but none of them went into serial production. Then, in 1926, he moved his operation to a rented factory at College Point on Long Island Sound just east of Glenn Curtiss Field. Along with other projects, Sikorsky began constructing and testing a seaplane.[31]

Early in 1928 and only a step or two ahead of bankruptcy, Sikorsky began to design his thirty-eighth aircraft. The model S-38 was a twin-engine flying boat that also had wheeled landing gear that could be raised or lowered creating an amphibian equally at home on land or sea. Observers often described the S-38 as "a collection of airplane parts flying in formation." Below a big parasol wing were two Pratt & Whitney Wasp engines rated each at 420 hp; underneath hung a hulled fuselage and a smaller wing that bore two floats, one on each side to balance the craft in water. Extending aft of the large upper wing were two booms that held two rudders, an elevator, and a rear horizontal stabilizer. Keeping all these airplane parts together were a series of external wires, braces, and struts that made the S-38 borderline ugly but with a unique and easily recognizable profile. Carrying eight passengers and two crew members in comfort and safety (the plane could fly on one engine) and with a top speed of 130 mph, the amphibian matched or exceeded the performance of existing commercial aircraft.[32]

In a small way, de Seversky would assist his old family friend in selling or getting leads for selling over one hundred amphibians. Between January and April 1930, he flew his wife and two Sikorsky mechanics to Palm Beach, Florida, and, later, to Havana, Cuba, where he put on demonstration flights of the S-38 for the wealthy and the Cuban navy. Regardless, Sikorsky enjoyed such success in S-38 sales that he reorganized his company, garnered $5 million in capital, and moved into a state-of-the-art manufacturing plant close to the water in Stratford, Connecticut. Part of the move and funding were made possible by a merger with United Aircraft Corporation (today, United Technologies). Later, Sikorsky would build huge Flying Clippers, which pioneered air routes across the oceans to Europe and Asia. By decade's end, however, competition from other flying boat manufacturers forced United Aircraft to temporarily close the Sikorsky Division. Igor moved on to a different type of aircraft and with such success that Sikorsky is now an informal synonym for the technology he developed—the helicopter.[33]

Back in the spring of 1930, the onset of the Great Depression prompted Sikorsky to make a much less expensive spin-off version of the S-38. Almost half the size of the original, the S-39 had a single 300 hp engine and carried only five people. Since the company's main test pilot, Boris V. Sergievsky, busied himself with assisting customers in flying the S-38, Sikorsky asked de Seversky to test and demonstrate the S-39 at Roosevelt Field, where the company kept a branch facility. The Long Island location was ideal because of the short distance to water, the presence of numerous airports and pilots, and the nearby residence of many wealthy commuters who owned companies in New York. In May, the Russian-American began his demonstration flights. Among the notables who flew with him in the S-39 must be counted Charles A. Lindbergh and Harry F. Guggenheim, whose family fortune funded numerous aviation research projects and programs around the country. A less famous but equally important passenger flown by de Seversky was his friend and air attaché at the U.S. Embassy in Cuba, Lt. Phillips Melville, who had introduced Alexander to his bride, Evelyn.[34]

Unfortunately for Sikorsky, the S-39 attracted just a handful of customers; only twenty units came off the production line. The Depression, of course, certainly helps explain lackluster sales. De Seversky, though, felt the craft could have done better even in a weak market. In his view, Sikorsky might have considered a major redesign of the smaller amphibian to take advantage of the revolution in flight technology and design that reached fruition in the late 1920s. In terms of seaplanes, de Seversky was already a modest participant in this revolution. His long-term enthusiasm for seaplanes stemming from the Great War did not wane in the 1920s, when he engineered bombsights. In his spare time between projects, he designed and patented a testing device to create sound and sturdy all-metal floats, a new type of adjustable float to streamline the profile of a seaplane, and a unique wheeled landing gear for amphibians to reduce the drag in flight caused by exposed wheels. His close association with seaplanes and related inventions coupled with his intimate knowledge of the S-39's shortcomings led him to begin in the fall of 1930 sketching out a radically new kind of seaplane. Instead of trying to sell his patents and designs to an aircraft manufacturer, he took the extraordinary step of creating a new company to build his dream airplane in the depths of national economic calamity. On February 17, 1931, he chartered the Seversky Aircraft Corporation under the laws of the state of Delaware.[35]

## Reflections

There is an issue that transcends chapters 5 and 6. That issue is highlighted by a page that used to appear on the website of the Cradle of Aviation Museum on Long Island, the principal depository of the Alexander P. de Seversky Papers. For a long time, a website page outlined the Major's life, including a statement that he received $50,000 for his bombsight and applied those funds to the formation of the Seversky Aero Corporation in 1922. The statement is incorrect, but the error is perfectly understandable. It is found in several published articles and a number of highly respected biographical dictionaries. The source of this factual mistake is, of course, de Seversky. He made the assertion in interviews or wrote it down (or his secretary wrote it down) on forms used to build an entry on his life in various reference works.

There are several reasons why any careful researcher will question this claim. First, $50,000 was a fortune in 1922 dollars; yet there is no indication the Russian's lifestyle changed with the infusion of so much cash. And why would his company's creation require $50,000 when it produced nothing; required no office building, no factory, no machine tools, and no employees; and cost only a small fee to incorporate? Second, documents from the National Archives clearly reveal that U.S. Army Air Service chief Patrick refused to sign off on a contract that paid a government employee extra money or even a royalty for an invention or design created with government support. Finally, the C-1 bombsight was not completed and tested until 1923. Because de Seversky worked for Sperry Gyroscope Company then, he could negotiate a buyout for his calculator patent, though this occurred a year *after* the formation of the corporation.

One can speculate on the reason why this factual error emerged in de Seversky's mind in later years. No doubt the Major correctly remembered that Congress approved $50,000 to support the air service in bombing derelict naval ships in 1923. In some interviews and publications, de Seversky did in fact suggest that this huge sum went to Sperry to fund his bombsight, a suggestion that is partly, but only partly, correct. Late in 1923, when he received a check from the War Department for his calculator, he used the monies for his journeys in 1924 to seek patents in a number of European countries, patents assigned to, and controlled by, Seversky Aero Corporation. With the passage of time, it is likely these activities converged in his mind until it was logical to state that his first corporation was courtesy of major funds from the government for his bombsight.

# 7

# The Innovative Designer

Filling out a form and paying a fee of incorporation have little to do with actually establishing a company. Alexander P. de Seversky had to add flesh to a charter that by itself was all too easily accomplished in Delaware. It is fascinating to watch the Major maneuver around as he began building his corporation in 1931. Like a good carpenter or stone mason fashioning a house, his success as a builder depended heavily on working with familiar materials. He needed a place to construct the amphibian. Thus he logically arranged to secure space in a hangar at the Edo Aircraft Corporation (today, EDO Corporation) located at College Point by Long Island Sound. Sikorsky had been at the same location for several years. Moreover, Edo specialized in manufacturing seaplane floats, including those employed by Sikorsky, and de Seversky had worked with the company on a couple of his inventions.[1]

### Fleshing Out the Corporate Skeleton

The interconnections between Sasha and Edo set the pattern for his selection of key employees, the engineers, who could help him translate his ideas into a high-performing aircraft. One of the first and most important individuals he hired was Alexander M. Pishvanov, who had, in fact, worked for both Edo and Sikorsky Aircraft Corporation before joining Seversky. Like the Major, Pishvanov was a Russian émigré, a trained engineer, and a World War I ace pilot for the Imperial Russian Air Service, but for the army not the navy. Unlike de Seversky, who fled the country with his mother several months after the Soviets came to power, Pishvanov stayed and flew for the anti-Soviet Whites in the Russian Civil War. Victory by the Reds in that horrible conflict forced him to leave the land of his birth. He then served in the British Royal Air Force (RAF) as a flight instructor before immigrating to the United States in 1926. Fearless in battle, Pishvanov was a quiet, unassuming gentleman in peacetime. His native ingenuity combined with his engineering education and practical experience enabled him to become the future head of Seversky Aircraft Corporation's Experimental Department.[2]

In one respect, Pishvanov proved to be the most important engineer. His child, Nicholas, was treated like a son by the childless Major and Evelyn, especially after Pishvanov's wife, Nona, drowned in 1936. The Pishvanovs and de Severskys remained close long after the aircraft company they helped to create changed hands and names. Nevertheless, for a chief engineer, Sasha selected Mikhail Gregor, who had designed the *Bird* airplane prized by Alexander and sold by Evelyn. While the Major worked on the overall design, novel floats, wheeled landing gear, and control surfaces, Gregor and Pishvanov did the drawings for the fuselage. The unique wing would be the handiwork of the company's fourth engineer, Alexander Kartveli, who was born in the Russian Empire in what is now the Republic of Georgia. Formerly employed by Atlantic Aircraft Corporation, his superior skills in designing metal aircraft would result in his promotion by 1936 to the position of vice president in charge of engineering. Kartveli held a similar title when Seversky Aircraft became the Republic Aviation Corporation; hence he was ultimately responsible for the subsequent development of the P-47 *Thunderbolt*, F-84 *Thunderjet*, and F-105 *Thunderchief*.[3]

Naturally, Kartveli, Pishvanov, and Gregor were vital to de Seversky's plans for the company. No three-dimensional airplane could emerge until the four engineers completed their two-dimensional drawings and specifications for the airframe, landing gear, and floats. On the other hand, construction required expert "metal benders" like Judd Hopla and shop managers like Michael Bondar, the engineer in charge of actual construction. Hence the fledgling company started with a handful of well-qualified employees. Despite good personnel, the corporate puzzle remained unsolved because of the missing piece; de Seversky needed an "angel." He had printed 10,000 shares of stock, which, not surprisingly, remained unsold. Before the October 1929 crash, aviation securities on the New York Stock Exchange weighed in at a value close to $1 billion. By the end of 1931, their worth had plummeted to $50 million. Fortunately, de Seversky's fame as an air show star, inventive engineer, and ace combat pilot converged with his Russian charm enabled him to convince Paul Moore to invest in the Seversky Aircraft Corporation over the winter of 1931–1932.[4]

*Time* magazine described Moore as a "rich, barrel-chested Wall Streeter." Ten years older than de Seversky, he graduated from Yale in 1908 and then received a law degree from New York University. He began his career in the Legal Department of the Rock Island Railroad in Chicago. By the end of the Great War, he had moved to New York and became a partner with a brokerage firm. Over the years, success on Wall Street rewarded him with membership on the board of directors of American Can Company; Bankers Trust Company; Delaware, Lackawanna and Western Railroad; National Biscuit Company; and, of course, Seversky Aircraft. As of September 15, 1938, he had personally invested over $3.5 million in the latter company. De Seversky may have had his name on the front door, but the rest of the corporation fit nicely in Moore's wallet. It is important to keep in mind that the company "angel" held an absolute majority of whatever stock Seversky Aircraft issued. At the drop of the proverbial hat, Moore could remove de Seversky as company president and change the corporate name. And eventually, he did both.[5]

## SEV-3 Amphibian

It was a fiction often held as true by contemporaries and later commentators that the corporation bearing de Seversky's name belonged to him. The only reality is that Moore's investment gave motion to a company that was comatose from money starvation. Seversky Aircraft spent a pathetic $868 for salaries in 1931. By contrast, the company moved its headquarters in 1932 from the founder's apartment to an office with a prestigious address on Lexington Avenue behind New York's famous Waldorf Astoria Hotel; the de Severskys soon moved nearby to an apartment on East 53rd Street. At the same time, the first metal was cut starting construction at Edo Aircraft of de Seversky's SEV-3, so named because it would carry a pilot and up to two passengers. The company president was so excited by the sudden burst of activity that he announced to the press in March that the airplane "was more than half completed and would be flown within six weeks." De Seversky's optimistic prediction missed its mark, not by days or weeks, but by a full year.[6]

One reason for the delay in finishing the project had to do with the modest amount of initial help from Moore. He loaned an office for the company headquarters; he also supplied enough capital to pay for raw materials and salaries for a handful of men as de Seversky rented space and machine tools from Edo. The other setback was related to all the special features of the SEV-3 that bore the fruit of the dramatic changes in aircraft construction, changes some historians now describe as a revolution. Clearly de Seversky, an inventive engineer, understood the latest developments in manufacturing aircraft. He was, Kartveli reminisced in 1960, a "talented man" who revealed in the amphibian a "venturesome design" that demonstrated his "foresight." In a radio show broadcast over New York's WOR station on January 27, 1933, the company president explained in precise terms his goal. He was building a fast airplane for business and pleasure, one that carried three people in comfort and with the flexibility to land or take off from an airfield or water.[7]

To accomplish his goals, de Seversky decided to go with an all-metal airplane that had the potential of being stronger and safer than the materials of wood and fabric employed in most airframes built before the 1930s. Moreover, the twenty-five foot, eight-inch-long fuselage was designed as a single unit of monocoque construction. The wing design also contributed to the airplane's lighter weight and speed. De Seversky decided against the old-fashioned biplane configuration. He knew the extra wing, accompanied by multiple struts and wires, resulted in wind drag and a slower craft. The second wing also reduced pilot visibility and increased the danger of accident. Largely drafted by Kartveli, the elliptical monowing was novel even for such cantilevered structures. To be sure, Kartveli dispensed with all external elements of support, but he also designed the wing without the normal braces of two or more spars. Instead, the upper skin of smooth duralumin was reinforced inside by a second sheet of corrugated metal and shaped over a series of metal ribs. A channel running the full length of the thirty-six-foot span stiffened the bottom skin. Eliminating entirely the weight of separate fuel tanks, the engineering team chose to use the space between wing covers to carry gasoline.[8]

While basic elements of the fuselage and wing were drafted by Gregor, Pishvanov, and Kartveli, de Seversky added special touches to the airframe. For example, he compared the SEV-3 with a phaeton automobile or, in modern parlance, a convertible. He designed sliding glass canopies for the cockpits and adjustable seats that rose up so the adventurous could have the option of flying in an open cockpit. That decision required pilot and passenger(s) to wear headgear, goggles, and heavy flying clothes. De Seversky speculated that women especially might appreciate the other option of an enclosed cockpit because instead of cumbersome flight gear "they will be able to wear their usual smart dresses and have their curls unruffled when they step out of the plane." He also designed and patented a seaplane anchor, which the pilot could release or retrieve from the cockpit. Housed in the nose of one of the floats, the anchor reduced the danger of the amphibian drifting into a harbor obstruction at the end of a flight.[9]

Additionally, de Seversky created for the amphibian a structure contemporaries called a decelerator or air brake, now commonly identified as a flap. It was located on the trailing edge of the wing below the fuselage and extended from one aileron to the other. When lowered, the flap provided both lift and drag and enabled the amphibian to reduce its speed quickly to 60 mph for a slow and safe landing. Moreover, de Seversky's genius and the impact of his war experiences are revealed in his patented pontoons. He gave the floats an internal keel and hence such strength that in an emergency, the craft as seaplane could land not only on water but also on ice, snow, marshland, sand, and even rough ground. Mounted at the end of the floats were rudders that allowed easy maneuverability of the craft in water. But the crème de la crème was that, controlled from the cockpit, pontoons rotated and recessed wheels extended so that the SEV-3 could take off from water as a seaplane and later land on an airport runway. Finally, during the seventeen months of construction at Edo Aircraft, de Seversky's team implemented his idea to make the SEV-3 as flexible as possible so that two or three variants could flow from the basic plans of the amphibian. It drafted the SEV-3 to hold either the 420 hp Wright Whirlwind or the Wright Cyclone rated at 710 hp. Naturally, both engines would be encased in the superefficient cowling tested and developed by the National Advisory Committee for Aeronautics, the government-funded research agency and predecessor to the National Aeronautics and Space Administration (NASA).[10]

As the SEV-3 underwent construction, de Seversky continued to fly in air shows. Besides the fun of gratifying his avocation and the requirement of improving his cash flow, it now became important to lay the groundwork for future sales of his company's aircraft. He needed to maintain a favorable and well-publicized presence in the aviation world. Hence, for example, he entered the acrobatic event for an air show at Curtiss Field on June 19,

1932, that benefited the Convalescent Relief Fund of Bellevue Hospital. He shared victory with Clyde Pangborne, who, along with Hugh Herndon, became the first to fly nonstop across the Pacific Ocean. Later that summer, the Major flew from Roosevelt Field to St. Hubert Airdrome in Montreal, Canada, as one of the headliners for the Canadian Air Pageant. In August he entertained 25,000 spectators with his deadstick aerobatic routine in the *Bird* biplane at the National Air Races held at Municipal Airport in Cleveland, Ohio. He won the prize and plaque for the event.[11]

In the evenings over the winter of 1932–1933 when he was not flying in air shows or working on the airplane, de Seversky took the Dale Carnegie Course. The activity was the obverse side of the same coin that partly explained his participation in air shows. If he expected to succeed as a new aircraft manufacturer, he had to be able to present effective talks before varied audiences, deliver articulate interviews for print and radio media, and pitch convincing testimony before government agencies. When de Seversky registered for the course, it was structured around Carnegie's book, *Public Speaking and Influencing Men in Business*. It focused on enhancing the enrollee's self-confidence, public speaking abilities, salesmanship, and interpersonal skills.[12]

The course paid off in both the short and long term. Later in life, de Seversky would gain widespread recognition for his speeches and publications. Meanwhile, in the spring of 1933, he applied elements of the Carnegie class in giving interviews and preparing press releases, including a photograph and cutline of the nearly completed airplane. Compared with other aircraft, especially the Sikorsky S-39, the SEV-3 was stunning in its clean design and modern, even futuristic, appearance. De Seversky added a dazzling, eye-catching touch by painting the craft bronze. In June a secret test flight occurred over Flushing Bay at College Point. Fortunately, one of the few eyewitnesses included Evelyn de Seversky. She is the only reason the first test flight of the amphibian is documented via a transcript of her interview on June 21, 1933. She shared a microphone with Dagmar Perkins, hostess of the *Morning Talk Show* on New York's WMCA radio station.[13]

In the theatrical tone common to 1930s radio, Evelyn recounted,

> I watched the plane climb upward at a terrific speed as though shot out of a cannon. Being a pilot myself I realized as I watched it that everything was under perfect control, but my momentary confidence was instantly

destroyed at the thought of how the plane would land, the next most dangerous phase of any flight test. But this didn't arrive for a long time. My husband seemingly delighted with the ship was putting it through a series of evolutions. I could see that the plane was very fast and very maneuverable and every movement indicated my husband was happy. I was happy too, but not for long.

The next instant the noise of the engine died and I knew he was coming in for a landing. He was losing altitude in a graceful spiral in total silence. Soon he straightened out and scooted a few feet above the water, making a perfect landing.

A sigh of relief and joy could be heard from all the spectators. The test was a complete success.[14]

## Selling the SEV-3

Evelyn, of course, was not an objective observer, but indications are that the SEV-3 performed well. De Seversky realized he and his small team had designed and built an advanced machine. If it were not for the Great Depression, the smooth lines and superb performance of the amphibian would automatically attract interest and orders. But under the economic conditions of the time, the Major needed to bring the plane to the attention of as many different people as possible in and out of the world of aviation. He considered entering the craft in the Bendix Air Race in July, but without the more powerful Wright Cyclone engine, he had no chance to win. His better alternative was to establish a world speed record for amphibians at a venue that would grab as much far-reaching publicity as possible. Thus he focused on planning, promoting, and entering the National Charity Air Pageant scheduled for October 7 and 8, 1933, at Roosevelt Field. The event attracted hundreds of military and civilian pilots and proved to be one of the largest air shows in New York history. Sixty-five pilots alone signed up for the transcontinental air race that preceded and opened the pageant.[15]

The significance of the pageant can be measured by the fact that Eleanor Roosevelt, wife of the U.S. president, served as honorary chair. Additionally, the event attracted such international headliners as Maj. Ernst Udet, whose sixty-two aerial victories in World War I made him Germany's top surviving ace.

The combination of star performers and abundant publicity brought out over 50,000 paying spectators on the ground at Roosevelt Field when the National Charity Air Pageant opened in October to benefit the Judson Health Center and the Emergency Exchange Association. Thousands more parked nearby or found off-site vantage points to view the show. No one was disappointed. There were air races, aerobatic contests, autogiro demonstrations, parachute jumping, and imitation "dogfights." Moreover, the U.S. Army Air Corps flew pursuit planes in formation and transferred a flight of bombers from Langley Field to demolish the cardboard village of "Depressionville." Other marvels pleased the crowds, including the presence of entertainers such as radio singer Kate Smith, whose later recording of Irving Berlin's "God Bless America" nearly eclipsed the "Star-Spangled Banner" as the national anthem. Finally, two pilots attempted to set new world records for speed. Only de Seversky succeeded—or so it seemed.[16]

He had to comply with the Fédération Aéronautique Internationale requirements for amphibian speed records published in June. According to FAI provisions, the amphibian had to take off from water and fly a straight and level land course of three kilometers. An FAI-designated observer would have to time the run electrically and verify through a barograph that the airplane's altitude remained constant. Once finished, the pilot had to land the amphibian in water. The latter two specifications prevented a pilot from artificially ratcheting up the plane's speed by dropping floats after takeoff and diving through the timed run. De Seversky scrupulously followed FAI regulations. In midafternoon on October 8, he flew the SEV-3 from the waters off North Beach at Curtiss Field. To the cheers of the crowd, the amphibian roared full throttle from the west as it approached the three-kilometer course. The plane barreled straight and true three times through the course for an average of 177.79 mph.[17]

Spectators and journalists alike left the air show to tell friends and editors they had witnessed the creation of a new speed record by the sleek amphibian. Unfortunately, William Eynart, the FAI-designated representative and an official observer for the National Aeronautical Association, discovered that the airplane's sealed barograph failed to operate. It should have measured and recorded changes in atmospheric pressure, hence changes in the airplane's altitude. No proof, then, existed that de Seversky did not try to pick up speed by placing the aircraft in a descent attitude as it traversed the course. A day later, he had to repeat his pageant performance but for a much smaller crowd. This time, the Major and his SEV-3 established a verified speed record for amphibians of 180.3 mph. Two years later at the Michigan Air Circus held in Detroit, he broke his own record. With his cocker spaniel companion, Vodka, as copilot and with a 710 hp Wright Cyclone engine pulling the craft through the air, de Seversky officially reached 230.03 mph. It marked the amphibian as comparable to the best-performing land planes.[18]

Back in 1933, de Seversky's initial frustration over the barograph's failure was tempered by the amphibian's double exposure in the press. Newspapers published follow-up stories to explain why the speed test had to be run a second time. Despite great publicity, the SEV-3 did not secure any immediate interest from individuals, business, or the military in terms of ordering and purchasing a production version. Indeed, Alexander Kartveli speaks in his oral history reminiscences about a second period when the company suffered another near-death economic experience. Understandably, Paul Moore refused to invest additional funds until it was clear that the SEV-3 would actually attract paying customers. Meanwhile, even the company president explored other options. De Seversky accepted an appointment in November 1933 as consulting engineer from Byron C. Foy, president of De Soto Motor Corporation, a division of Chrysler Motors.[19]

As it turned out, the well-publicized flights of the previous month eventually produced a contract that saved Seversky Aircraft from oblivion. U.S. air shows gained the scrutiny of military aviators from other countries. By the 1930s, and for the first time since the Wright brothers, America had once again become a leader in aircraft technology. Consequently, military representatives especially from Europe and Latin America frequented U.S. air shows and sent reports as well as translations of newspaper and magazine articles about American aircraft to their home governments and military. Such was the case with the attaché at the Washington Embassy of the Republic of Colombia. The SEV-3 caught the attention of the Colombia Naval Air Service because the airplane seemed to fit its requirement for a modern reconnaissance amphibian. After late winter negotiations and demonstration flights by de Seversky, his company's chief test pilot, Colombia awarded a contract of nearly $92,000 to Seversky Aircraft for three amphibians plus parts for the SEV-3M(ilitary).[20]

## Making the SEV-3M

The contract exposed a serious problem. While Seversky Aircraft occupied a nice office in Manhattan and possessed a small team of good engineers, it did not have a workshop. And de Seversky was painfully aware of another shortcoming. The SEV-3 had been built by hand, and intuition had played a role alongside measurement in construction. Moreover, if a part did not fit, it was remachined until it did. By contrast, the Colombia contract mandated three identical craft with interchangeable parts. This, in turn, necessitated creating dozens of templates, or jigs, for major elements of the airframe; engines and propellers were purchased off the shelf from other companies. The jigs would be used to guide machine tools in fashioning components. After considering several options, de Seversky decided to subcontract Kirkham Engineering and Manufacturing Corporation to build the SEV-3M airframes. Located south of Farmingdale, Long Island, on a thirty-acre site just west of American Airport (today, Republic Airport), the company manufactured parts for Fairchild Aviation Corporation (today, Fairchild Dornier GmbH) and Grumman Aeronautical Engineering Company (today, Northrop Grumman Corporation).[21]

On May 16, 1934, de Seversky and Charles B. Kirkham signed a contract that, based on drawings and specifications from Seversky Aircraft, handed responsibility to Kirkham Engineering for building three SEV-3M amphibians for the price of $75,000. It was further agreed that as soon as the Colombian government made its contracted deposit, Seversky Aircraft would fund Kirkham Engineering with 35 percent, or $26,250, of the total purchase price. The balance of 65 percent, or $48,750, would be due within ten days after delivery of the three airplanes. In addition, the contract covered the scenario of what would happen should Colombia order more airplanes. Finally, the Seversky-Kirkham agreement allowed Seversky Aircraft to buy for $10,000 all jigs Kirkham Engineering prepared as part of the manufacturing process.[22]

The contract details only become interesting when it is realized that Kirkham Engineering did not manufacture a single airplane. Obviously, something went terribly awry. To be sure, the first part of the agreement was fulfilled. Seversky Aircraft made its 35 percent deposit on the purchase price of the three amphibians after receiving close to $46,000 from the Consulate General of the Republic of Colombia on May 25. De Seversky and his team, however, failed to release in timely fashion all the specifications and drawings for the SEV-3M. As late as July 26, Kirkham Engineering complained that it still needed plans for eighty-two major components. As a result, it could not even establish a schedule for the airplane's production. The delay, of course, was partly attributable to the amphibian's redesign. An airplane built for sport or business was simply not the same as a war machine carrying both guns and bombs.[23]

This hold-up alone jeopardized meeting the November 1 delivery date for the three amphibians. But matters got worse. As summer gave way to fall, Kirkham Engineering realized the deposit it received from Seversky Aircraft would not begin to cover the costs of materials, tools, and salaries associated with building all three aircraft. President Kirkham began requesting, and then requested repeatedly with greater urgency, for a new arrangement that would transfer at least $4,000 a week from Seversky Aircraft to Kirkham Engineering. On top of the financial issue, President Kirkham claimed de Seversky and his team of engineers prepared faulty drawings and specifications since preliminary machining revealed that adjacent parts failed to fit together. From the distance of time, it is impossible to know for certain whether blame should be assigned to those who drew the plans or those who interpreted them. De Seversky, never known for his business sense, should have asked his friend Alexander Pishvanov to camp at the Kirkham factory and coordinate the work there with the Seversky office in Manhattan.[24]

Regardless, what is abundantly clear is that Kirkham Engineering could not fulfill the contract unless it received an infusion of cash. By mid-November, Seversky Aircraft expressed a willingness to negotiate a new agreement. Unhappily for President Kirkham, he had signed an indemnity agreement for a $33,750 bond with the National Surety Corporation. It obligated him to indemnify the surety against all liability, loss, costs, and expenses related to the Seversky Aircraft contract. In December de Seversky notified the bonding company of his troubles with Kirkham Engineering. National Surety lawyers then reminded President Kirkham on December 20 of his signed commitment. Faced with the possibility of serious legal and financial penalties, Kirkham decided to settle the issue out of court. At the beginning of 1935, Seversky Aircraft took charge of all jigs, materials, and machine tools built or purchased by Kirkham Engineering as part of the SEV-3M project. The items were transferred next door to Kirkham Engineering's warehouse, which was leased by Seversky Aircraft for $100 a month. After hiring several Kirkham craftsmen, de Seversky's company actually ended up manufacturing the three amphibians for Colombia.[25]

## Basic Trainer No. 8 (BT-8)

Part of the impetus for de Seversky's move against Kirkham came from the interest of another government in buying even more units from Seversky Aircraft. As early as March 1934, and by using his negotiations with Colombia as an opening gambit, the Major made the rounds in Washington, D.C. He delivered testimony of the SEV-3 before an executive session of the U.S. House of Representatives Military Affairs Subcommittee. The latter investigated U.S. military procurement procedures. Considering de Seversky's fame as the designer of an extremely advanced, all-metal plane that he flew to establish a world speed record, it seemed surprising to several politicians that the American military had not sought to at least examine the craft. Through his lobbying efforts with Congress and his rounds in the capital's Munitions Building that headquartered the U.S. Army Air Corps, he secured an invitation to have the U.S.A.A.C. Materiel Division at Wright Field evaluate the amphibian.[26]

The springtime flight of Evelyn and Sasha to Wright Field in Dayton, Ohio, turned into something of a homecoming for the Major. He had spent so much time there working with the Materiel Division (and its Engineering Division antecedent) on in-flight refueling and bombsights that a local newspaper labeled him the "Flying Stepson of Dayton." Indeed, de Seversky's friend and pilot who flight-tested the C-1 bombsight, Lt. (eventually, Col.) John F. Whiteley, flew and evaluated the amphibian. As the testing proceeded, the designer and his wife engaged in social activities, such as a Sunday party offered by the assistant chief of the Materiel Division, Col. (later, Maj. Gen.) Oliver P. Echols. De Seversky supplied the party's entertainment by offering his synthetic right leg to the resident and excitable Boston bull terrier that liked to nip at the leg of a guest. Meanwhile, and no surprise, the SEV-3 earned a favorable evaluation from Whiteley. The positive review, though, could not overcome the fact that the army was not in the market for a seaplane.[27]

On the other hand, the advanced qualities and fine performance of the amphibian resulted in an invitation to bring the SEV-3 back to Wright Field in August as a land plane and compete for a major contract to build aircraft for the air corps flight training program. Hence, in June and July 1934, de Seversky and his small team converted the amphibian into the SEV-3XAR (eXperimental ARmy) by removing the floats and installing spatted fixed landing gear. In addition, the canopy and seats were raised to expand the viewing area for pilot and instructor. Finally, the engine was moved forward to rebalance the aircraft after removal of the floats. The time spent reworking the aircraft is the other part of the explanation as to why de Seversky and his engineers delayed issuing drawings and specifications to Kirkham Engineering that led to the first of several conflicts between Seversky Aircraft and its subcontractor. The SEV-3XAR won the August competition to build the BT-8. It would be the army's first modern, all-metal monowing trainer with cantilevered wing and monocoque fuselage.[28]

On January 2, 1935, the U.S. War Department awarded a contract worth $754,738 to Seversky Aircraft Corporation to build thirty basic training planes plus parts equal to five more. From de Seversky's standpoint, the only disappointment was the unyielding stipulation to comply with an air corps regulation on engines. It specified a power rating maximum of 400 hp for such BT aircraft. As a result, the powerplant installed in the BT-8 would be a 400 hp Pratt & Whitney engine. It left the craft somewhat underpowered. Student pilots practicing touch-and-go landings would have to be warned not to power down excessively when landing and not to pull up abruptly on takeoff; otherwise the plane might stall and crash. Regardless, the contract theoretically elevated the company to the status of a significant aircraft manufacturer. In reality, it was a small design bureau that had leased a warehouse, borrowed some workers, and struggled to build three airplanes in a twelve-month period. It could not begin to match such contemporary firms as Boeing, Curtiss-Wright, Martin, and Vought, which also held important military contracts.[29]

It was because of de Seversky's lengthy collaboration with the military and his reputation as a prolific aeronautical inventor and an innovative designer that the company he represented could get around the fact that it was in no way prepared to fulfill such an ambitious production run when he signed the contract. The U.S. Army Air Corps expected BT-8 deliveries to begin well before year's end. It never happened. Nevertheless, de Seversky made a valiant, if tardy, effort to resize the company in 1935. Later that year, Seversky Aircraft moved to a vacant factory, one of three located at Farmingdale's American Airport. A subsidiary of Fairchild Aviation, American Aviation

Corporation, controlled the property. Seversky Aircraft shared the airport and facilities with Grumman Aeronautical and another Fairchild subsidiary, the Ranger Aircraft Engine Corporation. In November 1936 the company, after registering with the newly created Securities Exchange Commission and issuing 840,000 shares of stock, bought and occupied the entire property. It gave Seversky Aircraft 200,000 square feet of factory space, a 127-acre airfield, and a modern brick, steel, and glass hangar of 16,000 square feet. For obvious reasons, the field was renamed Seversky Airport.[30]

By the beginning of 1936, the company had hired 391 men, including thirteen foremen. The impressive increase in personnel must be balanced against the fact it failed to result in the manufacture of a single BT-8. Indeed, a very frustrated Materiel Division representative, Capt. J. S. Gullet, noted that over time de Seversky had supplied four different production schedules to the U.S.A.A.C. and had not met any of his own deadlines. One explanation for the delay is that de Seversky could not afford the $5 million he estimated it would take to buy new and advanced machine tools and stamping equipment. As a result, production involved a tremendous amount of individual labor on older machines that required greater skill on the part of operators to cut, shape, fit, and weld parts for the metal airplane. Moreover, in the last six months of 1935, many of these new factory workers had to be trained. The company recorded 903 salvages, which were materials that had to be thrown away or, if possible, reworked in the process of training employees, to meet air corps expectations for a high-quality product. Regardless, salvages were costly in money and time. De Seversky also blamed the delay in production on the Materiel Division's requests for changes in the BT-8 after the contract had been signed. Whatever logic they might have had, Gullet dismissed the Major's excuses and, in turn, countered with his own reasons why Seversky Aircraft ended up one year behind in meeting its contractual obligations. First, there were months after the contract was signed when de Seversky devoted more attention to the Colombian project and the design of a pursuit prototype than to the BT-8. Second, frequent turnovers in the factory manager position strongly suggested serious flaws in setting up the manufacturing process. Third, just as the construction phase of the BT-8 was about to begin in 1936, de Seversky pulled his most skilled metalworkers from the line to help build experimental aircraft.[31]

The tardy start to the serial production of the BT-8 cannot diminish the genuine accomplishments of the innovative designer. De Seversky and his team engineered and built documentably the most advanced amphibian in the world and then converted it successfully into the first modern low-wing, all-metal trainer accepted into service by the U.S.A.A.C. Its precursor, Consolidated's BT-7, resembled nothing so much in profile and construction as a World War I biplane. By contrast, de Seversky's BT-8 had the look, feel, and sound of a contemporary warplane and a performance level nearly 50 percent higher than the BT-7. At the same time, Seversky Aircraft kept the SEV-3 flap or air brake so that the landing speed for the novice pilot measured comfortably near 60 mph. Finally, and unlike earlier open cockpit trainers, pilot and instructor enjoyed the warmth and safety of the enclosed cockpits that kept hurricane-force winds outside the BT-8 during flights.[32]

### Reflections

In mid-August 1934 Alexander P. de Seversky first met Lt. Col. (later, General of the Army) Henry Harley (Hap) Arnold. It is almost surprising that they did not know each other—one explanation being Arnold had spent much of his service time since 1919 at army bases and airfields in California and Kansas. The occasion of their meeting came as a result of both men visiting Wright Field: de Seversky to participate in the BT-8 competition and Arnold to rest during a stopover from his round trip of 7,630 miles between Washington, D.C., and Alaska as head of a flight of ten B-10 bombers. For its time, the latter event was a stunning portent of how quickly air power could be projected over great distances. The Major, as a hopeful manufacturer of military aircraft, applied his Russian charm widely among officers, including Arnold, and usually with good effect. One never knew which personnel change might impact the makeup of air corps leadership over the Materiel Division or Procurement Board.

At any rate, Arnold and several other officers accepted de Seversky's invitation to dine with him and Evelyn at their hotel in Dayton. By all accounts, dinner was excellent and everyone had a nice time. This moment is so fleeting and insignificant that the event is not mentioned in either the narrative or the endnotes. Two years later and without any contact or communication whatsoever between the two men, Arnold orally attacked de Seversky in a meeting of the U.S.A.A.C. Procurement Board. As Brig. Gen. Warner Robins informed the Major, Arnold denounced de Seversky and indicated that as far as he was concerned Seversky Aircraft would not supply any more airplanes to the air corps. As will be seen in the next several chapters, the animosity that emerged between these two figures was enhanced by their philosophical differences over the design and deployment of air assets in war.

The clash with Arnold played a background role in de Seversky's loss of the company he founded in 1931 and in the direction of his comments as a widely read and respected prophet of air power. Meanwhile, and to his dying day, de Seversky remained puzzled as to why Arnold suddenly turned against him in 1936. Chapter 7 solves the puzzle that escaped de Seversky for the next thirty-eight years. When the Procurement Board met, Brigadier General Arnold was assistant chief of the U.S. Army Air Corps. He had a special responsibility for aircraft acquisitions and reviewed the serious trouble the Materiel Division had with Seversky Aircraft over completing the BT-8. Philosophical differences between the men are important and will be explored later on. But the starting point for Arnold's verbal assault against de Seversky began with his perception that the innovative designer either poorly supervised or poorly understood the aircraft manufacturing process and repeatedly missed deadlines and thus proved to be unreliable.

# 8

# The P-35 Manufacturer

There is irony in the fact that Alexander P. de Seversky ended up manufacturing pursuit or fighter aircraft for the U.S. Army Air Corps. After all, he had spent years trying to enhance the destructive value and deadly accuracy of multiengine bombers via his C-1 and succeeding bombsights. Beginning with Gen. Billy Mitchell and extending through the 1920s, more and more of America's military airmen came to believe large airplanes carrying both offensive explosives and defensive guns represented the winning technology of future wars. The idea gained credence by the writings of early philosophers of air power, including Italian officer Giulio Douhet, who wrote *The Command of the Air* (1921), and British historian Basil H. Liddell Hart, who authored *Paris: Or, the Future of War* (1925). Their writings, in turn, were influenced by the savage and grisly course of the terrible conflict that ended in November 1918.[1]

### Bomber versus Pursuit

These ideas gradually embedded themselves in the Air Corps Tactical School (ACTS), which moved to Maxwell Field near Montgomery, Alabama, in July 1931. It did offer a course on pursuit aircraft, and in the first half of the 1930s it was taught by the former Louisiana teacher turned fighter pilot, Capt. (later, Maj. Gen.) Claire Lee Chennault. He supported a balanced air force composed of both bombardment and pursuit. Chennault based his position on the principle that victory in war could only

113

be achieved by establishing air supremacy in which enemy air power was severely checked. While acknowledging the importance of the bomber in reducing the enemy's capacity to fight, he hammered in class and in print that air supremacy depended entirely on pursuit aircraft. Unfortunately for U.S. bomber crews in World War II, Chennault and his course were marginalized by bomber partisans. They claimed bombardment would destroy enemy planes on the ground and that future air battles belonged to the realm of fantasy and fiction. His course would later be deleted from the curriculum as Chennault retired from the air corps in March 1937. In July of that year, he began a new military career in China, which suffered invasion by Japan—in one sense the opening round of the Second World War. Chennault trained fighter pilots for the Chinese air force and later created the American Volunteer Group (Flying Tigers). Belatedly, the latter proved bombardment proponents wrong. The Flying Tigers inflicted heavy damage against Japanese bombers while protecting the skies over the Chinese wartime capital of Chongqing.[2]

In the early 1930s, Chennault did have a few allies. One of these was a World War I Russian naval fighter pilot. Major de Seversky sided with the ACTS instructor when he wrote the first of hundreds of articles on air power. This initial offering appeared in the March 1934 issue of *U.S. Air Services*, a journal widely read by aviators and especially those in the military. De Seversky answered his own question, which he posed in the title: "How Can Pursuit Aviation Regain Its Tactical Freedom?" Since 1918, bombers enjoyed exceptional development that gave them more speed and defensive firepower. Deplorably, pursuit aircraft of recent vintage carried the same small caliber weapons as in 1918. As a result, de Seversky remarked, "[B]ombardment aviation, carried away by the success of its performance, considers itself immune from the attack of any aircraft." To regain its prominent if not preeminent role, the author suggested that pursuit aviation needed to upgrade its weaponry by employing some form of cannon. The article introduced de Seversky to Chennault. It indirectly supported the ACTS instructor's unsuccessful effort to convince the armament engineers at Wright Field to increase the firepower of the single-seat warplane. Chennault wanted to replace the standard two-gun emplacement on pursuits with four .30-caliber machine guns synchronized to fire through the propeller.[3]

Besides Chennault, Billy Mitchell also read the article, and this prompted him to renew his 1920s friendship with de Seversky. An apparent outcast after his court-martial, Mitchell still maintained many contacts among the circle of officers who directed the air corps. Most of these contacts considered Mitchell to have been an exceptional assistant chief of the U.S. Army Air Service and a great prophet of air power who was wrongly maligned by nearsighted, ground-immured army generals. The latter were colorfully described by Chennault as "foggy-brained brass." In addition, Mitchell had a tie-in with the War Department through his long-term association with Assistant Secretary of War Frederick P. Keppel. These inside connections helped de Seversky immensely. Between March 1934 and his death in February 1936, Mitchell briefed the Major regularly over dinner or the phone on the military's views and plans for pursuit aircraft.[4]

### P-35 Prototypes

The article de Seversky wrote in 1934 clearly anticipated his views and plans. He wanted to convert the SEV-3 into something more than a military trainer. Over the winter of 1934–1935, as Seversky Aircraft completed its first Colombian contract and began the setup for the BT-8, metal was cut to produce another land plane variant of the original 1933 amphibian. This one would be the SEV-2XP (2 crew eXperimental Pursuit). The prototype carried a 750 hp Wright air-cooled, radial engine; a three-bladed propeller; and a fixed undercarriage with wheel pants. Aside from the much larger engine, the SEV-2XP differed little from the BT-8 except for machine-gun emplacements, including one for the second or aft crew member. De Seversky designed and later patented a flexible mount for a gun in the second cockpit to protect the rear of the plane from enemy air attack. In May 1935 he decided to enter the prototype in the U.S. Army Air Corps competition. The company that sponsored the winning aircraft would secure a handsome contract to build a replacement for the outdated Boeing P-26.[5]

It should be noted that de Seversky responded to the air corps specifications issued in May with a two-place aircraft when the air corps requested a single-place plane for the pursuit competition. On top of this self-imposed handicap, de Seversky learned that the competing aircraft, Curtiss 75 and Northrop 3A, had retractable landing gear. The ability to retract the wheels meant a serious reduction in drag and hence better performance in speed. Fortuitously, if not conveniently, the SEV-2XP prototype suffered damage when transported to Wright Field on June 18, 1935. Because of the limited number of competing companies and to avoid another congressional investigation into procurement procedures, the U.S.A.A.C. extended the competition period to enable Seversky Aircraft to repair its demonstrator.[6]

As it turned out, the air corps had made the right decision. When the Northrop 3A was tested at Wright Field, it developed vibration problems. Northrop Company, then (1932–1938) associated with Douglas Aircraft in California, also received permission to rework its plane to eliminate unwanted characteristics. On July 30, 1935, the Northrop 3A flew over the coastal waters of the Pacific Ocean during a test flight. Neither pilot nor plane ever returned. Northrop subsequently sold its design to Vought Aircraft, which built the plane as the V-141. Technically, this left the Curtiss-Wright Aeronautical Corporation, builder of the Curtiss 75, as the only active competitor. Had the contract for pursuit aircraft fallen by default into the hands of Curtiss-Wright, it would have raised eyebrows and hard questions among members of the administration of President Franklin D. Roosevelt and their friends and opponents in Congress. Thus the Materiel Division could only mark as good news when it learned Seversky Aircraft would have its pursuit prototype repaired and ready for testing in August.[7]

Meanwhile, de Seversky had wisely decided to have his engineers and shop workers do more than simply fix damage to the company's demonstrator. He dropped the challenge to air corps specifications by converting the plane from a two-seat to a single-seat aircraft and redesignating it the SEV-1XP. Moreover, the dorsal fuselage running from cockpit to tail was reshaped as a razorback spine, a feature characteristic of the P-35 and descendants, including the P-47. Additionally, retractable wheels, both main and tail, replaced the fixed landing gear. Instead of disappearing into the wing, the main-faired wheels retracted back into additional fairings that fully enclosed the gear. The process resulted in two exposed, bulbous structures left and right of the ventral fuselage near the trailing edge of the wing. Finally, the original 750 hp powerplant was replaced by a more potent 850 hp Wright R-1820 air-cooled, radial engine. Use of an engine built by Curtiss-Wright did not prevent the company from complaining bitterly that Seversky Aircraft had not repaired a dinged prototype but had entered an entirely new competitor.[8]

Regardless, de Seversky brought the SEV-1XP to Wright Field on August 15, 1935. Shortly thereafter, the Materiel Division inaugurated a lengthy period of tests comparing the construction and performance of the two planes.

While the SEV-1XP failed to reach the promised 300 mph mark, it hit 289 mph, which was, nonetheless, better than the speed of the Curtiss 75. As discussed in the following, Seversky Aircraft had designed a better plane. This was certainly the view of Maj. (temporary rank) Claire Chennault. In fact, through air corps contacts, Billy Mitchell could tell de Seversky that the SEV-1XP definitely won the competition and that he could expect a sizable contract by year's end. An ugly surprise, then, jolted de Seversky on December 31. Over the phone, he read to Mitchell a U.S.A.A.C. telegram he had just received: "ALL BIDS ON CIRCULAR PROPOSAL THIRTY FIVE DASH EIGHT NAUGHT FOUR COVERING SINGLE PLACE PURSUIT AIRPLANES ARE REJECTED AND NEW CIRCULAR PROPOSAL WILL BE ISSUED UNDER SAME SPECIFICATIONS SCHEDULED FOR OPENING APRIL FIFTEENTH NINETEEN THIRTY SIX."[9]

On the surface, air corps rejection of both the Curtiss 75 and SEV-1XP occurred because neither plane achieved the expected 300 mph listed in Circular Proposal 35-804. Members of the Curtiss-Wright Corporation, however, convinced themselves that over time the U.S.A.A.C. had acknowledged the legitimate complaint of Curtiss-Wright that it was wrong to give Seversky Aircraft extra months to alter its prototype significantly. It had unfairly punished corporate representatives and the Curtiss 75. After all, the pursuit had arrived at Wright Field ready for trials on the original date set by the air corps. On the other hand, there may have been another issue entirely. In December 1935 Mitchell met with Assistant Secretary of War Keppel in Washington, D.C. Keppel informed the former air service officer that de Seversky had designed a great airplane but failed to show he had the facilities for manufacturing pursuit aircraft.[10]

It will be recalled that nearly one year after receiving a contract to build BT-8s, Seversky Aircraft had failed to produce a single one by December 1935. Was it really a coincidence that the U.S.A.A.C. decided that same month to reject both Curtiss 75 and SEV-1XP, especially since the apparent winner of the 1935 trial was Seversky Aircraft? By the same token, was it not favorable to the cause of the Seversky prototype that in the midst of the spring 1936 trials for pursuit planes, the first modern-looking, quality-made BT-8s roared over Wright Field before landing for acceptance tests on May 16? Between the December rejection and May trials, de Seversky and his team made changes to their prototype to improve their chances for a substantial government contract. For example, engineers designed and workers produced and positioned a modified vertical tail stabilizer or fin. And de Seversky decided to try a Pratt & Whitney motor to power the aircraft. As might be expected, Curtiss-Wright also switched engines. Despite the changes, both the Curtiss 75 and SEV-1XP experienced engine problems and recorded even slower speeds in 1936 than during the trials of 1935.[11]

Fortunately for these yearlong rivals, the other competitors in the pursuit trials self-destructed—one quite literally. The Consolidated PB-2A was heavy and underpowered and, tragically, experienced a fatal crash that disqualified the plane. Vought Aircraft copied too carefully the Northrop 3A design it inherited. The Vought 141 entry displayed some of the undesirable characteristics of the 3A, including flutter in flight and directional instability. Since the Curtiss 75 again failed to measure up, Seversky Aircraft received a contract on June 16, 1936, worth $1,636,250 to build seventy-seven P-35 pursuit aircraft plus parts equivalent to eight more planes. The production model differed from the demonstrator as follows: the oil cooler was moved from the side to the bottom of the engine cowl, the landing gear was changed to open wheel fairings, 3 percent dihedral was added to the wings for stability, and one .30-caliber and one .50-caliber machine gun was mounted in the cowl above the engine. The machine guns fired synchronously through the propeller. Finally, the contract stipulated that a Pratt & Whitney R-1830-9 Twin Wasp air-cooled engine be installed in each airframe. Rated at 950 hp, the Twin Wasp gave the P-35 a maximum speed of 281 mph.[12]

Since neither surviving competitor reached 300 mph, features other than speed secured victory for Seversky Aircraft, which ended up building America's first modern fighter plane. One clear advantage for the SEV-1XP emerged from the fact that the aircraft did not have traditional fuel tanks but stored gasoline in the wing cavity. As a result, the plane possessed a fuel capacity 50 percent greater and thus a combat range of 1,150 miles compared to 700 miles for the Curtiss prototype. By contrast, Curtiss had installed three tanks in the fuselage. One was ahead of the pilot, another below the seat, and a third tank was located behind the pilot. What would ordinarily be a survivable accident might very well kill a Curtiss flier, who could be crushed by one of the fuel tanks or bathed in ignited fuel. Another winning design focused on the cockpit of the Seversky plane, which was farther forward than the pilot's seat in the Curtiss.[13]

Two positive effects attended the feature. First, the SEV-1XP pilot had a clearer view over the nose and leading edge of the wing. This helped both in landing the plane and engaging enemy aircraft in wartime. Second, the flier sat over the airframe's center of gravity. It reduced discomfort a pilot might experience from rapid maneuvers during aerial combat or training exercises that simulated aerial combat. By comparison with Curtiss, the Seversky possessed an ample baggage compartment and an equally large compartment door. If necessary, the space was more than sufficient to carry a passenger. The obvious advantage was that the compartment could hold luggage, tools, equipment, and spare parts in quantity. Moreover, a device allowed the pilot's seat to descend into the baggage area, which then became an emergency exit. Lastly and conveniently, the generous space gave mechanics easy access to the radio, battery, oxygen equipment, and the tail wheel retracting mechanism.[14]

The final feature favoring the SEV-1XP over the Curtiss 75 was the cowl with movable flaps or shutters around the skirt or trailing edge. They facilitated the flow of cool air over the hot engine from the wash of the propeller blades. Unhappily, the Curtiss 75 possessed a tight cowl that caused the engine to overheat and be less efficient. It resulted in the Curtiss plane enduring engine malfunctions and mediocre speeds during the May trials. Curtiss-Wright Corporation received a second chance to correct the error. The government awarded the losing company a contract to build three preproduction Y1P-36 aircraft. Clearly, air corps decision makers felt the Curtiss prototype showed great promise. Moreover, for reasons already suggested, the military did not want to depend on Seversky Aircraft for all of its pursuit planes. The first production version of the P-36A carried a more powerful Pratt & Whitney Twin Wasp engine. With cowl flaps, constant speed propellers, and 100 octane gasoline formulated by Shell Petroleum, the airplane exceeded the 300 mph speed desired by the air corps.[15]

### Halcyon Days for Seversky Aircraft and Its President

Despite evidence that Curtiss-Wright not only remained a potent rival but one that attracted the active encouragement and even funding from the War Department, Alexander P. de Seversky was elated by his victory. It justified his optimism to hold a stockholders' meeting on May 16, 1936, and seek additional working capital even before learning the official results of the pursuit trials at Wright Field. Frankly, the meeting proved to be a small affair. Seversky Aircraft Corporation's fourteen stockholders fit comfortably in a modest office at 120 Broadway, New York City. Twelve investors, including Evelyn de Seversky, held 21.22 percent of the 280,000 shares of outstanding stock; the Major controlled 21.01 percent; and the rest, a whopping 57.77 percent, belonged to the company's angel, Paul Moore. During the meeting, stockholders decided to issue new stock, purchase Seversky Aero Corporation to control de Seversky's patents, expand the number of company officers, reelect de Seversky as president, and appoint Joseph A. Sisto to the corporation's board of directors.[16]

J. A. Sisto & Company successfully prepared a prospectus and filed on June 22, 1936, a registration statement for Seversky Aircraft with the Securities Exchange Commission to offer publicly 840,000 shares of $1.00 par value common stock. Of this package, 200,000 shares were offered directly by Sisto for $3.75 each. Paul Moore, agreed to purchase for $3.00 any unsold stock from this initial public offering. However, two hours after the sale opened on July 16, the stock was oversubscribed and the books were closed. On August 24, the New York Curb Exchange (American Stock Exchange after January 5, 1953) announced Seversky Aircraft Corporation would be added to its trading list. The next day, the first thousand shares sold for a low of 3⅞ and a high of 4. Even though the prospectus clearly showed the company under de Seversky's leadership had lost money every year since its founding, the stock generally sold for more than 4. It partly reflected the large government contract to build seventy-seven pursuits and partly revealed the continuing investment of Paul Moore, who would remain the company's dominant stockholder and its true underwriter. Regardless, President de Seversky and his corporate officers now had the working capital to hire more workers and purchase automatic machinery, stamping presses, and spot welding equipment for the serial production of the P-35. He also had resources to cover the construction of experimental airplanes as well as funds to demonstrate aircraft in both the United States and abroad. Moreover, the infusion of money enabled Seversky Aircraft to exchange its $15,600 annual lease for a permanent deed to what became Seversky Airport and manufacturing complex near Farmingdale, Long Island.[17]

On a personal level, Alexander P. de Seversky and his wife, Evelyn, joined the well-to-do elite precisely because the share price of the new stock bounced between $4.00 and $6.00 until near the end of May 1937. His 1922 Seversky Aero Corporation had borrowed $11,522.05 from the newer company. As Seversky Aircraft bought out Seversky Aero to secure patents, the indebtedness was forgiven plus the Major received 15,306 shares of the new stock as compensation. The value of the shares in this happy period of fairly robust stock sales gave de Seversky a paper fortune of $60,000 to $90,000. Moreover, the stock sales enabled the board of directors to increase the president's annual salary from a modest $4,000 in 1934–1935 to a spectacular $25,000 in 1936–1937. To grasp what these amounts mean, a person earning $2,000 a year in the same period could support a family of four. The Major's salary placed him and Evelyn in the top 5 percent in terms of American income.[18]

Such rewards whether in stocks or salaries enabled the de Severskys to move from apartment living to a mansion on the north shore of Long Island at Asharoken Beach near Northport. The couple owned vacant lots on both sides of the huge residence. Thus Sasha could enjoy absolute privacy as well as engage in one of his favorite activities, which generally produced noise. A musician of many parts, the Major proved to be every bit the son of a professional musician and singer. Alexander played accordion, balalaika, guitar, piano, ukulele, and a Hammond electric organ. Plus, as he banged away on his instruments during free moments, he would also sing. And he could do so with gusto and without fear that a neighbor in the next apartment might call the local gendarmes and lodge a complaint.[19]

To an amazing degree, de Seversky was not hampered in his activities by the loss of a sizable portion of his right leg. Not only did he enjoy fishing, but he occasionally removed his prosthesis and went swimming as well. He and Evelyn also enjoyed dancing at nightclubs and ice-skating in season. In fact, the amputee's social activities seemed to multiply exponentially with the company's success in securing War Department contracts for the BT-8 and P-35. Hence, separately or together, the Major and his wife received regular coverage in society pages of the local press while attending such events as the Army-Navy football game, the Vanderbilt Cup Road Race, or the wedding of Chrysler Motor Corporation's vice president. And, as might be expected with a beautiful mansion on the northern shore of Long Island, the de Severskys entertained prominent guests in aviation and politics; sometimes the two were combined as in the person of New York mayor Fiorello H. La Guardia, who had served in the U.S. Army Air Service in World War I. De Seversky met the mayor in 1935, when he served with Eddie Rickenbacker and Roscoe Turner on the entertainment committee that honored La Guardia during the Sixteenth Annual Aviators

Ball held in the Pierre Hotel in the city. Subsequently, the Major flew the mayor to Washington, D.C., when La Guardia delivered testimony in 1936 before Congress on the subject of establishing an airport on Governors Island.[20]

Money and position served as the lubricants to the machinery of high society that the de Severskys had entered. As the Major's status shifted from air show performer to aircraft manufacturer, he discovered the Dale Carnegie Course that he had taken several years earlier now assumed greater importance. Being the head of a company producing modern military aircraft prompted organizations and media to turn to de Seversky for commentary on aviation subjects and national security. For example, the *Forum Hour* program broadcasted by New York's WOR radio station turned over prime time in January 1937 to de Seversky for his views on "What 1937 Will Mean to Aviation"; the Rotary Club of New York City invited the Major to discuss "America's National Defense in the Air." The latter highlighted the growing concern over the rise of fascist or militaristic powers that destabilized peace through their expansionist designs. By 1937 Germany had rearmed and reoccupied the Rhineland, effectively destroying the Treaty of Versailles, which ended the Great War. Italy had conquered Ethiopia and joined Germany in a Rome-Berlin Axis supporting fascist rebels fighting the Republican government of Spain. Japanese forces had occupied Manchuria in 1931 and began a general assault on China in 1937.[21]

Small wonder the U.S. Army Air Corps took several steps in the mid-1930s to respond to the potential challenges posed by the aggressive behavior of several powers. First, within the larger air corps, General Headquarters (GHQ) Air Force was organized on March 1, 1935. It emerged from the recommendations of several high-profile boards or commissions that sought to define the role of military aviation in the nation's defense. GHQ Air Force employed frontline combat aircraft and trained pilots in simulated wartime exercises to shield ground troops and maintain coastal defenses alongside the U.S. Navy. It also functioned in planning independent air operations—a portent of the future U.S. Air Force. Second, the air corps pressed Congress and the War Department to fund the serial production of Boeing's Flying Fortress. Unfortunately, during 1935 bomber trials at Wright Field, human error caused the destruction of the Boeing prototype. Victory and a contract thus fell to Douglas Aircraft, which developed the B-18. This military version of the DC-2 airliner carried half the bomb load and flew half the distance at 40 mph slower than the Flying Fortress. The Douglas contract left only enough funds to build thirteen preproduction units of the Flying Fortress, or B-17, which, at the time, was simply the best strategic bomber in the world.[22]

Finally, during July 1937, the U.S. War Department awarded Curtiss-Wright a $4 million contract to build 210 P-36 aircraft. The news struck de Seversky like an undeserved slap in the face. Why Curtiss-Wright and not Seversky Aircraft? As mentioned in chapter 7, Gen. Warner Robins had warned the Major about Gen. Hap Arnold's criticism of Seversky Aircraft before the Procurement Board. Hence de Seversky quickly blamed the assistant chief of staff for the decision that favored Curtiss-Wright. Obviously, air corps logic of not depending on one manufacturer for all its pursuit aircraft failed to convince the Major. Moreover, de Seversky turned a blind eye toward his own culpability. Three preproduction P-36 planes arrived at Wright Field by March 1937 and had been found by Materiel Division engineers and test pilots to be good aircraft with even greater potential. By contrast, the first anniversary of Seversky Aircraft's P-35 contract came and went without a single P-35 entering the air corps inventory. It appeared to many air corps officers, not just Arnold, that Seversky Aircraft lacked the manufacturing and leadership abilities to be a reliable producer of military planes.[23]

### Long-Distance Racer

When General Arnold visited Seversky Aircraft eight months after the company had received the P-35 contract, he failed to see even a glimmer of the pursuit being built. Regrettably, de Seversky had promised that the first P-35 would be delivered to Wright Field within six months. In reality, the first plane arrived on May 5, 1937, nearly five months late. It could not be evaluated by the Materiel Division because of construction deficiencies especially associated with the installation of the engine. Later, the Major fired the engineer in charge of putting the plane together. Meanwhile, the problems that delayed production of the P-35 resembled those that interrupted completion of the BT-8. Seversky Aircraft spent time in 1936 completing a second order of military amphibians for the Colombia Naval Air Service; P-35 construction forced the company to purchase and upgrade machine tools and train additional workers. A couple of individual P-35s were finally accepted for preliminary testing by the Materiel Division at the beginning of September 1937, but the full production line did not begin operations until November. Nevertheless, once the sundry parts of the assembly process had been set up, Seversky Aircraft could produce 150 or more aircraft a year. As a result, de Seversky firmly believed the air corps had made a terrible mistake in contracting a second company to build pursuit aircraft. To prove this to air corps leaders, if not to Congress and the public, he chose to demonstrate the superior characteristics of the P-35 through a high-visibility program of long-distance flights and races.[24]

De Seversky focused more on distance than speed. The Curtiss-Wright demonstrator was not quite as fast as the P-35, though with a more powerful engine the production P-36 did, in fact, perform better. But that would also be true of the P-35. The last article produced under contract possessed landing gear that retracted flush into the wing and a Pratt & Whitney engine rated at 1,150 hp. This modified P-35, redesignated as XP-41, had a top speed of 323 mph or 10 mph faster than the serially produced P-36A. While the speed of either the P-35 or P-36 could be altered by the type of engine, propeller, and/or fuel employed, the proportional difference in range would remain approximately the same. Here the P-35 held a tremendous advantage. Its longer range, easily augmented further by the addition of a fuel tank in the fuselage, would allow the P-35 in wartime to accompany and guard bombers on lengthy missions, permit the plane to stay airborne longer to protect ground assets such as troops against enemy aircraft, and enable the planes to mobilize quickly through nonstop flights from interior airfields to combat stations.[25]

Thus de Seversky chose to place P-35s in the September 1937 Bendix cross-country air race flown from United Airport in Burbank, California, to Municipal Airport in Cleveland, Ohio. Sponsored since 1931 by industrialist and inventor Vincent Bendix, whose several corporations built automotive and airplane parts, the Transcontinental Free-for-All Speed Dash preceded and opened the National Air Races in Cleveland (now held in Reno, Nevada). For this first effort to generate publicity and enhance legitimacy for the P-35 as a high-performing distance racer, de Seversky had a newly minted twin of the SEV-1XP modified. Engineers and machinists cut down the cockpit canopy to reduce drag, stripped away excess weight, and installed a bigger engine to create the SEV-S2 (Special #2). At the same time, he contacted the president of Fuller Paint Company, sportsman pilot Frank W. Fuller of San Francisco, California, and secured his enthusiastic agreement to fly the plane in the Bendix Race. For good measure, Seversky Aircraft test pilot Frank Sinclair also registered for the race and flew the SEV-S1, the original SEV-1XP demonstrator used in the 1936 pursuit trials at Wright Field.[26]

With only three hours sleep and no breakfast, Frank Fuller took off in the SEV-S2 from Burbank at 7:55 a.m. (4:55 a.m. local time) on September 3, 1937. He made one fuel stop for the plane in Kansas City and picked up one small bottle of milk for himself. Regrettably, no one heeded the message he had sent earlier requesting a prepared meal. With an empty stomach but a fully fueled aircraft, he roared off to Cleveland. He flew over Municipal Airport with the fastest time among the six competitors who completed this phase of the race. As a result, he won the $13,000 prize accompanying the Bendix Trophy. Instead of landing at Cleveland, he chose to continue flying on the optional second leg of the race, which took him to a flyover of Bendix (today, Teterboro) Airport, New Jersey, before landing at Floyd Bennett Field in Brooklyn, New York, at 5:35 p.m. Hence, he completed a true transcontinental flight in record time for the Bendix at an average speed of 258 mph and earned an additional prize of $2,500.[27]

### Jackie Cochran

Engine problems dropped Frank Sinclair to fourth place. Among the remaining competitors who survived and completed the Bendix Race, de Seversky's attention was drawn to the third-place finisher, Jacqueline Cochran. She was almost as attractive as the Beechcraft Model 17 (Staggerwing) that she flew. This rising star in the air show circuit replaced her friend, Amelia Earhart, as America's best-known aviatrix. Tragically, Earhart had disappeared two months earlier over the Pacific Ocean during her attempt to be the first female pilot to circumnavigate the world. Cochran, like Earhart, was a skilled pilot who possessed remarkable courage. De Seversky also appreciated the fact that Cochran was a woman driven to win any competition she entered. What motivated her and propelled her to be victorious in every situation she faced was her lengthy battle to gain freedom from bone-crushing poverty.[28]

Born in 1906 to a migrant family in the Florida Panhandle, Cochran escaped her impoverished surroundings by becoming a sought-after beautician who took her talents and business acumen to New York City, where she met and eventually married Floyd Bostwick Odlum, lawyer, financier, and head of Atlas Corporation. He could help Jackie establish the Jacqueline Cochran Cosmetics Company, and he encouraged her to use an airplane to manage her far-flung business affairs. Her first long-distance flight as a novice pilot took place in August 1932, when she flew from Long Island's Roosevelt Field to Montreal for the Canadian Air Pageant, where she watched headliner de Seversky perform his deadstick aerobatic routine in the *Bird* biplane.[29]

Before the Bendix Race, de Seversky and Cochran met by chance at Roosevelt Field in July 1937. The Major had test-flown the SEV-S2 to the field where Cochran had a more powerful engine installed in the Beechcraft. Naturally, Cochran knew about the high performance level of Seversky Aircraft's latest creation. When the aviatrix saw the sleek, metal-silver plane, she wanted to fly the aircraft and jumped at the opportunity to talk with the P-35 manufacturer. Their conversations led to de Seversky's invitation for Cochran to fly a demonstrator at Wright Field two days after the Bendix. The Major, in fact, was eager for a female to fly the P-35. More than one test pilot at the Materiel Division felt the pursuit was difficult to handle probably because it was faster both flying and landing than aircraft normally flown. On the other hand, the narrow stance of the main wheels made it too easy to nose-over or ground loop the P-35. If a female could safely handle the plane, de Seversky hoped it would quash the complaints of testosterone-ladened military pilots.[30]

De Seversky's ploy worked; military pilot complaints diminished. He now modified his strategy and moved it into the public arena. The Major chose to demonstrate the outstanding features of the P-35 through a female. To be sure, he was one of the most experienced pilots in the world and served as his company's first test pilot. He constantly flew the P-35 and its variants and officially broke numerous speed records such as flights between New York and Washington, D.C., New York and Havana, Cuba, as well as the east to west transcontinental record between New York and Los Angeles. Despite de Seversky's certified air accomplishments, he understood that a female pilot setting new records would gain more recognition and attract more attention to the P-35. Playing on contemporary attitudes, de Seversky essentially told the U.S. military, public, and politicians that the P-35 was so easy to fly at combat speeds and distances that "even a woman can do it." Hence he turned over the SEV-S1 to Cochran two weeks later for the air show held near Detroit, Michigan, at the Wayne County Airport. On September 21, 1937, she flew the plane six times over a measured three-kilometer course at full throttle. Timed by a representative of the National Aeronautic Association, Cochran's top speed reached 304.62 mph; her record speed— average of her best four runs—was 293.05 mph. It bequeathed Cochran the title fastest female pilot in the world. She was ecstatic. "Ever since I started flying five years ago," she exclaimed, "I dreamed of doing this!" The priceless publicity showered on the P-35 spurred de Seversky to encourage Cochran to fly the same plane in December from New York to Miami, Florida, to open the All-American Air Maneuvers at Miami Municipal Airport. On December 3, she broke the long-distance speed record then held by racing pilot, Howard Hughes, founder of Hughes Aircraft Company. Subsequently, on December 13, she flew over a 100-kilometer course and established a new national women's speed record.[31]

Later, de Seversky and Cochran conducted negotiations about a P-35 variant designed expressly for Jackie. On March 12, 1938, the pair signed a letter contract specifying Seversky Aircraft would build a plane for her use. The Major then asked his engineering team, headed by Alexander Kartveli, to refine the airframe to promote speed by reducing drag, for example, the cockpit canopy took on a triangular shape that merged seamlessly with the altered fuselage. The engineers' designs became the template for the XP-41, the last pursuit built under the government's original order. That last plane flew 42 mph faster than the P-35; it differed from "Jackie's plane," though, as it had a more powerful engine and a different landing gear. The contract left the plane's ownership in the hands of Seversky Aircraft, which listed it as the AP-7. One would suspect that only an airplane genealogist wants to learn that, two years after the first P-35 demonstrator was built, Seversky Aircraft decided all potential military pursuit prototypes should receive the AP (Army Pursuit) label. As an illustration, the second SEV-1XP became the SEV-S2 but also acquired the classification AP-2.[32]

Leaving aside these multiple designations, the contract gave Cochran use of the AP-7 for a series of enumerated speed trials, but especially for the Bendix Race. She would not have to share potential winnings with Seversky Aircraft or its president because she pledged to contribute to the developmental expense of the plane by either paying $30,000 in cash or securing a buyer for $100,000 worth of Seversky stock. The aerodynamically improved P-35 was constructed, tested, and flown to Burbank by de Seversky before the start of the Bendix race on September 3, 1938. Jackie Cochran took off at 3:13 a.m. local time. Unlike Fuller the previous year, the aviatrix faced not only bad weather but equipment failure as well. An obstruction (a wad of paper) in the fuel line running from the right wing to the engine nearly terminated her flight. Inadvertently, Cochran discovered she could still transfer fuel from one side of the wing to the other by lowering her left wing. Fortunately, the port side fuel line to the engine remained open.[33]

Even handicapped, Cochran still flew nonstop to Cleveland and with a faster time than her nine male competitors. Her biggest concern arose as she landed at Municipal Airport and noticed the onrush of 20,000 jubilant witnesses to her victory. Fortunately, she and her plane suffered no damage. After refueling in Cleveland, smoking a cigarette, and meeting her husband, the aviatrix took off and flew eastward to complete and win the final leg of the transcontinental derby. Because of the fuel line and bad weather issues, plus the extra time it took to clear the crowd and gas the AP-7, Cochran "only" established a new female record for the Bendix. Nevertheless, it was not very surprising that most published photographs of the event showed Cochran and de Seversky together and sporting incredible smiles. If Jackie was the star of the show, the Major with his P-35 won best supporting actor. Except for Boeing's B-17, no other U.S. military aircraft received so much favorable press in so little time. On the surface level of symbols and slogans, the raw publicity amassed for the pursuit via Cochran's record flights marked de Seversky's strategy as a huge success. But what exactly was accomplished?[34]

## Reflections

It is a mixed blessing that a significant figure in this chapter, Jacqueline Cochran, prepared with the help of a stenographer an autobiography that was expanded and published after her death by Maryann Bucknum Brinley. Cochran needed the help of a stenographer because her impoverished childhood left her semiliterate as an adult. On the other hand, her more recent biographer (Doris L. Rich, *Jackie Cochran*) noted she had excellent "oral literacy." Cochran worked hard to learn and use correctly new words in her conversations and, much to her credit, significantly improved her vocabulary over time even though writing and spelling and reading words remained difficult for her. Nevertheless, her efforts at autobiography fall into the category of oral history, which depends on the memory of the speaker rather than on notes, diaries, letters, newspapers, or other documents.

Obviously, it is easy for mistakes to occur in oral history when the subject or speaker might forget, confuse, transpose, diminish, or embellish a memory. One mistake Cochran made was her explanation of why she flew the P-35 at Wright Field in September 1937. She stated that by then, seventeen P-35s had been destroyed in accidents. According to her, de Seversky wanted her to fly the pursuit to counter its horrifying record. Over time, the pursuit certainly experienced some accidents, but the air corps had flown only two of the five preproduction P-35s built by September. As discussed in the next chapter, the Major informed U.S. Secretary of War Harry H. Woodring on November 4, 1937, that the first eleven P-35s were on the production line. A company production report indicated the eighth one of the initial eleven was ready for its first motor test on January 7, 1938. If Cochran spoke the truth in her autobiography, the U.S. Army Air Corps destroyed and rebuilt two P-35s a total of seventeen times.

# 9

# Troubled Times

The rush of publicity enjoyed by the P-35 seemed to favorably influence everyone except the Procurement Board of the U.S. Army Air Corps. Meanwhile, a series of events marked the end to Alexander P. de Seversky's halcyon days as an aircraft manufacturer. A minor irritant and a major loss started the walk down a less fortunate path. In the fall of 1936, the Major had to submit to a thorough investigation before he could secure a $100,000 policy from the Mutual Life Insurance Company of New York (today, Mutual of New York). Besides requiring multiple application forms, Mutual sent an investigator to look at de Seversky's "domestic environment" and interview neighbors and acquaintances. The good news was the Major possessed a gossip-free reputation, decent health, and had given up stereotypical Russian behaviors of drinking vodka like water and smoking cigarettes with each waking breath. The bad news was the one-legged pilot flew really fast planes for long distances. Mutual finally condescended to approve a life insurance policy, but with the stipulation that if Sasha died in an airplane crash, his bride, Evelyn, would receive only the balance of his account at the time of death.[1]

## Foreboding Signs

A more grievous moment arrived with the news that Evelyn's mother, Evelyn Kennedy Olliphant, passed away on March 19, 1937. The former president of the Louisiana State Society in New York had returned to her native state and died in the care of her younger sister in Lafayette. Surely, Olliphant's daughter, Evelyn, and son, a New York lawyer, were saddened by the loss, but so was her son-in-law. The Major and Mrs. Olliphant had enjoyed good relations cemented by their partnership in trading on the stock market. Naturally, some of their investments included Seversky Aircraft Corporation. It may have been a small comfort to Sasha that Seversky stock began its negative drift only after Olliphant's funeral. The air corps decision in July to award Curtiss-Wright and its P-36, rather than Seversky and its P-35, a contract to build an additional 210 pursuit planes lubricated the downward slide. From a 1937 high of 6½, Seversky Aircraft stock descended in value to hover around 1¾ by year's end.[2]

Even before Curtiss-Wright received its large contract, the Major had decided to try to augment his army business by also selling the P-35 to the navy. To get his company's foot in the door, he proposed to give the U.S. Navy Department a variant article for testing purposes without cost to the government. The navy accepted his free offer. It would fly the NF-1 (Navy Fighter No. 1) and use the data for comparison against the XF4F-2 of Grumman Aeronautical Engineering Company and the XF2A-1 of Brewster Aircraft Company. Because the NF-1 was borrowed from and later returned to Seversky Aircraft, it retained its civil registration and never received an official naval designation. Nevertheless, Sasha asked Alexander Kartveli and his engineering team to take a straight-wing SEV-1XP and modify it to meet naval specifications.[3]

The Brewster F2A *Buffalo* won the naval trials. However, similar to what happened to Curtiss-Wright and the P-36, the navy continued to provide development funds to Grumman that also eventually led to a large contract to build the F4F *Wildcat*. Regardless, de Seversky had suffered another setback. Shortsightedly, the P-35 manufacturer failed to consider that time spent on the NF-1 as well as the racing program discussed in the previous chapter took time away from setting up his factory complex for the serial production of the army pursuit. This, in turn, explains why assistant chief of the U.S. Army Air Corps, Gen. Hap Arnold, saw little progress on the part of Seversky Aircraft toward building the P-35 during his two visits to the Farmingdale, Long Island, facility in March and June 1937. In a 1970 interview with Dr. Murray Green, U.S. Air Force deputy chief for research and analysis, the Major painfully, but probably accurately, mimicked Arnold's clipped response in 1937: "'Seversky promised us the first article in six months, it's now eight months, I don't see a sign of an airplane. I told you he cannot produce.' A year has past and he comes again, and again no airplane." And quoting Arnold a second time, de Seversky mimicked, "'I told you he cannot produce.'"[4]

De Seversky compounded his poor relations with Arnold by opposing the future air corps chief's notions about the appropriate powerplant for pursuit aircraft. By 1937 Arnold and other air corps leaders considered big air-cooled engines best for bombers, and they encouraged pursuit or potential pursuit manufacturers to examine the use of liquid-cooled engines such as the Allison V-1710 model. Two phenomena drove this position. First, liquid-cooled engines presented a smaller front to an airplane and allowed airframe engineers to design an aerodynamically smoother line to reduce drag and increase speed. All things being equal, an airplane powered by a 1,000 hp Allison should fly somewhat faster than the same plane equipped with a 1,000 hp Pratt & Whitney. Second, that same year, high-performance fighter aircraft entered German and British air squadrons in the form of the Messerschmitt Bf 109 and the Hawker Hurricane. Liquid-cooled engines propelled both fighters, which reputedly moved comfortably to the 300 mph mark that had become the air corps standard for a successful pursuit.[5]

De Seversky did not endear himself to Arnold by his refusal to consider an Allison as anything more than a poor choice as a powerplant. "So I was in his way," the Major spoke of Arnold, "because I thought the Allison was a junk engine, and I wouldn't be on an airplane with an Allison. As a designer with combat experience, I knew from design analyses, that they were flying coffins." De Seversky's hyperbolic expression should not hide the fact that his reservation about switching engines was based in 1937 on sound reasoning. Liquid-cooled engines tended to have more malfunctions and maintenance problems attributable to the paraphernalia associated with the cooling process, such as pumps, radiators, and tubing. Even more importantly from the Major's perspective, no engineer could blueprint an airplane around the 1,000 hp Allison that matched in speed a well-designed aircraft powered by a 1,200 hp Pratt & Whitney. By August 1937 Allison was left in the lurch when Pratt & Whitney tested the R-2800 Double Wasp 18-cylinder twin row radial air-cooled engine rated at 1,800 hp, soon to reach 2,000 hp. Installed in the XF4U, the engine enabled the Vought *Corsair* prototype in 1940 to become America's first aircraft of any type to fly faster than 400 mph in level flight.[6]

It should not, then, come as a shock that Seversky Aircraft and Curtiss-Wright sharply differed in the way they responded to Arnold's ideas. Belatedly, in 1938, de Seversky asked his Engineering Section to modify the nose of the original P-35 demonstrator, now identified by the company as the AP-1. The team drafted and metalsmiths built a smaller, tight-fitting cowl and added a large spinner to the propeller hub. It gave the front of the airplane an appearance similar to the business end of a bullet. To be sure, the engineers drew up a marvelously aerodynamic nose, equal to the look of a fuselage built around a liquid-cooled engine. Unfortunately, in terms of operating the AP-1, the design was flawed. The cowl was so clean to reduce drag that it starved the cylinder heads of cooling air and created an overheated and inefficient engine. De Seversky's alternative approach to a streamlined plane simply did not work.[7]

Months earlier, in July 1937, Curtiss-Wright engineers initiated a major project to redesign the P-36 around the V-1710 engine. The resulting prototype flew in October 1938 as the XP-40 *Warhawk*. Eventually, over 13,700 of the pursuits would be manufactured. Never considered one of the top-performing aircraft of World War II, it nonetheless was sturdy and adaptable and appeared on every major front of the global conflict. When Japan's attack on Pearl Harbor vaulted the United States into the two-year-old war on December 7, 1941, the P-40 had supplanted both the P-35 and P-36 as America's frontline fighter aircraft. To illustrate how far de Seversky had wandered from air corps thinking, on the same date of April 27, 1939, when Curtiss-Wright signed a huge production contract for the P-40, Lockheed Aircraft and Bell Aircraft received awards for development batches, respectively, for the P-38 Lightning and P-39 Airacobra. All three combat planes sported Allison liquid-cooled engines. By then, de Seversky had convinced himself that General Arnold had a chummy connection with General Motors (GM), which owned Allison.[8]

The final foreboding sign, one that indicated serious trouble for Seversky Aircraft with the federal government, arrived at the company's Farmingdale headquarters on October 17, 1937. It came in the form of a letter of reprimand from U.S. Secretary of War Harry H. Woodring. The key sentence in the terse message stated, "It is desired to invite your attention to the failure of your company to comply with the requirements of Contract W 535 ac-8892 relative to delivery of P-35 Airplanes." De Seversky's reply was constructed and massaged to perfection. It is a model of the best response a contracted business could make to a letter of censure from the highest official in the U.S. War Department. The Major certainly learned his lessons from the Dale Carnegie Course. Gently but effectively, de Seversky replied on November 4 by placing the delay of airplane shipments squarely on the doorstep of the air corps.[9]

The Major pointed out that the Materiel Division had not started to test the preproduction plane until September 1, to determine final changes for the production model. Only on October 21 did Seversky Aircraft receive, and then unofficially, a release to go ahead with the manufacturing process. The official release arrived on November 1, nearly two weeks after Seversky Aircraft opened Secretary Woodring's letter of rebuke. "In spite of all these uncertainties and handicaps, recognizing the need for airplanes by the Air Corps," de Seversky wrote the war secretary, "this company did proceed with the work prior to final approval. This meant the investment of a great deal of money in labor and material, at the risk of losing the investment should the Government desire to make further modifications at the last minute." As a result of taking this chance, de Seversky could proudly state that as of November 4, eleven airplanes were in the final stages of assembly. Moreover, all the parts necessary to build forty additional P-35s had been machined and readied for use on the assembly line.[10]

Those unfamiliar with the details of the relationship between the air corps and Seversky Aircraft might describe the letter as a tour de force. Unfortunately for de Seversky, Woodring knew better and understood that the Major had cleverly shifted the argument to hide his culpability. Delay in the delivery of P-35s had absolutely nothing to do with the fact that the air corps gave Seversky Aircraft official release to begin production at the start of November 1937. The real problem began when the company took fourteen months after signing the contract to supply the Materiel Division with a preproduction P-35 suitable for testing to determine final modifications. Having antagonized both the U.S. secretary of war and the assistant chief of the U.S. Army Air Corps, whose main job was aircraft procurement, it finally occurred to the Major that the federal government was unlikely to hand him a happy surprise by awarding his company a second big contract to build more P-35s. Frank Fuller winning the Bendix Race and Jackie Cochran setting speed records in September 1937 in P-35 variants had not moved the military away from its purchase program for the Curtiss-Wright P-36.[11]

## *Seversky Super Clipper*

As reality set in, de Seversky took stock of the assembly process. He and his administrative staff, especially Executive Vice President F. William Zelcer and Production Manager George A. Meyerer, possessed all the information necessary to know that once the assembly line was up and running, Seversky Aircraft would fulfill its air corps obligation in a matter of months. Indeed, the production schedule established on October 27, 1937, for the seventy-seven aircraft called for delivery of two P-35s a week. It took several months for the company to reach that level of production, but by June 1938 the Farmingdale factory complex at Seversky Airport turned out sixteen P-35s. It enabled the company to complete its air corps contract by August. During the interim, the Major had the presence of mind to assume he had a relatively short fuse before his company would explode apart unless he could find a new project or new buyers for the P-35. Hence he set a course to design a commercial airliner and sell P-35s abroad.[12]

On December 23, 1937, Vice President Zelcer telephoned Franklin Gledhill, vice president and purchasing agent for Pan American Aviation Supply Corporation. Through newspaper articles, de Seversky had learned that America's only significant overseas airline looked to augment its three Model 130 Ocean Transports and projected Boeing flying boat with even larger and better-performing sea airliners. Designed and built at a loss by the Glenn L. Martin Aircraft Company, the Model 130s (*China Clipper*, *Philippine Clipper*, and *Hawaii Clipper*) initiated flights across the Pacific Ocean in 1935, carrying passengers, mail, and express cargo between San Francisco and Manila with several island stops on the way. A year later, the flights to Asia extended to Hong Kong. The future Boeing flying boat, the Model 314 then on order, was actually part of Pan American Airways Yankee Clipper Project, created in 1935. Obviously, the airline wanted to push the performance level even higher since the goal was to create an airplane capable of flying nonstop between New York and various European cities. At de Seversky's urging, Zelcer asked Gledhill to send a copy of the letter provided to manufacturers that explained the required performance level and passenger accommodations of the new sea airliner as well as the process and time frame for submitting a proposal. Proposals were to be sent to Charles A. Lindbergh, chair of the Technical Committee of Pan American Airways.[13]

One day before the deadline of March 15, 1938, de Seversky sent Lindbergh the company's written proposal accompanied by drawings and models. The Major sometimes described the design as a "flying yacht." The plane did bear some resemblance to a huge trimaran. Three structures crossed and divided the 250-foot wing: a central pod-like fuselage housed pilots and crew as well as a pusher propeller driven by two engines in tandem; spaced both sides from the plane's control center were two hull-fuselages holding the main passenger staterooms, each headed by the same tandem engines but positioned to pull the craft. All motors, including two additional single engines on the trailing edge of the wing, could be serviced, if necessary, by mechanics during flight. The portion of the wing between the fuselages held a galley, lounge, promenade, and a large dining room. A segment of the wing outward from the fuselages contained more passenger staterooms. According to de Seversky's letter to Lindbergh, the novel design could come to life in two years with $7 million and the collaboration of Edward G. Budd Manufacturing Company in the plane's stainless steel construction.[14]

Not unexpectedly, the Major claimed his company's proposal would exceed Pan American's requirements. The pressurized *Seversky Super Clipper* with its eight 2,000 hp powerplants would carry 120 passengers and sixteen crew members in comfort across the Atlantic Ocean at a cruising speed of 250 mph. Its 17,000 gallon fuel capacity allowed a flight range in excess of 5,000 miles. Without a doubt, it was the most revolutionary of the five designs actually submitted to Lindbergh. The expensive, complex, and awkward joint venture construction of the *Seversky Super Clipper* might have guaranteed its rejection anyhow. As it turned out, though, Pan American Airways delayed making a final commitment on the submissions for the Yankee Clipper Project. On June 7, 1938, the Boeing flying boat was test-flown. Unmatched in luxury and performance, the Model 314 proved to be the largest, most magnificent sea airliner in the world. It absorbed Pan American's project as the Boeing aircraft took the name *Yankee Clipper*.[15]

While the *Seversky Super Clipper* failed to ensure the financial future of the company, press releases about it kept the Seversky name in the public eye as an innovative airplane manufacturer. It indirectly helped the other strategy to keep the company alive by selling versions of the P-35 to customers other than the U.S. War Department. Only two such aircraft entered the American market. Frank W. Fuller purchased the Seversky racer he used to win the 1937 Bendix Race. He subsequently flew the plane to set several intercity speed records and then finished first in the 1939 Bendix Race. The other aircraft, similar to Fuller's plane, was a straight-wing replica of the original air corps demonstrator. Shell Oil Company bought the SEV-DS (Doolittle Special) in 1937 for Jimmy Doolittle, future lieutenant general of the U.S. Army Air Forces, but then head of Shell's Aeronautical Division. Rather than American sales, a more promising strategy focused on selling aircraft abroad.[16]

## Export Sales: Soviet Union

Indeed, the company's very first sales sent three SEV-3M amphibians to South America for service in the naval air arm of Colombia. The Major was personally involved in negotiating that particular contract, but by 1937 Alexander A. Toochkoff had become the firm's export manager. Similar to de Seversky, the French spelling of his last name surfaced from his Russian passport when he led the Russian Naval Aviation Mission to America in the fall of 1917. Formerly one of de Seversky's superior officers during World War I, Toochkoff enjoyed a lifelong friendship with the young, heroic combat pilot he had appointed to his mission. If de Seversky was the Major, Toochkoff was the company's "admiral." Pleasant and good-natured, he helped de Seversky with his 1922 corporation and did the same for the one established in 1931, serving in both cases as an assistant to the president. In May 1937 he worked out a sales agreement with the Amtorg Trading Corporation.[17]

Amtorg had been incorporated in the state of New York on May 27, 1924, to conduct commercial activities in the United States on behalf of the Union of Soviet Socialist Republics. Moscow strictly controlled the agency since the Soviet State Bank or its offspring the Bank of Foreign Trade held Amtorg's paid-up stock. Soviet interest in Seversky Aircraft arose because of pivotal events in international affairs. Japanese militarists occupied Manchuria. As a result, an expansionist empire that coveted Siberian resources suddenly appeared on the Soviet border in the east. Shortly thereafter, Adolf Hitler became chancellor of Germany in the west. He not only rearmed the country and shredded the Versailles Treaty, but his book *Mein Kampf* (My Struggle) promised Germans living space at the expense of Slavic peoples in Eastern Europe. Hence, the Soviet Union's worst nightmare came to life by the mid-1930s. It was caught in a vise between two militant enemies who might very well attack the U.S.S.R. simultaneously to fulfill their dreams of securing resources and territories.[18]

Procrustean dictator Joseph V. Stalin sought salvation through two steps. First, he and his minions promoted collective security by strengthening ties with democratic countries inherently opposed to the fascist-militarist powers. For example, in 1935 the Soviet Union signed a trade treaty with America and military agreements with France and Czechoslovakia. Second, the U.S.S.R. tried to quickly upgrade its military technology through selective imports from major industrial powers. For obvious reasons, Germany, Italy, and Japan were stricken from the Soviet roster of potential suppliers. In the United States, the Soviets focused on buying advanced aviation technologies, a left-handed compliment to American leadership in the field. The Russians bought hydraulic presses to stamp aircraft panels and machinery to bend tubular steel employed in aircraft frames. They also signed contracts with petroleum firms to gain information on how to refine high-octane aviation fuels.[19]

In addition, Martin Aircraft transferred plans for a modern bomber to the U.S.S.R.; Vultee Aircraft sent technicians to Moscow to set up a new warplane factory near the capital. Among the twenty or so U.S. firms that marketed aviation accessories or one or two aircraft to the Soviets, the most publicized agreement occurred on July 15, 1936, when Douglas Aircraft sold the Russians not only the airplane but also the complete plans and manufacturing rights to its world-famous DC-3 passenger plane. The Soviets would make 3,000 copies as the Li-2. In one sense, then, Seversky Aircraft's agreement to sell planes and plans to Amtorg only confirmed that the company built high-profile, high-performing aircraft comparable to the best products of larger and longer-established airplane manufacturers. What seemed to make this an odd arrangement was that Seversky Aircraft had formed around a coterie of Russian émigrés who had fled, and in some cases fought, the Soviets. Since the Amtorg agreement represented the third largest contract in company history, it apparently swept aside personal or political feelings that otherwise might obstruct collaboration with communists.[20]

Press releases issued in the name of Seversky Aircraft's president announced that the Amtorg contract totaled $780,000. Clearly, de Seversky wanted stockholders and the aviation public, especially competitors and the air corps, to know that a major foreign country desired his company's airplanes. Technically, the amount of the purchase agreement placed second in the hierarchy of the firm's business. In reality, the deal fell to third place behind the thirty BT-8s when two months after signing the contract the

Soviets chose not to exercise a $410,000 option to buy two additional planes and the templates and tooling for building them. The actual sums received by the Farmingdale corporation were $80,000 each for an amphibian and a long-distance fighter plus $210,000 for plans and manufacturing rights to the aircraft. The latter option was never exercised, though the Russians may have employed construction features from the plans on their aircraft. Amtorg's first payment of $42,000 entered the company's coffers on August 2, 1937. By March 9, 1938, when the two planes were being built, the Russians had paid $250,000 of the $370,000 tab.[21]

The Russian contract served as a great excuse for de Seversky and his team to revisit and revise the two-place pursuit they had worked on in the late winter and early spring of 1935. Fortunately, Amtorg and the Major agreed on a fighter aircraft that differed significantly from the American concept. Four years after the air war began in China and two years after it began in Europe in 1939, Maj. Gen. Hap Arnold, then air corps chief, and Col. Ira C. Eaker, then 20th Fighter Group commander, coauthored *Winged Warfare*. In their book, they narrowly defined the pursuit as a short-ranged interceptor protecting "ground forces from air attack and preventing enemy observation aviation gleaning information as to our disposition and movements." Apparently, these air corps leaders considered the pursuit to be a flying foot soldier with multiple machine guns. By contrast, Amtorg asked for a long-range fighter that served roles beyond defender of Soviet troops. Not for nothing did Russians use the Slavic word for "destroyer" as their name for fighter aircraft. The "destroyer" was an offensive weapon ruggedly built and heavily armed to obliterate the enemy's air force, disrupt the enemy's rear, and kill the enemy's ground troops.[22]

By 1937 the Soviets observed a fourth use for the "destroyer" in offensive operations. It was a discovery also made by General Arnold and other air corps leaders who failed to act on the knowledge for longer missions until after the United States had entered the Second World War. Bombers employed by Russians and Germans in the Spanish Civil War enjoyed a better survival rate when accompanied by fighter aircraft. Coupling this fact with the Russian experience of the First World War, when the eastern front stretched 2,000 miles, one can understand why the Soviets wanted to consider the development of a long-distance "destroyer." And from de Seversky's viewpoint, the P-35 could be readily converted to what he called the "convoy fighter." Add the maximum number of fuselage fuel tanks and the plane could have a cruising range sufficient to fly nonstop 2,500 miles across America and with fuel to spare. Add a few extra spars to the airframe and the integrity of the aircraft could survive multiple hits from enemy machine guns. Add bomb racks and up to seven machine guns and the convoy fighter could become a formidable tactical weapon to destroy enemy soldiers and their supply infrastructure. Add a second cockpit, crew member, and the third, fifth, or seventh machine gun and the "destroyer" could protect itself from many angles of attack by enemy aircraft.[23]

Alexander Kartveli and his assistants, especially Alexander Pishvanov, who headed the Experimental Department, worked out the changes for the new craft. The company's chief engineer, however, credited the airplane's basic concept to de Seversky. In fact, the Major clearly contributed a key feature. It was the design of the aft cockpit for the second crewman and the rear machine gun. De Seversky dispensed with a heavy gun turret that would weigh hundreds of pounds and stick out in the airstream. The weight and drag from such a turret would seriously impair the plane's performance. Instead, the spacious rear cockpit and sliding canopy allowed the gunner seat to be mounted within a lightweight metal ring that retracted into the fuselage when not in use. And the ring permitted the gunner to traverse his weapon 260 degrees. When the convoy fighter and amphibian were completed in March 1938, the Major took the unusual step of flight-testing the aircraft himself and with the company's chief engineer in the second cockpit. Meanwhile, Export Manager Toochkoff had labeled both Amtorg planes as 2PA (2-placed Russian Aircraft, but using the Cyrillic "PA" for the initials). The company subsequently applied 2PA to other fighters sold for export. De Seversky and his company officers were very excited about the 2PA and the possibility of selling a large number of the planes abroad. After all, tensions were high in Europe and war had started between China and Japan.[24]

### Export Sales: Japan

Of the two warring countries, perhaps it was unfortunate that Japan turned to Seversky Aircraft to augment in this case its naval air arm. De Seversky had mixed feelings when he learned from a third party, Miranda Brothers, Inc., of Japan's interest in buying twenty fighter-bombers capable of a 2,000 mile range. Japan's American agent, I. J. Miranda, informed Seversky Aircraft on March 1, 1938, that Tokyo had sent "Mr. Yamamoto" to inspect the 2PA for the potential order. As a businessman who had received the cold shoulder from air corps leadership, de Seversky had to be grateful for a million-dollar deal that would help the company financially and keep the factory complex humming. On the other hand, he had spent the last twenty years of his life in almost daily contact with U.S. Army pilots, a fraternity he officially joined in 1928. The Major knew the American military considered Japan the most likely opponent in a future war.[25]

If such a terrible event took place and his planes attacked American forces, de Seversky also knew his reputation with the military would descend to the lowest and hottest rung of the netherworld. As might be expected, he tried to keep news of his business relations with Japan from entering the public domain. The other side of the same coin found Japan sensitive to its role as an American pariah. It had conquered Manchuria, invaded China, and, in the 1930s, terminated the naval limitations it agreed to during the Washington Naval Disarmament Conference of the 1920s. The cold icing on the cake took place in December 1937, when Japanese warplanes attacked and sank the U.S. Navy's *Panay*, a gunboat operating on the Chang Jiang (Yangtze) River. Even worse, the aircraft strafed the lifeboats of the abandoned *Panay*. Hence representatives for Japan and Seversky Aircraft decided to conduct the negotiations and purchase of convoy fighters in absolute secrecy. It was the only sale activity of the 1930s not publicized to the hilt by the company's president. The 2PA-B3 (3 bomb racks) airplanes were built between May and July and shipped to Japan in the late summer of 1938.[26]

Cleverly on the part of Japan and to the relief of de Seversky, Miranda Brothers arranged for the American Trading Corporation to purchase the airplanes. Its impressive-sounding name belied the fact it was a dummy firm that operated out of a law office in New York City. The American Trading Corporation did not even have a separate telephone number. Despite the byzantine arrangement to hide the connection between Seversky Aircraft and Japan, the concealed effort failed; the *New York Times* caught wind of the sale through, perhaps, a disgruntled company employee who considered the deal malodorous. Of course, when a reporter asked de Seversky whether his company had built P-35s for Japan, he could "honestly" reply in the negative. Certainly, the client *was* the American Trading Corporation, which bought the twenty 2PAs and then transferred them to a West Coast export company. So who knew—wink, wink—which country had actually bought them? All of this fooled neither the newspaper nor the air corps, which marked the sale as the third and final strike against Seversky Aircraft.[27]

Once the airplanes arrived in the land of the rising sun, the Japanese labeled them A8V1 and formed them into two squadrons. The convoy fighters escorted and protected Mitsubishi G3M, twin-engine bombers on missions dropping ordnance on targets of interest in China's interior. Later, the A8V1 served a reconnaissance role. Well before Japan's Pearl Harbor attack, the Seversky-built aircraft had been withdrawn from frontline service much as the United States had done with the P-35. (Some Republic Aircraft P-35As engaged Japanese forces in the Philippines in December 1941.) The retired A8V1s served as trainers or provided transportation services for officers. Two of the planes went to the *Asahi Shimbun* newspaper group to facilitate Japanese press coverage over the far-flung territories and islands acquired by the Nippon empire. Thus de Seversky's fear proved unwarranted. His planes did not kill Americans—unless a U.S. missionary in China fell victim inadvertently to the guns of the A8V1.[28]

### Reflections

Occasionally, a person or happening touches the life or works of a biographical subject without making any impact whatsoever. Then the issue becomes whether it is even worth mentioning at all. This is especially a point of concern for chapter 9, which rests uneasily on the border between biography and institutional history. Exploring in detail a fascinating but extraneous tale that completely failed to influence the life of de Seversky seemed to this author a gratuitous error that would align the chapter with some genre other than biography. Reference here is to the fact that Germany joined Colombia, the Soviet Union, and Japan in expressing an interest in the products of Seversky Aircraft. On June 23, 1938, a special federal grand jury issued indictments charging eighteen individuals with espionage against the United States. What is extraordinary in this case is that one of the indictments was directed at Erich Pfeiffer, an officer in the German War Ministry and head of its Secret Service. Small wonder prosecutors in the case paid visits to the White House and State Department since the forthcoming trial would also be an indictment against the government of Adolf Hitler and his Third Reich.

In America, the espionage ring was led by German-American Ignatz T.

Griebl, M.D., who presided over the Friends of New Germany. When issued a subpoena in May to appear before the federal grand jury, the doctor fled to Germany, where he found safety with thirteen other coconspirators. That left four "soldiers" at the bottom of the ring to be arrested by the Federal Bureau of Investigation. One of the four pled guilty and served as witness against the other three. Only two of the spies convicted on November 30, 1938, are of interest here. Johanna Hofmann, a beautician on the German passenger ship *Europa*, transmitted American defense secrets to the German War Ministry from Otto Hermann Voss, who worked as a mechanic for Seversky Aircraft. In a confession, he later recanted; Voss admitted he passed information (but no blueprints) to Johanna on the BT-8 and NF-1. Since one was a trainer replaced by 1938 and the other was rejected by the navy, the U.S. military was not overly alarmed. And certainly no one blamed de Seversky for the security breach. The incident is, of course, important but for the study of intelligence gathering and social history rather than biography. It said as much about German methods for gaining information as it revealed to many Americans the Nazis' implacable behavior.

# 10

# The P-35 Manufacturer
# Loses His Company

By June 1938 Alexander P. de Seversky had reached a point of near crisis. He saw that the light at the end of the tunnel belonged to a locomotive barreling down the track leading to the destruction of his company. That month production at Seversky Aircraft stood at one plane each workday. By July 1 the firm needed to assemble only twenty P-35s to finish the 1936 contract. At some point in August, with both air corps and Japanese orders completed, the only work left would be building experimental aircraft and manufacturing spare parts for the BT-8 and P-35. Each week the workforce, composed originally of more than a thousand employees, was diminished by layoffs; survivors knew their time would come soon enough. Production Manager George A. Meyerer, the Major's classmate at the Imperial Russian Naval Academy, reported on July 5 that the unit cost of the last P-35s might increase as "men will naturally slow down on their work so as to have it last longer."[1]

## The Letter Campaign

De Seversky began what can be described only as a frantic letter-writing campaign. He knew from the original contract that the air corps had the option of ordering up to twenty-five additional P-35s. On June 25 the Major sent the Materiel Division a lengthy four-page, single-spaced letter that served as his plan for the air corps to exercise its option for additional airplanes. He argued,

It appears to us that the plan for the development of aircraft should be followed along three distinct lines. First, the development of very advanced and speculative types which may, if successful, revolutionize, or at least result in a remarkable step forward in tactical utility. Such projects, naturally, require considerable time and the resulting aircraft cannot be expected to reach the service for a number of years.

The second type of development is the design and construction of conventional aircraft of marked refinement. The procurement of such aircraft must go through the process of competition and, therefore, would also be unavailable for a period of more than two years. Since hostilities usually break out unexpectedly, a third line of development should also be followed. We must constantly and unceasingly strive to improve our present equipment in service. In the event of an emergency, only airplanes of tried designs would be immediately put into mass production, but their performance would have to be boosted to the utmost. This cannot be accomplished unless modifications which improve the performance of service aircraft, without rendering them obsolete, have been continuously and zealously incorporated and service tested.[2]

Too bad for Seversky Aircraft and the company president, the air corps rejected de Seversky's third argument and chose not to request twenty-five additional, though revised, versions of the P-35. De Seversky had spelled out the changes he proposed for the modified pursuit and upgrades for engine and armament, and modestly suggested a sales contract for only twenty-one planes. The implication, however, was that all or most changes could be applied to the P-35s already produced. It would give Seversky Aircraft a chance to build or alter nearly one hundred pursuits. On the other hand, the Materiel Division did encourage de Seversky to apply his proposed improvements to the seventy-seventh, or final, P-35 built under the 1936 contract. Moreover, the air corps promised a careful evaluation of the revised plane and with the possibility that favorable test results might lead to a purchase contract.[3]

In one sense, Alexander Kartveli's Engineering Section had already drafted plans for what became the seventy-seventh P-35. The engineers reworked the canopy and made other changes to improve the aerodynamic profile of the P-35 in the spring of 1938 as they designed a racer for Jackie Cochran. The Seversky AP-7 served as the template for the last aircraft constructed under the 1936 contract. The XP-41 (Seversky AP-9) differed from Cochran's racer not only by its more powerful Pratt & Whitney engine and newly designed center wing section containing an inward contracting landing gear but also by a General Electric supercharger installed near the left underside of the wing root. The latter supplied pressurized air to the engine to increase power output and maintain sea-level conditions at altitude. Tested in March, April, and May 1939 at Wright and Langley Fields by both the air corps and National Advisory Committee for Aeronautics, the XP-41 had a maximum speed of 323 mph. However, that was not enough improvement to warrant a production contract.[4]

Quite clearly, the Materiel Division, with its Procurement Section that included branches for contracts, purchases, and inspections, wielded significant power over the procurement process. In fact, it wielded so much power that general officers decided in the late 1930s to transfer the Materiel Division chief from Dayton, Ohio, to a desk at air corps headquarters in the Munitions Building in Washington, D.C. On the other side of the procurement coin, de Seversky realized three echelons separated him (and all aircraft manufacturers) from the U.S. secretary of war, who legally had the final say on all contracts. The key personnel/organizations were the Materiel Division chief and his staff, the U.S. Air Corps chief and his staff, and the assistant secretary of war and his staff. All these echelons played a role in determining the categories, characteristics, numbers, and/or performance levels of aircraft to be procured or upgraded.[5]

Understandably, then, between June 7 and July 1, 1938, de Seversky also mailed a dozen letters of two or more pages each to such influential leaders as Louis A. Johnson, U.S. assistant secretary of war; Maj. Gen. Oscar Westover, U.S. Army Air Corps chief; and Maj. Gen. Frank M. Andrews, GHQ Air Force chief. He personalized the letters in some respects, but they all contained the identical paragraphs quoted earlier that supported his argument for building improved P-35s and modifying existing pursuits. The main exception was the Major's letter to General Andrews, with which he included a copy of the letter he had sent to General Westover that did contain those key paragraphs. Finally, de Seversky did send a letter to Gen. Hap Arnold, U.S. Army Air Corps assistant chief, but it was short, structurally different, and did not employ any phrases from the master missive sent to the Materiel Division.[6]

Reasons for Arnold's special treatment have been addressed in previous chapters. The Major knew he faced an obstacle in the form of the general who headed the U.S. Army Air Corps Procurement Planning Board. At minimum, the manufacturer had to convert the assistant chief to benign neutrality toward Seversky Aircraft if he ever expected his company would receive another contract. Initially, he did not send Arnold a letter but tried unsuccessfully to talk with him via telephone. When that failed, he mailed the assistant chief a letter on July 1, inviting him to visit the factory complex and spend the night at his Asharoken home. The letter's contents suggest the Major hoped to "make up" with Arnold. He certainly wanted the general to see the plant in full and efficient production. It might negate the image imprinted on Arnold's mind from his 1937 visits when he failed to see even a glimmer of a production line a year after the P-35 contract had been signed.[7]

Arnold took nearly two weeks to reply to the de Seversky letter. His response was kind, but he claimed other demands prevented him from traveling to Farmingdale, Long Island. "As it is," Arnold wrote, "I have the idea and I have the desire, but don't know when I will be able to carry both out." De Seversky had also invited in a separate letter General Westover to visit the plant. He took the occasion to remind the chief of his correspondence of June 7 that suggested the government might want to exercise its option to buy additional P-35s. If Arnold's response to de Seversky was kind, breezy, and unhelpful, Westover's was officious, frosty, and bluntly negative. "Regarding exercise of option under the contract," the chief declared, "the Pursuit Airplane requirements of the Air Corps for Fiscal Year 1939 are to be met by competition.... It is of course hoped and expected that the airplane winning this competition will have performance much superior to that of the P-35."[8]

### Playing the Last Cards: AP-9, AP-4, EP-1, and 2PA

It may not be necessary to point out that General Westover did turn down the invitation to visit Seversky Airport. In fact, he would never see Farmingdale again because he tragically perished in a September airplane crash that resulted in the elevation of Arnold to the position of air corps chief. Meanwhile, the July responses of Westover and Arnold made it abundantly clear to de Seversky that no last-minute reprieve awaited his firm. Within weeks, Seversky Aircraft struggled to keep a skeleton workforce of 160 men composed of foremen and machinists. Many engineers and upper-level managers such as Vice President F. William Zelcer fled the failing company. Fortunately, the "Russians," including the Russian-Georgian and chief engineer Kartveli, stayed. His now small group of designers along with a crew of workers made replacement parts for the BT-8 and P-35 as they constructed a 2PA and three redesigned P-35s, the AP-9, the AP-4, and the EP-1.[9]

Actually, the preliminary plans for the AP-4 had been completed on January 11, 1938. The two-dimensional drawings had not yet been translated into a three-dimensional article, which explains why the AP-9, or XP-41, was built at the same time as the AP-4. Regardless, it would be a high-altitude, long-distance fighter powered by a Pratt & Whitney 1,200 hp, turbo-supercharged engine. In this flush riveted model, the basic P-35 profile changed by raising the deck, lengthening the fuselage, and reducing the transparent areas aft of the pilot's seat. With the bigger engine and improved aerodynamics, the plane could fly 349 mph. In the long run, the AP-4 proved to be one of the most important airplanes designed and built during the Major's tenure as company president. As the future P-43, the AP-4 was father to the P-47, which served a critical role in World War II in the effort to protect American bombers, destroy the German Luftwaffe, and attack the enemy's ground forces.[10]

In the short term, the third so-called new plane built in the fall of 1938, the EP-1 (Export Pursuit #1), symbolized a potential alternative to the hope of a future U.S. military contract for either the AP-4 or AP-9. The Major decided foreign markets could help save the company. His expectation of significant sales abroad rested on the fact that Europe stood on the brink of war. Immediately after the Austrian Anschluss in March 1938, Germans in the Sudetenland of Czechoslovakia began agitating for the border region to join the Third Reich as Austria had done after the German occupation. Adolf Hitler, with the help of Heinrich Himmler and Reinhard Heydrich, orchestrated the actions of the Fifth Column movement through the Schutzstaffeln, or SS. When the Czechoslovakian government refused to surrender the German-populated Sudetenland—a hilly, defendable land protecting western Czechoslovakia—Hitler mobilized thirty-six Wehrmacht divisions in anticipation of a full-scale invasion of the uncooperative country.[11]

Because Czechoslovakia had military agreements with France and the Soviet Union and because Great Britain had pledged to assist France should war break out, a conflagration of major proportions threatened European peace. The Munich Conference of September 1938 temporarily allayed the crisis. Leaders of Great Britain and France chose to defuse tensions by agreeing to a German takeover of Sudetenland. This policy of appeasement, however, soon soured when it became obvious that Germany intended to

destroy Czechoslovakia, a Slavic not Germanic land, by creating a protector-
ate over the Czech lands and turning the Slovakian rump over to a fascist
dictator who did Hitler's bidding. Once the British and French experienced
an epiphany and dumped the appeasement policy, they pledged support
to Poland, which Germany had identified as its potential next victim. The
tremendous insecurity across the continent from spring 1938 through summer 1939 encouraged some European nations to consider the purchase in
America of additional military hardware, including warplanes.[12]

This is why the EP-1 was built. It would serve as a demonstrator for foreign buyers, particularly European air force personnel. The specifications
for the plane were completed on July 12, 1938. It would be the first of the
new aircraft to be constructed precisely because it nearly mirrored the P-35
profile, including the rearward retracting landing gear that resulted in wheel
bulges near the trailing edge of the wing roots. Only a military observer
who focused on weapons could distinguish the EP-1 from the P-35. The aft
portion of the EP-1 fuselage was a few inches longer, the armament consisted
of two machine guns in the cowl and two more in the wing, and Pratt &
Whitney supplied a Twin Wasp fourteen-cylinder, air-cooled powerplant
rated at 1,050 hp. At an altitude of 15,000 feet, the plane flew 316 mph. In
fact, the upgraded P-35 was exactly the modified article de Seversky first
tried to sell to the air corps.[13]

In addition to the EP-1, de Seversky assumed some foreign buyers might
also be interested in the two-place, long-distance convoy fighter purchased
by both the U.S.S.R. and Japan. The unchanged 2PA and minimally altered
EP-1 could be readily built by a small number of workers. They used leftover
parts already manufactured or machined new parts from P-35 and 2PA jigs,
dies, and patterns. As a result, the two demonstrators for examination by
foreign buyers were completed at the end of the summer. By contrast, the
AP-9 built by a group under supervision of Kartveli in the large production shop and the AP-4 constructed by a team led by de Seversky (or, in his
absence, Alexander Pishvanov) in the smaller experimental shop, took nearly
six months to finish. Different airframe dimensions meant P-35 templates
were often useless. Eventually, the AP-9 and AP-4 had to be handcrafted
with many one-of-a-kind machined parts. Nevertheless, by August 1938
de Seversky had set in motion a logical two-pronged plan for saving the
company. He would have by February 1939 two high-performing aircraft,
one of which might attract a U.S. military contract; he would soon have two

demonstrators that the air corps did not want and hence found acceptable for production and sale in markets abroad.[14]

In terms of the latter, de Seversky also worked out a plan to interest European buyers in the EP-1 and 2PA. In August he brought his brother, George Seversky, to America. George later adopted the name George Pro-cofieff de Seversky to prevent confusion over his relationship to Alexander. A well-known Parisian singer and nightclub entertainer, George informally watched over his brother's patents in a half-dozen countries after 1924. He also maintained the family's three-decade tradition of flying airplanes. Naturally, many of his friends were French or Belgian aviators. On Long Island, when the Major had to conduct other business, George and Evelyn de Seversky took turns piloting her Savoia Marchetti Amphibian and a rented Stinson *Reliant*. A different moment of fun occurred when George joined Sasha in attending what turned out to be the last Seversky company picnic. Otherwise, George's visit tended to focus on company exports. The brothers worked on developing a package of materials (pictures, specifications, and price lists) on the EP-1 and 2PA that George could use in approaching European procurement officials.[15]

Unless European countries eagerly sent military aviation missions to Seversky Airport, the Major understood demonstrator aircraft and pilot(s) might have to be sent abroad. Either way, the brothers were helped in their plans when Sasha set a new east to west transcontinental flight record on August 29, 1938, and Jackie Cochran flew the same P-35 variant west to east to win the famous Bendix Race on September 2. With this excellent national and even international publicity still echoing in the background, George returned to France on the payroll as the official European representative of Seversky Aircraft Corporation. In one sense, though, he was a tiny part of a colossal problem. The company approached the edge of a precipice leading to bankruptcy. It survived after August 1938 on borrowed money rather than earned revenue. An auditor's certificate verified on December 31 that the deficit for the year was $553,819.[16]

## Dealing with Debt

A huge portion of the company's loss was attributable to the expense of constructing two fundamentally new airplanes. The AP-9/XP-41 and AP-4/XP-43 cost over $365,000 to build, with $250,000 of that amount devoted to the future P-43. Meanwhile, as the AP-4 soaked up money, Paul Moore examined Seversky Aircraft payroll figures in September and realized the company's remaining cash funds would soon disappear. He told his lawyer, Livingston Platt of the firm Bleakley, Platt & Walker, to order a stop to all work not under contract and to terminate excess workers. Insulted by this abrupt action from the company angel, de Seversky hotly refused the order and responded with a sharply worded telegram on September 15. "Regardless of the merit of the proposed measure," he told Moore, "I resent and protest against such high handed inconsistent and unbusinesslike interference on the part of [Bleakley, Platt & Walker] with the administration of the affairs of Seversky Corporation." The immediate dispute centered on the AP-4, which was being built on speculation, while the AP-9 had been encouraged by the air corps, which would pay for the machine once delivered.[17]

The unspoken issue between the Major and Moore lay in the fact that under de Seversky's leadership, the company never operated in the black. Before the half-million dollar shortfall of 1938, Seversky Aircraft began the year with an earned deficit of $1,296,299. Since Moore had invested over $3 million in the company, one can understand the frustration revealed in his letter to de Seversky on September 16, which stated in part,

In your wire you mention "high handed" and I toss it back to you doubly as I can read figures and was horrified on my return to realize that our huge payroll still continued and in a short time we would be bankrupt. I have told you repeatedly that my credit in the bank is at its limit, and yet you seem to consider that borrowed money which I keep putting up belongs to the company for you to play with for new designs. We have a top plane [i.e., AP-9], so get out and sell what we have and forget something [i.e., AP-4] that may surpass the world until we are on a decent financial basis. At present, new financing is impossible and we must stop everything except the completion of our last Army plane and orders for spare parts. The alternative is that I am out financially and that you are repudiated for anything other than the great flier and designer that you are.[18]

What really irked Moore was not the Major's telegram but the fact that the company president ignored the instructions he received in July from the board of directors. The board gave de Seversky a green light to build the AP-9, EP-1, and 2PA; it also instructed him to end all plant activities not under contract, release unneeded workers, and do everything in his power to con-serve cash. Thus he should have been able to predict Moore's reaction—and in one sense he did. In August the Major sought additional outside funding for the company to avoid being constrained in developing new military air-craft. Through his friends, Jackie Cochran and her financier husband, Floyd B. Odlum, de Seversky gained access to White, Weld & Co.[19]

The latter was a well-connected New York investment bank. It signed an agreement with board chairman Moore on October 27, 1938, which restruc-tured Seversky Aircraft's stock into first and second preferred categories. The restructuring sought to preserve a major portion of the chairman's multi-million-dollar investment in case of bankruptcy. White, Weld & Co. also sold, at a steep discounted rate, convertible notes (notes convertible to preferred stock) with a face value of $610,000. Moore actually received $530,000; he kept $110,000 for himself. The rest of the funds had to be used to keep Seversky Aircraft alive long enough to give the company a chance to secure a substantial contract or contracts for the production of multiple aircraft. Hence the document signed by Moore obligated him to maintain Seversky Aircraft for at least eight months after October 1938. Specifically, he was required to fund the company with up to $420,000: $60,000 in cash for each of the first two months; $50,000 in cash for each of the next six months. The money, of course, would take care of the firm's payroll, utilities, and supplies for office and shop. Happily, the agreement worked exactly as intended by Moore and White, Weld & Co. By the end of June 1939, the company had signed the first of several contracts with each of two governments for the serial manufacture of two different airplanes, the AP-4 and EP-1.[20]

There is no hiding the fact that de Seversky also proved to be a beneficiary of the agreement. Within a year, his large stock holdings nearly doubled in value. Moreover, in the short term, the company acquired enough capital to enable the Major to pursue and then finish constructing the AP-4. A broader perspective, however, also reveals the agreement worked against him. In return for raising funds for the corporation, White, Weld & Co. expected leadership changes in the company, changes that gave the invest-ment bank a serious role in Seversky Aircraft's operation. As a result, the board of directors was reorganized by replacing "resigned" members with John J. Daly, Joseph W. Powell, and W. Wallace Kellett. These three direc-tors, in essence appointed by the investment bank, joined Moore and his lawyer, Platt, who was also a director, to form an unbeatable majority block of votes on the board that left de Seversky powerless.[21]

On top of everything else, one of the new board members, Kellett, also became the company vice president. His actual role was greater. He served as the eyes and ears of the investment bank, which presumed all company information and correspondence would cross his desk. Within days, de Seversky would be reporting to Kellett as the Major moved into the role of promoter and sales manager for the firm. In fact, Kellett and his role were mentioned specifically in the October agreement by White, Weld & Co. The company's new vice president had founded Kellett Aircraft Corporation in 1920 and served as its president until his death in 1951. An American pioneer in constructing autogiros purchased by, among others, the air corps, his company also built airplane parts as a subcontractor to several airframe manufacturers. It was in Kellett's best interest to see Seversky Aircraft succeed because of the potential new business he could guide and direct to his own company. His experiences, connections, and motivations were exactly what attracted the investment bank to Kellett.[22]

### Seversky Aircraft in Europe and Farmingdale

Meanwhile, the reorganized board of directors met on November 11, 1938. The minutes of that meeting make it clear that Vice President Kellett would be the officer in charge of company affairs. It would give the Major "necessary relief and freedom from business routine and details, thus enabling him to devote all of his energies to development work, sales, and the major policy problems of the Corporation." If the minutes are accurate, the latter quotation actually summarizes de Seversky's own comments about his new role at Seversky Aircraft. Indeed, he asked for and received financial backing from the board for his planned sales mission to Europe as a follow-up to his brother's foundational work in distributing information to various governments about the EP-1 and 2PA. One can only ponder over the unrecorded motives of Kellett and other board members in supporting the mission. After all, they sided with Moore in blaming the Major for the company's economic distress. And absence would not make their hearts grow fonder.[23]

While Kellett, Moore, and their associates on the board may have been pleased for the wrong reasons that de Seversky went to Europe, the level of their support for a sales abroad program was very limited. Perhaps that would be expected no matter what because the company tottered near bankruptcy. Directors rejected as too expensive, for example, de Seversky's request for funds to send a parallel sales mission to Latin America. Additionally, he received a restricted line of credit and travelers checks of $10,055 to cover the expense of travel, room, and board for himself, his wife, two mechanics, and another pilot. The tab alone for transporting the airplanes back and forth across the Atlantic Ocean and for storing, fueling, and servicing the EP-1 and 2PA in Europe would eat up much of those funds. Then, too, if the sales effort failed with his primary targets of France, Belgium, and England, the Major planned to work his secondary prospects of Poland, Portugal, and Scandinavia. Since he expected to come home with at least one contract, de Seversky placed no time limit on his European excursion.[24]

There is only one reason we know that the Major and his small entourage sailed from New York on the French liner SS *Normandie* on November 26, 1938. One of his fellow passengers was Myron C. Taylor, who served as vice chairman of the Intergovernmental Committee for Political Refugees. Taylor and the other committee members would try to address the problem posed by how to aid tens of thousands of Jewish refugees. They had fled Austria after the German occupation of that country in March. Thousands more escaped Germany following the horror of Kristallnacht, when Nazis destroyed Jewish stores, homes, and synagogues in a weeklong brutish rampage beginning November 10. Taylor and de Seversky were unacquainted, but the Major appeared in a newspaper story about the vice chairman because loading the EP-1 and 2PA on board the ship delayed its departure by thirty minutes.[25]

More than likely, de Seversky made sure his planes were safely loaded before joining Evelyn in their stateroom. Regardless, a letter awaited him there from Gurdon W. Wattles, one of the representatives of White, Weld & Co. who had authored the clever scheme to raise money for Seversky Aircraft. Better than any other document, the letter reveals the level of authority the investment bank presumed to exercise over the Farmingdale corporation during this awkward period between contracts or between contract and liquidation. Wattles delivered the bank's instructions to de Seversky. He was told to stay within his budget and even be frugal during his European stay. Beyond money, Wattles told the Major to make neither commitments nor sign contracts without the prior approval of the board of directors. Above everything else, he had to work through and report to "Kellett . . . all developments and plans, as well as people being contacted."[26]

When, after a stop in London, England, the SS *Normandie* finally arrived at its home port of Le Havre in France and unloaded, de Seversky chose to make the Hotel George V his permanent headquarters in Europe. It was, and is, one of the most prestigious and expensive hotels in Paris. While faithfully reporting his plans and activities to Kellett, de Seversky refused to be frugal. After extending him another $7,500, the corporation would not repay his excessive expenses. It only confirmed the board's opinion of the president as an irresponsible spendthrift as it forced him to arrange in January and April 1939 the sale of thousands of shares of his stock to keep the sales campaign supplied with cash. Logic nourished the Major's extravagance. He wanted European governments and military to be convinced that he was the head of a preeminently successful airframe company possessing all the financial and material resources necessary to produce serial copies of the high-quality aircraft he demonstrated.[27]

While de Seversky employed impression management to improve his chances for negotiating a procurement contract with a European government, he promoted at the same time several other strategies to improve his chances for success. For instance, to garner general publicity as well as the favorable attention of West European military aviators, the Major flew in January a series of noteworthy flights in the EP-1. When he had finished, he had established a number of international intercity speed records: Paris to Brussels, 35 minutes; London to Paris, 45 minutes; London to Copenhagen, 2 hours, 12 minutes; Copenhagen to Paris, 2 hours, 40 minutes. Two other plans of action directly involved his brother. In the evenings, George de Seversky headlined the entertainment at the Monseigneur nightclub on Rue Pouchet in Paris. During the day, he spent time at the Hotel George V with his brother and sister-in-law going over tactics and reviewing correspondence received or preparing correspondence to send.[28]

In the fall of 1938, George had established good relations with military aviation officials in France and various foreign legations in Paris. He now cashed in on those contacts by employing them to set up demonstration flights for his brother and evaluation sessions for the EP-1 and 2PA. Alexander and George worked together on the last strategy. They prepared and George distributed a series of press releases on the airplanes and biography of Alexander. Because George was himself a well-known aviator, he had no trouble placing the press releases or getting aviation writers to use the press releases as a basis for articles in such journals as *Gazette-Bruxelles* (Belgium), *L'Avion* (Belgium), *Le Petit Parisien* (France), and *L'Aero* (France). In France and Belgium especially, the press releases also focused on Alexander's record as an ace pilot in the Great War. It reflected only too well past events and current concerns. Many readers relished information that the Russian-American had shot down thirteen German aircraft during the Great War.[29]

As de Seversky prepared his campaign to win some type of contract in Europe, developments in America gave hope for the company's turnaround in Farmingdale. The use or threat of using military force to gain territory and influence by Germany, Italy, and Japan prompted a U.S. response. By the fall of 1938, President Franklin D. Roosevelt had concluded that America must rearm in face of these expanding and menacing dictatorships. On November 14, FDR opened in the White House a meeting of his key political and military advisors. Since he had already talked individually about the international situation with those in attendance, including General Arnold, he did not seek counsel. Instead, he issued his administration's policy. He expected to match, for example, German air power through increasing U.S. Army Air Corps strength by 870 percent to 20,000 aircraft backed by the annual production of 24,000 warplanes.[30]

Before the end of the month, news splashed across America about the subject of the November 14 meeting. The administration in Washington eagerly sought such publicity to gather citizen support and hence congressional votes for appropriation bills to rearm America, especially its air force. U.S. Assistant Secretary of War Johnson held meetings with aircraft manufacturers under air corps contract and issued public statements about the mobilization plans for producing thousands of planes. When Congress considered legislation in February and March 1939 to supply the air corps with an initial $57 million for new equipment, General Arnold delivered key testimony on March 1. The air corps chief observed that the ambitious expansion program could be easily accomplished because several important airframe companies possessed factories that were "practically idle." He mentioned specifically Chance Vought, Consolidated, Northrop, and Seversky.[31]

Such encouraging news about mobilization plans for aircraft factories allowed Kellett to wax enthusiastic about the prospects of selling in quantity the AP-9, or XP-41, to the air corps. In comments he made during a meeting of the board of directors on December 29, 1938, he obliquely criticized the company president. Kellett stated "the XP-41 was a more advanced plane than the AP-4," which was de Seversky's expensive project that endangered the company's coffers. Nowhere is it recorded that, figuratively speaking, Kellett had to eat his words. Nevertheless, when the air corps received both planes in February, the military quickly concluded that the AP-4 was far superior. True, the XP-41 was tested extensively to see if any design features were worthy of emulation. It was also compared with the XP-39 as a potential backup pursuit to the plane winning the frontline position for a big contract through competition. But unlike the XP-39 and despite Kellett's misplaced optimism, there was never more than one XP-41.[32]

While the air corps examined the XP-41 for its technology and points of comparison with another aircraft, it assigned the AP-4, now the XP-43, to an entirely different category. The plane went head-to-head in competition with the Curtiss-Wright P-40 to be America's next primary pursuit. It will be recalled that the P-40 was the redesigned P-36 that had competed with the P-35 in two lengthy air corps evaluations held in 1935 and 1936. Curtiss-Wright altered the P-36 airframe to accommodate the P-40's liquid-cooled, in-line engine rated at 1,000 hp. De Seversky had his team design the XP-43 to carry four different air-cooled, radial engines rated from 1,200 hp to 2,000 hp. Later, he would be furious when he discovered Kellett had sent the XP-43 to Wright Field with the smallest of the four possible powerplants. Despite the least powerful engine, the turbo-supercharged XP-43 gave an early indication that it could fly faster and higher than the P-40.[33]

Poor maintenance caused the XP-43 to catch fire during one of its initial flights. The pilot bailed out of the cockpit, and naturally, the plane crashed. Destruction of the only demonstrator allowed the P-40 to win by default an April contract for Curtiss-Wright to build 524 pursuits. The excellent performance, though, shown by the XP-43 persuaded the air corps to award Seversky Aircraft a "service test" contract to build fifteen airplanes for $934,324. Section 10k of the 1926 Air Corps Act permitted development orders for fifteen or fewer aircraft without conducting a formal competition. As war headed for a collision course with the United States, the notion of competitive contracts quickly underwent a radical change. Quantity production replaced lower cost as the important factor in the rearmament equation. And speaking of equations, when in early April the air corps started lengthy negotiations to purchase the P-43 from Seversky Aircraft, the talks led to life-transforming events for de Seversky both in Europe and Farmingdale.[34]

Kellett realized the Major's European sales effort had suddenly lost its luster. After all, production agreements often followed a service test order. This is exactly what happened. Multiple follow-on contracts were eventually negotiated and signed to build a total of 272 P-43 *Lancers*. Some 20 percent of those pursuits went to China as part of the Lend-Lease program of U.S. aid to countries fighting the fascist, militaristic powers. Meanwhile, as instructed by White, Weld & Co., Vice President Kellett had become the gatekeeper of all communications coming to Seversky Aircraft from the Major. According to Kellett's secretary, in statements made on October 31, 1940, and November 6, 1940, the vice president kept and hid a number of de Seversky's cablegrams and letters. These were the ones that reflected de Seversky's positive experiences in Europe or his criticisms of Kellett's judgment. Such edited information, coupled with P-43 contract negotiations and stockholder approval on April 11 of the capitalization changes, led the board to elect W. Wallace Kellett president of Seversky Aircraft on April 18, 1939. Immediately, he sent telegrams to the U.S. military and cablegrams to foreign governments to inform them of the corporation's change in leadership.[35]

Such cablegrams, and this was exactly what Kellett intended, undermined de Seversky's position. The Major had spent his own money on luxurious accommodations with a prestigious address and on first-class restaurants and entertainment for European officials. All of these efforts and expenses went to give the appearance that de Seversky headed a stable and successful aircraft company. Because of the good publicity he generated with his record flights and because of the excellent groundwork provided by his brother, de Seversky and his aircraft received a warm welcome in February and March by officials in such countries as Belgium, England, and France. The Belgians expressed an interest in the EP-1 and the British asked to examine the 2PA convoy fighter. In England, the Major formed such good relations with Royal Air Force officers that they accorded him the unusual honor of letting him fly the Supermarine *Spitfire*—later viewed by many as England's savior in World War II. Despite such close associations, Kellett's cablegrams disturbed and ultimately closed de Seversky's promising discussions about aircraft sales in both Belgium and Britain.[36]

Two weeks before he would be replaced as president, the Major departed

England and flew to Scandinavia. There he demonstrated the EP-1 for military procurement officials in both Norway and Sweden. The governments were so pleased by the pursuit that each expressed an interest in buying fifteen aircraft. Kellett, however, lost Norway's business when he hesitated in permitting Norway to merge its purchase with Sweden's to save money as a result of a bulk order for thirty airplanes. Reflecting circumstances that seemed to promise war for Europe, Sweden really wanted modern fighter aircraft. It chose, then, to continue negotiations. The day before he lost his position, de Seversky sent a letter with appendices to the chief of the Swedish Royal Air Force. It explained costs, equipment, and delivery schedules in great detail for a projected purchase agreement. Not only did Kellett withhold from Paul Moore and most board members information about the Major's success, he added insult to injury by sending a copy of de Seversky's Swedish air force letter to the company's lawyers for use as a basis for the contract later signed between Seversky Aircraft and the Swedish government. Subsequently, Sweden bought forty-five more planes in October and sixty additional EP-1s in January 1940. The U.S. government requisitioned the latter and sent most of Sweden's pursuits to the Philippines as P-35As that flew operationally against Japanese forces after Pearl Harbor.[37]

Notwithstanding Seversky's sales triumph with Sweden (or because of it), Kellett refused to authorize the Major to fly the EP-1 to Switzerland and Poland. Through their Paris legations, the two governments asked de Seversky to give their militaries a chance to evaluate the pursuit. Admittedly, Switzerland would have been a speculative trip. Poland, by contrast, had been clearly identified as the next subject of interest for Third Reich expansion. Moreover, Poland's frontline fighter, the PZL P-11, had a top speed of only 242 mph. The country's envoys told de Seversky at his Hotel George V headquarters that they expected a decent demonstration session would lead to an order for 250 aircraft. After several go-rounds with Kellett about Norway, Switzerland, and Poland in late April and early May, Kellett won a vote from the board of directors on May 9, ordering de Seversky to cease talks with foreign governments. Thereafter, such negotiations would be conducted only in America. The order, of course, terminated the Major's sales efforts in Europe. He stayed several weeks longer only because Evelyn endured an unspecified illness and convalesced in the American Hospital. Perhaps she suffered hypertension stress from her husband's dismal treatment at the hands of the company he had founded. Shortly before Evelyn and Sasha boarded the SS *Normandie* for the cruise across the Atlantic on May 30, 1939, de Seversky received a cablegram informing him that he was fired; his employment would end on the last day of June. Thus the trip home would not be a bon voyage.[38]

## Reflections

One can readily understand why de Seversky was angered and aggrieved by his treatment from Kellett and the reorganized board of directors. It cannot be much of a surprise to reveal that the next chapter includes comments about the Major's lawsuits against his former company, lawsuits designed as much to heal his psyche as line his pockets with cash. The pain caused by losing his executive position and then even his employment only grew worse over the next several months. De Seversky soon realized that his AP-4 project and EP-1 sales pitch to Sweden resulted in over $20 million worth of business, a result that should have made him the company hero rather than its pariah. The puzzle, then, is not how de Seversky reacted to his ouster in the short term, but how he felt three decades later. In interviews near the end of his life, he actually expressed gratitude to White, Weld & Co. for raising money he could use to finish the AP-4 project. Furthermore, he made no reference to his obvious nemesis, W. Wallace Kellett. Instead, the focus of his ire fell on Gen. Hap Arnold, who suggested to the Procurement Board that it avoid future contracts with de Seversky.

There is, however, no smoking gun proving Arnold caused the P-35 manufacturer to lose his company. One-third of the Procurement Board members changed every year, and it is documented that de Seversky was well known and well liked by hundreds of air corps officers. So a comment made by Arnold late in 1936 would not necessarily carry over to, for example, 1938. Moreover, hundreds of contracts for all types of air corps equipment passed through Arnold's office each year on their way to the U.S. secretary of war. It is very unlikely he sat around waiting to pounce on a Materiel Division contract for Seversky Aircraft. In addition, Arnold praised in his memoir the P-35, which in 1938 broke the air corps record for a transcontinental flight. Finally, before de Seversky lost his position as president, the air corps initiated negotiations for the company to build the P-43 and Arnold gave congressional testimony indicating that Seversky

Aircraft would be a participant in the projected expansion of the air corps. Neither of these events would have taken place if Arnold were devoted to destroying the career of the Russian-American. The crux of the problem is that Arnold made decisions about aircraft engines that worked against Seversky Aircraft. These decisions, however, happened to be the ones most open to serious criticism as the United States entered war in 1941. When the Major found new life as America's best-known prophet of air power, he used his position to attack the leadership of the newly renamed U.S. Army Air Forces. As a result, the two men turned against each other. For his part, Alexander P. de Seversky's smoldering dislike of Arnold evolved over time into an uncontrollable flame that prompted him in later interviews to state baldly that Arnold flat-out took his company away from him.

# 11

## The Making of an
## Air Power Prophet

Alexander and Evelyn de Seversky arrived in New York on board the SS *Normandie* on Monday, June 12, 1939. At the 21 Club, the Major held an impromptu news conference. Newspapermen were intrigued by the views of this former combat pilot who designed military aircraft. He had just spent six months in a Europe deeply troubled by the expansionist behavior of Germany under its Führer, Adolf Hitler. During the session, de Seversky appeared annoyed by his recent shipmate, Dr. Nicholas Murray Butler. The Columbia University president had stated facetiously that Hitler's timetable for whatever he might want to do was set by astrologists. "It's time," the Major countered, "to take our opponents seriously, give them due credit and get ready ourselves." De Seversky then told reporters that Hitler had "carefully planned" his next conquest, which would take place in September. War erupted on September 1. The correct prediction "touched off a flourishing reputation for Sasha as a 'prophet,'" according to Eugene Lyons, a contemporary journalist and editor of *The American Mercury* magazine.[1]

### Months of Meandering

While de Seversky played the prophet and foretold the start of war in Europe, he had no idea about his own future. Alexander and Evelyn stayed in New York for three weeks in an apartment at River House, guests of Jackie Cochran and her financier husband, Floyd Odlum. He was not surprised Sasha had lost his position with Seversky Aircraft. Certainly, the Russian-American was such a great designer that Odlum had invested $10,000 in the company.

On the other hand, the financier understood the Major was out of his league trying to match the business skills and schemes of the revised board of directors. After evening meals, de Seversky bored his hosts recounting how he had lost the presidency and then even employment in the firm he had created. After several nights of repetitive tales of tragedy, Odlum took out his accordion and placed the instrument on the Major's lap. The trick worked. De Seversky happily provided the cozy group musical entertainment by playing, among others, Gypsy songs his father had recorded in 1910 on phonograph disks for the Gramaphone Company of St. Petersburg, Russia. Evenings for the Odlums became tolerable.[2]

After several weeks in the company of consoling, music-loving friends, a calmer de Seversky couple left the city and returned to their mansion at Asharoken on the north shore of Long Island. Their home was a scant twenty-five-mile drive away from Farmingdale and the company headquarters. The Major made an emotionally painful trip to Seversky Airport to pick up his things. It was not a pleasant experience. While several of his "Russian" colleagues welcomed de Seversky, W. Wallace Kellett and his handpicked assistants made it clear he was persona non grata. Moreover, it quickly became obvious he lost access to selected company files pertaining to his European trip. Despite his election by stockholders on April 11 for another term on the board of directors, de Seversky realized that he had absolutely no influence with the board. Proof of the latter occurred the day Germany attacked Poland and two days before England and France declared war on Germany. On September 1, 1939, a majority of board members voted to change the company's name to Republic Aircraft (later, Aviation) Corporation.[3]

The name change coupled with the advent of war in Europe prompted de Seversky to move on with his life and in familiar ways. Since 1918 he had worked directly or indirectly with American military aviation. He assumed this pattern would continue. The added impetus of war might enable him to provide a needed technology or product to the U.S. Army Air Corps, which, in turn, would lead to financial compensation. Thus, in the fall of 1939, he laid the groundwork for the formation in 1940 of not one, but three companies through the benign registration laws of the state of Delaware. Aviation Development Corporation replicated his 1922 firm in holding his patents. He also had some hope of making a light gun turret or other war materiel for the military through the Aircraft Ordnance Corporation. Third, just as he had done in building the SEV-3 amphibian, de Seversky decided once again to follow his friend Igor I. Sikorsky's lead by trying to build a helicopter via the Rotoflight Corporation.[4]

To assist him with his multiple projects, he hired away from Seversky/ Republic Aircraft Alexander M. Pishvanov, who became his aide, and Mary P. Albert, who had been his personal secretary when he was company president. Albert helped the Major organize his papers, prepare correspondence, complete applications to incorporate companies, and secure information or submit applications for patents. It just so happened 1940 proved to be a fruitful year in terms of receiving patents from previously filed applications. Documents of exclusive rights were granted for the gun turret, a stratospheric fighter aircraft, a retractable crash protector for pilots, an improved cowling design, and a movable pilot's seat. It was, however, hard to determine whether de Seversky could translate these patents into something saleable either as a patent or manufactured product. It will be recalled that he had folded, for 15,306 shares of new stock, his patent-holding Seversky Aero Corporation into Seversky Aircraft. By September 1938 the Major had assigned or proportionately assigned on a 70-30 basis, fifty-two of his inventions to the company. Hence one ongoing task given to Miss Albert was to research patent documents to determine which of the hundred or so patents belonged to the Major, the company, or proportionately to both.[5]

As this activity took place, de Seversky decided to lease in November 1939 a New York office to be on the inside of America's business and financial center. His personal headquarters would be a small suite on the seventeenth floor of the RCA Building with an imposing address of 30 Rockefeller Center. Evelyn and the Major also decided to rent an apartment in Manhattan where they could stay during the week. It enabled them to entertain guests in the city, participate in various organizations, and enjoy the many cultural and pleasurable diversions of the urban setting. After a couple of false starts, they settled on an apartment at 40 Central Park South that became their permanent Manhattan home. On the surface, then, things seemed to be going well for the Major and his wife. He bustled about with various business schemes during the day, and in the evening Evelyn could join him in visiting friends, attending shows and concerts, or dancing at their favorite nightclubs. Evelyn, the former professional dancer, made her amputee husband look great on the ballroom floor.[6]

Moreover, the Major continued to be a popular figure because of his record flights and airplane designs. He became a spokesman in print ads for Bromo-Seltzer. In February 1940 Sasha and Evelyn traveled to Los Angeles as guests of the Pacific Aviation Club. On Tuesday, February 20, the group honored de Seversky with a trophy to recognize his east–west transcontinental speed record achieved in a P-35 variant on August 29, 1938. Among P.A.C. members offering words of praise were Brig. Gen. Frank D. Lackland, in charge of GHQ Air Force First Wing; Col. Rush B. Lincoln who commanded March Field (today, March Air Reserve Base); President Robert E. Squier of Lockheed Aircraft Corporation; and Vice President Irving Taylor of the Aeronautical Chamber of Commerce based in Washington, D.C.[7]

De Seversky's acceptance speech expressed gratitude as the Major pressed all the right buttons for his audience of military officers and airplane manufacturers. "Before many months roll by," he predicted near the end of his short talk, "we shall see aviation dominating every form of transportation—performing junctions where older agencies have failed. Air power will be recognized as the first line of national defense and its strength the yardstick of the might and power of a nation. If there are any skeptics left they will be quickly converted this coming spring." Once again, de Seversky proved to be memorably accurate since the European war was in the midst of a most peculiar hiatus at the time these remarks were delivered.[8]

Poland's defeat and disappearance in occupation by Germany and the Soviet Union fulfilled secret clauses in the infamous Nazi-Soviet Pact of August 23, 1939. The real benefit of the pact for Germany kept the U.S.S.R. a friendly neutral in the east as it granted the Wehrmacht the good fortune of fighting only a single-front war against France and Great Britain in the west. After the blitzkrieg (lightning war) conquest of Poland in September, a strange interlude occurred. True, the Soviet Union fought a brief and costly conflict with Finland, but the main event in the west fizzled. Germany substituted a "sitzkrieg" for the blitzkrieg; France, which made a gentle penetration of German territory, ordered its troops on October 24 to retreat to the fortified Maginot Line. Additionally, some 250,000 British soldiers who crossed the English Channel took up nonthreatening defensive positions along the Franco-Belgian frontier. Except for naval battles, the war seemed incredibly peaceful. Americans described it as the Phony War until Germany pounced on Denmark on April 9, 1940. As de Seversky foretold, spring witnessed the resumption of full combat with aircraft playing a vital role in its conduct.[9]

## Taking Stock

De Seversky, who was intimately acquainted with, and a victim of, the horrors of war, would never have admitted publicly that he hoped to profit from the conflict that had erupted in Europe. As it turned out, he could not, in fact, take advantage of the enormous increase in demand for military aircraft and related technologies from the air corps and foreign markets, especially England and France. For example, one of his more promising inventions received a patent in February 1940. It was for split flaps on the wing's trailing edge. The flaps could slow down fast fighter aircraft for safer landings or serve as an air brake for dive-bombers or torpedo planes. Patent assignment, however, went to Seversky/Republic Aircraft. Additionally, he never found another "angel" like Paul Moore to supply several million dollars to bankroll the startup costs for one of his incorporated companies. As a result, the Major's income was so minimal and inconsistent, an occasional honorarium for a talk or a print ad, that he began selling stock to support himself; his bride; his two homes; his dog, Vodka; his office; and his secretary and assistant. Early in November 1939, he had to dispose of 3,500 shares of his Seversky/Republic stock.[10]

There is irony in the fact that the Major's stock holdings had actually increased to more than 60,000 shares because of the notes converted to preferred stock from the refinancing process created by White, Weld & Co. Moreover, even the common stock he held matched the value of the preferred stock. The trading price on the New York Curb Exchange for the former ranged between five and six dollars precisely because of his success in developing the AP-4/XP-43 for the air corps and selling the EP-1/P-35A to Sweden. De Seversky continued the process he had begun in November by cashing out 14,000 shares of stock in January 1940, 3,900 shares in February, and 7,700 shares in May. The $150,000-plus derived from stock sales would keep the Major and his extended family in the lap of luxury for several years. By contrast, such an amount would make only a dent in the total funds de Seversky required to give life to one of his corporations. He would have to buy or lease a plant and then fill it with expensive machinery and a food service and staff it with workers, foremen, engineers, draftsmen, managers, accountants, secretaries, a lawyer or two, and a company nurse—all this in order to design and build airplanes or manufacture airplane parts.[11]

When de Seversky was not reelected to the board of directors in May 1940, he sold all but 507 of his remaining 34,329 shares of Republic Aviation stock. With a portion of the resulting small fortune in cash, he retained Eugene L. and Earl J. Garey of the high-priced Wall Street law firm of Garey & Garey. The Major had earlier consulted with these attorneys before the May meeting of Republic stockholders. His preliminary consultations expanded in June and July in expectation of taking serious action. On August 21, 1940, Garey & Garey initiated two lawsuits against Republic Aviation Corporation. The first was filed in the U.S. District Court (Brooklyn) and claimed the company owed de Seversky $2,497,069 for experimental research, development work, flight testing, and foreign sales between June 1938 and April 1939. A second lawsuit entered the docket of the Manhattan Supreme Court to recover for stockholders $20 million in damages for mismanagement by Kellett, Moore, Platt, and the other named board members. Co-plaintiffs were de Seversky and Alexander Pishvanov.[12]

Besides securing the services of a prominent law firm, the Major also hired a private investigator, Paul C. Dunn, to uncover sensitive information on Kellett for use in the lawsuits. If one can believe the statements Dunn collected from individuals who worked with (and in some cases were fired by) Kellett, the president used every trick in the book to steal de Seversky's position. Finally, the Major employed a public relations firm, H. A. Bruno & Associates, to bathe Republic Aviation in the glare of a negative spotlight. All these expensive activities, subsidized paradoxically by the sale of company stock, served potentially a couple of needs. Victory on one suit would restore de Seversky's pride and reputation as the founder and administrator of the company that designed and built America's first modern fighter aircraft; a win specifically in the Federal District Court would give him the financial resources necessary to start up a new company.[13]

The legal process dragged on for more than two years; then it ended abruptly and with several surprises. On October 16, 1942, Republic Aviation announced the lawsuits had been settled amicably and the litigation discontinued. A settlement may have been eased by the fact Ralph S. Damon, former vice president of American Airlines, had replaced Kellett as president of Republic. Moreover, at the moment of this public announcement, the company was in the midst of constructing thousands of P-47s. Republic and subcontractors built a total of 15,683 of these pursuits, making the plane America's top fighter in terms of numbers produced in World War II. Designed by a team led by Alexander Kartveli, the P-47 clearly descended from the P-35 and P-43. Multiple contracts from the U.S. Army Air Forces to build the plane endowed the company with an abundance of funds. It could afford both to acknowledge the Major's tremendous contributions to the company and settle the lawsuits through a very generous, though unpublicized, amount of money to de Seversky.[14]

## The Prophet Goes Public: Radio

Equally important for understanding the quick end to litigation was the fact that de Seversky no longer aspired to administer or even be employed by Republic. Beyond that, the Major's interests and career had changed so much that he stopped trying to create a new company to build airplanes or airplane parts. De Seversky's altered life emerged in one sense because his prediction about the resumption of full-scale European war in the spring came true. By June 1, 1940, Germany had conquered Denmark, Norway, Belgium, Luxembourg, and the Netherlands. It had also successfully invaded France and then cornered hundreds of thousands of British, French, and Belgian troops in Dunkirk, a modest-sized French port on the English Channel. Under blitzkrieg victories that made German arms appear to be invincible, American print and radio journalists, especially in New York, fell over each other seeking individuals who could make sense of Germany's rapid triumphs and comment as well about U.S. national security in the face of a militaristic power whose thirst for expansion seemed unquenchable.[15]

Naturally, de Seversky attracted media attention as a potential expert and commentator on the air war. Since 1930 his name and face had made regular appearances in newspapers and magazines because of participating in air shows, designing the world's fastest amphibian, and, most importantly for the media in 1940, manufacturing America's first modern fighter aircraft. Thus it only made sense for Gabriel Heatter to contact him. Heatter, a popular newscaster for New York's WABC radio station, gained de Seversky's agreement to join him, June 4, on his weekly interview show, *We the People*, broadcast each Tuesday at 9:00 p.m. The newscaster opened the program by pointing out to his radio listeners and live studio audience that Paris had been bombed just twenty-four hours earlier. Heatter used the bombing attack to introduce de Seversky and ask him several questions that focused on the state of America's air defense.[16]

In response to these questions, the Major praised the quality of both the

Nicholas and sons Alexander (left) and George (right) circa 1900.
*Courtesy of Diane M. A. P. de Seversky*

De Seversky as a young military cadet circa 1906. *Courtesy of Diane M. A. P. de Seversky*

De Seversky after his first solo flight for the Russian military in March 1915. *Courtesy of the Cradle of Aviation Museum*

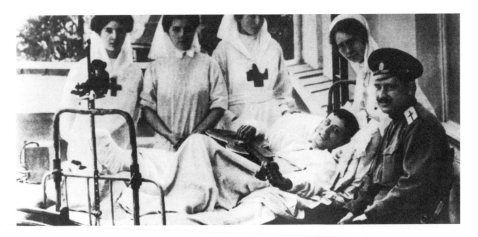

A hospitalized de Seversky recuperating from the partial amputation of his leg during fall 1915. His father, Nicholas, is to the right; his talisman, Iasha, is to the left. *Courtesy of Jack Herris*

The Baltic region. *Courtesy of Robert Carberry*

De Seversky in his wartime flight gear circa 1916. *Courtesy of Flying Machines Press*

De Seversky in Washington, D.C., in 1918. *Courtesy of Flying Machines Press*

Brig. Gen. William (Billy) Mitchell in a Thomas Morse MB-3a biplane at Selfridge Field in 1922. *Courtesy of the National Air and Space Museum, Smithsonian Institution (SI 82-11868)*

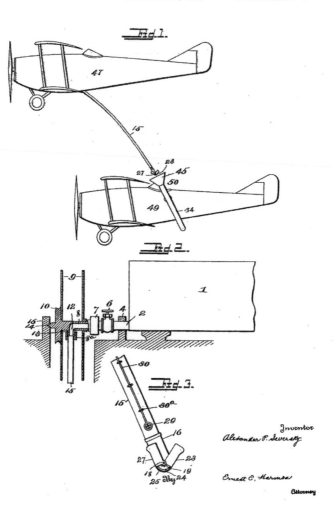

Illustration for de Seversky's in-flight refueling system of 1921.
*Courtesy of the U.S. Patent Office*

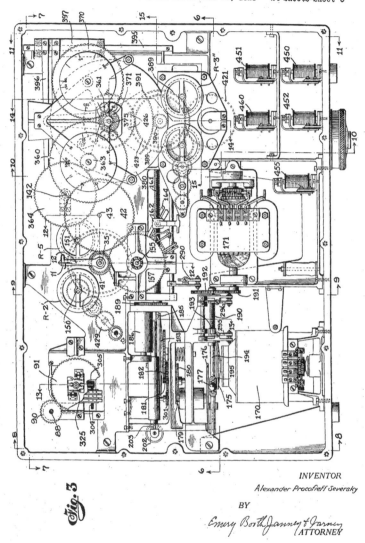

INVENTOR

*Alexander Procofieff Seversky*

BY

*Emery Booth Janney & Varney*
ATTORNEY

Illustration of one portion (in this case the analog calculator) of de Seversky's complex bombsight of 1923. *Courtesy of the U.S. Patent Office*

De Seversky's wife, Evelyn, shortly after receiving her pilot's license in 1930.
*Courtesy of the Cradle of Aviation Museum*

De Seversky and his SEV-3 amphibian aircraft in 1934.
*Courtesy of the Cradle of Aviation Museum*

The BT-8 production line in the Seversky Aircraft Corporation plant, 1936.
*Courtesy of the Cradle of Aviation Museum*

Seversky Aircraft facilities in Farmingdale, New York, in 1937.
*Courtesy of the Cradle of Aviation Museum*

Seversky Aircraft's founder and president in his Farmingdale office circa 1936.
*Courtesy of the Cradle of Aviation Museum*

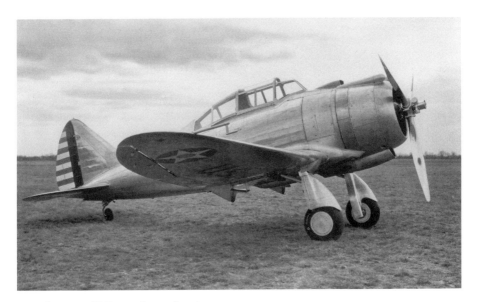

Seversky Aircraft's P-35 military plane in 1937.
*Courtesy of the Cradle of Aviation Museum*

De Seversky and Jackie Cochran with one of Seversky Aircraft's racing plane versions of the P-35 in 1938. *Courtesy of the Cradle of Aviation Museum*

Jan. 3, 1939.  A. P. DE SEVERSKY  Des. 112,834

AIRPLANE

Filed April 15, 1938  6 Sheets-Sheet 1

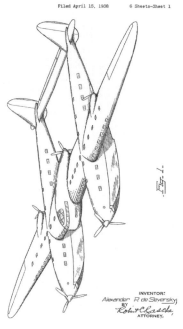

Patent illustration of de Seversky's Super Clipper of 1938. *Courtesy of the U.S. Patent Office*

Seversky Aircraft's 2PA long-distance/convoy fighter airplane. *Courtesy of the Cradle of Aviation Museum*

Seversky Aircraft's XP-43 and the basis for Republic Aviation's YP-43. *Courtesy of the Cradle of Aviation Museum*

President Franklin D. Roosevelt congratulating de Seversky on receiving the Harmon Trophy on December 19, 1939. *Courtesy of the Cradle of Aviation Museum*

Charles Lindbergh at a reception during one of his six visits to Germany between 1936 and 1938. *Courtesy of the Lindbergh Pictures Collection, Manuscripts and Archives, Yale University Library*

General of the Army
Henry (Hap) Arnold circa
1944–1945. *Courtesy of the
National Air and Space
Museum, Smithsonian
Institution (SI 86-13271)*

Walt Disney presents de
Seversky with a "Winged
Oscar" for the movie
*Victory through Air Power*
in June 1943. *Courtesy of the
Cradle of Aviation Museum*

Alexander and Evelyn at home with their famous flying dog, Vodka, 1942.
*Courtesy of the Cradle of Aviation Museum.*

The one-legged major proving he can still cut a rug with his wife, Evelyn, at a New York nightclub, mid-1940s. *Courtesy of Diane M. A. P. de Seversky*

(*across*) President Harry S. Truman congratulating de Seversky on receiving the Harmon Trophy on June 24, 1947. War Secretary Robert P. Patterson is between them, and Evelyn de Seversky is to de Seversky's right. *Courtesy of the Truman Presidential Library*

De Seversky operating his Ionocraft in his Long Island City laboratory/factory circa mid-1960s. *Courtesy of the Cradle of Aviation Museum*

De Seversky in the P-35's cockpit at the time of the plane's acquisition by the U.S. Air Force Museum on June 1, 1974. *Courtesy of the Cradle of Aviation Museum*

planes and pilots possessed by the U.S. military; he saved his criticism for quantity. For this reason, de Seversky strongly endorsed the ideas embedded in a speech President Franklin D. Roosevelt delivered before Congress on May 16. As the Allies in Europe confronted annihilation from German arms, FDR called for appropriations sufficient to procure at least 50,000 warplanes a year. The Major perceptively noted such large numbers of aircraft mandated an equally large number of ground organizations, maintenance facilities, and trained personnel (pilots, mechanics, navigators, bombardiers, etc.). He also pointed out that the best defense is a vigorous offense. Hence he argued that the United States must develop long-range fighters and bombers to strike at the source of danger. Despite listing several significant shortcomings in U.S. preparations for a strong air defense, he concluded, "But we have the materials, we have the experience, we have the manpower and above all, we have the will to protect ourselves. And protect ourselves—we will." De Seversky captured the favor of the studio audience, which showered him with loud applause.[17]

Once they got past de Seversky's heavy Russian accent, radio listeners marveled at his thoughtful comments. The reality, of course, is that all such shows were completely scripted to stay within time constraints of the program's length including commercials—for Sanka Coffee in the case of *We the People*. The Columbia Broadcasting System (CBS), which then owned WABC, employed a professional radio production company, Phillips H. Lord, Inc., to prepare the script. The latter was based on the guest's written answers to the host's written questions. Additionally, guests were assigned so many minutes and even seconds and told to time themselves for compliance before turning the material over to the production company for final preparation. The resulting transcripts are fascinating to examine. Besides last-minute changes and corrections, the Major marked his pages with his own creative pronunciation key. For example, he placed "ee" above words like "sea" and "these" and эй (Cyrillic for the "ai" sound) above "nation" and "stake."[18]

As he gained experience speaking on the radio and before sundry groups, de Seversky outgrew his need to devise multilingual markings on typescripts. He also became adept at doing unscripted interviews with, for example, print journalists. In the short term, the favorable audience response on June 4 gave de Seversky the opportunity for return visits to *We the People* and other WABC programs. Moreover, his success on WABC led to his name being inscribed on an unpublicized short list of military experts to be invited as a special commentator or good interview on numerous other radio stations. Over the next twenty years, the Major would take part in hundreds of radio and, by 1950, television shows including such well-known programs as *Meet the Press*. Simultaneously with de Seversky's meteoric rise as a radio personality, he began writing air war articles for such wire services as United Press (United Press International after 1958) and North American Newspaper Alliance (now defunct). The print and on-air activities dovetailed to enhance the Major's reputation in both media. And, naturally, many of his radio scripts bore some resemblance to his wire service articles.[19]

## The Prophet Goes Public: Print

De Seversky's first article in collaboration with United Press appeared in newspapers nationwide on June 1, 1940. Its content unintentionally defined the Major as an extraordinary prophet who reflected the two secular meanings of that term: predictor and spokesman. At a time when Anglophile pundits convinced themselves Germany would soon invade England, de Seversky predicted the British Isles would remain safe as long as the Royal Air Force functioned. Germany had to control the skies over the English Channel or its invading forces faced bloody annihilation. Because in 1939 the Major had flown and appreciated the superior qualities of the Supermarine *Spitfire*, he knew the Germans would be hard-pressed to gain anything resembling air supremacy. Unlike the Great War, when the airplane occasionally made important contributions to the combat struggles on the ground, the second round of global war witnessed air power playing a decisive role in determining the outcome of most battles on land and sea. Such was certainly the case for the event discussed by the Major in his second United Press article. This one focused on Dunkirk, from which, between May 26 and June 3, 1940, 850 private vessels and naval warships evacuated 338,000 Allied soldiers to England. Viewed by many as both victory and miracle, the evacuations at Dunkirk and other French locations handed the British government of Prime Minister Winston S. Churchill an army of over a half-million men to help defend England.[20]

In his article, de Seversky noted that many commentators claimed the successful evacuation of hundreds of thousands of soldiers from the German snare demonstrated British sea power. "I would not for a moment," he wrote, "attempt to detract from the work of the British navy, but as one who has trained in naval warfare and graduated from it to the field of aerial combat I am compelled to assert that this withdrawal operation was accomplished primarily because of British local superiority in the air." Hindsight confirms the Major's assertion and in ways he could not have known from the sanitized and slanted press releases issued by the belligerent countries.[21]

Gen. Gerd von Rundstedt, who led the Wehrmacht's Army Group A, which slashed across northern France, asked Hitler to spare his armored columns from trying to cut the British off from the sea at Dunkirk. He feared the action might bog down his forces and prevent them from responding to a French counterstroke from the south. Hitler agreed to von Rundstedt's request because Field Marshal Hermann Goering enthusiastically promised that his Luftwaffe would halt the withdrawal, kill the evacuees, and finish off the valiant French First Army, which defended the land perimeter around the embattled port of Dunkirk. Surely, the German air force caused damage and killed troops, but the withdrawal proved successful. The RAF protected the site with 3,561 sorties, losing in the process 177 aircraft to the Luftwaffe's 240. The numbers are not nearly as important as the fact that for the first time in the European phase of the war, German air power failed to carry out its mission.[22]

As wars in Europe and Asia continued, it seemed more and more likely that the United States would somehow be caught up in the maelstrom of these multiple conflicts. The tentacles of the militaristic powers reached out and threatened American interests. Japan coveted the Philippines and other U.S. territories in the Pacific; German victories in Europe disturbed U.S. security in the Caribbean over the potential transfer of French, Dutch, and Danish colonies to the Nazis. Just as de Seversky spoke of the need for more and better aircraft on the radio, he began to argue in print that American air power must be strengthened. His radio interviews and newspaper articles opened the door for the appearance of his first lengthy article in a well-known and highly respected journal of commentary, *The American Mercury*, edited by Eugene Lyons. The piece, "Hard Facts on Air Power," typified in the words of Lyons the Major's "hard-hitting" arguments, attracted "extraordinary attention," and gave the prophet's "crusade" for American air power "the big push in public opinion it needed."[23]

In this first extended article, de Seversky devoted most of his narrative to three "hard facts." First, a rapid increase in warplane production was necessary, but too many commentators claimed the task could be accomplished by employing the automobile industry. The Major noted, though, that the simplest warplane was far more complex than the most intricate automobile. Besides tremendous differences in constructing an air frame with hundreds of pieces of metal and stamping a car body, he cited such warplane technologies as bombsights, gun sights, armament, communications equipment, retractable landing gear, control surfaces, and navigational instruments. He went on to point out that automakers had neither the right kind of factory setup and machine tools nor the specially trained skilled workers and aeronautical engineers appropriate for aircraft production. To be sure, Ford Motor Company later built 6,792 B-24 heavy bombers designed and produced originally by Consolidated Aircraft Corporation (absorbed by General Dynamics after 1953 and now part of Lockheed Martin). Ford successfully accomplished a very important production run but only after a lengthy period devoted to building an airframe factory at Willow Run in Michigan and investing millions of dollars in government funds to secure the necessary special machinery and trained personnel. In short, history proved de Seversky correct. Car manufacturers simply could not provide a quick fix to increase the number of warplanes.[24]

Another "hard fact" reflected the controversy over the relative merits of air and sea power. "It is," de Seversky stated, "as inane as an argument about the superiority of the train over the steamer. Each operates in its own medium, and when we span a waterway with a bridge, the medium suddenly changes—the train or automobile suddenly becomes more effective than a ferryboat in crossing the river." Keeping this analogy in mind, the Major claimed that any time warplanes could "bridge a water gap," whether river, channel, lake, or ocean, it is self-evident that air power is "more efficient than sea power." De Seversky's recent articles and radio interviews concerning military actions in Norway and Dunkirk allowed him to conclude "that no land or sea operations are possible where control of the air is in the hands of the adversary [emphasis original]."[25]

The Major actually focused on the image of the airplane as a bridge over water. Taken to its logical conclusion, such a bridge would leave the navy with a limited tactical role. Based upon the revolution in aircraft design of the 1930s to which he contributed, de Seversky assumed in his article that within five years warplanes would be able to carry ordnance across an ocean, drop it on an enemy target, and return to a home base. Presumably, in the Pacific theater of World War II, this capability would have made the air, sea, and land battles on or near Saipan totally unnecessary since the American attack on the island occurred primarily to create and secure a B-29 airfield for a bombing campaign against Japan. Because such technology did not exist in 1940, de Seversky admitted it would be suicidal for the United States to maintain anything less than a strong navy. Regardless, the Major's prediction was off. It would be eight years before America possessed a true intercontinental bomber in the form of Convair's B-36. By 1955 Boeing's B-52 Stratofortress entered service with the Strategic Air Command of the U.S. Air Force, 1947 successor to the U.S. Army Air Forces. The B-52 had a 10,000-mile range. With the application of de Seversky's 1921 patent on in-flight refueling, the Stratofortress ignored the boundaries of oceans and continents by taking on fuel supplied by the Boeing KC-135 Stratotanker.[26]

The final "hard fact" in this first extended article centered on the need for aviators to be in charge of military aviation and to recognize the importance of air power by creating a U.S. Air Department parallel and equal to the U.S. War and Navy Departments. Fascinatingly, he suggested the U.S. Navy should have aircraft to help protect American vessels against enemy fleets; and the U.S. Army should have ground attack and observation planes to assist in locating and destroying enemy troops. This would mean the proposed Air Department would provide leadership and direction over a strategic air force designed to defeat enemy air power, disrupt its military organization, and bomb those war industries and transportation systems supplying the enemy with war materiel. De Seversky used Germany as his example of a country that recognized the significance of military aviation. Proof was the fact that an experienced combat aviator, Hermann Goering, headed the country's Air Ministry and hence the Luftwaffe. Until the Battle of Britain, however, the Major may not have fully realized that Goering narrowly defined military aviation as an extension of combat ground forces. Thus, unlike the United States and the United Kingdom, Germany did not develop and serially produce strategic bombers. The latter failing proved to be one of many reasons Germany lost the war.[27]

Even as the August issue of *The American Mercury* went to press early in July, Lyons and his editorial staff knew they had a hot item on their hands. They sought to expand magazine sales and perhaps even subscriptions by sending postcards announcing the Major's article to leaders of aeronautical associations, executives in the aviation industry, air corps officers in or near

Washington, D.C., plus a lengthy list of army and navy officers de Seversky had worked with over the previous two decades. Magazine sales were not hurt by the corresponding appearance nationwide of what may very well be described as de Seversky's most extraordinary United Press article in 1940. It enhanced his reputation and elevated him to the highest echelon among military aviation commentators.[28]

Published on August 15, the article both described and defined the Battle of Britain. The Major was one of the first American analysts to recognize that the Luftwaffe's air attack on England was not simply a preliminary softening up exercise before the real battle would begin. Germany had to gain mastery of the sky before it could expect the English to surrender or succumb to an invasion. De Seversky speculated leaders of traditional military forces around the world might be surprised to learn that the air war over England and the English Channel was, in fact, the main event. Neither armies nor navies would decide the battle's outcome. If England lost the air battle, it lost the war. The nation would be defenseless against crushing blows from the sky; its navy, imperiled if not bombed to oblivion, could not prevent Germany from landing troops on British shores. If England won the air battle, however, the country would be free from accepting German suzerainty under duress or enduring invasion and occupation.[29]

When de Seversky's United Press press release crossed the desk of H. V. Kaltenborn on Wednesday August 14, the article struck him as so perceptive and persuasive he made it the subject of his evening broadcast on New York's WEAF radio, flagship station for the coast-to-coast network of the National Broadcasting Company (NBC). Kaltenborn, with his highly precise diction, was the best-known news commentator in the United States. His distinctive voice and style of presentation were so much a part of Americana that he played himself or a caricature of himself in such Hollywood movies as *Mr. Smith Goes to Washington* (1939) and *The Day the Earth Stood Still* (1951). Kaltenborn added luster to the Major's prominent position. While de Seversky continued to write articles about other aspects of the air war during the fall, the victory of the RAF over the Luftwaffe in the Battle of Britain led *Look*, one of America's more popular magazines, to ask the United Press analyst to explain Germany's defeat.[30]

De Seversky's article, "Why Hitler's Planes Failed to Beat England . . . A Lesson," handed the writer a vehicle for making a couple of key points. Without knowing the crucial role of British radar, the Major decided Germany lost the Battle of Britain because it lacked the right equipment. The Luftwaffe's inventory of warplanes consisted of short-range fighters and light or medium bombers. Before July 1940, these airplanes had operated near the front lines and supplied the Wehrmacht with excellent, close air support as mechanized forces advanced to victory in a Poland or a France. Add the thirty- to hundred-mile-wide English Channel that intervened between the Luftwaffe on the continent and its targets in England and the result only highlighted a disastrous blend of the wrong aircraft. Germans lacked long-range fighters and large, four-engine bombers that could carry tons of ordnance. The inadequate mix of German aircraft confronted a disciplined and determined RAF invested with a superb interceptor in the form of the *Spitfire*. By the end of October 1940, over 1,700 German aircraft had been transformed into pieces of junk. Since the Luftwaffe did not secure the skies, even Adolf Hitler understood an invasion of England was absolutely impossible.[31]

As implied in the title, the other important point de Seversky made in the article was the "lesson" the Battle of Britain held for the United States. Here the analyst stood tall in both shoes of a prophet by foretelling and proposing the future of American air power. "We must," he argued, "build huge, long-range bombers that will be capable of discharging many tons of explosives. . . . They must be protected from enemy planes by convoys of specially designed fighter planes." The bomber he had in mind was Douglas Aircraft's XB-19. Its projected performance would allow it to fly nonstop, round-trip between a U.S. airfield and a target in Europe, where it could drop eighteen tons of explosives. The XB-19 never went into production. The air corps/air forces, however, did order a total of 31,000 B-17 and B-24 heavy bombers. Moreover, the Major's nemesis, Gen. Hap Arnold, pushed to completion the development and production of Boeing's B-29. This most advanced long-range bomber of World War II could carry six tons of ordnance up to 4,000 miles.[32]

De Seversky, of course, thought the 2PA variant of the P-35 with its 2,000 mile range would be a good start on the way to developing a long-distance fighter. It could match the range of the B-17. The Major's comments about the 2PA were an unspoken rebuke directed at air corps leaders who showed little interest in the plane his company had built in 1938 for the U.S.S.R. and Japan. Nevertheless, the future proved the prophet correct. During the second half of 1943, two superior fighter aircraft, the rugged and hefty

Republic P-47 and the sleek and speedy North American P-51, were altered by having additional, droppable fuel tanks installed on the wing. It enabled the pursuits to fly round-trip between English airfields and traditional German territory. A combination of heavy bombers accompanied and protected by long-distance fighters could then attack targets deep in enemy territory. This combination, at one and the same time, allowed U.S. air power to visit horrendous destruction on, and gain air superiority over, Germany during the course of 1944. Indeed, many U.S. bomb runs were actually designed to lure, engage, and exterminate German warplanes and their pilots.[33]

Two days after *Look* magazine published the article, President Franklin D. Roosevelt greeted de Seversky in the White House on December 19, 1940. In short order and with the glare of photographers' popping flash bulbs, FDR presented the Major with the Clifford Burke Harmon Trophy. The Ligue Internationale des Aviateurs had selected him to receive the trophy as the world's outstanding aviator for the year 1939. Naturally, the award recognized his lifelong work in aviation as a combat pilot, prolific inventor of aircraft technologies, record holder for distance and speed flights, and designer and developer of advanced military aircraft. Additionally, the Ligue acknowledged him as a leading authority on military aviation as evidenced by his public addresses, radio interviews, and published articles. "His analyses," the Ligue noted, "of the present aerial warfare, as well as his forecasts of the tactical, strategical and technical developments, have been unusually accurate and have won for him a reputation of creditability." Thus, by the end of 1940, de Seversky managed to complete his transformation from an apparently failed aircraft company president to a highly renowned air power prophet. He now pursued with relish his new vocation.[34]

## Reflections

Different writers have used different terms to characterize and define Alexander P. de Seversky in his redesigned role as commentator on air power. The dozen descriptors one can identify range from futurist to theoretician. Generally, however, the various labels fall into two sets of related terms: publicist/promoter and disciple/prophet. These discrete sets appeared respectively four decades apart in two distinct edited books that nevertheless bore the same title, *Makers of Modern Strategy* (Princeton, 1943, 1986). An updated exploration of de Seversky's work thoughtfully employing his critics to elaborate the publicist/promoter category appeared as two articles in the journal *Air Power History* (Summer, Fall, 1993) by Russell E. Lee, National Air and Space Museum curator. And an interesting reevaluation of the Major in the disciple/prophet classification can be found in *The Rise of American Air Power* (Yale, 1987), a book written by Michael S. Sherry, Leopold Professor of History at Northwestern University.

As made clear in this and earlier chapters, the author favors the latter appellations, though he appreciates the value of the former. The term "prophet" is appropriate because the Major's written and oral commentaries in the media seem to fit comfortably within two definitions of the term; in other words, he was both a predictor and a spokesman for a cause. There is, of course, a third and perhaps more commonly understood definition for a prophet: a person who expresses or interprets the will of God. If not in the twenty-first century then certainly in the 1940s, U.S. military aviators perceived the late Gen. William (Billy) Mitchell as the secular god of air power, and de Seversky viewed himself as the god's primary "disciple." He served to interpret and bring to fruition the substance of the master's teaching. Sasha was a genius at design and invention, but even he admitted he was not an original thinker when it came to air power. Billy Mitchell gave shape to his basic ideas. Indeed, the Major repeatedly acknowledged his indebtedness to the man who became his guide and friend in the 1920s. This, in turn, explains why chapter 12 begins with a section titled "The Prophet's Mentor."

# 12

## Prophet of Air Power

Because Alexander P. de Seversky inherited the fundamental concepts of air power from Gen. Billy Mitchell, it is worth a few moments to examine the source and substance of Mitchell's ideas. Chapter 4 discusses briefly the general's experience and appreciation for the importance of aircraft in attacking enemy troops and safeguarding American soldiers against enemy airplanes when he served as chief of air service for the First Army of the American Expeditionary Force in World War I. Thus, while some air power enthusiasts saved all their affection for bombers, Mitchell endorsed a "balanced air force" that contained a mix of specialized aircraft. He accepted, for example, pursuit planes as not only vital in destroying enemy aircraft but also in protecting bombers. Five years after his 1925 court-martial and resignation from the military, Mitchell wrote a popular book on aeronautics, *Skyways*, in which he detailed his latest and mature views on military aviation.[1]

### The Prophet's Master

In *Skyways*, he narrated in considerable detail an unfortunate episode experienced by a bombardment squadron during the St. Mihiel battle in September 1918. Mitchell sent eighteen bombers behind German lines to drop ordnance on the hillside village of Conflans, which housed enemy soldiers and supplies. Regrettably, the squadron failed to connect with its escort of pursuits. Even though each of the bombers carried two or more guns, the squadron was attacked with devastating effect. Over German-held territory, the bombers were pounced upon from different angles by enemy fighters that were fast and maneuverable. Only five planes of the bombardment squadron made it to Allied lines, but not safely. All surviving aircraft were damaged and most crew members were wounded. While Mitchell readily acknowledged that bombers needed fighters and guns for protection, he also recognized that the exercise of air power occurred primarily through bombardment. The bomber, then, must be the centerpiece of any air force. Moreover, he argued that aviation cannot dig trenches in the sky or otherwise play a strictly defensive role; it "must attack to bring results."[2]

In addition to the lessons he learned in 1918 as an American commander of military aviation, Mitchell enhanced his understanding of air power through reading commentaries and holding conversations on the subject with numerous Allied aviators. Three contemporaries, however, played special roles in advancing or affirming Mitchell's views. Maj. Gen. Hugh Trenchard of England symbolized a pathfinder for a process Mitchell fervently hoped to duplicate in the United States. When the Royal Flying Corps and Royal Naval Air Service merged to form the Royal Air Force on April 1, 1918, Trenchard served as the first RAF chief of air staff. The notion of an independent air force on equal terms with that of an army or navy was also the focal point of Giulio Douhet, the second personality to impact Mitchell. The Italian general published *Il Dominio dell'Aria* (The Command of the Air) in 1921. Mitchell borrowed Douhet's argument: Aerial warfare would raise such havoc in the enemy country that it would force a quick resolution to the conflict in contrast with the lengthy horror of trench warfare experienced during the Great War. Finally, Mitchell also valued the work of British historian Basil H. Liddell Hart. The title of his 1925 book, *Paris: Or the Future of War*, is a reference to Homer's epic poem about the Greek conflict with Troy. In *Skyways*, Mitchell adopted Hart's "vital center" concept and paraphrased Hart's thesis: "Aircraft enables us *to jump over* the army which shields the enemy government, industry, and people and *so strike direct and immediately at the seat of the opposing will and policy* [emphasis original]."[3]

Between 1921, when Mitchell and de Seversky first worked together, and 1936, when Mitchell died, the general impressed and bequeathed his ideas on air power and a separate air force to the Major. To be sure, by 1940 de Seversky had updated Mitchell's examples and modified his arguments because circumstances and aircraft had changed dramatically since *Skyways* appeared. After 1930, the general had a hard time getting his ideas in print. Many book publishers and magazine editors felt the air power topic had been milked dry along with its audience of readers. Disappointed over the Great War and distressed over the Great Depression, most Americans adopted an isolationist position in the early 1930s that ignored problems abroad. However, two things happened by 1940 to re-create an audience not only for the air power debate but specifically for a discussion of that debate by de Seversky. First, as depression waned, wars and the resulting threats to American interests by the expansionist powers caused a substantial number of Americans to shift away from isolationism. Second, as discussed in chapter 11, the Major had attracted much ink nationally. He also possessed a significant level of authority to back his printed and spoken word for reasons that ranged from flying combat missions in World War I to manufacturing combat planes in the late 1930s.[4]

### Independent Air Force

In between preparing short pieces for wire services and commentaries for radio programs, de Seversky spent time in his RCA Building office suite writing and revising a feature article on the subject of the independent air force. Naturally, the late Billy Mitchell's shadow crossed his desk. The immediate inspiration for the article, however, came from Maj. Gen. Frank M. Andrews, who was then Panama Canal air force commander at Albrook Field in the Canal Zone. The two men had become acquainted in 1938, when the Major was the manufacturer of the P-35 and Andrews was chief of General Headquarters Air Force. By 1941 they were exchanging letters and telegrams on a monthly basis. They continued to communicate with each other regularly until Lieutenant General Andrews, then air commander for the European theater, perished in a B-24 Liberator on May 3, 1943. Andrews Air Force Base was named in his honor six years later.[5]

When General Headquarters Air Force was first established on March 1, 1935, with Andrews serving as chief, it gave promise of being the first step in the formation of a separate air force. A whole series of issues, though, denied fulfillment of the promise. A flawed organizational structure plagued the new unit. While the General Headquarters Air Force functioned as the operational or combat arm, the U.S. Army Air Corps controlled the crucial support elements of training, finances, and procurement. Meanwhile, both air corps and air force chiefs reported to the deputy chief of staff for air of the U.S. Army, which continued to exercise ultimate authority. Then, too, the situation at the local level bordered on the bizarre since tactical airfields belonged to neither air corps nor air force but to army commanders who were ground soldiers first and airmen last. On top of everything else, Andrews wanted to develop a force that could project air power against an enemy by securing a great strategic bomber. "Flying Fortress Frank" Andrews pushed relentlessly with the press, Congress, and army brass for a huge production run of B-17s. His strident efforts were rewarded by his removal as chief and "exile" to a unit in Texas in March 1939. Even after war in Europe began, Andrews had to watch as the army delayed for months signing a contract for only thirty-eight B-17s in order to haggle with Boeing over its already bargain-basement unit price. And earlier, the U.S. Navy insisted the air corps not operate aircraft more than one hundred miles from American shores.[6]

As the year 1941 opened, de Seversky began to add all this up: the prospects for an independent air force seemed more hopeful in 1935 than 1941; by the latter year, the best candidate to head such an air force, Andrews, was squirreled away and out of sight in Central America; the traditional armed forces, both army and navy, seemed to have done everything in their power to keep the United States from securing and effectively using the world's best strategic bomber; and the organizational nightmare of America's air arm was not only cumbersome but positively archaic when compared with such wartime belligerents as England and Germany. Small wonder de Seversky decided to expand ideas that were presented briefly in such other publications as *The American Mercury* and *Look* to write a feature article titled, "Why We *Must* Have a Separate Air Force." It appeared as an original piece in the March 1941 issue of *Reader's Digest*, then the magazine with the nation's widest readership.[7]

As proof of the wrongheaded infantry view of aviation, de Seversky cited anomalies associated with pursuit armament in the late 1930s. Army Ordnance insisted ammunition had to be fed into aircraft machine guns on just one side when, for design purposes, aircraft engineers wanted guns that could accept the belt from either side. Regulations further specified only two machine guns on pursuits as if nothing had changed in military aviation since the Great War had ended two decades earlier. Moreover, the pair of guns had to be placed on the nose of the fuselage in front of the cockpit and no more than fourteen inches, according to the P-35 manufacturer, from the pilot's eye. The army apparently conceived the pilot as an airborne trooper with a rifle butt on his shoulder. All this at a time when the English strung eight machine guns along the wing of their fighters and the Germans added cannon for good measure. Thus it made no sense for U.S. infantrymen to be in charge of aviation. Only airmen of vision, the Major asserted, should make decisions about combat planes.[8]

De Seversky believed the establishment of a U.S. Air Department would guarantee those visionary aviators would be in charge of military aviation. It would be comparable to, and independent of, the War and Navy Departments. Backed by an American aircraft industry fully capable of, the Major claimed, excellent design and quality production, Air Department experts would employ U.S. industrial superiority to create long-range bombers like the B-19. Theoretically, it could operate from American airfields, flying bombs to a target in Europe but capable of returning nonstop to its U.S. base. Additionally, such experts would encourage the aircraft industry to create a long-distance fighter with the speed and firepower to protect bombers from enemy planes during combat missions. "But if we allow," de Seversky concluded, "the outworn, terrestrial-minded thinking of the Army and Navy to dominate, we shall find ourselves fatally handicapped—losers in the race for air supremacy, which we ought to win."[9]

De Seversky finished revising the article and sent it to *Reader's Digest* through the publisher, DeWitt Wallace. By the end of January, the author received a check for $1,800. Along with printing in the magazine in February, numerous offprints of the Major's article were prepared and mailed to members of Congress, the White House, and commanding officers of the military. Not long after newsstands and subscribers received the March issue, the White House was inundated with a flurry of letters supporting or demanding the formation of an independent air force. Although de Seversky moved on to address other issues, he continued to write and speak about the subject. Besides wire service articles and radio interviews, he participated in a debate over a separate air force that gained national attention. The Mutual Broadcasting Company (defunct after 1998) sent the debate, hosted by the American Forum of the Air, on May 18 over its national network from the New York flagship station, WOR. The Major also spoke on the subject on June 19, 1941, before the city's influential Advertising Club.[10]

The very next day and almost on cue, the U.S. Army Air Corps enjoyed a facelift. Secretary of War Henry L. Stimson made a public announcement on June 21 concerning the reorganization on the 20th of military aviation into the U.S. Army Air Forces. The announced change centered on two key ingredients. A short while earlier, Robert A. Lovett had been named assistant secretary of war for air, an office that had been vacant since 1933. The appointment clearly showed the Roosevelt administration's determination to elevate the visibility and status of the air arm. Second, Maj. Gen. Henry H. Arnold not only headed the new air forces, including its Combat Command (formerly, General Headquarters Air Force), but also served as deputy army chief of staff to Gen. George C. Marshall, army chief of staff. Thus the administrative structure of the revised organization was simple and clear. Moreover, in the person of Hap Arnold, the air forces had a seat at the highest level of the army's hierarchy.[11]

It would be wrong, of course, to credit de Seversky with causing the reorganization. He was responsible, however, for helping to create a political and public atmosphere that supported a separate air force. Indeed, one reason for the air corps makeover was to knock the wind out of the sails of legislation sponsored by the Major's correspondents in both the U.S. Senate and House to mandate the establishment of the American air force. Forewarned by friends in the air corps about the June 20 reform, de Seversky publicly revealed and reviled the War Department's initiative a day before it happened. The *New York Post* quoted de Seversky calling the proposal a "trick," "compromise," "half-measure," and an "insult to the American people." His friend, General Andrews, took a less negative approach describing it as a "step in the right direction." Nevertheless, he remained unhappy that the new air forces continued to be under the army's thumb. "The prime consideration," Andrews wrote de Seversky on June 27, "in the technical development of the airplane should be its strategic role not its auxiliary function of supporting ground troops."[12]

### Confronting the Isolationists

In this period, de Seversky almost always found occasion to mention the need for an independent air force no matter what the larger topic of his article, speech, or radio commentary was. But one of those larger topics that he spent quite a bit of time on in 1941 was American isolationism. It was a subject that also concerned and plagued the efforts of Billy Mitchell, precisely because it diminished support for air power. The isolationist impulse that influenced American thinking in the 1920s and 1930s was undermined by the brazen expansionist activities of Germany, Italy, and Japan. As a result, the Roosevelt administration felt it had enough public approval to extend in June 1940 the sale of war materiel to the "opponents of force." With the disheartening collapse of France later that month, American arms became available for purchase not just to England, the only European country still at war with the Nazis, but also to its British Empire and Commonwealth of Nations. Presidential executive orders to the U.S. War and Navy Departments caused the release for sale of older aircraft, machine guns, and cannon to private corporations for transfer to the British. On September 2, President Roosevelt signed another executive order exchanging fifty older American destroyers to the British Navy for leases on a series of bases extending northward from the Caribbean and ending at Newfoundland.[13]

These measures served as catalysts for the start of a great debate. It pitted Americans who supported the president by intervening (short of war) to supply military goods to countries fighting the Axis powers against those who opposed the president by seeking to keep America out of the war through the preservation of absolute neutrality toward all belligerents. During the course of 1940, two pivotal organizations formed, one on each side of the debate and embodying other groups: isolationists sided with the America First Committee and interventionists joined the Committee to Defend America by Aiding the Allies. The controversial event that heightened and defined the debate and led to vocal attacks between the groups was the Lend-Lease Act passed by Congress on March 10, 1941, and signed into law the next day by FDR. The measure granted the president the right to exchange, lease, lend, or otherwise dispose of military goods to any nation whose defense he deemed crucial to the defense of the United States.[14]

The America First Committee's response to passage of the Lend-Lease Act came from its chief spokesman, Charles A. Lindbergh, the heroic aviator who had garnered international fame by his solo flight from New York to Paris in May 1927. He wrote a "Letter to Americans" published in the popular *Collier's* magazine on March 21, 1941. Lindbergh maintained that the United States was "being led toward that war . . . by every conceivable subterfuge" such as all-out aid promised to Britain via Lend-Lease. One retort to his "letter" appeared as a feature article in *The American Mercury*, "Why Lindbergh Is Wrong," by de Seversky, who was also a member of the Committee to Defend America by Aiding the Allies. Following a tribute to the Lone Eagle's 1927 accomplishment, the Major cleverly chose to argue the technical aspects rather than the political views expressed by Lindbergh in *Collier's*. After all, de Seversky claimed,

> Colonel Lindbergh would be the first to admit that sitting for 33 hours in the cramped cockpit of a single-motored plane between New York and Paris . . . [did] not thereby automatically [transform him] into an authority on military tactics and strategy, the design and manufacture of airplanes, the organization of Air Power, or other matters which he has since then been maneuvered into discussing.[15]

By stark contrast in terms of military affairs, the Major was everything the Colonel was not. De Seversky graduated from Russia's naval academy; studied military engineering; flew fifty-seven combat missions in World War I; served as consultant to Gen. Billy Mitchell; invented and patented a number of key military technologies, such as the world's most accurate bombsight; and designed, tested, and manufactured advanced military aircraft. Lindbergh in his "letter" called on readers to demand from experts practical answers to questions he raised about national defense. Thus de Seversky, a true expert, felt comfortable to respond to three technical issues raised by Lindbergh both in his letter and current speeches. First, the Colonel firmly believed that the United States would waste its treasure aiding a losing cause. Great Britain, Lindbergh predicted in speeches and articles, would lose the war. Naturally, de Seversky repeated in his article's reply old arguments about air supremacy, the RAF, and the *Spitfire* as safeguarding the British Isles from Nazi invasion.[16]

Second, the America First spokesman stated that aid to Great Britain would diminish the amount of equipment available to American forces and hence weaken national defense. Once again, the Major adroitly overturned Lindbergh's case by taking a different perspective. "Far from weakening us," he stated, "the conversion of America into an arsenal for other nations is forcing the organization of a military industrial machine, strengthening national muscles, making Americans conscious of their exposed position in a predatory world." Finally, Lindbergh could afford to hold an isolationist viewpoint since he knew the country had nothing to fear from, for example, Germany because of the expanse of the Atlantic Ocean and the presence of the U.S. Navy. De Seversky thought Lindbergh gave far too much credit to the ocean as an impediment. The Germans had developed an airliner, the Focke Wulf 200 Condor, which flew nonstop from Berlin to New York in 1938, and converted it to an antishipping aircraft. Alone or in communication with German U-boats, the plane was responsible for destroying vast quantities of ships as it could operate nearly a thousand miles into the Atlantic. Using current technology, de Seversky noted the Fw 200 or its successor could be redesigned and reequipped to fly round-trip across the ocean.[17]

The piece in *The American Mercury* resulted in an invitation for de Seversky to speak on the subject of "Aviation vs. Isolationism" at Yale Club's Federal Union Dinner on May 20, 1941. A dominant theme in the talk was the fact that technology, in the forms of travel and communication, had made the world smaller and interconnected and thus reduced American isolationism to the level of an ideology that was downright silly. The Major warned that in the atmosphere of war it would be a few short years before the range of aircraft would increase enough to convert the Atlantic Ocean obstacle into nothing more than a wide English Channel. Frighteningly, he suggested that an aggressive Germany could then turn the air Battle of Britain into the air Battle of America. The speech was broadcast over New York's WMCA radio station and received such attention that a transcript was published in *Vital Speeches of the Day*. In fact, the favorable notice, if not notoriety, attached to de Seversky's talk gave Simon & Schuster the perfect opportunity to announce publicly that it had agreed to publish a book on air power by the Yale Club's speaker.[18]

The capstone to de Seversky's efforts to undermine and weaken the isolationist position came in October 1941 with the publication of "Air Power Ends Isolation" in *The Atlantic Monthly* (now *The Atlantic*). Founded in Boston in 1857 by a group of writers that included Harriet Beecher Stowe, Ralph Waldo Emerson, and its first editor, James Russell Lowell, the cultural commentary journal appealed to America's intellectual leaders. De Seversky's article centered on a paradox. U.S. military leaders opposed isolationists politically but remained isolationists themselves in their military planning. High-ranking officers prepared American ground and naval forces for the archaic tasks of slogging it out in mile-by-mile combat over land and water to destroy navies and armies and to occupy territories. They ignored the new airplane technology that could wreak havoc on a country by flying over soldiers and warships. De Seversky went on to state provocatively that Secretary of the Navy W. Frank Knox and Secretary of War Henry L.

Stimson were America's foremost isolationists. "Self-consoling isolationist optimism," the Major concluded, "has no place in the modern world. Physical remoteness with all its attendant comforts and automatic safeguards, has been abolished."[19]

## Questioning Sea Power

In the June issue of *The American Mercury*, de Seversky attacked his mentor's favorite target, the U.S. Navy. The Major brought together ideas he expressed in various other newspaper and magazine articles to prepare "The Twilight of Sea Power." It irked the author that Congress funded a multi-billion-dollar program to build a huge, two-ocean navy. Construction would be completed in five or six years—"just in time," de Seversky wrote sarcastically, "to have all of its battleships scrapped." The war in Europe made clear that warships simply could not sail in waters controlled by enemy air power. The exception that proved the rule occurred in the Mediterranean Sea, where old-fashioned naval battles were possible only because of the dismal performance of Italy's warplanes. When Luftwaffe units came to Italy's aid, the situation returned to the normal pattern that banished warships under skies dominated by enemy aircraft.[20]

According to one of de Seversky's axioms, as aircraft range expanded, ocean areas open to naval activity would diminish until they disappeared entirely. The U.S. Navy, however, possessed half a dozen aircraft carriers and could argue its sea-based fighters would protect naval fleets against enemy planes. To this, de Seversky responded with his second axiom: land planes were superior to carrier planes. In 1941 there was some truth to the claim. The U.S. Navy's top carrier fighter, the F4F Wildcat, could not begin to match the performance of such contemporary land planes as the RAF's *Spitfire* MkV and Luftwaffe's Bf-109F. On the other hand, by war's end the U.S. Navy's F4U *Corsair* built by Vought Aircraft equaled the world's best fighter aircraft. The Major's better notion focused on the limited number of aircraft, generally under eighty, housed on an individual carrier. Also, a single, well-placed bomb on a carrier's deck could terminate the carrier's ability to launch or land aircraft. Thus even an aircraft carrier could not operate in seas within range of a substantial, land-based enemy air force.[21]

De Seversky's final axiom stated "*[t]hat only Air Power can effectively fight Air Power*" (emphasis original). If readers accepted all three axioms, it was self-evident that sea power was sailing toward extinction. Readers could then only nod their heads in agreement with the author that it made no sense to build for the future a large number of battleships at a cost of $100 million each. The sum for one capital ship could better be spent on building hundreds of long-range bombers. Each bomber could theoretically destroy or put out of commission an enemy's capital ship. More importantly from the prophet's perspective, the bombers could simply ignore and fly over an adversary's ships to pulverize the foe's homeland into submission. Fortunately for the Major's credibility, he did not advocate abandoning the U.S. Navy immediately. To the contrary, he accepted the absolute need for a transition period when both warships and warplanes would be crucial to U.S. security. He warned readers, though, not to continue to cling exclusively to the outdated strategy of depending on the navy for America's defense—to do so would be suicidal.[22]

## Substandard Military Aircraft

The same month de Seversky questioned the effectiveness of sea power, he also marked shortcomings in U.S. Army planes, which he wrote about for *Coronet*. A popular magazine owned by *Esquire*, *Coronet* resembled *Reader's Digest* in format and competed for the same type of readers. The Major's feature article, "Is America Flying Blind?," followed in the footsteps of Billy Mitchell by expressing concern over the quality of frontline warplanes. It should be noted that neither Mitchell nor de Seversky blamed American industry for the shortcoming. In Mitchell's time (circa 1920), Congress and the U.S. Army starved the air service and prevented it from buying new, high-quality equipment. In de Seversky's time (circa 1940), Congress abundantly funded the traditional armed forces, but the leadership treated aircraft as extensions of existing weapons and focused on numbers rather than performance. Unlike artillery, de Seversky observed, airplanes were both newer weapons and ones with constantly improving levels of effectiveness. They necessitated (the article's key thesis) new forms of administration under air-minded officers who exhibited the vision to seek the type of innovations that created combat planes superior to those of any potential enemy.[23]

What prompted de Seversky's article were recent press disclosures that the American frontline pursuit and bomber sent to England simply failed to measure up as combat aircraft. Clearly identifying the planes without actually naming them, de Seversky noted that neither the P-40 nor the B-17 could function in the European theater of operations. In the spring of 1941, Great Britain received the first of twenty B-17Cs from a cash purchase contracted before passage of the Lend-Lease Act. The authoritative *Jane's All the World's Aircraft* described the Flying Fortress as "just a huge flying target." Fortunately, the problem with the B-17, inadequate defensive armament, could be remedied especially with tail guns. Unlike the B-17, the P-40 never evolved into anything more than a second-rate combat plane. The first batch of 140 P-40Bs, designated by the British as Tomahawks, arrived in England beginning in April 1940. The RAF quickly concluded that the "model was unsuitable for combat duties." De Seversky in his *Coronet* article explained why. Compared with the Supermarine *Spitfire*, the P-40 carried six fewer machine guns, flew thirty miles per hour slower, and lacked self-sealing fuel tanks and appropriate armor to protect pilot and machine. In short, the Tomahawk was simply obsolete before it arrived in the British Isles.[24]

Meanwhile, in October 1941, de Seversky continued his criticism of the P-40 in "America Repeats Europe's Aviation Mistakes," another feature article published by *The American Mercury* and the last one he wrote in 1941. The P-40, or more specifically, its engine, came under fire in the fourth and last section of the piece. The powerplant was built by the Allison Engine Company, a division of General Motors. After five years of development, the Allison V-1710 produced only 1,150 hp, which allowed the 1941 P-40E to reach a top speed of 362 mph. At the same time, the United States could have availed itself of England's Napier Sabre liquid-cooled engine, which generated 2,100 hp. Placed in the Hawker *Typhoon* Mk IB, the Napier propelled the craft to 405 mph. When all was said and done, de Seversky believed his proposed U.S. Air Department, with a unified command under farsighted officers, would lead to quality equipment and the development of true American air power. In this piece, the Major all but placed a neon sign on the forehead of Gen. Hap Arnold blaming him and his procurement staff for the shortcomings in military aircraft. "The backwardness of our aviation, after all, was not due to lack of aeronautic brains," he claimed, "but the incompetence and limited outlook in high places. Many of the officials chiefly responsible are still entrenched in those places." De Seversky concluded his article by recommending a radical housecleaning to weed out the "inertia" and "self-interest" that impeded the progress of military aviation.[25]

## Pearl Harbor

De Seversky's October article for *The American Mercury* was completed in late August in time for editorial review and last-minute revisions before being printed during the early portion of September. While he participated in several radio shows, the Major stopped writing articles and, after August, devoted his full attention to completing his book-length manuscript for Simon & Schuster. The company expected to publish the work, tentatively titled "The Future of American Air Power—The Road to Victory," in January or February 1942. As the working title indicated, the manuscript was constructed around a discussion of the way U.S. military aviation should prepare for a future conflict. However, events intruded and powerfully disturbed the basic concept. The Japanese attacked Pearl Harbor on December 7, 1941, and suddenly the book's title and thesis changed from the tentative to the immediate, *Victory through Air Power*. De Seversky requested and received from his publisher additional time to revise, rearrange, and add new material to the book as his secretary, Mary P. Albert, was kept busy typing altered drafts.[26]

It was not de Seversky's fault that Japan clinched his judgment about the crucial nature of air power in modern war. Pearl Harbor certainly confirmed the vulnerability of warships in the face of coordinated and nearly unchallenged air attack. Enemy aircraft sank six battleships and two destroyers and seriously damaged nine other naval vessels, including three cruisers and three battleships. Naturally, most American citizens riveted their attention on the devastating blow to the U.S. Navy at a port in U.S.-controlled territory. President Franklin D. Roosevelt, however, in his next-day address before the U.S. Congress noted specifically that Japan also attacked on the same "date which will live in infamy" Malaya, Hong Kong, Guam, the Philippines, Wake, and Midway. The floor of the Pacific Ocean would soon be littered with the hulks of ships bombed or torpedoed by airplanes, including the British battleships *Prince of Wales* and *Repulse*. Moreover, air power proved key to the later success of Japanese ground troops as they descended upon U.S., British, and Dutch possessions in the Western Pacific.[27]

Five days after Pearl Harbor, Adolf Hitler and Benito Mussolini made a terrible blunder. Going beyond the requirements of the Tripartite Pact with Japan, Nazi Germany and Fascist Italy declared war on the United States. Their Axis Allies—Bulgaria, Hungary, and Romania—soon followed suit.

Since both the United States and United Kingdom then faced the daunt-
ing task of fighting armed conflicts on several fronts, Roosevelt, British
prime minister Winston S. Churchill, and their military staffs held joint
meetings in Washington beginning December 22. Numerous issues were
raised and addressed during lengthy sessions that ended on January 14,
1942. Three actions deserve mention. First, Churchill and FDR drafted a
military alliance, Declaration by United Nations, signed initially by twenty-
six countries, including China and the Soviet Union, on January 1, 1942.
Second, unlike the other signatories to this document, the United States
and Great Britain established more than a paper alliance by creating the
Anglo-American Combined Chiefs of Staff, which attempted, not always
smoothly, to coordinate military activity. Third, the two countries resolved
to contain Japan but first defeat Germany and Hitlerism.[28]

Churchill's and FDR's determination to give priority to the war in Europe
inadvertently helped de Seversky. The decision made the Major's book-length
manuscript after Pearl Harbor not merely salvageable but absolutely pertinent. His writings about air power before December 7 employed examples
exclusively from the European conflict, not the one in China. In addition,
his articles and radio commentaries were compelling to many Americans,
not to mention his book publisher, precisely because by the fall of 1941 it
appeared likely that the United States would go to war with Germany. Not
only had the United States extended Lend-Lease aid to Soviet Russia then
battling the Wehrmacht, but the U.S. Navy protected as far as Iceland British
convoys sailing across the Atlantic Ocean. As a result, an undeclared naval
war between Germany and the United States had begun, pitting American
destroyers against German submarines. The U.S. focus on Europe, rather than
Japan, sustained de Seversky's original approach to his book manuscript, in
which chapters were built out of revised versions of his featured articles. Not
only did the author acknowledge the fact, he also gained permission from
*The American Mercury*, *The Atlantic Monthly*, *Coronet*, *Reader's Digest*, and
*Look* (for his December 1940 piece) magazines to use updated renderings
of previously published materials. Appropriately, the prophet dedicated the
book to his ultimate source, the American god of air power—Gen. Billy
Mitchell.[29]

## Reflections

Alexander P. de Seversky possessed his fair share of strengths and weaknesses common to Homo sapiens. Perhaps one of his baser motives is embedded in the articles described in this chapter. The aircraft manufacturer-turned-commentator used his new position to get even with Gen. Hap Arnold. It will be recalled that de Seversky blamed Arnold for the loss of Seversky Aircraft Corporation. In his anger and disappointment, the Major overlooked the huge, multilevel military staff involved in planning and procurement. No single individual served as a gatekeeper to decide, for example, whether to end or extend the production of the Seversky P-35. And de Seversky never appreciated Arnold's effectiveness in his position as chief of the U.S. Army Air Forces.

The general, however, exhibited political skill in gaining resources from Congress and the president and in placing the air forces in the strongest possible position within the larger military establishment. By way of illustration, he formed a close and beneficial working relationship with Gen. George C. Marshall, U.S. Army chief of staff. Arnold also supported research to improve aircraft performance. He developed a long-term association with Dr. Theodore von Karman, America's foremost aerodynamicist and head of the Guggenheim Aeronautical Laboratory at the California Institute of Technology. Arnold's extremely important contribution to the success of American air power in World War II was his thorough understanding of all the support services, facilities, schools, personnel, and supplies required to maintain, equip, man, and fly military aircraft. He realized, for instance, that in wartime, U.S. production of aircraft had to reach a level capable of replacing 20 percent of all planes employed in combat each month.

As a result of understanding the nuts and bolts of air force operations, Arnold proved to be an extremely effective wartime administrator. Most importantly, as Dik Alan Daso has noted in his biography of the general, his private flaws matched Billy Mitchell's public ones, but Arnold "was far more politically correct than Mitchell" and hence more effective in developing the independent air force.

# 13

# Victory through Air Power

By New Year's Day 1942, the war front presented a grim spectacle from the American point of view. After Pearl Harbor and despite many hours of warning, the U.S. military in the Philippines under the surprisingly irresolute leadership of Gen. Douglas MacArthur suffered Little Pearl Harbor. Japanese aircraft attacked Clark Field, destroying on the ground sixteen B-17s, fifty-five P-40s, plus an assortment of thirty other military planes. Besides a number of frontline aircraft at other fields, the surviving aircraft available to the U.S. Far East Air Force were a few Martin B-10s, Douglas B-18s, and P-35As—all woefully obsolete aircraft whose very presence in harm's way served as tangible symbols of bad decisions and tight budgets. In some respects, Little Pearl Harbor proved more decisive than Pearl Harbor. The latter continued in operation under American control; many of the sunken capital ships were raised, repaired, and returned to duty. By contrast, Little Pearl Harbor established Japanese air superiority that doomed American ground forces and condemned the Philippines to occupation.[1]

The Japanese also used air power to strike at Guam and Wake Island. A U.S. Marine Corps VMF-211 squadron composed of F4F *Wildcats* protected the latter. Unfortunately, the bulk of the *Wildcats*, like P-40s at Clark Field, were caught and destroyed on the ground; others were victims of Nippon's superior A6M Zero. As it had in the Philippines, enemy air power aided the ground assault and occupation of these islands. Rising Sun victories in the Western Pacific had a direct impact on the application of U.S. air power in Europe. True, Gen. Hap Arnold promoted Ira C. Eaker to brigadier general and appointed him as U.S. Army Air Forces bomber commander in Great Britain in January. Eaker undertook the gargantuan task of setting up staff and facilities and organizing the Eighth Air Force with its prime mission of conducting a strategic bombing campaign against Germany. The catch? No one was eager to send America's long-distance bomber, the B-17, to Europe until America's long-distance war in the Pacific seemed containable.[2]

### Before *Victory*: Pearl Harbor and the Major

It was under these extremely dark circumstances that Alexander P. de Seversky revised and rewrote his feature articles in book form and added comment about U.S. losses to Japanese air power that occurred in December 1941. Obviously, the environment in which he wrote helped sharpen his criticism of the leadership, organization, planning, and procurement of military aviation. The prophet certainly had to modify over time his views about carrier planes and his prediction about when a bomber could fly round-trip across the Atlantic Ocean. He missed that mark by several years. However, his other comments about air power issues proved to be absolutely correct. December events in the Pacific verified the European experience—air power would be a key to most victories in the battles of war. Additionally, Japanese ascendancy in the air, not just British and Russian evaluations, painfully confirmed de Seversky's argument that the United States had to upgrade its military aircraft to successfully confront the air forces of Germany and Japan.[3]

In addition, deadly Japanese air attacks on American battleships at Pearl Harbor and British battleships off the coast of Malaya served to confirm the prophet's claim that aircraft had eclipsed and hedged naval operations. Only the presence of American air power or the absence of enemy air power enabled U.S. Navy vessels to anchor safely in harbors or sail the seas openly. Certainly, the war in the Pacific terminated the isolationist debate, but it also validated the Major's repeated arguments on the need to extend the range of military aircraft, especially pursuits. In terms of the latter, a battle-ready P-38F with a combat range of 425 miles would not be available until later in 1942. Only by the end of 1943 would external fuel tanks provide top-performing fighters, P-47 and P-51, the ability to accompany bombers on longer missions. The failure heretofore to employ fighter escorts on lengthy bomb runs led to frightful losses of enemy aircraft. Based on the notion of such early air power philosophers as Giulio Douhet, U.S. military air leaders continued to reassure each other by mouthing the unthinking incantation: "bombers will always get through." In the case of the Eighth Air Force, however, a staggering 3,908 bombers and their precious crews never came back.[4]

Finally, as de Seversky considered his feature articles for the foundation of his book, Pearl Harbor only confirmed in his mind the need for a U.S. Air Department to administer and merge the air forces of the U.S. Army, Navy, and Marine Corps. Shortly after the "date which will live in infamy," the Major gave an interview which was later published in *Who: The Magazine about People*. The periodical was one of many precursors to *People* magazine but with longer stories and fewer pictures. During the interview, de Seversky pointed out the absurdity of the artificial divisions in military aviation. On American territory of the Hawaiian Islands, the U.S. Navy had air bases at Ford Island and Kaneohe Bay, the U.S. Marine Corps parked their planes at Ewa, and the U.S. Army operated from Bellows, Wheeler, and Hickam Fields. Ignoring the marines, the army and navy air forces possessed especially a "different command, different training, different psychology, different equipment." Such fragmentation added nothing to the possibility of a coordinated American response to the Japanese air invasion on December 7.[5]

Interestingly, de Seversky communicated this and other air power concerns on a regular basis via letters or article offprints to the head of the Truman Committee. Senator Harry S. Truman (Dem., Missouri) chaired the U.S. Senate Special Committee to Investigate the National Defense Program. Political scientists generally recognize the Truman Committee, as it was universally known, as one of the most objective, respected, and successful investigative committees in congressional history. Established on March 1, 1941, the committee helped turn the national spotlight on Truman for his role as the no nonsense guardian over the costs, quality, and effectiveness of industrial goods purchased with the people's money for the nation's defense. By 1944 Franklin D. Roosevelt felt compelled to ask the Missouri senator to join the presidential ticket for the Democratic Party. The pair's victory followed by FDR's death on April 12, 1945, abruptly thrust Truman into the White House. While there is no immediate link between de Seversky and the committee's conclusions, the Truman Committee agreed with the Major's public statements that the lack of unity of command among the armed forces contributed to the Pearl Harbor disaster.[6]

## *Victory*

Right before Simon & Schuster released de Seversky's *Victory through Air Power* on April 20, 1942, he published new articles for *The Atlantic Monthly, American Magazine,* and *The American Mercury.* He also managed to place a piece in the *Sunday Magazine* of the *New York Times* one day before the official publication of his book. Coupled with his preparation of United Press commentaries and participation on radio shows, the articles by the Major built a foundation for a receptive audience in both the media and public. Moreover, a war event seemed to conspire to promote widespread interest in de Seversky's work. Two days before its general release, newspapers nationwide headlined in large, bold print stories on the use of American air power to bomb Tokyo. Initially, the news came from Japanese radio and lacked specifics. Eventually, Americans would learn all about the audacious raid against Tokyo by sixteen North American B-25 twin-engine bombers under the command of Lt. Col. (soon to be Brig. Gen.) James H. (Jimmy) Doolittle.[7]

Print and radio commentators quickly realized even before any U.S. government statement had been issued that army bombers could hit Japan only after being transported to within so many miles of the target by a navy aircraft carrier. In some quarters, it substantiated the Major's criticism of the military for not requiring the U.S. aircraft industry to develop and produce a number of different long-range warplanes. Thus de Seversky's relentless and controversial approach must partly explain why his articles, broadcasts, and now his book drew so much attention. Even the early favorable reviews of *Victory* focused on his hard-hitting narrative. "Angry Sascha" captioned *Time* magazine's article about the book. *The New Republic*'s Joseph G. Harrison concluded his review, "Perhaps no airman today has a more devoted following and a more bitter opposition than Major de Seversky.... Be that as it may, his book is interesting, provocative and instructive reading." Orville Prescott of the *New York Times* in an otherwise lengthy review managed to capture the book's flavor in a single phrase: "A more crucially vital subject has rarely been discussed with a more staggering array of authoritative facts and opinions or with more righteous wrath and controversial gusto."[8]

The contentious nature of *Victory* attracted the attention not only of reviewers but also their readers. Within days it became a best seller in New York and would shortly achieve the same status in major markets coast-to-coast. The brisk sales that kept the book among the top five sellers for weeks prompted the Book-of-the-Month Club to adopt *Victory* as its June selection. The club, however, took the extraordinary step of requiring the publisher to insert a four-page "Warning to Laymen" as a special preface for subscribers who picked *Victory* as one of their four annual book selections required to maintain club membership. The warning, of course, referred to the author's disquieting remarks that panned the leadership of the U.S. War and Navy Departments. Harry Scherman, the organization's president, who wrote the preface, did not need to be concerned. So many subscribers selected and praised *Victory* that the club decided to use it in a later advertising campaign to entice new members to join.[9]

### General Arnold and *Victory*: The Meeting

By the fall of 1942, over 400,000 books had been sold at $2.50 each, netting de Seversky close to $100,000 in royalties. While the book remained on best-seller lists for months, giving tangible proof of its popularity, it received a mixed assessment within the military and specifically from Gen. Hap Arnold, who was both chief of the U.S. Army Air Forces and deputy chief of the U.S. Army. *Victory*, though, was not the only publication flashing a negative spotlight on Arnold because of the shortcomings of the early P-38s, P-39s, and P-40s when measured against fighter aircraft of other countries. Much to his credit, the general got into the habit of inviting his critics to his Munitions Building office (the Pentagon was not dedicated until January 1943) so that he could point out that no pursuit could claim absolute superiority in all circumstances. Except for firepower, aircraft speed as well as maneuverability and climb varied with altitude and the use, or lack, of superchargers. Moreover, pursuits varied in the quality of their performance depending on their roles in attacking enemy ground forces, intercepting bombers, or counterattacking other fighters.[10]

Thus Arnold brought to his headquarters at different times in 1942 what he called the "worst offenders" among his critics: Geoffrey Parsons of the *New York Herald Tribune*; Tex McCrary of the *New York Daily Mirror*; and Alexander de Seversky, a freelance commentator. Conversations with Parsons led to Arnold going to New York and making a presentation to the editorial staff of Parsons's newspaper. "From that time on," Arnold declared proudly, "the *New York Herald Tribune* was one of the best friends the Air

Force had." When he talked with McCrary, Arnold did such a convincing job the journalist accepted an army commission and shipped out to England, where he prepared public relations materials praising the success of the Eighth Air Force. But with de Seversky, Hap struck out. The former aircraft manufacturer and experienced combat pilot knew as much or more than Hap did about the performance variables of warplanes. When the general asked the Major what he should be doing differently, de Seversky appeared "shocked." *Victory's* author needed a week or more to think that question over according to Arnold. He noted de Seversky never returned. From this he reached the interesting, perhaps even rosy, conclusion that "[c]onstructive criticism was certainly hard to get in those days."[11]

There is, however, more to this account. Sasha and his wife, Evelyn, not only owned a mansion on Long Island and an apartment on Manhattan, they also kept in this period an apartment in Washington. De Seversky frequented the capital and shared meals with friends and associates, especially air officers he had known, in some cases, for twenty years. Perhaps inadvertently, these officers supplied him with insider information on aircraft development and the war's progress. Two enduring acquaintances were Brig. Gen. (later, Maj. Gen.) Harold L. George and Brig. Gen. (later, Maj. Gen.) Laurence S. Kuter. Both belonged to the camp of officers who believed de Seversky, despite his criticisms, correctly championed the quest for air power and an independent air force. These two men were the ones who convinced Arnold he should meet with and try to convert de Seversky into a personal ally. When Arnold agreed to the suggestion, he tapped George to make the initial contact with his sharpest critic.[12]

It only made sense. George had known de Seversky since 1921, when the Major served as consulting engineer to Gen. Billy Mitchell. At that time, George flew one of the bombers that sank the *Ostfriesland* via the water-hammer technique recommended by de Seversky. Later, George became director in the 1930s of the Department of Air Tactics and Strategy at the Air Corps Tactical School housed at Maxwell Field. In this period, he emerged as a strong advocate for defeating a future enemy by sending massive bomber formations to attack the opponent's homeland. After a stint commanding the only B-17 unit in the air corps, George ended up in the Munitions Building as an assistant chief of staff. In July 1941 Arnold appointed Lieutenant Colonel George to head the Air War Plans Division (AWPD).[13]

Two important elements clarify the background scenario to the Arnold–de

Seversky meeting. First, the AWPD project allowed George to approach membership in Arnold's inner circle, which included such notable general officers as Ira C. Eaker, Carl A. (Tooey) Spaatz, and George C. Kenney. Arnold would soon appoint George to head Air Transport Command. Second, this Arnold advisor contacted de Seversky just a few days after the crucial Battle of Midway on June 4, 1942. Although technically a naval clash between Japanese and American forces, the opposing ships did not engage each other. The battle was waged exclusively by aircraft. Specifically, the United States enjoyed victory primarily because Douglas SBD Dauntless dive-bombers sank four Japanese aircraft carriers. In the short term, Japan lost its platforms to project air power against U.S. forces on land and sea around Midway Island; in the long term, the battle reversed the course of the Pacific War by ending Japan's ability to conduct offensive operations.[14]

But Midway proved to be a disaster from Arnold's perspective. The Seventh Army Air Force had a Midway detachment of B-17Es. Nine bombers of the 431st Bombardment Squadron located Japanese transport ships over 500 miles west of Midway. The squadron dropped from altitude thirty-six 600-pound bombs but scored zero hits. A second mission the following day against Japan's carrier strike force produced the same results. As might be expected, U.S. Navy staff officers clobbered Arnold with their comments. After all, the initial argument used by the air corps in the 1930s to develop a large, long-distance bomber centered on the plane's ability to protect the United States and its territories against enemy ships. In Arnold's mind, however, the B-17s failed because the U.S. Navy refused to share their 1,000-pound bombs with the army. The more powerful ordnance might have destroyed Japanese ships through the water-hammer effect. Hence when Arnold talked with George about setting up a meeting with de Seversky, he let his guard down by also expressing his anger with the navy and frustration with military politics caused by the air force link to the army. Deputy chief to General Marshall, Arnold had to check his true feelings about the seaborne service in the midst of war.[15]

Thus after a brief telephone call, George came over to de Seversky's Washington apartment and talked with him about a meeting with Arnold. He received the Major's enthusiastic agreement, mainly because George read Arnold as holding identical views with the Russian-American, that is, a degree of antipathy toward the navy and support for an autonomous air force. On this basis, de Seversky immediately accompanied George to the Munitions Building, where they met Kuter before the three men entered Arnold's office. But by the time Arnold and the Major greeted each other, the air forces chief had regained his normal politician's composure of mouthing cooperation with the navy and reserving discussion of an independent air force for the postwar era. Small wonder Arnold observed de Seversky as in a shocked state. The Major turned down Arnold's offer to be de Seversky's pipeline for information on the war. He also turned down Arnold's request for a list of air force errors, saying,

> Harold George told me you brought me in here because you were incensed over the Battle of Midway, and you wanted to fight for an independent Air Force, and you wanted my assistance. I am perfectly willing to play ball with you along these lines. But I will not write you any essays on your judgment of what you have done, what you didn't do. This is not my job. If I have something, I will tell it to the American people.[16]

### General Arnold and *Victory*: The Counterattack

According to de Seversky, Arnold then shouted, "I want this list. When you have this list, I will see you again." At that point, the amputee got up and limped out of the office. Arnold did, in fact, see the Major again but three years later in another country and without receiving the infamous list. Meanwhile, the air forces chief was so upset with *Victory* and de Seversky's articles that he contacted Col. Arthur I. Ennis, director of the Army Air Forces Division, War Department Bureau of Public Relations (AAFPR). Based on the suggestion from Arnold, Ennis worked out a strategy to discredit de Seversky. Ennis, though, had to be remarkably circumspect in his approach. De Seversky did not simply have numerous acquaintances in the army air forces. Several high-ranking officers endorsed the prophet's views; among them were Frank M. Andrews, future head of U.S. Army Air Forces in Europe; William E. Keppner, head of the Eighth Air Force Fighter Command; Hugh J. Knerr, future head of Eighth Air Force Service Command; and Claire L. Chennault, head of the U.S. Army Air Forces in China.[17]

As a result, the AAFPR wisely chose not to issue any comment or materials directed against the Major. Instead, Ennis worked stealthily through third parties who were not active members of the air forces. Since de Seversky sharply criticized the P-40, its engine, and the military leadership for buying inferior technologies, the first attack came from the engineer who designed the P-40 and the corporation whose Allison Division built its engine. On August 22, 1942, Donald R. Berlin, an aeronautical engineer with General Motors Corporation, gave a talk that trashed de Seversky's book at the GM Institute of Technology. His presentation was excerpted and distributed widely as a formal GM press release. Berlin, future president of Piasecki/Vertol Helicopters, had formerly served as chief engineer of the Curtiss-Wright Corporation. In the latter capacity, he led the design team for the Curtiss-Wright plane that lost the P-35 contract to Seversky Aircraft. He also helped design the P-36 and P-40 that won military competitions and shoved the Seversky Company down the path toward bankruptcy.[18]

Describing de Seversky's book as "slightly entertaining," Berlin went on to state, "[But] it is time to call a halt to the comedy where the Chief of our Army Air Forces is singled out for attack because the Army Air Forces did not continue to order Mr. Alexander P. de Seversky's pursuit airplanes." The comment obviously struck a nerve with the Major, and it was not anywhere near his funny bone. Only one day after newspapers published Berlin's comments on August 23, de Seversky issued his own scathing press release. He claimed to be "horrified" by Berlin's charge and called it "childish" and "hitting below the belt." He went on to point out recent press reports quoting Americans flying British *Spitfires* against the Luftwaffe. These U.S. combat pilots expressed gratitude that they did not have to face German warplanes in P-40s. De Seversky argued that one can forget about the old rivalry between the Seversky P-35 and the Curtiss P-36: "The only competition that counts is our competition with the Axis." He wondered how Berlin's smear campaign against him improved the performance level of an inferior plane.[19]

On the other hand, the Major had to admit that

it is true that the Army master minds brushed aside my designs for longer ranges, greater firepower, heavier armor, higher operational ceilings. It is true that the prototype of the P-47, now belatedly advanced as the white hope of American fighter aircraft, was discarded when I pleaded for it years ago. In all these respects the war has justified my ideas. Should the fact that I was right seal my lips now, for fear that small-minded men might question my motives?

Indeed, the Truman Committee agreed with de Seversky in a July 1943 report when it rebuked the air forces for continuing to procure an outmoded P-40 at a time when advanced aircraft such as the P-47 and P-51 were being developed.[20]

Meanwhile, evidence the campaign continued occurred when advanced copies of two magazine articles ended up on the desk of General Arnold. Confessing insider information, David Brown published "Victory through Hot Air Power," a two-part article in *Pic* magazine, while William S. Friedman wrote "Listen, Major de Seversky—Wings of Victory" for *Popular Science*. Moreover, Arnold personally encouraged the efforts of Paul B. Malone. A highly decorated veteran of the Spanish-American War and World War I, Malone retired as major general and commander of the U.S. Fourth Field Army. In the late summer of 1942, he went after de Seversky on San Francisco's KGO radio. He also prepared a lengthy article, "Victory through Air Prophets?," that appeared in the November issue of *Skyways* magazine. As might be expected, General Malone was deeply troubled by de Seversky's assertions that neither the army nor the navy was as important in modern warfare as the air forces. Repeatedly, the retired soldier lamented the fact that the Major seemed willing to disrupt and question in the midst of war the valiant efforts of American land and sea forces.[21]

Disastrously for him, Malone made an awful gaffe that utterly destroyed the credibility of his article. He built his whole case against de Seversky around the premise that the Major had no military experience after his first combat mission, when he suffered the loss of a significant portion of his right leg. From this erroneous assumption, Malone could disparage de Seversky's claim to be a military expert. Alexander A. Toochkoff, one of the Major's commanders during the Great War, calmly and devastatingly corrected the "grave injustice" done by Malone's "unwarranted attacks" against the "brilliant career" of de Seversky in a letter published in a succeeding issue of *Skyways*. Toochkoff confirmed the amputee heroically returned to battle and became an ace pilot who flew numerous combat missions. Indeed, for his bravery and aerial victories he was awarded every decoration Imperial Russia could bestow on a naval aviator. De Seversky's expertise in combat was supplemented by a thorough grounding in military studies as he had graduated from the Imperial Russian Naval Academy and took advanced courses on warfare from both the Russian Army and Navy. Finally, Toochkoff reminded Malone that de Seversky's stunning military career led to his promotion as lieutenant commander and assignment as chief of Russian Naval Aviation in the Baltic theater of war at the young age of twenty-three.[22]

The anti–de Seversky campaign promoted by Arnold proved to be curiously modest and totally ineffectual. At the same time, America's best-known historian, Charles A. Beard, described *Victory through Air Power* as the nation's most significant book on the war, and the country's most famous racing pilot, Col. Roscoe Turner, credited the Major's critique of U.S. military aircraft for the subsequent improvements in war planes. "Let's have," Turner pleaded, "more of this kind of criticism." If anything, within a year of the campaign's start in August 1942, the Major became more widely known by the general public, more favorably received by print and broadcast media, and more genuinely appreciated in the highest echelons of the Roosevelt administration. Certainly, a big reason for the continued influence and success of de Seversky was linked to the fact that Walter E. Disney read a copy of the Major's book immediately after its release by Simon & Schuster. In the words of one of his biographers, Disney was "overwhelmed by the logic of the 1942 book."[23]

## Walt Disney's *Victory through Air Power*

Walt Disney telegraphed his New York representative to secure the Major's telephone number and mailing address. Soon de Seversky's secretary, Miss Albert, walked into his office and told her boss that Walt Disney was on the telephone. The Major had never had any dealings with Disney and wondered why the creator (and voice) of the Mickey Mouse cartoons wanted to talk with him. "He explained," Sasha later recalled, "that he had read my book and since it dealt with the future, he wanted to animate the events yet to come which would lead to victory (in the war)." The telephone call resulted in a movie contract for de Seversky and a copyright agreement for Disney. Shortly after the Major gave a speech at New York City's Hotel Commodore on July 8 to help raise $4.45 million for the U.S.O. (United Service Organization), he and Evelyn traveled to the West Coast. They were accompanied by their dog, Vodka, as well as de Seversky's assistant, Alexander M. Pishvanov, who served as the majordomo over the couple's summer home and expressed his genius with wood. Besides furnishing the de Severskys' Manhattan apartment with his work, the Russian-American engineer built various wooden set pieces and models for the live-action movie scenes. Disney arranged for the small group to stay in a luxurious residence not too far from the Burbank studios.[24]

Over the next couple of weeks, Disney and de Seversky spent their most intense time together in the yearlong process of making the movie. "We worked," the Major remembered, "in his studio at Burbank, in my bungalow at the Beverly Hills Hotel, sometimes in restaurants, sometimes while driving to and from the studio." The crux of the whole movie production process occurred at the beginning. Bouncing ideas off each other, Disney and de Seversky drafted an elaborate storyboard. It proved vital to the creative efforts of the live-action and animation directors. In August, once an outline of the film had emerged, the de Severskys went home to their mansion at Asharoken on Long Island Sound to take care of personal affairs and participate in a benefit for the U.S. Army hospital in England. After their return to California in September, the Major assumed the role of technical advisor for the movie. He drew sketches of scenarios, airplanes, and maps that served as guides to hundreds of Disney employees: layout men, animators, assistant animators, in-betweeners, inkers, and painters who prepared drawings by the thousands for the camera.[25]

Considering the number of shorts being produced at the same time, the animation portion of *Victory through Air Power* moved along relatively smoothly and in timely fashion. The live-action portion, which was originally scheduled to take up one-third of the movie, caused problems. Shooting began on October 13 but had to be rescheduled for evenings only. Disney studios were close enough to Lockheed Aircraft Corporation that the rumbles of multiengine airplanes could be heard in the daytime even on the soundstage. At first, the live-action sequences were set up as a news conference employing four professional actors as newspaper reporters. They asked de Seversky scripted questions to elicit scripted answers that were then illustrated via animation. After a couple weeks of shooting, two shortcomings were observed when film rushes were viewed by Disney and his staff in a projection room. The press conference format put everyone to sleep and de Seversky's heavy Russian accent did not help.[26]

Disney dropped the four actor-reporters, moved the live-action scenes to a lecture format, reduced de Seversky's on-screen time to 15 percent of the movie, and employed the voice of a studio professional, Art Baker, who narrated most of the animations. In addition, he hired an elocutionist to straighten out the Major's pronunciation. Sasha and Evelyn went home for the holidays to enjoy the season, take care of personal business, and, for de Seversky, participate in radio shows. Meanwhile, Disney negotiated the film's release with United Artists, which had also distributed *Snow White and the Seven Dwarfs*. In January 1943 de Seversky worked with the elocutionist on the script. By the time Evelyn did a radio program with Cathryn Cragen on "Women in America," for WNEW, Los Angeles, on February 6, her husband was back before the cameras. The studio indicated the movie would be released in the near future.[27]

Then something dramatic happened to delay matters. Shortly before Christmas, U.S. Treasury Secretary Henry Morgenthau Jr. called Disney and requested an urgent meeting with him in Washington. The Treasury Department wanted Walt Disney Productions to create a cartoon before March 15 (then tax day) that would encourage Americans to pay their income taxes on time as a patriotic duty in support of the war effort. Disney had only two months to produce *The New Spirit*, starring Donald Duck. The pro-tax cartoon required 1,100 prints to saturate the U.S. movie theater market before the income tax deadline. Only then did Disney have a chance to review and ponder thoughtfully the studio's progress on *Victory through Air Power*. As animators returned to finish their work on the feature film, Walt critically examined de Seversky's filmed lecture. He felt uncomfortable. The new scenes did not seem much better than the old ones in the news conference format. Meanwhile, the Major was back in Manhattan attending a reception for Crown Prince Olav and Crown Princess Martha to raise money for Norwegian charities. He had thought his days as a movie actor were over.[28]

Disney, the perfectionist, had a different idea. He decided to reshoot the live-action scenes. Understandably, de Seversky at a much later point in his life glibly stated he had spent an entire year working in the Burbank studios. Walt hired H. C. (Henry Codman) Potter to be the new live-action director. A graduate of the Yale School of Drama, Potter had directed Broadway plays before heading for Hollywood in the mid-1930s. He would direct more than twenty feature films during his West Coast career. Two qualities endeared Potter to Disney. His recent films included *Second Chorus* (1940) and *Hellzapoppin* (1941), which gave him a reputation for being the master of movement. As importantly, he was an avid pilot who was well acquainted with the one actor to appear in *Victory through Air*

*Power.* The new director and the lone actor got along famously during the late May reshoot. In the hands of Potter, de Seversky would not be a stiff, unmoving lecturer. The moviegoer would be transformed into an invited guest to de Seversky's office, where the Major casually moved about while conversationally explaining and expertly illustrating his views on air power. Adroitly, Potter captured a relaxed, articulate, and authoritative de Seversky, whose expressive and clear voice charmed the moviegoer by its tinge of an exotic accent. Moreover, Potter's camera angles and careful timing erased the amputee's limp as the Major moved effortlessly about his office. The shooting was finished on June 6, but de Seversky stayed to do some radio work in Los Angeles while the film went through final editing and then to Technicolor for copies. In mid-June Disney threw a big bon voyage party for de Seversky and awarded the Russian-American a studio-made, winged Oscar for his role in the film.[29]

In July United Artists distributed *Victory through Air Power* to theaters in the United States. Some copies also went to England and Commonwealth Nations, though box office receipts could not be transferred in wartime. A short feature with a running time of only sixty-five minutes, the film, like the book, was dedicated to Billy Mitchell. It contained five animation sequences interspersed with four live-action segments. Besides introducing the animations and tying the film together, the latter segments stressed the importance of the United States controlling the skies, exercising air power offensively, and forming a single command over America's military air forces. The first animation, and the only one to be a true cartoon, gave a humorous history of aviation from the Wright brothers to the Douglas B-19. Despite the lighthearted tone, it emphatically demonstrated how quickly aviation technology progressed in forty years. Thus the first flight of the Wright Flyer was shown to be shorter than the wing span of the B-19. The remainder of the movie followed key portions of de Seversky's book. One animation, for example, illustrated the crucial importance of air power to the course of the war. It ranged from exploring the use of military aircraft in the German blitzkrieg and conquest of Crete to the Battle of Britain and Japan's attack on Pearl Harbor. Other animations persuasively showed air power flying over war vessels and ground forces to attack and destroy the enemy's industrial infrastructure and hence its ability to continue the conflict. The Major argued that the United States and Great Britain had the right equipment, such as Fortresses and Lancasters, to strike Germany's vital centers. But like the book, the film ends with de Seversky's notion that victory over Japan would best be accomplished by deploying large and numerous long-distance bombers to strike the archipelago from bases in Alaska.[30]

The most interesting aspect of the movie is not the material it covered but the subjects it neglected. The film made it very clear that ships were vulnerable to air attack; they needed an umbrella of friendly air power for protection. On the other hand, neither the animations nor de Seversky repeated the book's sharp criticism of the U.S. Navy's persistent love affair with battleships. Moreover, the Major made no negative evaluations of General Arnold or America's military leadership. Finally, not a word was spoken and not a scene was drawn about the mediocre performance of America's frontline military aircraft at the start of war. It was, of course, Walt Disney's decision to sanitize the movie version of de Seversky's book for practical reasons. Geography prompted the army to occupy portions of the Disney studios during the war, and most Disney wartime revenue came from the U.S. military. The father of Mickey Mouse and Donald Duck was not about to kill the goose that laid the golden egg.[31]

### Impact of the Movie

Obviously, a few leading members of the military did not know about Disney's practical nature. Fleet Adm. William D. Leahy, who was chief of staff to President Roosevelt, did everything in his power to prevent reels of *Victory through Air Power* from entering the White House. Leahy, who considered de Seversky a crackpot, feared the movie would suggest that either the U.S. Navy or at least its battleships should be scrapped. By the same token, Gen. Arnold, who viewed the Major as a spiteful enemy, initially refused to see the picture even after Gen. Larry Kuter sent him a note and a clipping from Hedda Hopper's column. Hopper, the famous gossip columnist of the Hollywood scene, argued that "every man, woman, and child in America" should see the film. "I do think," Hopper enthused, "'Victory through Air Power' is one of the most stupendous things we've ever put on the screen."[32]

Both Arnold and Roosevelt would see the film soon enough. Meanwhile, *Victory through Air Power* premiered in New York City at the Globe Theater on July 17, 1943. By the time United Artists distributed the picture across the country, ending in the West Coast in October, millions had seen the movie. At an average price of ten cents for children and twenty-five cents for adults, not enough millions had seen the film to cover all the costs for producing, copying, and distributing the picture in the United States; markets abroad eventually handed Disney a profit. Nevertheless, it had an impact among moviegoers and media. The *New York Times* called *Victory through Air Power* a *"tour de force"* and praised its technical "combination of ingenious diagrams, persuasive argument by de Seversky himself and tremendous sky battles as terrifying as Goya etchings." The *Los Angeles Times* felt the film would "jolt you off your comfortable spine"; and the *Washington Post* acknowledged "the experience of seeing it is too impressive to keep it to one's self." *Time* magazine described the mixture of de Seversky and animation as "unorthodox" but labeled it "an exceedingly potent instrument of propaganda for untrammeled . . . air power."[33]

As the movie starring de Seversky opened on the East Coast, it prompted a renewal of the call for an independent air force. The *Washington Post*, for example, published a front-page letter-editorial addressed to President Roosevelt titled "Give Air Power Its Wings." In addition, the film encouraged the War Department to announce that an unspecified number of superbombers were in the process of being delivered to the U.S. Army Air Forces. Staff writer for the Associated Press, Sterling F. Green, wrote that the "new dreadnought of the sky" had "a greater bomb capacity and longer range than any existing bomber." Philip K. Scheuer, a reporter for the *Los Angeles Times*, noted that the existence of the superbomber demonstrated "that the message of 'Victory through Air Power' is no longer a mere potential. It is being acted upon now." Naturally, the emergence of the Boeing B-29 heightened de Seversky's reputation as a prophet. True, his notion of using Alaska as a base proved erroneous because of distance and weather, but the end of his book and film predicted correctly that with a superbomber Japan would suffer massive destruction.[34]

Today, Americans who know something about World War II are likely to link the B-29 and the end of the Pacific War with the dropping of two atomic devices. The "massive destruction," however, described in de Seversky's book and depicted in Disney's movie actually occurred via air power and not nuclear technology. Beginning in March 1945, formations of B-29s dropped tons of incendiary bombs that utterly devastated sixty-six Japanese cities, including the capital. For example, on the night of March 9–10,

1945, a B-29 raid against Tokyo wiped out sixteen square miles of the city, razed 267,000 structures, killed or maimed 125,000 residents, and created a homeless population of one million. The level of horror, carnage, and destruction exceeded the effect of the atomic blast at Hiroshima. The U.S. Strategic Bombing Survey later discovered that the incendiaries, not two atomic bombs, made 64 percent of the Japanese people feel they were "personally unable to go on with the war" prior to the surrender. In addition to the bombing campaigns that reduced industrial production by two-thirds, B-29s also dropped mines in harbors as U.S. Navy aircraft and submarines sank 8.9 million tons of Japanese shipping. Blockade of the resource-poor archipelago left Japan without the ability to import the food necessary to sustain the population and the raw materials necessary to build or operate military hardware: oil, rubber, iron ore, coking coal, bauxite, manganese, chrome, nickel, cobalt, tungsten, tin, lead, and mercury. Except for senseless and bloody suicidal attacks, Japan was incapable of conducting a sustained military counterstroke against invasion.[35]

Besides demonstrating de Seversky's ability to predict how *Victory through Air Power* could be accomplished in Japan, the movie played a role in determining the course of the war in the European theater. On August 17, 1943, the Quebec Conference, code-named Quadrant, opened in the Citadelle with working sessions also in the Château Frontenac. President Roosevelt, British prime minister Winston S. Churchill, and their Anglo-American Combined Chiefs of Staff met to decide, among other issues, the timing of the cross-channel invasion of Nazi-occupied Europe. Unlike the British, the Americans wanted the invasion to occur sooner rather than later. Gen. Hap Arnold remembered in his autobiography, "At those meetings in Quebec behind closed doors, there were some very rough, tough sessions. Angry words were sometimes thrown back and forth."[36]

In the midst of these difficult sessions, Churchill turned to Roosevelt and asked him if he had seen the American movie that was then popular in England, *Victory through Air Power*. The president admitted he had not but agreed to get a copy. Arnold immediately contacted General Kuter, who secured a print in New York and flew it in a military plane to Quebec. Churchill and Roosevelt saw the film twice and then had it shown a third time for the benefit of the Combined Chiefs of Staff. Roosevelt was impressed by de Seversky's comments and excited by Disney's animations that demonstrated naval vessels being blown apart by aircraft. After the movie, it was decided that the final date for what became known as Operation Overlord would be determined by the availability of sufficient air power to protect ships and their precious cargoes of 132,000-plus soldiers and war materiel as they crossed the English Channel. Thus on D-day June 6, 1944, Allied Supreme Commander Dwight D. Eisenhower had access to 13,195 aircraft of which 8,000 served as a virtually impenetrable shield over the Normandy invasions. The Luftwaffe made only a token appearance.[37]

## Reflections

The narrative for this chapter includes a quote from de Seversky that is controversial. It is found within his response to Donald Berlin's critique of *Victory through Air Power* and its author. In essence, in 1942 the Major claimed that he had pleaded with the air corps "years ago" to put a prototype of the P-47 in production. Keep in mind that he had lost his company in 1939; the P-47 was designed in 1940, flew in May 1941, and entered production in March 1942. Surely, one must wonder why the Major made such a seemingly outlandish claim. The notion emerged full blown as a factor in his lawsuit against Republic Aviation. Since the matter was settled out of court, his claim should probably fall somewhere under the category of the proverbial footnote to history. Nevertheless, he earnestly believed he had designed one of America's best fighter aircraft of World War II. The foundation for this belief was built on airplane genealogy. The family lineage among the SEV-3, BT-8, P-35, P-43, and P-47 was clearly evident. And chapter 7 makes it abundantly clear that de Seversky served as chief engineer for the SEV-3. That aircraft was his baby from first to last. Not only did he personally engineer portions of that plane, he established the amphibian's innovative (for 1931) parameters: monowing, all-metal, radial engine, NACA cowl, cantilevered wing, and monocoque fuselage.

On top of this foundation, de Seversky planned and then supervised much of the construction for the AP-4 in 1938. It will be recalled from chapter 10 that the AP-4 served as the prototype for the military P-43 *Lancer*. Anyone who has seen the *Lancer* and the P-47 *Thunderbolt* will understand that outwardly the P-43 is not the "father" of the P-47 but rather the identical twin who had an unfortunate diet deficiency and suffered stunted growth. In engineering terms, however, the two airplanes were not twins but very distant cousins. And they had to be. The R1830, 1,200 hp *Lancer* engine was replaced by a huge R2800, 2,000 hp powerplant in the *Thunderbolt*. As a result, the P-47 airframe had to be totally redesigned from one end to the other—the fuselage was nearly eight feet longer and the wing span was almost five feet more than the P-43. The big engine required double the fuel tankage. It also used a four-bladed, twelve-foot diameter propeller, which forced the creation of an unusual landing gear system that extended the main wheels nine inches after being released from the wing cavity to provide clearance for the blades. Add four more machine guns to the P-43's four and the *Thunderbolt*'s empty weight almost doubled the *Lancer*'s; yet the P-47's maximum speed, 433 mph at 30,000 feet, was 77 mph faster than the best speed of the P-43. One can acknowledge de Seversky and his SEV-3 for the elliptical wings and deep fuselage that characterized the *Thunderbolt*, but P-47 historians are correct in crediting Republic Aviation's chief engineer, Alexander Kartveli, with designing the P-47.

# 14

## The Prophet at Home
## and Abroad

Near the time when the movie *Victory through Air Power* opened in New York City, Walt Disney, wife Lillian, and daughters Diane and Sharon stayed for several days at the de Seversky mansion on Long Island Sound. Alexander and Evelyn de Seversky often had company at what they considered their summer home. Because the pair participated in so many functions in the city, the rest of the year was spent mainly at their Central Park South apartment. The Long Island Railroad, however, made it easy for them to commute to their stand-alone residence whenever they had a free weekend. Obviously, their neighbors in Asharoken saw the Major enough times or at least appreciated his fame enough to elect him mayor of the village at war's end. It was more honor than office. Besides the Disneys, another summer guest in 1943, and one who came every summer, was Nicholas, the son of Alexander Pishvanov, who supervised the domicile and servants in the absence of the owners. The rest of the time, Nick lived north of the city near the Catskills on a farm with his grandmother and step-grandfather and attended school in Livingston Manor.[1]

### Wartime Activities

"Uncle" Sasha and "Aunt" Evelyn treated Nick like the son they never had. Thus the highlight of the youth's school year was to spend his Christmas vacation in the city and be pampered and peppered with gifts by the de Severskys. The interesting arrangement for Pishvanov's son emerged from the fact that the father did not remarry until the late 1950s. Moreover, as

Sasha's friend and assistant, Pishvanov had to be prepared to go on a trip or commute to the city at a moment's notice, leaving his son without a parent if he had lived with his father. Summers, however, brought every-one together in a relaxing environment for nearly three months. Summers also gave Pishvanov the chance to enjoy his favorite hobby. He cultivated and planted two vacant lots next to the house to produce an abundance of fresh vegetables and flowers to the delight of neighbors, the de Severskys, and any guests who stayed with them. He also maintained a fully equipped workshop that allowed him to repair or make almost anything whether in wood or metal.[2]

After gasoline rationing went into effect in seventeen eastern states on May 14, 1942, nonessential vehicles were limited to two or three gallons of fuel a week. The maximum allotment for essential vehicles was six gallons. Pishvanov responded to this necessary wartime restriction by making and adding a large rectangular container to a three-wheeled Cushman motor scooter. He could then ride the modified, gas-efficient scooter as often as he wished to the nearby town of Northport, where he picked up food and supplies for the house. The round-trip was approximately six miles. In summers, he actually began each day by going to town for newspapers for Sasha and Evelyn and any guests they might have. During the visit by the Disney family, Pishvanov plopped his son and Disney's daughters—their ages ranged from seven to ten—in the large container for the short ride to Northport. Though squeezed together, the children relished the excursion. After picking up newspapers, he treated the children to breakfast at the popular Peter Pan Diner.[3]

During the day, the three families spent quite a bit of time outside the waterfront home and by the shore. Walt Disney joined in the fun, but he also put in some work reviewing a script in the house. While Evelyn and Lillian watched the children splashing about the water, the Major and his assistant fished. The fact that de Seversky surrounded himself with Russian-American friends, such as Pishvanov and Alexander A. Toochkoff, helps explain why he carried with him a strong Russian accent throughout his life. Later, Nick fondly remembered the Disney family visit and especially the creator and voice of Mickey Mouse. "Walt Disney," he recalled, "was a most engaging person with a wonderful sense of humor. . . . We had an intercom from the house to the beach and you could count on Walt broadcasting various hilarious announcements from time to time." If de Seversky and Pishvanov caught bluefish, the Major cooked supper. Afterward, he strapped on his accordion and provided the evening's entertainment by playing and singing songs his father made popular in Imperial Russia thirty-five years earlier.[4]

Besides the de Severskys and Pishvanovs, the home had one other resident cherished by all—Vodka, the silky-haired cocker spaniel. Evelyn and Sasha had acquired the dog in the days when the SEV-3 was being designed in 1931. Vodka soon shared the cockpit with the de Severskys and became the Major's copilot for all of his record flights and air shows. As a result, the dog shared the spotlight and appeared in newsreels, magazines, and newspapers to become a nationally recognized celebrity. He showed up in one iteration of Disney's *Victory through Air Power*. Even though he failed to make the theater version of the movie, his owners claimed that Vodka supervised the film's production and made friends with one of Disney's cartoon stars, Pluto. During a Cleveland Air Show of the 1930s, when he participated in a flight contest along with the Major, Vodka was asked to say a few words to the multitudes on alighting as victor. The dog graciously consented to bark his greetings into a microphone.[5]

Vodka enjoyed a long, adventuresome life and passed away at the ripe old age of sixteen. Before then, the dog racked up over 2,000 hours of flight time making him one of the more experienced flyers in America. The war, however, interrupted his aviation career. Civilians could no longer fly for fun, contests, or records. In addition, since his owner lost access to advanced military aircraft, Vodka could only watch as his and the Major's flight accomplishments were surpassed: a North American P-51 would soon break their 1937 record flight from Havana to Washington, a Lockheed P-80 would cancel their 1938 record flight from New York to Washington, and a Lockheed P-2 would erase their 1938 record flight from New York to Burbank, California. The war, in fact, left the family, both pilots and their dog, without even an airplane.[6]

The U.S. War Department's Office of Military Director of Civil Aviation pressed many airplane owners to contribute their aircraft for military use. Fortunately, owners were compensated under a generous government appraisal formula. As it turned out, the de Severskys had an airplane prized by the military as a liaison aircraft for transporting high-ranking officers and War Department officials. Over the telephone on June 2, and by letter contract on June 24, 1942, the Major agreed to transfer the family's Beechcraft Model D17R. It was popularly called the Staggerwing because of the unusual negative configuration of the biplane's wings. Designed in 1932 by Theodore A. Wells for Beech Aircraft Company, the Staggerwing and later variants have been described by more than one aficionado as the most exquisite planes ever built. Contemporaries marked it as the flying equivalent to the luxurious Duesenburg automobile. The single-engine beauty carried a pilot and four passengers in comfort and style. With a speed in excess of 200 mph and a range of 1,000 miles, the D17R flew faster and farther than the standard commercial airliner of the day, the Douglas DC-3. The military paid the de Severskys $16,675 for the plane, which was not that far removed from its 1940 list price.[7]

There were other ways Sasha and Evelyn contributed to America's war effort. They were generous with their time and talents in supporting charities and programs often related to the global conflict. After they sold their plane to the military, Evelyn applied for membership in the Civil Air Patrol to serve as a pilot courier, chauffeuring officers and transporting documents or materiel for the army. In interview articles published by the *New York World Telegram* and Associated Press, she revealed that she did not follow the Amelia Earhart stereotype of wearing slacks and helmet when flying. To the contrary, Evelyn's flying attire consisted of attractive dresses that accompanied and accentuated her well-groomed hair and immaculate makeup. Such qualities elevated her to America's most glamorous sportswoman according to journalists Mary Anderson and Willa Martin. Besides attending functions with her husband, Evelyn participated singly in benefits for the city's United Neighborhood Houses and the Russian War Relief Society. The latter gained $6 million to purchase medical supplies for Russian war victims.[8]

Evelyn's husband, meanwhile, served several groups supporting war bond drives. He also joined the Executive Committee of the Legion for American Unity. He worked alongside such distinguished immigrants as lawyer and diplomat Henry Morgenthau, whose son, Henry Morgenthau Jr., headed the U.S. Treasury Department from 1934 to 1945. Like the Russian-American, other members were naturalized U.S. citizens who crusaded against ethnic and religious bigotry in contradistinction to America's fascist enemies. Perhaps most effectively, de Seversky donated his speaker skills and fame to benefit several organizations. For example, he gave an informative talk on war developments to members of the business and professional communities in midtown Manhattan as part of the half-century tradition associated with the Town Hall program. Moreover, along with actress Tallulah Bankhead and journalist-author William L. Shirer, he headlined a rally at the Waldorf Astoria for Freedom House. Founded in 1941 by Eleanor Roosevelt and Wendell Willkie, Freedom House advocated democracy and human rights in a world besieged by dictatorship and tyranny. Finally, the Major shared the speaker's podium with Joseph E. Davies, former U.S. ambassador to Soviet Russia, at a United Nations Victory Rally in White Plains, New York. Sponsored by the Westchester lodge of B'nai B'rith, the rally attracted an audience of three thousand that donated funds to ten Allied agencies.[9]

De Seversky could and did offer a very special and very personal service to those war heroes returning home minus a limb. In the spring of 1944, he wrote an extraordinary autobiographical article for those men, but targeted to their wives, mothers, and sisters. "I Owe My Career to Losing a Leg" appeared in the May 1944 issue of *Ladies' Home Journal*. The Major admitted that when he first lost his leg in World War I combat, his thoughts turned to despair. He soon learned, however, the loss of one faculty can be quickly replaced by the development of others. He wrote,

> I mean, quite literally, that my bodily disability awakened powers and aptitudes within me which were dormant. It focused mental energies which otherwise would probably have been dissipated. It enforced invaluable habits of caution and studious interests that would have escaped me had my limbs been intact.

In the article, he went on to explain in detail how his apparent disability helped him become a better combat pilot, inventor, airplane designer, writer, and student of aerial warfare. He even suggested the loss of his leg enabled him to succeed in romancing his bride, a professional dancer who admired his courageous efforts to become a decent ballroom partner. The article garnered such favorable national attention that the U.S. Army Signal Corps Photographic Center decided to briefly resurrect de Seversky's role as a "movie star." In the summer of 1944, he appeared in the army short, *Swinging into Step*, a film designed to build hope and confidence in combat amputees.[10]

Besides the army film, memberships in several organizations, and speaking engagements before different associations, de Seversky prepared, with the help of his new secretary Anita Yale, a significant quantity of correspondence. The book, movie, and articles generated as a matter of course numerous letters. In addition to fans, critics, publishers, and politicians, he kept in touch with American air officers, including Gen. Frank M. Andrews and Gen. Carl A. (Tooey) Spaatz. He also exchanged letters with various acquaintances in England, such as Lady Dorothy Beatty, RAF Wing Commander James G. Findlayson, RAF Air Chief Marshal Sir Arthur (Bomber) Harris, and Aircraft Production Minister Lord Brabazon of Tara. The Major, of course, had many acquaintances in the city's Russian community, but he also corresponded with an old family friend in Connecticut, Igor I. Sikorsky, who had moved from building flying boats to designing helicopters. The two men, both Russian-born aviators and inventors, were often confused in the media. When a *New York World Telegram* reporter asked his views on the frequent mix-up, Sasha could only laugh and joke: "Why straighten it out? Sikorsky gets credit for my work. I get credit for his. Two hundred per cent for each!"[11]

The quip for the newspaper displayed a sense of humor that also enlivened his public speeches and radio programs. In terms of the latter, he briefly had his own radio show on NBC shortly after the publication of his best-selling book. Each Saturday night at 7:45, de Seversky presented his take on the *War in the Air*. Although he had to give up the program in the fall of 1942 because of his work with Disney, the Major's voice could be heard on the radio from time to time on the subject of air power. His delivery and mannerisms became so well-known that actor Reginald Gardiner, famous for his movie and later TV roles as a butler, did a perfect parody of the Major during a Hollywood party at the home of Basil Rathbone. Gleeful guests, including de Seversky, found the impersonation an absolute delight. At home in Manhattan, de Seversky became a listener of, rather than a performer on, radio. In his den in the Central Park South apartment, he kept a shortwave radio and a recording machine to take down foreign broadcasts, especially BBC, that focused on war news.[12]

### The Syndicated Columnist

Shortly after his radio broadcast for New York City's WOR Forum on a separate air force on August 24, 1943, de Seversky received an offer from the McNaught Syndicate of wire services to prepare a column on air power that would be published three times a week in dozens of major newspapers. It would be one way to translate his fame from the book and movie into a regular paycheck. The Major, however, was under no illusion. It would be grueling to meet multiple weekly deadlines with a fresh and insightful column that often required considerable research. It would be the equivalent of preparing four or five major magazine articles each month. Since he received a check for $27,000 (today, $400,000) for his Walt Disney movie, Sasha and Evelyn decided to enjoy a break before inaugurating the column. They took a Florida vacation in September; it was their first real time off together since 1936. The couple could renew their relationship as de Seversky recharged his mind for the writing marathon to come.[13]

Back in Manhattan at the end of September, de Seversky began a regimen of life that lasted for one solid year. Like some other well-known Russians, including the infamous Joseph Stalin, the Major did some of his best work after midnight. Surrounded and inspired by a photomural of six Seversky aircraft in his den, de Seversky began a draft of his first syndicated column. Later that day, he took the draft to his Rockefeller Plaza office, where his secretary typed it up. He would then revise and refine the short manuscript to guarantee the narrative flowed smoothly and logically and stayed within the thousand-word range required by the wire services. Titles for the column were left up to individual newspapers though after time they generally employed some variation of "War and Air Power."[14]

The introductory column appeared on October 4, 1943. Considering how flush he was with cash from the book, movie, and settlement of the lawsuit against Republic Aviation, de Seversky may have told the truth when he stated he undertook the chore of writing a regular column as a duty. He earnestly believed Americans needed to understand the impact of aviation on the conflict. The air power angle influenced every battlefront as well as every discussion on how to shape and preserve the peace at war's end. The author lamented the fact that the United States lacked something resembling the British Air Ministry. As a result, American air power developed haphazardly among civilian elements and various components of the U.S. Army, Navy, Marines, and Coast Guard. One casualty was truth. Americans received news about the role of aircraft that was filtered by "Army and Navy minds." Thus the Axis defeat in North Africa was reported as a wonderful victory for Allied infantry, but without recognizing the role of aviation. Allied warplanes, however, had protected friendly troops and supplies as they had ravaged Axis soldiers and provisions. The victory was actually shared by both ground and air forces. "I do not for a moment presume," de

Seversky concluded, "that [my] dispatches can balance accounts as against the prevalent surface mentality and earthbound information. But they may help."[15]

Precisely because the exercise of air power occurred during every major battle, one could follow the course of World War II by reading the Major's column. His object, though, was not to give the reader a nice summary of war events but to focus on several basic principles: victory in warfare depends on air power; advances in aviation technology diminish the role of navies; air power radius must equal the battlefront's dimensions; aircraft quality, not quantity, enhances air power; and air power requires unity of command. In his last column, published September 29, 1944, de Seversky recognized that in a democracy the voters are ultimately responsible for national security. He hoped that by enlightening "public opinion on the implications of air power and on the decline of the functions of surface forces," the American people might support a strong, perhaps inclusive, administrative structure for military and civilian aviation.[16]

During the year when de Seversky prepared weekly columns, he had little time for anything else. It certainly became one of the reasons he decided to give up such a constraining obligation. He virtually ceased participating in radio programs and stopped writing, for example, feature articles for leading magazines. The lone exception was his lengthy piece for the May 1944 issue of the *Ladies' Home Journal*. He also managed to prepare three short essays for *The American Mercury*, where he had become a semi-regular contributor; however, the articles mimicked the subject and length of his columns. He also wrote a short book review for the Book-of-the-Month Club publication. Despite his grinding schedule, Sasha and Evelyn did manage to take a couple brief trips during his employ by the McNaught Syndicate. The Major, though, had to plan these excursions carefully by preparing in advance columns that were not time sensitive and made no reference to current events. Hence, he wrote summary or thought pieces about air power as well as a column about his mentor, Billy Mitchell, and one that celebrated the first flights by the Wright brothers.[17]

One of de Seversky's brief trips took him early in 1944 to Winter Park, Florida. There, Rollins College acknowledged him for his life's endeavor to promote air power as a combat pilot, inventor, manufacturer, and writer. On behalf of the college faculty and board of trustees, President Hamilton Holt awarded the Major an honorary Doctor of Science degree to recognize, among other attributes, his courage to say "the United States should no longer consider the airplane as the adjunct of the Army and Navy, but as a powerful co-equal with them." While similar accolades in the citation for the honorary Ph.D. were gratefully received by the Major, it could not begin to match the welcomed plaudits he received from military airmen. Except for Gen. Hap Arnold and his immediate staff, most air officers warmly endorsed de Seversky's work as a publicist and promoter of air power. De Seversky especially valued praise from General Spaatz. He later replaced Arnold and, in 1947, assumed the chief of staff post of the newly designated U.S. Air Force. Coincidentally, Spaatz became an air power columnist when he retired.[18]

Shortly after the German phase of the war had ended, when Spaatz served as commanding general of the U.S. Strategic Air Forces in Europe, his staff shared with him a file folder containing copies of de Seversky's column as published by the *New York Times.* In June 1945 Spaatz sent to "Dear Sasha" a letter praising the Russian-American:

> I have read what you have stated very carefully and feel that you have sensed in an extraordinary manner the basic ideas which were involved in the utilization of our air power at that time. It goes without saying that the primary task is to secure control of the air. . . . This, in the Air War over Europe, meant in concrete terms that it was necessary to destroy the German fighter force. Until that was secured, all other application of armed resources would have been ineffective. That you from a remote position could sense so thoroughly the essential facts involved in the application of our Air Power against Germany is to say the least remarkable.[19]

### De Seversky's Nemesis

Arnold's future replacement joined other air officers in applauding de Seversky's column, especially since the prophet discontinued any direct criticism of early fighter aircraft and air forces leadership. It is understandable that Arnold, and the staff who knew his views, held a different opinion. Unbeknownst to the Major initially, Arnold blocked de Seversky's post-column plans. At the beginning of August 1944, the writer visited Robert P. Patterson, undersecretary of war and future secretary of war (1945–1947).

Patterson appreciated de Seversky's column because it was less strident and more thoughtful than his earlier work. He listened receptively as the Major explained that he wanted to collect materials for a new book by visiting aircraft factories and air bases. But the official gave him the only answer he could under the circumstances. He had to be sure air staff officers such as those in charge of materiel and intelligence would permit a civilian to have access to sensitive plants and bases in wartime. After de Seversky left his office, Patterson sent a memorandum to Arnold on August 3. He explained to the air forces commander de Seversky's request and closed, "I am satisfied that a good and useful purpose would be served by his collection of the material, and I would appreciate your facilitating his trip in every proper way. Please let me know your views on the matter."[20]

Arnold asked Maj. Gen. Oliver P. Echols, assistant chief for materiel and services, and Brig. Gen. Thomas D. White, assistant chief for intelligence, to work up a response to Patterson's memorandum. Echols, who knew exactly what Arnold wanted, made a laundry list of reasons to deny de Seversky access to aircraft factories and air forces installations. White agreed with Echols and sent a confidential memorandum to Arnold on August 6 that summarized Echols's list and accompanied a draft response for Arnold to send to Patterson. The list included the fact that de Seversky was a "sensational and controversial writer" who had attacked in print air forces equipment, policies, and chief "prior to Pearl Harbor and shortly thereafter." Since Patterson clearly favored granting the Major his request, White's draft for Arnold's signature avoided any negative comments about de Seversky by focusing on the issue of consistency. Similar requests from well-known aviation writers had been turned down "because of the inconvenience which would be caused our contractors and installations with the result that production and training programs would be interrupted." White's draft, which Arnold sent to Patterson on August 10, concluded on a positive note: "At some future date his [de Seversky's] request could be reconsidered."[21]

Frankly, the columnist did not have much time to fret about this setback to his idea for a book. Once he finished his commitment to the wire services, he took on a couple of projects that kept him busy in the fall. He wrote and polished a lengthy keynote speech for delivery before a meeting of the American Engineering Association. His address later appeared as a feature article in the group's magazine, *The American Engineer*. De Seversky also joined Irving S. Olds, chairman of the board of directors of the U.S. Steel Corporation, and Harvey S. Firestone Jr., president of Firestone Tire and Rubber Company, for a presentation on the outlook for postwar industry at a dinner of the Economic Club held in the grand ballroom of New York's Astor Hotel. With the conclusion of these events in December, de Seversky contacted Patterson again. This time he hoped to gain permission to go to Europe as the war ended. He could see the effects of strategic bombing and investigate the wartime products of German ingenuity in the form of jets, rockets, and robot planes. For a second time, Arnold stepped in to smother de Seversky's request. It became clear that Arnold would never allow the Russian-American to gain any special access or favor from the air forces.[22]

Shortly thereafter, Arnold suffered a serious health problem that, nonetheless, lifted the barriers he had constructed around de Seversky. A smoker and an overweight workaholic with a family history of heart problems, Arnold experienced a serious blockage on the morning of January 19, 1945. After a major heart attack, he was carefully airlifted from Washington to the army hospital near Coral Gables, Florida. Because it was several years before the availability of bypass surgery, Arnold's condition kept him in the hospital for almost two months and on a restricted diet that featured daily salads. He lost weight, and doctors believed his body may have developed a natural bypass. As he gradually regained his strength, doctors kept him isolated from stress. It meant he did not see his staff members and he received no briefings until near the end of his hospital stay. When he did return to his office in Washington, five-star General of the Army Arnold certainly commanded the air forces, but all normal day-to-day work stopped at the desk of his deputy.[23]

### The Special Consultant: Europe

With Arnold out of the nation's capital and secluded from his office, de Seversky took this window of opportunity to resume his conversations with Patterson in February about a trip to Europe. The undersecretary obviously liked the writer and had a high regard for his publications. He secured Secretary of War Henry L. Stimson's approval to appoint the Major as a special consultant to the War Department; moreover, he won the endorsement of Lt. Gen. Barney M. Giles, deputy commander and chief of staff, who headed the air forces during Arnold's absence. De Seversky reported directly to the secretary or designee, but he was assigned to, and supported by, the Headquarters, U.S. Army Air Forces. The government contract of March 2, 1945, awarded the Major only a token salary of one dollar a day; however, the air forces furnished him all necessary transportation, food, and housing. De Seversky listed his specific tasks in his final report. The latter was issued on September 27, 1945, as a War Department press release by newly appointed Secretary of War Patterson. "My mission," de Seversky revealed in his report's opening paragraph, "was to study and appraise the role of Air Power in those areas of conflict in terms of strategy, tactics, equipment, operations, supply, scientific research and development, bomb damage, organization and psychology; and to render a report on my findings."[24]

The special consultant to the secretary of war left for Europe on April 5, a full month before the war ended, and he returned nearly five months later on August 28. During that interval, he conferred with numerous high-level military officers and civilian administrators and manufacturers who played a role in air power or aircraft development. To hold these consultations, de Seversky visited the Allied countries of Great Britain and liberated France as well as the neutral nations of Switzerland and Sweden. Naturally, once the war ended with the Third Reich's unconditional surrender on May 8, he spent most of his time in Germany. He visited forty towns and cities and flew over another seventy urban areas to witness firsthand the impact of American daylight and British nighttime bombing. De Seversky also inspected German aviation facilities and fields where he viewed and even flew advanced Luftwaffe planes such as the Me-262, the world's first jet aircraft to enter combat. Indeed, as a result of flying jet aircraft in both England and Germany, he became a strong proponent of replacing reciprocating engines with jet propulsion.[25]

Besides piloting German planes and admiring jet engines, de Seversky assisted in interviewing Luftwaffe leaders as well as German pilots, technicians, and researchers. In no sense were his personal observations built around the extensive and measured data collected by American teams for the U.S. Strategic Bombing Survey. Nevertheless, to a surprising degree, his views mirrored the results of the survey teams. When they differed with the Major, it had more to do with the way a particular issue was defined. For example, the survey concluded that air attacks reduced German confidence in leaders. The bombings failed, however, to impact morale to the extent of reducing efficiency in the workplace. By contrast, de Seversky believed air power did produce a serious morale problem. He focused, however, on the morale of industrial managers. They suffered frustration when forced to quickly disperse the manufacturing process after Allied bombers hit key assembly plants for complex machinery. Dispersal added time, fuel, transportation, and labor costs to a finished product.[26]

Of all the interviews de Seversky participated in, the most extraordinary occurred in Augsburg, Germany, on May 10, 1945, two days after the Nazis surrendered. One captive held in Augsburg's Ritter School by the Seventh U.S. Army was Reich Marshal Hermann Goering, former head of the Luftwaffe. The Major joined an interrogation team led by General Spaatz, commanding general, U.S. Strategic Air Forces Europe. Unit staff members included Brig. Gen. Edward Curtis, Brig. Gen. Paul Barcus, and historian Dr. Bruce Hopper. Besides a translator, the seven-member team also included Lt. Gen. Alexander M. Patch, head of the Seventh Army, and Lt. Gen. Hoyt S. Vandenberg, chief of the Ninth Air Force. In 1948 Vandenberg succeeded Spaatz as commander of the U.S. Air Force. During the two-hour interrogation, Goering was cooperative and forthcoming in his answers. De Seversky was not alone, however, in noticing that the Luftwaffe leader made empty boasts and self-serving statements. He frequently blamed Luftwaffe shortcomings on others especially the Führer, Adolf Hitler, who had committed suicide in his Berlin bunker days before Germany's collapse. Goering claimed, for instance, that he strongly opposed the invasion of Russia and that "higher authorities" often made basic decisions about the Luftwaffe's war role after 1940, when the German air force lost the Battle of Britain.[27]

During the lengthy interrogation session, Spaatz, Patch, and Vandenberg asked most of the questions. They covered many of the principal events and issues related to air power and the war. These ranged from the Battle of Britain to the controversy over area bombing versus precision bombing. As practiced by the British and Germans, area bombing was supposed to interfere with war production and lead to the demoralization of civilians. Neither premise possessed more than occasional substance. The only other team member to quiz the Reich Marshal was de Seversky. He asked a question about why tremendous resources were diverted to the development and manufacture of *vergeltunswaffen* (vengeance weapons). The Major noted the V-1 (robot plane) and V-2 (rocket missile) appeared at a time when the

Luftwaffe desperately needed expansion to defend Germany against the Allied onslaught by land and air forces in the second half of 1944. Goering could only agree. "Prior to the [Normandy] invasion," he replied, "the V-1 would have been effective. After the invasion, our effort should have been concentrated on the Me-262 [jet]. The decision on the V-2 project was made at higher headquarters [by Hitler]."[28]

The second issue that perplexed de Seversky was the failure of Germany to develop a strategic bomber, which led to this exchange:

**Seversky**: I know that four-engine Focke-Wulf planes were in production in 1939. When you found out, after the Battle of Britain, that your planes did not have sufficient fire power and bombing power, why didn't you concentrate on these four-engine planes as a heavy bomber?

**Goering**: Instead of that, we were developing the HE-177 and tried to develop the ME-264, which was designed to go to America and return. We did use the Focke-Wulf against shipping from Norway. Because our production capacity was not so great as that of America we could not produce quickly everything we needed. Moreover, our plants were subject to constant bombing, so that it was difficult to carry out our plans for heavy bomber production.

**Seversky**: The reason why I asked the previous question was because I wanted to establish whether you failed to build big bombers because you did not believe in strategic air power or because your productive capacity was restricted to the production of tactical aircraft for the Russian campaign.

**Goering**: No, I always believed in strategic use of air power. I built the Luftwaffe as the finest bomber fleet, only to see it wasted on Stalingrad. My beautiful bomber fleet was used up in transporting munitions and supplies to the army [of] 200,000 at Stalingrad. I always was against the Russian campaign.[29]

In his comments about the Heinkel He 177 *Greif* (Griffin) and strategic air power, Goering's response was half truth and half hokum. He subsequently admitted on June 29 in an interview with a team member from the U.S. Strategic Bombing Survey that the He 177 had terrible "bugs." When born in 1938, it was an orphan with little sustenance from the Luftwaffe hierarchy. It suffered engine fires, structural flaws, and repeated and unrealistic design changes. Thus it never had a chance to fulfill its intended primary role after production finally began in 1942. By 1944 it was grounded because it consumed too much fuel. Moreover, as Goering pointed out in the June interview, "the expenditure of material for one He 177 is the same as for four fighters." On the other hand, he was correct to lament its use as a transport to carry supplies to German troops surrounded by Russians at Stalingrad. Almost unbelievably, this large, four-engine plane with a wingspan in excess of 100 feet was also employed as a dive-bomber. Historians of the German air force know, however, the first Luftwaffe chief of staff Gen. Walther Wever promoted the creation of a strategic bomber fleet. His death in a 1936 air crash allowed the future Reich Marshal to bury the strategic bomber initiative alongside Wever. Goering favored larger numbers of smaller bombers that could assist ground forces. "The Führer," Goering said at the time, "will not ask how big the bombers are, but how many there are."[30]

Following the Goering interview, de Seversky remained with the Spaatz team of interrogators to question a series of Luftwaffe general officers who headed such units as engineering, quartermaster, and fighter aircraft as well as technical, flight, and flak training programs. Results from these interviews were incorporated in his final report. As mentioned earlier, he then visited German bomb sites and aviation facilities before deciding to conclude his European trip by attending the Potsdam Conference. American, British, and Soviet political and military leaders gathered in the Berlin suburb for their final wartime meeting, July 17 to August 2, 1945. Because of travel limitations and restrictions on accommodations in Potsdam, de Seversky had to make his plans with the air forces representative to the high-level meeting, that is, with General Arnold. In reality, details for War Department personnel going to Potsdam were in the hands of Gen. Joseph Cannon, commander of the Twelfth Air Force. Cannon, however, could not add or delete someone on his list of attendees without Arnold's approval.[31]

After his lengthy hospital stay, Arnold returned to Washington in mid-March and entered a series of frank conversations with U.S. Army Chief of Staff George C. Marshall. Among other subjects, they discussed Arnold's near future replacement. The top candidate was, and would be, Spaatz. Meanwhile, it was clear Arnold was in no condition to handle the stress of directing on a daily basis the immense staff operations at headquarters. With General of the Army Marshall's active encouragement, Arnold brought back to Washington Lt. Gen. Ira C. Eaker, who was then chief of Mediterranean Army Air Forces. The new deputy commander joined Deputy Commander

Giles in jointly serving as acting heads of the air forces. The team allowed Arnold to become, in essence, semiretired before his official tour of duty ended on March 3, 1946. Thus at the end of March 1945, Arnold, in the company of a medical doctor, could take a relaxing three month, April–June, therapeutic victory tour to the air forces command centers in both Europe and the Pacific.[32]

Barely had he returned from the Pacific when Arnold had to get ready for another flight to Europe, this time to participate in the Potsdam Conference. Surrounded by a capable and solicitous staff, Arnold would generally face activities no more stressful than ceremonial meetings and dinners plus an extensive tour of Berlin in Hitler's open-top car to view the results of aerial bombing. Surely, he would engage in serious discussions. Top U.S. officials met secretly to ponder the best target in Japan for the recently tested atomic bomb. Additionally, the Combined Chiefs of Staff (American, British, and Russian) held sessions related to the U.S.S.R.'s imminent invasion of Japanese-held Manchuria. The Combined Chiefs also reviewed a draft proclamation encouraging Japan to surrender. The Potsdam Declaration of July 26 was sent to Chinese Generalissimo Jiang Jieshi (Chiang Kai-shek) for his approval but was signed by U.S. President Harry S. Truman and U.K. Prime Minister Winston S. Churchill—shortly before elections replaced the latter at Potsdam with Clement R. Attlee. Officially, Soviet leader Joseph Stalin, who held innumerable titles, had nothing to do with the declaration since the U.S.S.R. remained neutral toward Japan until August 8. Regardless, Arnold departed Washington for Potsdam on July 11. Following a stopover in Canada to do some fishing, he and his staff arrived at Orly Airport near Paris on July 13.[33]

Although his father did not survive the war, de Seversky came to Paris to see his brother, George; half-sister, Nika; and his French cousins before meeting Arnold's party at the airport. He requested and was granted a meeting with Arnold at the Hotel Raphael, a stone's throw from the Arc de Triomphe. The general had to meet the Major because of his official position with the war secretary, but he actually looked forward to seeing de Seversky because he expected an apology for the attacks he had endured in print from the Russian-American. When it became obvious de Seversky wanted to go to Potsdam and had no intention of expressing his regrets, the meeting turned sour. Arnold demanded to know why he wanted to attend the conference. The Major replied that he hoped to keep track of what the

Russians were up to and had an advantage because he could speak their language. His response to Arnold led to this exchange, later recorded by de Seversky:

> Arnold says to me: "I'm not interested about Russia. This goddamned backward country will never amount to anything. We might as well forget about it. After I get through with the Potsdam Conference," Arnold said, "I have to go and lick Japan. That's my business. But the Russians, we can forget about them. They are never going to amount to anything. I'm not worrying about them." And I said: "I have a different opinion. I came from there and I know what the people are capable of, and I'd like to keep my eye on them." Arnold said: "Well, if you want to waste your time, go ahead and waste your time. Joe [Cannon], come here! Seversky wants to go to Potsdam, make arrangements."[34]

This terse and tense session in a foreign country was the last time de Seversky and Arnold would see each other. Ironically, the pair thought as one on the subject of how air power should be reorganized after the war. Nonetheless, both went to their graves with a grudge against the other. Arnold went first, suffering a fatal heart attack on January 15, 1950. Meanwhile, Arnold's claim that de Seversky's presence at Potsdam would be a waste of time came close to the truth. As the Major well knew and had commented in his column, the Russians were devoted to the Red Army and had discounted the importance of strategic air power. Their air hero in the Great Patriotic War was the Ilyushin Il-2 *Shturmovik* (storm trooper). The heavily armored plane often carried multiple cannon and bombs as well as eight 82 mm rockets. It was virtually a flying tank that destroyed or disrupted the German enemy in the path of advancing Soviet ground forces. Only near war's end did the Russians realize their vastly expanded power position mandated a long-distance bomber. As a result, they quickly copied and put into production a replica of the Boeing B-29—the Tupolev Tu-4. Finally, with Stalin nearby, no Soviet staff officer would dare make an unguarded comment to the Russian-American. De Seversky, though, did not waste his time entirely. Like Arnold, he saw the catastrophic effect of bombing on Berlin as he prepared an initial draft of his report for the war secretary.[35]

The report contained eleven main points. One of them, the effect of bombing on German morale, has already been discussed. The other ten can be divided into six observations and four recommendations/predictions. His observations were as follows: (1) As he had noted in his book, movie, and articles, air power was decisive in most land and sea operations. The key moment in the war arrived, as German commanders admitted to de Seversky, when the Allies gained air superiority during the first half of 1944 followed by air supremacy thereafter. (2) The American doctrine of daylight bombing proved successful but only when a fighter escort accompanied bombers. (3) Bomb damage was immense and forced diversion of German resources to repair, rebuild, disperse, and, ultimately, build underground sites to protect manufacturing processes. (4) The interrogation of German leaders confirmed that the Luftwaffe's loss of air superiority impeded Wehrmacht operations. Hence, the Major argued, Allied victory in the air defeated Germany. (5) Hitler's dictatorial government proved to be a major handicap. The tactical brilliance of the German army on the battlefield was nullified by Hitler's strategic folly. His government did not have to answer to public opinion and its war strategy froze as Allied strategy adapted. (6) And Allied adaptability was crucial because its equipment did not measure up at the start of war. In terms of equipment, de Seversky became the first official observer to state publicly that precision bombing was not so precise.[36]

The report also recommended or predicted the following: (1) "The Germans excelled," the consultant noted, "in aerodynamical research of high-speed flying, jet propulsion, the study of ballistics, rocket projectiles and synthetic fuels." De Seversky considered German scientific data and even scientists in these areas as prizes of war that should be acquired and exploited to America's advantage. (2) Congress and citizens needed to be educated to the fact that jet propulsion made existing aircraft obsolete. Thus the air force must discard current equipment and acquire this new technology that would lead to "revolutionary changes in aircraft design and performance." (3) De Seversky remarked that once radar went into use, jamming appeared to counteract it. Therefore the air force had to understand that U.S. electronic capacity should exceed that of any potential enemy. Indeed, future battles, the Major predicted, will be won by those who control "electronic space." (4) De Seversky was convinced that "the entire air potential of our country should be organized into one single military force to achieve unity of command in the air." The Major chose not to engage in the current Washington debate over the creation of a single department of national defense. Regardless, he claimed, "Air Power should at once receive recognition as a force co-equal with the Army and Navy with an autonomous organization and budget."[37]

A summary of the massive U.S. Strategic Bombing Survey that employed the services of 1,150 civilians and military personnel generally agreed with the report prepared by de Seversky as an independent observer. The summary first appeared several days after publication of the Major's findings and recommendations; only time, of course, would validate his predictions about a revolution in aircraft design and electronic warfare. Secretary of War Patterson received a preliminary briefing of the survey's conclusions, which only confirmed his earlier judgment that de Seversky would be a perceptive and articulate witness to the results of strategic bombing in Europe. Small wonder Patterson chose as one of his first official acts as the new secretary of war to have de Seversky's report distributed in its entirety through wire services to newspapers nationwide. In fact, as will be seen in the next chapter, Patterson was so pleased with the Major that he extended his role as special consultant. De Seversky would continue in that position for more than twenty-five years, though from 1947 on he served General Spaatz and successor chiefs of staff of the U.S. Air Force rather than the defense secretary.[38]

## Reflections

Carl L. Norden developed and manufactured the bombsight employed by U.S. strategic air forces. During the war, the press and even commercial advertisements praised the Norden device because it enabled U.S. aircraft at altitude to drop a bomb into the proverbial pickle barrel. It comforted many Americans to learn that the United States took the moral high road even in wartime. Precision bombing seemed to promise that only the enemy's military targets would be attacked while preserving the lives and properties of innocent noncombatants. Remarkably out of step, then, with popular opinion, de Seversky stated in his report that the "miraculous powers" of the Norden were a "gross exaggeration." Indeed, the Major was disappointed "by the comparatively small progress that had been made in this connection in the last two decades." To people in the know, de Seversky's criticism seemed like a self-serving comment. Two decades earlier, of course, he had designed the gyroscopically synchronized bombsight that evolved into the C series, which the Norden replaced in the 1930s. Despite his apparently gratuitous assessment of his bombsight competitor/successor, de Seversky was absolutely correct.

The Norden bombsight was only as good as the quality of the manufacturing process. Unfortunately, the rushed, mass-production techniques of wartime led to the use of materials and methods that caused friction in the delicate cogs, discs, and gears. The friction reduced the accuracy of the computations analogically accomplished by the instrument. Thus the serially produced bombsight was 5.6 times more inaccurate than its original specifications. Along with fallible bombardiers, bad weather, antiaircraft fire, and German fighters, the imperfect bombsight contributed to, for example, the mixed record of the Eighth Air Force strategic bombers. Seventy percent of the time they dropped ordnance more than a thousand feet from the target. As a result, some German factories attacked by U.S. bombers resumed full production in a matter of days. A true anomaly occurred in 1944, when the United States directed bombing missions against enemy aircraft plants. Despite such deadly attention, the German aircraft industry more than doubled its 1942 production to deliver 39,807 warplanes to the Luftwaffe. The U.S. Strategic Bombing Survey discovered that only repeated bombings of the same site gave some success. By way of illustration, the survey noted that the synthetic fuel plant, Leuna, finally had its production reduced to 15 percent of full capacity after being struck over time by twenty-four separate formations of U.S. and RAF bombers.

# 15

## The Prophet Challenged

Alexander P. de Seversky returned to the United States on August 28, 1945, to a warm welcome from Evelyn and Vodka, as well as to a grateful reception from Secretary of War–designate Robert P. Patterson. The latter soon received the major's revised and polished report on air power in the European theater. Once he read the report, Patterson was so pleased with the end product that he decided not only to share it with the American public but to ask its author for a repeat performance, this time in the Pacific theater. Thus, barely four weeks after returning home, de Seversky packed and left on September 26 for the Japanese archipelago. Flights were supplied by Air Transport Command, then under the leadership of Sasha's friend, Maj. Gen. Harold L. George. "My mission," de Seversky stated later, "was to observe and appraise the role of air power in the attainment of victory over Japan; to study the magnitude and character of aerial destruction; to study the air power, strategy, tactics and equipment of the Japanese." Naturally, he was also interested in comparing the impact of aerial warfare in Japan with what he had seen in Germany.[1]

### The Special Consultant: Pacific

In some respects, the Major's travels and interviews on the Japanese home islands resembled his activities in Europe and, specifically, in Germany. He consulted with numerous U.S. officials and military officers, such as General of the Army Douglas MacArthur, who led the occupation forces, and Franklin D'Olier, who chaired the U.S. Strategic Bombing Survey. Additionally, de Seversky visited on the ground twenty of Japan's leading cities, noting bomb damage in such urban centers as Kobe, Tokyo, and Yokohama. He also flew over dozens of other cities that had been assailed by B-29 bombers and noted the general pattern of destruction by U.S. ordnance. Finally, as in Germany and again with interpreters, de Seversky interviewed key figures among the Japanese, including Emperor Hirohito, revered by many of his compatriots as both god and ruler. Perhaps more importantly, the Major spent time with Lt. Gen. Saburo Endo, who had directed aircraft and engine production for the Japanese Empire.[2]

On the other hand, the final report of February 11, 1946 (released to newspapers for publication on February 19) differed in content and volume from the one about the European phase of the conflict. Various reasons explain the difference. For starters, it was longer and contained an additional sixteen-page supplement on the atomic bombings of Hiroshima and Nagasaki. Moreover, the bulk of the basic report explored a number of shortcomings and limitations to Japan's use of air power. The Major analyzed, for example, Nippon's failures to consider air power beyond support for surface forces, produce in quantity an effective strategic bomber, build robust and high-performing aircraft, form joint chiefs of staff to coordinate land and sea operations, avoid the horrible waste of suicide bombing, create larger bombs to destroy concrete structures and capital ships, and overcome the handicap of a totalitarian system that lacked the flexibility to alter outmoded strategic plans. Two other parts of the report were strikingly different.[3]

First, de Seversky openly rebuked U.S. military and political leaders for not giving the development of a long-distance bomber the same urgent attention and financial backing as the Manhattan Project, which delivered the nuclear weapon. Consolidated Aircraft Corporation had won the original design competition for the B-36 in 1941; however, the huge plane with a projected range of 8,000 miles received such low priority during the war it did not reach the production stage until 1948. By then, Consolidated had merged with Vultee Aircraft and adopted the truncated and unofficial (until 1954) name of Convair. Meanwhile, de Seversky castigated U.S. military policy in the Pacific theater as "a museum of lost aeronautical opportunities." According to him, thousands of American lives and billions of dollars in equipment were forfeited in the bloody and totally unnecessary effort to wrench from Japanese forces island bases close enough to the enemy's home archipelago to employ the much shorter-ranged B-29. The Major balanced his criticism by offering high praise to one official in the administration, his patron. Despite other military cutbacks following the end to hostilities, Secretary of War Patterson had endorsed the continued evolution of the XB-36 prototype that served as the template for the 386 intercontinental bombers subsequently built.[4]

The second significant difference between de Seversky's two reports concerned the influence of air power on the war's outcome. In Europe, commanders such as Gen. Dwight D. Eisenhower and Gen. Omar N. Bradley readily acknowledged the importance of air power in protecting U.S. troops and in disrupting, if not devastating, enemy operations. It is easy to imagine the horrible consequences for U.S. ground troops if the Luftwaffe had suddenly attained air superiority shortly after the Normandy landings. Therefore, it was not out of line for de Seversky to claim U.S. and Allied air forces made victory possible. This conclusion did not detract from the role of surface forces. Air power facilitated the brave work of Allied soldiers who gave their lives and blood to conquer and occupy the Third Reich. By contrast, the end to the Pacific war sharply differed from the European conflict. "In the Pacific," the Major exclaimed, "a complete victory was scored through the air, without the need for surface invasion and bypassing the enemy's immense surface forces."[5]

De Seversky's conclusion that air power alone beat Japan coupled with his slanted view of the U.S. Navy and enthusiastic support for the B-36 combined to elevate him to the role of public relations point man in the U.S. War Department's struggle with the U.S. Navy Department. At the end of World War II, the normal jealousies, sport rivalries, and funding competitions between the two military services ballooned into a major conflagration. The navy's admirals came to believe that if the army's generals reserved exclusively the strategic combat role to the air forces, the U.S. Navy's status would decline to the level of an auxiliary. As a consequence, its budget would be slashed and naval morale would tumble. Worse, and like de Seversky, most army air officers expected all military planes to fall under the command of a single air force. And, if possible, matters seemed even more ominous as army ground commanders, such as General Eisenhower, questioned why the navy should have its own army in the form of the U.S. Marine Corps.[6]

The U.S. Navy's dire concerns about its future help explain the great anomaly found in the summary of the U.S. Strategic Bombing Survey. Naval aviation had a very small role in the strategic bombing of Japan. Nonetheless, the survey's summary contained major naval-related subsections, such as "The Advance across the Pacific" and "Destruction or Isolation of Japanese Ground Forces." These and other navy-focused subsections, and the longer reports upon which the summary was based, emerged at the insistence of the U.S. Navy's chief representative on the survey, Rear Adm. Ralph A. Oftsie. Using the other side of the same coin employed by de Seversky, Rear Admiral Oftsie claimed that the navy and marines played a strategic role in projecting U.S. air power by leveraging from Japan island bases used by army B-29s for the actual strategic bomb runs. The War Department recognized naval contributions but accepted as the unvarnished truth the widely published conclusion of its special consultant about why Japan surrendered.[7]

## Atomic Bombs

Unlike the official bombing survey, de Seversky did not waffle. Air power won the war. And it was ended by two B-29s dropping one atomic device each on Hiroshima and Nagasaki. When these bombs fell on August 6 and 9, 1945, the Major was in England testing British jets and waiting for military air transportation back to the United States. He avidly read and listened to newspaper and radio accounts that led him to visualize, like other readers and listeners, the complete destruction of Hiroshima and Nagasaki in the twinkling of an eye. The image included the vaporization of people and buildings at ground zero, a shock wave that pulverized buildings and homes for miles, heat of incalculable intensity, and radioactive fallout from the atomic explosion almost as lethal as the original blast. Before de Seversky left for Japan, he saw the Hiroshima photograph that came to symbolize the massive destruction and horror and death suffered by citizens of that devastated city. The picture showed an annihilated municipality except for a lone, multistory building that served as a grim sentinel over the Hiroshima grave.[8]

Repeatedly published in newspapers and magazines, the photo caused widespread anxiety over the new atomic weapon. It also inspired debate and discussion posed by the dilemma of killing noncombatants in wartime. Later, talking points for America's conversation about the atom bomb were embellished by John Hersey's best-selling book, *Hiroshima*, based on interviews with Japanese survivors. De Seversky fully appreciated the dreadful level of death and destruction. On the other hand, as a trained military engineer who invented bombsights and understood the physics of exploding ordnance, he was intrigued by the obvious question raised by the Hiroshima photograph. Why did a single, multistory building survive so close to ground zero? When he got to Japan after brief stops in Guam, Saipan, Tinian, and Iwo Jima, he began visiting and flying over Japanese cities that had been incinerated by B-29s loaded with firebombs filled with jellied gasoline or other incendiary materials. The Major then made not one, but five separate observation flights over Hiroshima and Nagasaki before spending four days on the ground touring the two cities and talking with survivors.[9]

When the Major flew over, for example, Hiroshima, he was genuinely surprised by what he saw. Unlike the images he acquired from photographs or media sources about the instant annihilation of that Japanese city, he saw nothing from the air that differed from the sixty-six burned-out urban centers visited earlier by B-29s. Hiroshima and Osaka had the identical two-square-mile area of pinkish ash caused by a holocaust of largely wooden structures mixed with bricks, roof tiles, and rusted metal. A couple individual concrete and steel structures did stand out in isolation, but from a different perspective a cluster of modern, multistory buildings in the city's downtown section remained upright. Moreover, after he spent two days on the ground traveling about Hiroshima, he saw nothing that changed the impression he had received from the several flyovers. For instance, there was no bald spot at ground zero where everything had been vaporized and boiled into dust. From this, he surmised (correctly) that the actual atomic detonation must have occurred in the range of 2,000 feet above the city.[10]

"What I did see," de Seversky remarked in his report, "was in substance a replica of Yokohama, Osaka, or the Tokyo suburbs—the familiar residue of an area of wood and brick houses razed by uncontrollable fire." From this he concluded, "The horror was as profound as reported. But the character of the damage was in no sense unique." He estimated the identical level of destruction could have been caused by two hundred B-29s dropping napalm bombs. What was so incredible is that one atomic weapon from one B-29 could equal the devastation of two hundred bomb-loaded aircraft. On the other hand, the key to the widespread destruction in Hiroshima and Nagasaki was the fact that only a small percentage of structures were built out of steel-framed concrete. Most other buildings and dwellings were of wood or load-bearing brick construction, topped with heavy tiled roofs. The shock wave and massive air pressure from the detonation of the atomic bomb collapsed these structures under the weight of tile, trapping residents under rubble, expanding the holocaust because of the presence of open flames, and multiplying the deaths and injuries of residents.[11]

De Seversky merged these observations about Hiroshima with what he saw during his two-day tour of Nagasaki. There, despite the detonation of a 42 percent more powerful plutonium bomb, less destruction and fewer deaths occurred because of a varied topography that deflected the blast. "In Hiroshima," he reported, "4.7 square miles were razed; in Nagasaki, only 1.45 square miles. The improved atom bomb, in other words, was only about one-fourth as effective!" It reminded the engineer that the impact of an exploding device is determined, in part, by the type and location of the target. Extraordinarily, and as later proven at the Bikini Atoll site, de Seversky predicted correctly that an atomic bomb would not be very effective against naval vessels at sea. In a subsequent interview with radio personality Bob Considine, the Major illustrated the point about the relationship between target and ordnance: "[I]f a target consists of four square miles of hay or kindling wood, then the efficiency of the atomic bomb would not only be reduced to that of a 10 ton blockbuster, but also to one match—because either of them would destroy the target completely."[12]

The ten-ton blockbuster used as an example by de Seversky in his interview with Considine is significant. He came to the conclusion that if Little Boy, the Hiroshima atomic bomb, were dropped in the middle of a modern city like Chicago or New York, its effect would be no more extensive than the blockbuster. On the surface, this seems downright ridiculous. Little Boy possessed the explosive power of 14,000 tons of TNT (trinitrotoluene). Given the fact that the casing took up half the weight of the blockbuster, Little Boy was 2,800 times more powerful. Two years later, de Seversky gave a lecture at the Air War College and Command and Staff School of the Air University in which he explained the physics behind his idea. He noted at the outset that as a target Hiroshima was no Chicago or New York. Although there were nearby hills, the Japanese city itself was relatively flat with mainly low-rise buildings and homes with insubstantial, load-bearing walls.[13]

By contrast, the central portion of a major U.S. city is dominated by multistoried buildings, each buttressed by an immensely strong frame of steel beams. Dropping an identical Little Boy atomic device among such structures would cause horrendous damage and loss of life, but it would not be as widespread as in Hiroshima. The shock wave and compressed air crashing into a building near the detonation point might put, according to the Major, 1,900 pounds of pressure per square inch against the building's face. The hydrostatic or side-on pressure enveloping an object would be 300 pounds per square inch. With such terrific force, it is easy to imagine the facing wall crumbling, floors collapsing, steel beams twisting, and occupants perishing. Nevertheless, the buildings immediately behind the first one would experience a rapidly diminishing side-on pressure. In essence, the buildings themselves would be comparable to the hills of Nagasaki in deflecting and absorbing the bomb's energy and sharply reducing the radius of its impact.[14]

If not his physics, the logic employed by de Seversky helped demystify what happened at Hiroshima and Nagasaki. Regardless, the most obvious shortcoming in his observations centered on his inability to detect any evidence of radioactive fallout. He knew from atomic testing in New Mexico that energy emitted from fission included nuclear particles harmful or fatal to humans. In his report, de Seversky revealed he did in fact question survivors and even Japanese medical personnel at the hospital about radiation sickness in Hiroshima. The hospital, about a mile from the bomb's detonation point, survived the holocaust because it was not surrounded by flammable structures. Perhaps in his interviews he phrased his questions poorly, bumped into a cultural cover-up, or engaged a terrible translator. Nevertheless, he received no direct confirmation about the presence of radioactivity or casualties related to radiation.[15]

### Atomic Firestorm

Armed with these views and peeved by what he perceived as media exaggerations about the two atomic bombs, de Seversky returned to Tokyo where he proceeded to share his impressions with American newspaper correspondents. He made it very clear to journalists that his comments focused not on future and more powerful bombs but exclusively on the two devices unleashed over Hiroshima and Nagasaki. Little Boy and Fat Man possessed onerous attributes that de Seversky fully appreciated, but he preferred to compare nuclear ordnance with traditional bombs and in the process redefine atomic bombs as simply another weapon in the arsenal of the air forces. He told reporters,

The same bombs . . . if dropped in the same manner on a modern city like New York or Chicago, would have done no more damage than a ten-ton blockbuster; and the results obtained in Hiroshima and Nagasaki could have been accomplished by about 200 B-29s loaded with incendiaries, though the loss of life in that case would have been much smaller.[16]

Considering his multiyear, intimate participation with both broadcast and print media, the Major had to have some inkling that his comments might cause a firestorm of controversy. And it could be the type of controversy that would diminish, not enhance, his reputation. Nevertheless, given his official position with the War Department, he felt duty bound to present his expert assessment. He did not want the military to be unduly influenced by media accounts that suggested the same atomic bombs used against Japan would be just as devastatingly effective against the cities of a future enemy. Moreover, there was a subtle problem stemming from the quick and dramatic end to the Pacific War. The flash of exploding atomic devices brilliantly lighted the conflict's finale. It also shoved the full measure of air power's victory into the shadows as Japan lost the war months before the atomic age struck Hiroshima and Nagasaki. Napalm bombs destroyed or severely disrupted Japan's urban-industrial culture.[17]

This fact was brought home to de Seversky when he interviewed such Japanese leaders as Emperor Hirohito. It was clear that the government had recognized the country's defeat by the spring of 1945. Damaged cities and mined ports coupled with the sinking of much of its merchant marine denied Japan food and raw materials. Hence, in isolation, the country's people and war industries were starved. As a result, the pro-war administration ended on April 7, 1945, when retired admiral Kantaro Suzuki became the new premier. He appointed war critic Shigenori Togo to serve as his foreign minister. Unfortunately, the powerful Supreme War Council composed of army and navy chiefs of staff opposed peace. Despite the council's stand, early in May the government initiated talks with the Soviet Union, which remained neutral in the war with Japan until August 8. Tokyo hoped Moscow would help mediate an end to the war. The effort failed. At his own initiative, Hirohito met with council members on June 18 and 20, and July 7, to impress upon the Supreme War Council the importance of negotiating peace.[18]

The atomic bomb certainly precipitated the end to war but only because key leaders in Japan already recognized the country's defeat. It became a face-saving device. "The atom bomb," de Seversky noted, "provided a perfect excuse for surrender. [Japan's leaders] could now pretend that they were not to blame for the defeat—an almost supernatural element had intervened to force their hands." Nevertheless, when the Major talked with Hirohito, the emperor indicated his surrender announcement was based on logic. He fully appreciated the fact that U.S. air power had taken control of the skies. Along with atomic weapons, American aircraft exposed Japan's technical and scientific backwardness. De Seversky observed that Hirohito "urged the Japanese people to endeavor to improve their scientific knowledge in the years of peace to come."[19]

Overshadowing de Seversky's intriguing interview with Emperor Hirohito was his subsequent press conference in November. It was followed in February 1946 by the public release of his report, which appeared in revised form that same month in *Reader's Digest*. His comments and publications caused an explosion of criticism. Shortly after the Major's Tokyo statements were published, three scientists at the University of Chicago who had worked on the Manhattan Project rejected the Major's assessment that two hundred B-29s with incendiaries could have destroyed Hiroshima to the same extent as the atomic bomb. To the contrary, Drs. William Rubinsen, Melvin Friedman, and Leonard Katsin argued that if de Seversky's infamous two hundred B-29s carried one atomic weapon each they could, without question, wipe out any two hundred cities in the world the size of Hiroshima. Another scientist, Dr. Karl T. Compton, president of the Massachusetts Institute of Technology, later claimed that the Hiroshima bomb "would take all the masonry off practically every building in New York City."[20]

Besides these scientists, de Seversky managed to maximize the number of his critics by adding angry and articulate commentators from another field. Beyond the controversy started by his Tokyo press interview, War Department report, and *Reader's Digest* article, the Major published a piece with the immensely abrasive title, "Navies Are Finished," in the February issue of *The American Mercury*. Among other naval supporters, Fletcher Pratt went after the Major in articles published by *The New Republic* and *Sea Power*. Pratt, a popular writer with eleven naval history books to his credit, had often debated de Seversky during radio programs that focused on air versus sea power. The naval historian scoffed at de Seversky's efforts to minimize the destructive impact of nuclear weapons on Japan. Pratt's central point in both articles is that the Major carried forward the flawed logic of the U.S. Army Air Forces "that neither atom bombs nor the Navy had anything much to do with the defeat of Japan, which was accomplished by bombing alone."[21]

De Seversky's most difficult moment in this period of controversy occurred on February 15, 1946. He spent a grueling day at the witness table before the U.S. Senate's Special Committee on Atomic Energy. Senator Brien McMahan, Democrat from Connecticut who chaired the committee, and his Republican colleague, Senator Thomas Hart from the same state, sharply disputed de Seversky's ideas. Naturally, both senators championed U.S. Navy interests because of submarines and carrier aircraft produced in Connecticut. Hart was later quoted as saying, "The objective is very clear. The effects of the atomic bomb were clouding the destruction caused by ordinary bombing, and whoever was behind Mr. de Seversky was interested in changing that impression." Despite being confronted by adversarial senators, the most injurious comments that undercut de Seversky came from another witness, Brig. Gen. Thomas F. Farrell. He had been the executive officer and deputy to Maj. Gen. Leslie R. Groves, who headed the Manhattan Project. Farrell told the special senate committee that according to his calculations, it would take 730 B-29s loaded with conventional bombs to inflict the same damage on Hiroshima as the one atomic bomb.[22]

### The Prophet's Rewards

Happily for the Major, the attacks against him ceased abruptly on July 1, 1946. On that date, the U.S. Strategic Bombing Survey published its summary report on the Pacific phase of World War II. After a team of U.S. experts carefully weighed and measured evidence of the atomic bomb's impact on every square foot of Hiroshima, the official survey concluded 220 B-29s carrying normal weapons would have caused the same amount of damage as Little Boy. It clearly affirmed de Seversky's expertise on ordnance and his powers of observation. This one man came close to matching in two days the months of work of dozens of men. The survey in Japan employed over one thousand civilian and military personnel and maintained for six months one of its four subheadquarters at Hiroshima. Moreover, survey experts agreed with the Major that modern cities would not suffer the extensive damage experienced by Hiroshima. Dr. Charles Krieg, for example, esti-mated that if the Hiroshima atomic bomb were dropped at a much lower altitude, it might destroy up to one-quarter square mile of New York City, which would represent only a fraction of the size of just one of the city's five boroughs. Just as the survey vindicated de Seversky, another event on July 1 corroborated the Major's comments on limitations associated with the early nuclear weapons.[23]

During his presentation before the senate committee in February, de Seversky continued his efforts to demystify the atomic bomb. As before, he stated that the effectiveness of the nuclear weapon depended on its type of power, altitude, target, and surrounding topography. Besides his argument that the same Little Boy bomb could not begin to destroy New York City as it had Hiroshima, the Major predicted the forthcoming atomic test against a naval fleet would fizzle. It was the wrong target for an atom bomb. De Seversky aimed the prediction at Senator McMahan, who had been the first public official to call for such a test in August 1945. The U.S. Navy and its congressional supporters hoped to challenge the army's monopoly on strategic air power. By the start of 1946, the admirals were planning to build a huge, flush-deck aircraft carrier capable of launching multiengine, long-distance aircraft armed with atomic bombs. Presumably, the navy would use the new strategic weapon system to attack a future enemy's sea power as well as land targets.[24]

Meanwhile, under the auspices of the Joint Chiefs of Staff, the U.S. military planned an atomic test against ships at the Pacific site of Bikini Atoll in the Marshall Islands. On July 1, 1946 (June 30, in the U.S.), a B-29 dropped a Mark III atom bomb that detonated at an altitude of 550 feet above a fleet of eighty-eight unmanned ships, Japanese and surplus American war vessels. Fulfilling de Seversky's prediction but surprising many experts, the nuclear explosion sank only five ships. None of the other vessels suffered underwater damage, and most retained their military serviceability. The results undercut one reason for the U.S. Navy to acquire large aircraft carriers and bombers capable of carrying atomic bombs. A second test occurred on July 25, which verified the Major's notion that the bomb's detonation altitude would play a key role in its effectiveness against a specific target. In the test, the atomic device was suspended in water ninety fleet below a naval landing ship. This explosion sank or capsized nine ships. Moreover, a number of the seventy-four vessels arrayed closest to the bomb received extensive radioactive contamination caused by the splash of irradiated water. Presumably, if manned and functioning in a real war, some ships would have been hampered or withdrawn from operations owing to widespread radioactive sickness among crew members. Together, the two tests suggested that in a future war a submarine with nuclear-armed torpedoes designed to explode at a specified depth and distance would be the best equipment to attack an enemy fleet.[25]

Thus the Bikini atom bomb tests and the disputes and surprises over their limited effectiveness against naval vessels only bolstered de Seversky's reputation as prophet and air war expert and helped silence his critics. The Major, in fact, witnessed the tests in his continuing role as consultant to Secretary of War Patterson. In the fall, the latter nominated de Seversky for the Medal of Merit, an award established for fidelity and service by Gen. George Washington near the end of the Revolutionary War. As the citation indicated, Patterson asked President Harry S. Truman to honor de Seversky with the medal because the Major had "contributed to the formulation of a sound public opinion through the medium of his writings from September 1939 to September 1946." Additionally, the special consultant brought to the secretary of war "his shrewd analysis" and "remarkable ability as an observer" to summarize the value of the air war in Europe and the Pacific. President Truman and Secretary of State James F. (Jimmy) Byrnes signed the citation on December 18, 1946.[26]

In the presence of Evelyn and numerous air officers, including Gen. Carl A. Spaatz, chief of the U.S. Army Air Forces, Secretary of War Patterson presented the Medal of Merit to de Seversky on February 6, 1947. Many commentators in print and radio media remarked how incredible it was for the government to grant such an award to a severe critic of its air strategy during the war. Damon Runyon Jr., son of the famous writer and himself an International News Services correspondent, interviewed the Major on February 22. "The Russian-born airplane designer and flyer observed," Runyon recorded, "that it could happen in few nations outside of the United States where a citizen can knock his government in time of war without getting ventilated by a firing squad." Even during the ceremony itself, de Seversky paid tribute to America's freedom of the press that allowed him to present views that initially were contrary to the positions of wartime leaders directing U.S. surface forces.[27]

The plaudits for de Seversky continued when President Truman presented the Russian-American with his second Harmon Trophy from the Ligue Internationale des Aviateurs in White House ceremonies on June

24. Besides the Major's wife, those in attendance included several cabinet members: a U.S. Supreme Court justice and eleven aviation officers, such as Lt. Gen. Hoyt S. Vandenberg and Lt. Gen. James H. (Jimmy) Doolittle, plus Maj. Gen. Lauris (Larry) Norstad and Maj. Gen. Curtis E. LeMay. The citation accompanying the trophy praised de Seversky for his "contributions to American victory through his farsighted advocacy of strategic air power, and his courageous labors in support of a modern and adequate Air Force." The latter explained indirectly all the official government publicity lavished on the Major. It became part of the larger campaign supporting passage of the National Security Act signed into law by Truman on July 26, 1947. Among its provisions was the formation of the National Military Establishment, soon renamed U.S. Department of Defense, containing three equal branches of army, navy, and air force coordinated by a secretary of defense. The lengthy quest for a separate air force that began with Billy Mitchell finally came to fruition, at least to a modest degree, through the fervent effort of Mitchell's disciple.[28]

## The Prophet Responds to the Cold War

The honors showered on de Seversky did not, however, spotlight and clarify the path his life should follow. For the twelve months after he received the Harmon Trophy, his career took two sharp turns as he tried to respond meaningfully to the emerging Cold War. Coined by British author George Orwell and popularized by American journalist Walter Lippmann, the term "Cold War" described the hostility without direct combat between the United States and U.S.S.R. after the defeat of Germany and Japan. Early controversies erupted over the Soviet failure to settle its wartime Lend-Lease debts with America and the U.S. failure to provide the Soviets a significant loan. In the midst of these squabbles, East and West seemed to announce the start of the Cold War. In February 1946 Stalin delivered a speech predicting the inevitability of war as long as capitalism existed. The next month, at Westminster College in Fulton, Missouri, former British prime minister Winston S. Churchill declared the Soviet Union had built an "iron curtain" to segregate Eastern from Western Europe.[29]

When Soviet plans to carve a permanent empire out of territory east of the Elbe River became obvious, President Truman moved from his "get tough" policy of 1946 to his famous doctrine issued before a joint session of

Congress on March 12, 1947. The Truman Doctrine stated that the United States should "support free peoples who are resisting attempted subjugation by armed minorities or by outside pressures." In short order, Congress passed a major spending bill to help Greece, suffering a communist insurgency, and Turkey, experiencing Soviet intimidation over control of the straits between the Aegean and Black Seas. In June Secretary of State George C. Marshall made a stunning proposal at Harvard University's commencement about a project that would carry his name. As subsequently implemented, the Marshall Plan provided funds to rebuild war-torn Western Europe. It gave recipient nations strength to stave off internal communist challenges and external Soviet threats. Together, the Truman Doctrine and Marshall Plan served as the centerpiece for America's containment policy that sought to end further expansion of the Soviet Union. The capstone to this process occurred with the 1949 formation of a western military alliance directed against Soviet-controlled Eastern Europe, the North Atlantic Treaty Organization (NATO).[30]

Regardless, by the summer of 1947 it had become clear to de Seversky that another global war might break out in the near future. The terms "Russia" and "the Soviet Union" appeared more regularly in the lectures he delivered at the Armed (today, Joint) Forces Staff College in Norfolk, Virginia, and the Air University at Maxwell Air Force Base in Alabama. Meanwhile, thanks to the out-of-court settlement of his lawsuit against Republic Aviation, the Major regained the right to use his name for a new corporation. Moreover, lawsuit funds coupled with the Disney movie income and book sales that eventually reached close to 500,000 copies supplied de Seversky with investment capital. As the looming Cold War gave him inspiration for action, the Major worked on a plan to create the new Seversky Aviation Corporation. In his office at 30 Rockefeller Plaza, and with the help of his secretary, Lucy D. Costello, he completed a draft prospectus for the organization on October 20, 1947. It proposed raising $50 million. Sixty percent of those funds would be invested in aeronautical companies manufacturing airframes, engines, and/or instruments; 40 percent would go for research and development. Based on research and development, the new or improved aeronautical hardware would be manufactured in facilities that had received Seversky Aviation investments.[31]

In December 1947 de Seversky turned his attention briefly away from the establishment of a new corporation and reentered the public arena. On

December 1 he gave testimony before President Truman's Air Policy Commission; on December 9 he published a featured article in *Look* magazine titled "We're Preparing for the Wrong War." As might be expected, his testimony before the commission bore some resemblance to the narrative in the article. On both occasions, de Seversky forcefully argued against what he often called America's "triphibious" or balanced approach to defense, in which air, land, and sea power were considered coequal and funded accordingly. Adm. Chester W. Nimitz, who preceded the Major before the commission, described it as a "three-legged stool." Whether triphibious or stool, it had seemed to work during the Second World War, but at a terrible cost in men, money, and materiel. Long-range bombers could have destroyed, for example, Japan without the bloody and sometimes lengthy island battles across the Western Pacific from Guadalcanal to Okinawa.[32]

The logic of de Seversky's argument was not entirely lost on civilian and military leaders. As postwar belt-tightening placed a premium on selecting the most effective military technology, Defense Secretary Louis A. Johnson made an extraordinary decision. With the support and encouragement of Air Force Chief of Staff Hoyt S. Vandenberg, Army Chief of Staff Omar N. Bradley, and President Truman, on April 23, 1949, Johnson canceled construction of super aircraft carrier, the USS *United States*. The projected vessel would have displaced twice the tonnage of standard aircraft carriers and would have been capable of launching multiengine aircraft large enough to carry nuclear weapons a combat radius of 2,000 miles. Clearly, the navy planned to duplicate and compete with the air force for the strategic bombing role; yet hundreds of land-based aircraft could be built for the price of just the one floating airfield. With thousands of personnel to operate the gigantic ship plus its complement of aircraft and nuclear ordnance, the carrier would have been the most expensive piece of military equipment in world history. In wartime, the captain of such an expensive carrier would want to keep the ship as far away from enemy aircraft as possible. A single, well-placed bomb on the flight deck would turn the carrier into an 80,000 ton hunk of useless floating metal.[33]

Meanwhile, two events in June 1948 put the corporation on hold—permanently as it turned out. First, de Seversky simply failed to attract investors, prompting his lawyers to question on June 17 whether he could "complete the organization of the corporation." It would seem the entrepreneur could not find investors who were willing to place $250,000 on the table and then share 50 percent of the uncertain profits from Seversky Aviation with two hundred other investors and the remaining 50 percent with the Major. Second, between June 18 and 24, Soviet security forces implemented a blockade of the British, French, and U.S. sectors of West Berlin, which were approximately one hundred miles inside the Soviet zone of occupied Germany. Initially, the U.S.S.R. avoided using the Russian term "blokada." The Soviets claimed they were closing down road, rail, and river traffic in order to repair war-damaged bridges. In reality, the blockade represented Russian chagrin over the loss of influence over the British, French, and U.S. zones of occupied Germany. The three western zones had formed an economic unit, Trizonia, which decided in June to replace worthless occupation script with a viable currency, the Deutsche mark. Moreover, the Russians wanted to expel the Americans, British, and French and their island sectors of capitalism from Berlin. The Cold War seemed to degenerate into a bitter and brittle freeze that threatened to shatter the postwar peace. Under these twin circumstances, it was logical for de Seversky to revert to his role as prophet. Thus he began writing his second book on air power.[34]

### Reflections

Because he made such an effort to demystify the atomic bomb in the newspaper interview, congressional testimony, *Reader's Digest* article, and U.S. War Department report, de Seversky seemed perfectly aligned with the position of the air forces hierarchy. This alignment certainly explains why he was honored with the prestigious Medal of Merit. Small wonder navy supporters such as Senator Thomas Hart considered the Major as something akin to the official mouthpiece for the air forces. While Arnold and de Seversky disliked each other intensely, the Russian-American interacted with a number of top air officers, many of whom—such as Gen. Harold L. George and Gen. George C. Kenney—he had known since 1921. It was only natural that his thoughts ran parallel with their opinions. When it got down to finer points, however, certain distinctions emerged that defined de Seversky as something other than a simple sycophant. His way of thinking about the value of the atomic bomb in the period of 1945–1950 was shaped by what he witnessed in Japan and wrote several years earlier in *Victory through Air Power*.

During his tour of Hiroshima, de Seversky discovered electric trolley service was restored in the city forty-eight hours after Little Boy's detonation. In addition, most of the city's bridges survived intact. These two facts impressed upon him that the type of target determined the effectiveness of the atomic bomb. The Bikini tests on naval vessels only confirmed his position. Atom bombs would be wasted on a variety of targets such as modern cities as well as roads, railroads, and ships; other targets such as bridges and facilities encased in steel and concrete could be taken out with greater certainty by traditional concussion bombs. And in terms of targets, de Seversky wanted to destroy the enemy's military machinery but not the enemy. War factories, not human lives, should be eliminated through precision bombing. This thesis expressed in his 1942 book was reasserted in his 1950 book. It served as a foundation for the Major's argument that nuclear weapons were both ineffective and inappropriate for use against an enemy's urban centers. By contrast, shortly after Gen. Curtis Emerson LeMay headed Strategic Air Command in 1948, he contributed to the deliberations held by the U.S. Joint Chiefs of Staff on a plan of action should war erupt between the United States and the U.S.S.R. The plan called for dropping 133 atomic bombs on seventy-seven Russian cities. By 1955 the revised version charged SAC with destroying 118 cities with thermonuclear weapons, which would terminate the lives of an estimated 77 million people.

# 16

## Return of the Media
## Personality

When de Seversky finally realized his extremely ambitious and newly minted aviation corporation was not going to succeed, he chose to return to his wartime position of, in the words of his editor friend Eugene Lyons, "airpower crusader." Conveniently, the formal headquarters of his now-ghost company was the same as his personal office at 30 Rockefeller Plaza in the RCA Building. To assist him in typing final manuscripts, he hired Ann Hamilton, who also took classes in music and history at Columbia University. Hamilton was a pilot who had ferried P-40s and P-47s during World War II as a member of the Women's Airforce Service Pilots (WASP). Jackie Cochran, a mutual friend and former WASP director, introduced Hamilton to de Seversky. In a 1976 interview, Hamilton expressed fond memories of the man and her work with the Russian-American in 1948–1949. Coincidentally, she later married William H. Tunner, who indirectly was related to her employment as de Seversky's secretary.[1]

### The Soviet Menace and the North
### American Newspaper Alliance

Tunner, a major general in July 1948, was in charge of the U.S. Airlift Task Force. It kept two and a half million West Berliners supplied with food, clothes, medicine, and coal as a counter to the Soviet blockade, which lasted until May 12, 1949. Fortunately, for the sake of world peace, the United States chose not to use military force to breach the blockade. The decision was made easier by the fact that the U.S. Army reputedly had only one brigade that was actually equipped, trained, and ready for battle. Fortunately, except for some harassment, the Soviets decided to uphold their agreement of November 22, 1945. On that date, the Allied Control Council, which theoretically supervised the four-power occupation of Germany, established through its Air Directorate three air corridors to Berlin from Hamburg, Hanover, and Frankfurt-am-Main in West Germany. Hence the key feature to the Berlin blockade was the American and British airlift that reached heroic proportions by transferring to West Berlin over 2.3 million tons of supplies through 277,804 aircraft flights.[2]

As the blockade and airlift response unfolded, it created a potentially explosive situation. It was easy to visualize a scenario in which Soviet aircraft could trigger, inadvertently or on purpose, a war between the United States and the U.S.S.R. by shooting down an American military transport plane flying in one of the Soviet-approved air corridors to Berlin. This dangerous event in the Cold War rivaled the Cuban Missile Crisis of October 1962, except it lasted months not days. The nearly yearlong Berlin confrontation prompted de Seversky to begin outlining ideas for his next book. Unlike his first text, the second one would not be a slightly revised collection of his previously published magazine articles that had to be acknowledged on the copyright page of *Victory through Air Power*. On the other hand, it was only natural that his second book would build on ideas explored in narratives published in periodicals in 1948 and 1949.[3]

Early on, the Major formed what turned out to be a lengthy relationship as a stringer with the North American Newspaper Alliance (NANA). The news service organization produced articles for sixty-five U.S. and Canadian newspapers ranging from the *Toronto Telegram* and *New York Times* in the East to the *Vancouver Province* and *San Francisco Chronicle* in the West. It also distributed material to twenty-nine foreign newspapers, including seven in Latin America. In general, NANA articles fell into the category of human interest stories or background pieces on national or international news. The wire service was reimbursed by publishers for pieces actually selected by editors to appear in print. No matter how many or how few newspapers picked up one of his articles, de Seversky was paid a flat rate of $200 for each item.[4]

Sasha's early press releases for NANA focused on the hemispheric nature of any future war fought between the United States and the U.S.S.R. Since Soviet Russia lacked a navy (by U.S. standards) and America lacked an army (by Soviet standards), the notion that either one could invade and defeat the other in a traditional land battle was simply delusional. As a result, de Seversky logically projected a wartime plan involving air power. Both countries possessed or had in production bombers patterned after the B-29—the American B-50 and the Russian Tu-4—and both were developing more advanced airplanes with improved range, speed, and bomb loads. Thus the Arctic Ocean would be the future no man's land over which American and Russian bombers would crisscross on their way to try and bomb each other into submissive defeat.[5]

On the surface, the air power prophet anticipated future war plans involving the polar ice cap. It may be, however, more than coincidence that such ideas gelled in his mind in the few months before he took up writing wire service articles for NANA. An interesting event took place at the beginning of April 1948 in the nation's capital. Just before he retired, Gen. Carl Spaatz, air force chief of staff, delivered testimony behind closed doors before committees in both houses of Congress. In the House Appropriations Committee, for example, his comments were not fully declassified by the U.S. Department of Defense until June 20, 1974. For the benefit of representatives, Spaatz elaborated in his testimony on what he called the "polar concept." Should war occur, air power was the only American weapon available to destroy the Soviet war industry. The goal could be accomplished, according to the air chief, by sending long-range bombers to Soviet targets via the Arctic Ocean from bases in Alaska, Maine, and Okinawa. Since the intercontinental B-36 had just entered production and only a partial production run of B-50s had been completed, Spaatz hastened to point out that Air Materiel Command had given the highest priority to developing air-to-air refueling devices for the shorter-ranged B-29s. Although there is no smoking gun, de Seversky's close ties with air officers including Spaatz suggests the Major may have learned, first- or secondhand, some elements of the chief's testimony.[6]

Whether prophet or publicist for the U.S. Air Force, de Seversky clearly understood a serious problem in a hemispheric war. The air force would prevent the U.S.S.R. from establishing bases in or near the Western Hemisphere; the Soviet air force would make untenable (with the possible exception of the British Isles) U.S. bases on or near Eurasia. America, though, imported vital products for the war industry from Eurasia, such as chrome, cobalt, tungsten, manganese, hemp, mica tin, and, among others, natural rubber—large aircraft, for example, used tires made from natural, rather than synthetic, rubber. Because Soviet air power had the potential of denying U.S. access to these products (a claim made more plausible the next year by the Communist victory in China), the Major argued that America must immediately expand and nurture its trade with Latin America. If certain items could not be found or developed within the Western Hemisphere, then the United States must establish a program to import and store an abundant supply of strategic materials that would be available to American industry should war erupt between the United States and U.S.S.R.[7]

As one might expect, newspapers in Latin America picked up and published de Seversky's articles. Associated embassies in Washington also forwarded copies or summaries of the stories to their governments. Three of those governments, Argentina, Chile, and Uruguay, invited de Seversky to fly to their countries for discussions on hemispheric security. In the spring of 1949, the Major conversed with defense ministers, cabinet officials, and three presidents: Jean Domingo Perón of Argentina, Gabriel Gonzáles Videla of Chile, and Luis Battle Berres of Uruguay. It was a mutual lovefest because of the fallout from the Marshall Plan. The U.S. Congress had already approved the first of several appropriation bills that eventually supplied nearly $13 billion in American aid to Western Europe. Understandably, many Latin Americans wondered when the United States would extend its largesse to them. As importantly, they could be harmed by the fact that Europeans received through the Marshall Plan American credits, not cash. It gave the United States control over where Europeans could buy supplies. The United States did permit some off-shore purchases by Europeans in the Western Hemisphere, but significant amounts of U.S.-generated Marshall Plan funds had to be spent in the United States.[8]

As a result, the Marshall Plan could diminish South America's export trade as it enhanced the U.S. economy. For this reason, South American leaders enthusiastically endorsed de Seversky's call for the United States to dramatically increase its hemispheric trade to improve its national security position. This endorsement caught the attention of the National Broadcasting Company, which put the Major on his first television show on July 16, 1949. It was a Saturday evening program devoted to the news behind the headlines and hosted by Leon M. Pearson. Similar to many radio programs, the TV show was scripted in the sense that de Seversky knew ahead of time all the questions Pearson might ask. It differed from radio, however, because the TV show's guest could not read his answers on air. Based on the length of the guest's answers, it was up to the host to add comments or delete questions to meet time constraints. Regardless, the Major used the show to initiate an idea he developed more fully in his second book. He asserted that the United States must create a hemispheric resources planning board to help America meet the challenge of potential conflict with the Soviet Union.[9]

## Feature Articles

Before his trip to Latin America, between January and April 1949 de Seversky prepared and published five feature articles that explored many of the themes that found their way into his next book. In January *Air Affairs* published a lecture the Major delivered a month earlier before the U.S. Strategic Intelligence School. In his lecture and article, the speaker and author claimed that possession of long-range air power had the best chance for maintaining peace as it saved money and preserved democracy. He firmly believed global air power would ensure American leadership over Pax Democratica similar to the previous century's Pax Britannica based on England's overwhelming sea power. And just as England had saved money by focusing military expenditures on a huge fleet at the expense of her small army, the United States should allocate most of its limited resources to the U.S. Air Force. Additionally, if the United States tried to match the Soviet Army's 250 divisions, it would bankrupt the federal government, disrupt the American economy, wreak havoc on the male labor force, and likely require a U.S. dictatorship.[10]

In February *Reader's Digest* published what it advertised as a condensed version of a chapter from de Seversky's forthcoming book. As it turned out, the text actually showed up in several chapters of the larger work. In "Peace through Air Power," both the title of the article and the working title of the book, the Major repeated much of the material he had written for *Look* magazine in 1947. Once again, he blasted the notion of balanced or equal funding for the three-member army-navy-air team, which he labeled cynically as the triphibious military. The Major logically presumed the only way the United States could harm the Soviet Union directly in wartime was through long-distance bombing. Hence military expenditures had to be skewed in favor of air power as the army and navy received fewer funds out of recognition of their auxiliary status. "*The nation,*" de Seversky pointed out, *"that is first in preparing for inter-continental aerial warfare will win the next war* [emphasis original]."[11]

For this reason, he championed Air Force Chief of Staff Spaatz and his successor, Gen. Hoyt S. Vandenberg, in their effort to secure public funding for an air force of seventy combat groups. Each group would contain several squadrons of planes and pilots. Twenty-five of the projected groups would be composed of bombers. This was fine up to a point, but de Seversky sharply disagreed with the plan for twenty groups of B-29 and B-50 medium-range bombers and only five groups of the long-distance B-36s. The Major knew Air Materiel Command worked overtime to install in-flight refueling devices for the B-29s and B-50s. In fact, the world became aware of this when in-flight refueling allowed a B-50 to complete the circumnavigation of the globe in a ninety-four-hour, nonstop flight on March 2, 1949. Even though de Seversky held the original patent on in-flight refueling, he opposed its use in both the *Reader's Digest* article and in a press release he prepared on March 4 for NANA. The technology, he argued, could be used only through the use of overseas bases that required significant land, sea, and air forces to hold and supply them against long-range Soviet air attacks.[12]

It was clear that de Seversky did not want the United States to disperse and thin its air power by trying to maintain numerous bases abroad. A number of the latter were already vulnerable to Soviet attack by medium-range Tu-4s; others could become vulnerable following a Communist victory in China, the development of long-range aircraft, or a Soviet ground assault in nearby territories. The Major wanted a substantial number of long-distance bombers but operating from North American bases and, possibly, the British Isles. By creating what de Seversky described as "invincible strategic air power," the United States could convince the U.S.S.R. that war with America was fraught with atomic dangers and unacceptable costs. This thesis explains why the author chose "Peace through Air Power" as the title of his *Reader's Digest* article. The same idea underlay the piece he wrote for the March issue of *The American Mercury*. From his perspective, it was "The Only Way to Rearm Europe." Massive U.S. air power would shield European allies as they rebuilt their military. Along with the U.S. air shield, once the West Europeans created a significant land force and a "tactical air armada," American allies would be impregnable to Soviet assault.[13]

Two other articles delved into the democratic theme that de Seversky consistently discussed in a number of longer publications and reports. In contrast to the stagnant strategy adhered to by wartime dictatorships, the United States and the United Kingdom had open societies that could expose, debate, and then correct military shortcomings. After the Second World War, the Major frequently expressed concern that the effort to build a massive military in response to the Soviet Union might force the United States to adopt the characteristics of a garrison state. The other side of the same coin was his fear that forcing the creation of an unrealistic, balanced military could be accomplished only by a defense secretary who exercised despotic leadership over the National Military Establishment (U.S. Department of Defense after August 1949). The latter scenario served as the subject of two feature articles published in April, one each by *The American Mercury* and *Pageant* magazines.[14]

The narrative in both articles centered on two subjects tied to James V. Forrestal. First, at the end of 1948, U.S. Defense Secretary Forrestal issued his initial annual report on the National Military Establishment. In the report, he suggested his office should hire the secretaries or civilian heads of the army, navy, and air force. Forrestal also thought his office should handle the budgets, legislation, public relations, and representation before the National Security Council for all three services. If these recommendations were implemented, de Seversky believed they would crown Forrestal as the American tsar over the U.S. military. Second, the tight control Forrestal hoped to exercise was made worse, in the eyes of the Major, by the fact that the defense secretary championed the navy. He had served in the posts of undersecretary (1940–1944) and secretary (1944–1947) of the U.S. Navy before being appointed by President Harry S. Truman and confirmed by the U.S. Senate to serve as the nation's first defense secretary. As it turned out, de Seversky wasted time and ink in attacking Forrestal. Late in March, as the April issues of *The American Mercury* and *Pageant* were being mailed or distributed to subscribers and newsstands, Forrestal was replaced by Louis A. Johnson, who had a strong affiliation with the U.S. Air Force.[15]

As might be expected, the narrative in de Seversky's book favored Johnson over Forrestal. Unlike the two feature articles, however, the Major measured carefully his comments about Forrestal in the longer text. Shortly after losing his cabinet-level position, Forrestal tragically committed suicide. Nevertheless, the book upheld the principles examined in these two articles, namely, the values associated with democratic processes and civilian control that guided the military. For the book-length manuscript, de Seversky rewrote and expanded all the information explored in the NANA press releases and feature articles discussed previously. He added chapters on air power history, atomic bombs, Russia, and making America invincible against the Soviet threat. As early as June 1949, de Seversky's publisher, Simon & Schuster, listed the book, *Peace through Air Power*, for an October release date.[16]

## The Book Is Published . . . Eventually

Just as de Seversky failed to meet his own deadlines for completing the BT-8, P-35, and his earlier book, he also missed his deadline by nearly a year for his second book. He later admitted in a *Reader's Digest* article that the project took two full years of writing. A whole series of issues caused this; if the Major were still alive, he could probably add several other reasons for the delay. The most obvious problem was de Seversky's optimism that he could turn out over 500 typescript pages of readable narrative in a single year. He could not, as he had for the first book, simply glue together earlier articles and present them as chapters in the larger text. This time, he had to rework completely and add new material to his previous magazine pieces and press releases. Several other complications emerged to put a hitch in the Major's timetable. Certainly, the most important of these was the health of his wife, Evelyn. This former dancer in off-Broadway shows gave up on keeping her svelte figure. Whether because of the rich foods she ate or the genes she inherited, she suffered an unspecified heart ailment in 1948. Future heart problems suggest hypertension. As a result, she could no longer pilot an airplane. From this point until her death in 1967, the condition plagued her and forced her to live a more quiet life close to home. Exceptions were her brief appearances with her husband to publicize his book on two television shows: *Success Story*, with Betty Furness on New York City's WJZ-TV, and *Eloise Salutes the Stars*, with Eloise McElhone on the City's WABD-TV.[17]

Besides the significant issue of Evelyn's health, there were always plenty of other events that cut into the Major's writing time. He continued to give, into the 1970s, lectures at the Air University and other military venues. He also delivered a presentation to the Sons of the Revolution in New York State. The latter occurred in the city's Waldorf Astoria Hotel on November 25, 1949—a month after his book was supposed to be published. Earlier that same month, de Seversky was invited by the National Society for Crippled

Children and Adults (today, National Easter Seals Organization) to join a special panel of six handicapped persons. Panel members told their stories of suffering and success in dealing with their afflictions to a plenary session of three thousand professional and lay workers who attended the society's convention in the city's Commodore Hotel. Three days after his November 6 appearance at the conference, de Seversky repeated many of his comments about being an amputee before a radio audience during an afternoon program hosted by Nancy Craig on New York's WJZ radio station.[18]

A welcomed complication appeared in the form of the Major's brother, George, and George's wife, Renée (a nickname), who arrived in the United States in the spring of 1950. Russian émigrés to France and then French émigrés to the United States, their names evolved over time from Georgii Nikolaevich Severskii and Elizaveta Aleksandrovna Severskaia to George P. de Seversky and Renée E. de Seversky owing to the fame of their American relative. Three years later, this family connection eased the change in their temporary status to permanent residents when President Dwight D. Eisenhower signed the enabling legislation on June 19, 1953. The brothers were reunited because George, a cabaret singer with numerous records to his credit and a professional pilot, had suffered a horrible accident in 1947. For the media, he was covering from the air the postwar resumption of the Tour de France bicycle race. Unfortunately, his airplane, a British-built Taylorcraft light observation plane was severely buffeted by brutal winds in the French Alps. His crash resulted in serious injuries and a monthlong hospital stay coupled with months of rehabilitation. The accident reminded the brothers of their mortality and their many years of separation that now ended.[19]

George's multiple fractures, including one in his hip, left one leg shorter than the other and produced a slight limp that matched his brother's. Beyond the limp, they were alike in their love of flight and music and the fact that their marriages were childless. The latter condition was also shared by their twice-married half sister, Nika, who won the title "Miss Russia" in Paris in 1931 and walked runways as a sought-after fashion model. Until her death in 1967, she lived in the French capital. Meanwhile, once George fully recovered from his injuries, Sasha invited him to come to America and help him with Seversky Aviation Corporation. Even though the new company was moribund when George and Renée came to the United States, Sasha had hopes of resurrecting it at some point in the future. During the interim, Alexander hired George to be his assistant and run the office in the RCA

Building during Sasha's many absences. Frankly, it is unclear whether de Seversky's new secretary, Florence Cummings, needed or welcomed George's help. "The relationship between the two brothers," observed mutual friend Michail Ryl, "was cordial but except for work, they had no interests in common. Major de Seversky considered himself an American and all his friends were wealthy Americans whereas his brother George considered himself a Russian and all his friends were Russian émigrés." After his pacemaker failed, George suffered a fatal heart attack in 1972. Ten years later, Renée passed away and joined her husband at the Russian Orthodox Novo Diveevo Cemetery in Nanuet, New York.[20]

Just as Pearl Harbor delayed his first book and led to a change in title, the same thing happened when the Democratic People's Republic of (North) Korea sent troops across the 38th Parallel border in an effort to conquer the Republic of (South) Korea on June 25, 1950 (U.S. time). The subtitle of *Air Power* changed from *Key to Peace* to *Key to Survival*. Such an alteration seemed logical because America's military response against North Korea obviously broadened the conflict. If North Korean allies the People's Republic of China and the Soviet Union officially entered the conflict, it would signal the start of World War III. Since the U.S.S.R. after August 1949 was a nuclear power, it constrained America's response to Russian and Chinese assistance for North Korea. As the Korean War began, de Seversky's text had reached the page-proof stage, when the author would correct spellings and minor errors and create an index from the printed version. To avoid destroying the page-proof setup, the publisher allowed the Major a little extra time to prepare a separate eight-page prologue, "The Lesson of Korea," and four footnotes that did not disturb the larger narrative's pagination. The prologue followed the "Publisher's Foreword" by Richard L. Simon of Simon & Schuster and "About the Author," a section focusing on de Seversky's qualifications for writing the book.[21]

Written just days after the start of the war, the prologue is an amazing document. In it, the prophet demonstrated that he understood immediately what proved to be, from the American perspective, a horrible problem that cursed the conflict especially after November 1950, when Chinese forces entered the fray and overwhelmed American and South Korean troops with cruel success. De Seversky explained why the United States could not achieve victory in a war that would eventually stop, but did not officially end, in an armistice signed on July 27, 1953:

It is important to realize that *strategic air power, the decisive modern force, does not enter into the Korean equation* [emphasis original]. This force is not designed to fight land wars in small and backward countries. There are no genuine strategic targets in Korea. The sources of North Korean war-making capacity lie elsewhere in Manchuria and Russia. Under the conditions of this localized "police action" we remain technically at "peace" and cannot attack these wellheads of enemy strength. We are constrained to deal with effects, not with causes.[22]

Arguing for a diminished role for soldiers and sailors, de Seversky's *Air Power: Key to Survival* hit the bookstores and arrived on reviewers' desks at absolutely the most inopportune moment, September 21, 1950. It was just a few days after the Inchon landings that destroyed North Korea's attempted conquest of South Korea. China's subsequent intervention, of course, gave new life to a Communist North Korea. Meanwhile, the American military basked in glory. The landings had engaged the U.S. Army, U.S. Navy and naval aviation, U.S. Marine Corps, and U.S. Air Force. Small wonder most book reviewers shook their heads and chided de Seversky for being opposed to a balanced military.[23]

In fact, before the Inchon landing, de Seversky's condensed book in *Reader's Digest* had already produced a chorus of critics. As a result, the magazine gave him space for a rebuttal: "Korea *Proves* Our Need for a Dominant Air Force." Even though the Soviet Union and United States never had the war he predicted, the Major certainly proved to be remarkably prescient. He argued that the Korean War played directly into the Kremlin's hands. It cost the precious lives of thousands of U.S. soldiers and billions of dollars in war materiel. The process weakened the United States without touching the Soviet Union's war-making infrastructure. Stalin, in fact, loved the war. Historians, such as Cold War specialist John Lewis Gaddis, point out that the Soviet dictator encouraged the Chinese and North Koreans to continue the conflict even when their losses prompted them to consider peace. Not surprisingly, an armistice became possible shortly after Stalin died in 1953. The astonishing part of de Seversky's article was not simply his ability from day one to understand the nuances of the war for both the United States and the U.S.S.R. He also predicted, "We are now wide open to the exhausting drains and humiliations of an endless series of militarily futile little wars—Korea today . . . Indo-China tomorrow." And that is exactly what happened.[24]

## The Media Personality

Precisely because his book received mixed reviews and did not climb into anyone's best-seller list, de Seversky undertook a yearlong active campaign to publicize the work in media interviews and speaking engagements. The heavy promotional pace kept his book selling at a modest rate and his air power message broadcasting to the public. He made regular appearances on programs in New York and Washington. He participated in shows with a national audience, including *Town Meeting*, moderated by George V. Denny Jr. and distributed over the ABC Radio Network; *The American Forum of the Air*, moderated by Theodore Granik and broadcasted on both radio and television by NBC; and television shows such as *Meet the Press* and *People's Platform*, produced, respectively, by NBC and CBS. In between programs, de Seversky traveled the country and delivered dozens of speeches to a variety of groups.[25]

De Seversky's full-time return to the public forum also made him attractive to politicians. As had happened in the past and would be repeated in the future, members of the U.S. Congress asked for his expert testimony. His criticism of the Korean War coupled with the disastrous events over the winter of 1950–1951 enhanced the Major's reputation, especially among conservative Republicans. Defeat of American and South Korean troops in the North led the Truman administration to decide to augment the two U.S. Army divisions stationed in Europe with four additional divisions. It was feared that the U.S. setback in Asia might encourage the Russians to consider an adventurous military policy in Europe. President Truman hoped the extra troops would deter the Russians from taking that step. Senators Robert A. Taft (Rep., Ohio) and Kenneth S. Wherry (Rep., Nebraska) wanted the U.S. Congress, not the president, to decide on whether the divisions should be transferred. Before voting on a resolution, the two senators and like-minded colleagues requested a joint session of the U.S. Senate Foreign Relations and Armed Services Committees to hear testimony from several experts. Two of those experts appeared on February 21, 1951, as senators questioned and heard comments from de Seversky and Lt. Gen. Curtis E. LeMay, head of Strategic Air Command.[26]

In their separate statements before the joint committee, LeMay and de Seversky agreed the transfer of more American soldiers would not deter a Soviet invasion force. The Russians could field more than thirty divisions for each American unit. Certainly, the U.S. Army in Europe could serve as a tripwire for the start of World War III, but the soldiers themselves would be slaughtered by the Soviet army. Both men also agreed that the only true deterrent against Soviet expansion was a large strategic air arm that could threaten the U.S.S.R. with nuclear holocaust. Unlike LeMay, who waffled, de Seversky strongly supported the resolution that required that large troop transfers to Europe be approved by the nation's legislature. The Major remained true to his long-standing position that the American public and the public's representatives should have a voice on the issue of military strategy. Early in April, the U.S. Senate did adopt Resolution 99, but it was a meaningless compromise. Under the resolution, the U.S. president and Joint Chiefs of Staff could send troops to Europe as long as they could certify to Congress that NATO partners also contributed an unspecified number of soldiers.[27]

De Seversky's one-day participation at the hearings on behalf of a resolution sponsored by conservative senators such as Wherry and Taft ultimately resulted in the Major adopting for the first time a very public and partisan approach to national politics. In his conversations then and later with Taft, de Seversky came to realize that the Ohio senator, though labeled an isolationist, shared the Major's belief that strategic air power held the key to preserving national security. Hence in 1952, when Taft competed with General of the Army Dwight D. Eisenhower for the Republican nomination for president, the Major publicly endorsed Taft at the candidate's New York headquarters in the Chatham Hotel on June 2, 1952. This commitment, in turn, led de Seversky to write a newspaper article for the New York *Journal American*. It attacked the president and Democrats as it applauded Taft and Republicans. The abuse of Truman seems unfortunate. Ten years earlier, de Seversky had marked Senator Truman as his most significant wartime ally; after the war, President Truman approved or presented the Major with his two most prized awards, the Medal of Merit and Harmon Trophy. In addition to the newspaper piece, de Seversky prepared a pro-Taft pamphlet on air power for distribution to all Republican delegates attending the national convention in Chicago, July 7–11, 1952.[28]

Despite the fact that Taft had more committed delegates than "Ike," Eisenhower swept the nomination on the very first ballot. Following his extraordinary victory, the Republican nominee for president took the unusual step of reaching out immediately to his opponent. Ike walked across the street to Taft's hotel room. He asked Taft—in essence, he asked conservative Old Guard Republicans—to join his team for a November victory and a place in the new administration. As a result, Eisenhower's advisors and cabinet nominees were open to appoint a number of Taft supporters to government positions after Eisenhower won the election over Democratic candidate Adlai E. Stevenson. A vocal Taft supporter, de Seversky benefited from Eisenhower's leadership style. Harold E. Talbott Jr., the new secretary of the U.S. Air Force, interviewed the Major to be his deputy. The fact that de Seversky was given first consideration for the post also speaks legions about his national reputation and his enduring membership in the air force fraternity.[29]

As the interview proceeded, however, it became clear from Talbott that de Seversky's appointment came with a condition. The Major had to support Eisenhower's opposition to Project Lincoln, a study by scientists and engineers associated with the Massachusetts Institute of Technology. Project Lincoln required sufficient funds and facilities to permit researchers to develop the technologies necessary to detect and defeat enemy air attacks. The initial price tag reached $21 billion. It would break the bank and unbalance the federal budget. On this basis, Ike not only disapproved of Project Lincoln, he expected his administrative team to support his decision. When it became obvious de Seversky both applauded Project Lincoln and would not abide by Eisenhower's team rules, the offer to make him deputy secretary of the U.S. Air Force was removed from the table. Nevertheless, a government-funded Lincoln Laboratory was later created to improve America's air defense system, but with a more modest startup cost.[30]

Regardless, de Seversky was left without a regular paycheck to help him maintain two homes, domestic and secretarial help, an expensive office at a prestigious address, a defunct aviation corporation, plus his wife and extended family. As will be discussed in the next chapter, he would begin to develop in the 1950s what was then an exotic propulsion system for aerospace craft. Because he lacked investors, the Major had to complete his inventive technology over time with personal resources. Meanwhile, for the ten years after 1952, de Seversky continued the pattern of life and livelihood he had experienced in the ten years prior. Thus he continued his public campaign for a large strategic air force modified to include not only aircraft but also a variety of atomic, rocket-powered, and electronic weapons. The Major continued, then, to write numerous wire service pieces for newspapers and feature articles for popular publications. His most rewarding work, at $2,500 per article, was associated with *This Week Magazine*, a Sunday supplement for newspapers nationwide. One such article, one speech, and several items for NANA earned de Seversky as much money in a month as the average annual salary of a public schoolteacher in 1954.[31]

In addition to NANA and the Sunday supplement, the Major received handsome checks for articles in such well-known monthlies as *Coronet* and *Pageant* as well as lesser gratuities from military aviation journals, including *Air Power Historian* and the *Air Force Magazine*. His most glaring publication failure was his botched effort to secure a publisher for his autobiography. He insisted unrealistically on a huge advance, at one point as much as $150,000, before writing a single word for the proposed book. De Seversky even rejected the promising advice of Alfred A. Knopf Jr. of the publishing house with the same name. Knopf, or more correctly his mother through him, suggested in December 1956 the name of a respected collaborator who could prepare a detailed outline and sample chapters about the Major's life. The outline and chapters could justify Knopf in offering a publishing contract before a fleshed-out manuscript existed. De Seversky decided he did not want to pay the proposed collaborator, Janet Mabie, $1,500 to prepare the framework for his autobiography.[32]

Fortunately for the Major, two other profitable activities served to offset his inability to sell his autobiography. First, he became very active in giving air power speeches across the country. He belonged to the W. Colston Leigh Speakers' Bureau and earned $500 plus expenses per venue. Each year, he could prepare a new talk, present it at dozens of locations before different audiences and organizations, and then sell a revised version to a magazine. Several of his presentations gained wide attention in the media and entered the pages of *Vital Speeches of the Day*. The latter published, for instance, his talk on the "Importance of Global Command of the Air" delivered at Southern Illinois University on October 12, 1956. University administrators were so pleased by the talk's national attention that they awarded de Seversky his second honorary Doctor of Science degree during the June 1957 commencement. In terms of support for his oratorical performances and travel, the Major was designated officially each year to 1973 as an advisor or consultant to the chief of staff of the U.S. Air Force. This position gave him the status and privileges accorded to a general officer. It meant he had free flights, temporary-duty pay, on-base living accommodations, and free ground transportation for his lectures for the Air University and for visits to various air force organizations and bases.

For example, on several occasions he visited a unit of the Strategic Air Command at March AFB (March Joint Air Reserve Base after July 1996) near Riverside, California. A mutual acquaintance, Herb Katz, introduced the Major to Leonora I. Wingenroth. Leonora, a vibrant thirty-three-year-old undergoing a divorce, was attracted to the stately and famous Major, who was three decades her senior. The pair found common interest in the fact that both were inventors. It appears likely de Seversky helped her prepare the first of five patents she successfully acquired for pharmaceutical instruments and technologies related to the female reproductive system. Eventually, she worked with the Johnson & Johnson Company on one of her inventions. Meanwhile, the May-December friendship turned over time to romance. The product of their liaison was a daughter, Diane, born June 15, 1958. With so much distance between them in terms of geography, the clandestine relationship between Alexander and Leonora gradually ended, although they kept in communication over a ten-year period. One can only speculate that Evelyn's ailing health was a factor in bringing them together and her resilience the cause of their demise. Apparently, Leonora hoped for something more; however, by the time Alexander's wife died in 1967, Leonora had bonded with a former pilot in the Royal Canadian Air Force.[33]

Second, de Seversky received stipends for each of his numerous appearances on television and participation on radio programs. He showed up or could be heard frequently in one or the other broadcast media through most of the 1950s. Like his famous dog, Vodka, in the 1930s, de Seversky approached the recognition level of being a household name. Samples of his television appearances include *The Mike Wallace Interview* show, presented by ABC; *Comeback*, hosted by Arlene Francis, also on ABC; and *Person to Person* with Edward R. Murrow on CBS. Among the radio programs the Major joined as a guest were *Time Capsule* with Melvyn Douglas and broadcasted by New York's WJZ as well as interview programs such as the one hosted by George Combs and, several years later, by Louis Sobol over WABC.[34]

Whether from genetics, diet, age, or the hectic pace he followed in delivering speeches around the nation and doing radio and television interviews in New York and other cities, the Major suffered a serious episode of cardiac arrhythmia in 1959. Ironically, it occurred when Evelyn and Sasha were vacationing in the Bahamas. On April 10 de Seversky caught a large shark off the shore of one of the islands. The effect, though, of trying to haul the fish into his rented boat resulted in the Major pulling a rib and experiencing a heart spasm. Because de Seversky possessed the status of a general, the U.S. Air Force promptly flew the couple from Andros Island to Miami, where both husband and wife were admitted to Jackson Memorial Hospital with heart-related issues. The fact that Evelyn enjoyed a quick recovery suggests that, without further information, her problem might have been stress-induced hypertension, which could be eased by rest if not sedation. Her husband, by contrast, continued to stay in the hospital in "fair condition." Subsequently, he was transferred to Houston, Texas, where world-renowned cardiac surgeon Dr. Michael E. DeBakey implanted a pacemaker for the Russian-American. Like Evelyn in 1948, the Major could now no longer pilot an airplane. The whole process also prompted him to temporarily reduce the number of his appearances for the media and at the speaker's lectern. He needed, however, to maintain cash flow to support his family and research. Thus he prepared his third and last book for publication, but it was not his autobiography.[35]

## Reflections

This chapter along with the previous five chapters have discussed to a greater or lesser extent key awards de Seversky received for his work as an aircraft manufacturer, air power commentator, military consultant, aeronautical inventor, and record-setting pilot. He was bestowed two Harmon Trophies, two honorary doctorate degrees, the Medal of Merit, and the U.S. Air Force Exceptional Service Award. The latter was briefly mentioned in chapter 4. Each of these awards fits smoothly in the narrative and contributed logically to the Major's story. But as one might imagine, the sixty years of de Seversky's very productive adulthood life resulted in many other citations. Any effort to mention or explain each honor would fail to advance the narrative or enhance the biography as it would play havoc with the prose. On the other hand, it might also be considered strange, if not a serious shortcoming, to ignore at least a sample of the many accolades he received.

He gained membership in the French Legion of Honor (1947) for his participation in the Inter-Allied Congress of Engineers (1945) that addressed reconstruction issues for postwar France. Because each year he made one or more presentations to senior officers at the Air University at Maxwell AFB, de Seversky was officially appointed lecturer for both the Air War College and Air Command and Staff School in 1952. He continued in this role into the early 1970s. The Major's work as an aeronautical inventor and designer prompted his election to the New York Academy of Science (1952) and his selection as Distinguished Engineer in Industry by the New York Society of Professional Engineers (1965). Additionally, a dozen aviation organizations acknowledged the Major's accomplishments: for example, the American Institute of Aeronautics and Astronautics elected de Seversky a fellow (1967); New York City's Aviator Post 743 of the American Legion awarded the Major what he described as "the highlight of my career"—the General William E. Mitchell Memorial Award (1962); his successful presentation at Brazil's National War College resulted in his receiving from President Juscelino Kubitschek the Brazilian Air Force Legion of Merit (1961); and the National Aeronautic Association named him Elder Statesman of Aviation (1959). Although not necessarily an honor, three of his many memberships deserve mention. Despite the Major's view that the U.S. Navy should be auxiliary to the U.S. Air Force, he became an associate of the U.S. Naval Institute. Once his nemesis, Gen. Hap Arnold, died, de Seversky not only joined the Arnold Air Society but had an Arnold "squadron" (a group of members) named in his honor. Third, the Major helped pick Harmon Trophy recipients as a member of the Harmon Advisory Committee. In the 1960s he was joined on the committee by such old friends and acquaintances as Jacqueline Cochran, Jimmy Doolittle, Curtis LeMay, Igor Sikorsky, and Carl Spaatz. The most prestigious aviation award to honor de Seversky, one that is viewed every day by hundreds of people, is saved for the last chapter.

# 17

## The Futurist

In April 1961 the McGraw-Hill Book Company published Alexander P. de Seversky's third book, *America: Too Young to Die!* The title alone might help explain why the book attracted so little attention. Major newspapers, for example, ignored it. The title can best be described as semi-hysterical, and to some people it would imply a shallow product slanted toward the sensational. Moreover, like Billy Mitchell in the 1930s, the Major may have cried wolf once too often about the weakness of American air power. This obviously was the judgment of Maj. Gen. W. H. Hennig, chief of staff, North American Air Defense Command (NORAD). Hennig noted, in an otherwise kind letter to de Seversky, that the book gave the impression that since 1941 top political and military leaders consistently made the wrong decisions about air power. The NORAD chief concluded, "The blanket criticism, I fear, may cause many people first to doubt, then reject your views, especially since somehow we have managed to survive!"[1]

### America: Too Young to Die!

While de Seversky examined in his book the latest technology and hardware available to the U.S. Air Force, his basic ideas on air power had not changed. From his perspective, a balanced military left the air force underfunded when, he claimed, a future war with the U.S.S.R. was inevitable. The United States could win such a war but only if it soon developed a preponderance of strategic bombers, guided missiles, and nuclear weapons. On the other hand, as suggested by Hennig, time seemed to be undermining the Major's basic argument. Civilian and military commentators alike have noted that the MAD (mutually assured destruction) concept operated to prevent a Soviet-American exchange of atomic bombs and warheads. Named by Secretary of Defense Robert S. McNamara and verified by the Cuban Missile Crisis, MAD had its origins in 1954. In a January speech before the Council on Foreign Relations and in a March article published by *Foreign Affairs*, Secretary of State John Foster Dulles announced that the United States might use nuclear weapons to retaliate massively against Soviet aggression. Before long, MAD would be recognized as the linchpin that locked the atomic wheel and kept it from moving. This is not to suggest that the world was safe during the latter decades of the Cold War. If not fear, reasonable concern remained that an inadvertent event or unstable personality might cause fulfillment of everyone's nuclear nightmare.[2]

Whether time, overexposure, or repetitiveness caused de Seversky to lose luster among readers and reviewers, McGraw-Hill had to place advertisements in newspapers and periodicals that otherwise failed to acknowledge the existence of his book. Frankly, the ads tried to scare people into purchasing it. The publisher headed the ads with quotes from the Major that figuratively screamed, for example: "*Unless our military posture is changed radically and immediately, war is inevitable—and we will be the losers* [emphasis original]." Despite his slower pace owing to his heart ailment, de Seversky did his best to promote the book. He remained close to home in New York but between April, when the book went on sale for $4.95, and July 1961 he visited four broadcast studios. The Major did interviews with Barry Gray on WMCA Radio, Lee Graham on WNCY Radio, Dave Garroway on NBC TV's *Today Show*, and Betty Furness on WNTA TV's *At Your Beck and Call.*[3]

Even with shortcomings in substance and limitations in popularity, *America: Too Young to Die!* contains interesting, if not fascinating, nuggets of ideas and predictions. De Seversky, for instance, rebuked Henry A. Kissinger for his 1958 book *Nuclear Weapons and Foreign Policy.* The future secretary of state and national security advisor for two Republican presidents argued that since atomic devices were so forbidding, the United States had to develop a "strategic doctrine" with "alternatives" that were "less cataclysmic than a thermonuclear holocaust." The Major mocked the Harvard University political scientist by employing some of Kissinger's own jargon. From de Seversky's point of view, "appropriate counterforce," "graduated retaliation," and "flexible response" to Soviet foreign policy adventures meant a future filled with inconclusive but painful Korea-type conflicts. But according to the cynical air power author, Kissinger's use of the "magic phrase *limited wars* [emphasis original] gave the old concept of balanced forces a new respectability." Such respectability guaranteed, de Seversky argued, that the United States would be unprepared for war with the U.S.S.R. It also ensured America's participation in hostilities that would accomplish nothing except to bleed the U.S. military of its manpower and materiel. As if to confirm the Major's prediction, the newly installed John F. Kennedy administration chose in 1961 to quadruple the number of U.S. military personnel in South Vietnam. In that same location and year, the first of an eventual 47,382 members of the U.S. armed forces died from hostile action—an additional 10,811 perished from other causes.[4]

## The Future of Aerospace

Besides predicting the unfortunate nature of limited war in his third book and serving as a prophet for air power, de Seversky also considered the future of flight. In addition to jets, he was very interested in reaction motors associated with rockets for military missiles and space travel. The Major was enough of an engineer to recognize the limitations of chemical reactions in solid- or liquid-fueled engines. While chemical-based engines release twenty-five or so electron volts (eV) per reaction, a controlled chain reaction of nuclear fission can release 200 million electron volts (MeV) per reaction. Because of the obvious magnitude of atomic energy, de Seversky became an early proponent of building nuclear-powered rockets. Apparently, he also thought it would be easy to store enough uranium-235 in a spaceship to sustain a chain reaction long enough not only to launch a rocket into space but also make a round-trip voyage to the moon or a planet. Only later could he appreciate the fact that a "direct drive" atomic engine would produce so much heat that the environment encasing it would be destroyed. When the U.S. Atomic Energy Commission and National Aeronautics and Space Administration jointly sponsored (circa 1960–1973) an experimental atomic rocket engine, they used liquid hydrogen to cool the reactor. The heated hydrogen that passed through the reactor then became the gas that jumped out of the engine's nozzle. Hence hydrogen, not the heat source, actually propelled the rocket and fulfilled Sir Isaac Newton's Third Law of Motion.[5]

Since de Seversky made bad assumptions about atomic-powered rockets, it is easy to dismiss the three articles he wrote on the subject between 1946 and 1952. To his credit, he admitted his limited expertise in this area in a speech he delivered at the University of Buffalo on December 7, 1951. The occasion was a convocation on technology's future in the year 2000. During the program, the Major noted he rarely attempted to speculate what might happen beyond a single decade. He understood his comments about atomic propulsion were "largely for the pleasures of climbing out on a limb in such distinguished company." While his notions about atomic engines for rockets only confirmed his ignorance of how best to apply nuclear fission to a reaction motor, de Seversky proved to be a bona fide soothsayer when it came to the topic of artificial satellites. In February 1952 his article titled "We'll Build Another Moon" was published in *The American Weekly* and reprinted in *Science Digest*. Except for pure atomic rocket engines, all his talking points came true and in a relatively short period of time. He suggested that, for example, unmanned satellites would measure cosmic radiation, forecast weather, relay ground signals, guide ships and planes in navigation, and provide telescopic images of planets and stars. He also believed that large satellites would be built, manned, and supplied by multistaged rocket shuttles equipped with wings. After a launched shuttle docked and unloaded its cargo at the space station, it would glide back to its home base on Earth. The large satellite would be built from modular units put together by astronauts in pressurized suits whose movements in space would be accomplished by small thrusters of compressed air. In appearance, the space station would look and perform like a giant rotating wheel. The centrifugal force on the outer rim would supply occupants with artificial gravity. The movie *2001: A Space Odyssey* later captured and brought this prose image to life, an image also suggested by Wernher von Braun. It is remarkable that de Seversky anticipated by a month most of the ideas presented by the German-American scientist in his first of several articles on space flight for the very popular *Collier's* magazine in March.[6]

### Electronatom and the Ionocraft

The article by von Braun served as the centerpiece for several essays written expertly by qualified scientists. Beginning with the magazine's cover, the issue contained spectacular illustrations to accompany faultless data on the subject of future space flight. Von Braun published two more pieces for *Collier's* before moving on to do programs on "Man in Space" for Walt Disney's television show on ABC. The German-American became a national celebrity who captivated many Americans with his notions of extraterrestrial exploration. It appears likely de Seversky was overtaken, if not overwhelmed, by von Braun's first article in March. The sensation it caused effectively ended the Major's budding program of writing speculative pieces about astronautics. He decided instead to participate in the future of flight by incorporating in the state of New York on March 13, 1952, the Electronatom Corporation—renamed Seversky Electronatom Corporation fifteen years later. De Seversky often commented that this new company was formed to develop, construct, and sell innovative equipment to control pollution.[7]

That may be, but the "Biographical Sketch" he prepared for the media before being interviewed suggested a different pattern. "The invention of the Ionocraft," the Major stated in 1970, "led to another technological break-through in the field of air pollution control." Whether first or in tandem with pollution-control devices, de Seversky decided to try and create a vehicle of flight propelled directly or indirectly by electricity. The idea was not original with the Major. Robert H. Goddard, America's pioneer rocket scientist, built and launched the world's first successful liquid-fuel rocket in 1926. Before that, he had worked extensively with solid-fuel reaction motors. During World War I, and for the U.S. Army, he used the latter technology to design ordnance fired from a tube on the shoulder of a soldier. It became the predecessor to the famous bazooka of World War II. Obviously, Goddard possessed an open mind over methods to achieve a reaction motor. One approach he considered was electrically charged particles, or the ionization process. He conducted experiments with "electrified jets" at Clark College (today, University) in 1916–1917 and applied for a patent for the "Continu-ously Acting Electrode" on July 16, 1926. Goddard failed to pursue that idea because it requires a significant amount of electrical power and hence a large and heavy generator with its own abundant fuel supply. The size and weight penalties did not fit the rockets he designed.[8]

Had Goddard lived beyond 1945, he might have revisited electric propul-sion given the potential of atomic energy to generate electricity, especially for long-distance rocket flights beyond the Earth's field of gravity. Mean-while, media criticism directed at de Seversky over his "direct drive" atomic engine certainly prompted him to rethink how to use the power released by nuclear fission. It could be applied, for instance, in the form of electricity to ionize a propellant for a reaction motor. There was no path, however, that he could travel to conduct nuclear experiments. In addition to publishing his ignorance in this area, he lacked financial resources, research facilities, and scientific personnel. These negative factors stopped him from gaining the ear of the U.S. Atomic Energy Commission. And that meant he would never have access to nuclear technology or fissionable material. Thus, the Major chose to labor off and on for seven years, not on atomic-powered spacecraft but on a vehicle that required atmosphere—truly an "air" craft. On August 31, 1959, four months and a pacemaker away from his heart spasm, de Seversky applied for a patent for his Ionocraft with the U.S. Patent Office.[9]

The Ionocraft not only worked, it flew on pure electricity. De Seversky installed a series of tall metal spikes above a grid of meshed wire. The spikes were biased at a high negative voltage relative to the positively charged wire grid. As the negative charge bombarded the surrounding air, negative air particles called ions flowed down to the positively charged mesh. When this happened, the ions collided with neutral air particles, which also dropped toward the grid. Since neutral air was not attracted to the actual wire mesh, the air flowed right through the open spaces to produce lift. The downwash of air a person felt standing underneath the Ionocraft resembled, in a less forceful way, that of an operating helicopter. By applying varied voltages to different parts of the grid via a joystick, the Ionocraft could be flown from one point to another in a slightly inclined attitude; it could also be steered in any direction. What was the catch? De Seversky's working models were tethered to the ground by an electric cord plugged into an outlet. At the time, the technology did not exist for a feather-light, self-contained generator that would produce enough electricity to power the craft.[10]

### Electronatom and the Hydro-Precipitrol

De Seversky kept the Ionocraft a secret until he received the patent on April 28, 1964. Another two years would go by before he received the basic patent for his first workable pollution-control equipment. The copyright for the final element was dated July 3, 1973. Regardless, the new device employed an ionization process like the Ionocraft; hence, technology transfer eased the development of both inventions. The Major's interest in pollution technology emerged naturally from his memberships and talks before engineering groups. Colleagues in these associations were attracted to the challenge of pollution problems as media stories inspired action. The issue first arose after World War II over radioactive fallout from testing atom bombs. The Major stated that this is exactly what attracted his initial interest. Additionally, cities such as New York and Los Angeles encountered smog or air pollution problems that posed serious health risks for citizens. Beginning in 1952, a number of municipalities and state legislatures approved statutes or ordinances designed to clean the air.[11]

In between speaking engagements, military lectures, writing assignments, and radio and TV appearances, the Major began work in the 1950s on what became by 1965 a successful device for removing from the air smoke and particulates as small as one-tenth of a micron. Progress was slow and expensive, but de Seversky had good help from an expert consultant on air pollution control, Dr. Bertram Spector, who served as vice president for research at the New York Institute of Technology. The result was the Hydro-Precipitrol. Smoke and gases entering a stack from an apartment, hospital, or hotel incinerator passed first through the Hydro, a scrubber using rapidly circulating water to remove larger particles and water soluble gases. The cyclonic swirl was then transformed into a smooth laminar flow that entered the Precipitrol, or precipitator. It consisted of a cylindrical dry discharge electrode surrounded by two concentric wet collecting electrodes. The discharge electrode ionized remaining tiny particles, which migrated to the collecting electrodes where they impinged on a film of water. Precipitated particles were then simply drained away.[12]

### Electronatom and Its Operation

Once this innovative purification equipment had been designed, and with the patent process under way, by 1964 it was time for Electronatom to actually build, test, and manufacture a full-sized Hydro-Precipitrol. Up to this point, the company had earned no revenue. Its personnel consisted of the Major and his employees: brother George de Seversky, friend Alexander Pishvanov, rotating secretaries such as Patricia Rittenhouse, as well as brother-in-law Samuel Rutherford Olliphant, who kept his day job but helped the firm with legal issues as a member of the New York Bar. The company not only owed its existence to de Seversky; the firm's president would also be responsible for raising its operating revenue when Electronatom moved from research to production. In the first instance, the Major loaned the company $144,000. He borrowed an additional $40,000 from Nicholas D. Biddle, a friend and private investor who, like de Seversky, kept an office in Manhattan's RCA Building. These two men also signed as guarantors a bank loan for $88,000. Moreover, the company president arranged for a $250,000 loan from Bessemer Securities Corporation. Finally, de Seversky issued 104,128 shares of stock, each valued at $2.50. Of these shares, 8,200 went for services rendered by employees and the consultant listed previously. The other 95,928 shares were sold for cash raising an additional $239,820. A number of those shares were purchased by the Major, Evelyn, and her brother.[13]

With this seed money, de Seversky rented a two-story brick building with 22,000 square feet of space for $38,500 a year. Located across the East River from Manhattan in Long Island City, it served the company as both laboratory and manufacturing plant. Besides his current employees, the Major hired eight more men, including Michail Ryl and Judd Hopla, to help bring the Hydro-Precipitrol to life. It may be recalled that Hopla was an expert metal cutter who had worked for Seversky Aircraft Corporation. Between 1965 and 1968, the small group of men under de Seversky's direction built twenty of the pollution-control devices at an uninstalled unit price of around $7,000. Regrettably, only five units were actually sold. The company simply lacked the financial resources to establish marketing facilities (sales and service centers) and an advertising campaign to promote business. Modest sales failed to cover even the factory's rent, not to mention the yearly rent of $14,616 on the company's office in the RCA Building plus salaries for twelve employees and funds for tools and materials to build the machines.[14]

In the midst of a growing financial crisis, tragedy struck the de Seversky household. Late in July 1967 Nicholas A. Pishvanov, whose father had passed away the previous year, came for a visit to the Asharoken mansion. He was on leave as a combat pilot for the U.S. Air Force. Years afterward Nicholas joked, "Heaven forbid I would pick the Navy!" When Nicholas, treated like a son by Sasha and Evelyn, graduated several years earlier from the USAF Aviation Cadet Training School at Greenville AFB (today, Mid-Delta Regional Airport), de Seversky came and delivered the commencement address. Late in the evening on the twenty-eighth, Alexander and his "son" sat at the kitchen table sharing a glass of spirits and reminiscing about previous summer guests and parties at the mansion. Suddenly, a

chilling report of a gunshot rang out from one of the second-floor bed-
rooms. The pair rushed upstairs and discovered to their horror and grief
that Evelyn, age sixty, had shot herself in the chest with a .38-caliber pistol.
She had become despondent over her years of poor health. Quite possibly
the financial strains of Electronatom, to which the de Severskys had invested
most of their wealth, may have added to her depression. Suffolk County
police were called and Dr. Sidney Weinburg, the county coroner, carefully
examined the deceased. Weinburg ruled the death a self-inflicted gunshot
wound. After the memorial service held a few days later, Sasha took home
his wife's cremated remains.[15]

Whatever personal pain Evelyn eliminated through suicide only added
heartache to the distress felt by her husband over Electronatom. As red ink
continued to spread gradually across the accounting ledger, de Seversky
must have felt vexation eerily similar to what he had experienced thirty
years earlier in 1938, when the Seversky Aircraft Corporation began sliding
toward bankruptcy. As of February 29, 1968, the company had access to only
$37,429 in cash according to the independent accounting firm of Lybrand,
Ross Brothers & Montgomery. On the plus side, the Major knew his Hydro-
Precipitrol was a technical improvement over existing pollution-control
devices for incinerators and smaller industrial plants. He needed, however,
to pay off debts, fund a marketing program, and possess a cash reserve to
maintain or expand operations. He decided to try and offer through public
sale 600,000 shares of stock for $12.50 each. On March 1, 1968, Seversky Elec-
tronatom signed a financial advisory agreement with the firm of D. H. Blair
& Company of New York City. Blair belonged to the National Association
of Securities Dealers—what later became the NASDAQ stock exchange.[16]

If not seriously, then half-facetiously, Americans often view New York
stock exchanges as Las Vegas East. Nevertheless, serious gambling did occur
when de Seversky signed the agreement with D. H. Blair. Beginning May
23, 1968, when the prospectus was issued, 180,000 of the 600,000 shares
had to be subscribed within thirty days. Why? It would raise the minimum
amount of money Seversky Electronatom needed to pay all debts and provide enough resources for operations and marketing with the potential to
reach a level of success that would make the stock worth its price. If the
number of subscribed shares fell below 180,000 by June 22, 1968, subscribers would be refunded their investments in full. Seversky Electronatom
would then sink into bankruptcy and disappear. D. H. Blair & Company,

however, worked hard to make Seversky Electronatom succeed. It sent the prospectus to its many customers as well as to other securities dealers; after all, if the 180,000 figure was reached, the NASDAQ firm stood to gain 6 percent of the deposited money to reimburse its services. The gamble paid off. Initial sales of 400,000 shares brought in $5 million. De Seversky's and Blair's venture was a financial success.[17]

Since the company was debt-free and had a bountiful cash reserve to guarantee continued operations, de Seversky and his small board of directors could afford to consider reducing the president's management load. After all, the Major was seventy-four. He had just been through a terrible year when his wife of forty-three years had died and the company he had founded nearly failed. To ease de Seversky's life, the company took advantage of its Chicago connections. The Windy City had purchased earlier through federal grants two Hydro-Precipitrol units for field testing. Installing the equipment and working with the municipal government, de Seversky and his team became acquainted with James V. Fitzpatrick, who headed the Chicago Department of Air Pollution Control. He held an electrical engineering degree from the Illinois Institute of Technology and two graduate degrees including an M.B.A. from the University of Chicago. From this position, Fitzpatrick served as a pollution-control consultant to various companies and government agencies.[18]

By 1968 Fitzpatrick had moved up the city's administrative ladder to become commissioner of streets and sanitation. In this new position, he supervised over six thousand employees and a budget of nearly $100 million. In July of that year, Mayor Richard Daley praised Fitzpatrick's authority in pollution control and management skills as he announced his commissioner's decision to join as president a revived Seversky Electronatom Corporation. Apparently, de Seversky and the board of directors had sufficient funds to make Fitzpatrick an offer he could not refuse. De Seversky became chairman of the board and consultant for the company. With significant financial resources, Fitzpatrick quickly led the company into a period of expansion. Larger manufacturing facilities were found at Roosevelt Field Industrial Park in Nassau County. Undoubtedly, the Major was pleased by the company's official address at One de Seversky Plaza, Garden City, Long Island.[19]

The expansion also overwhelmed the small colony of Russian immigrants with a number of highly educated, native-born Americans. Large advertisements were placed in newspapers to hire a chemical engineer, chief test engineer, fluid dynamicist, metallurgist, installation engineer, mechanical estimator, plus multiple sales engineers, designers, and draftsmen. For good reason, the Russians were not pleased. Nick Pishvanov, whose late father had worked with George de Seversky in building demonstration models of the Hydro-Precipitrol, remembered conversations he had had with the Major's brother:

> George was in despair when the CEO hired some high-powered "engineers," made organizational charts and dreamed of great days to come. Unfortunately, much needed capital was draining away. George was anguished [and] complained to me that early experiments and construction of scaled up versions cost huge sums of money in salaries, etc. The Chicago guy was always busy "lining up" some business with various cronies and/or the government. George told me that he and dad had made "scaled-up" versions [of the Hydro-Precipitrol] for $20,000 or less that worked beautifully and validated the design. But the [new] team of engineers would repeat the process at $100,000 and more.[20]

### Retrospectives

Regrettably, "great days" for the company never came. Its business or rather lack of business could be measured by following the NASDAQ exchange. Individual share prices for Seversky Electronatom fell from a little over $9 on November 1, 1968, to slightly more than $2 on the last day it was traded publicly, Thursday, February 22, 1973. Because so much of de Seversky's wealth was tied to stock that declined and then collapsed, there were personal repercussions. He sold empty lots beside his Asharoken mansion and then mortgaged the large house itself. These steps produced the cash he needed to feed and clothe himself and keep a modest office at 630 Fifth Avenue, Manhattan, as well as his apartment at 40 Central Park South. Despite his terrific disappointment over the failure of Seversky Electronatom and the unpleasant financial decisions he had to make, actions would be taken and words would be printed in his waning years that eased the pain of the descent and loss of his company. He was, after all, acknowledged and treated as a man of consequence.[21]

With passage of the Clean Air Act in 1970 and creation of the Environmental Protection Agency by President Richard M. Nixon's executive order, a number of publications did interviews or retrospective articles on the Major. Just as he seemed uncanny in his forecasts about aviation in the 1940s, he had become in the 1950s a pioneer in the environmental movement that came to fruition in the 1970s. On this basis, feature articles on de Seversky's new role appeared in various publications ranging from the *New York News Coloroto Magazine* to the *Los Angeles Herald-Examiner*. Coincidentally, Charles A. Lindbergh, America's best-known pilot, was also an environmentalist. The famous picture of Lindbergh hugging a tree became a basis for the tree-hugger sobriquet employed as a derisive term for ecologists by their opponents. On one issue, however, de Seversky and Lindbergh parted ways. The Major enthusiastically endorsed the use of federal funds to assist Boeing Aircraft in building America's SST (supersonic transport). His motivation came from the fact that Russian Communists had designed and tested the Tu-144 SST, which became the world's first civil aircraft to reach Mach 2 on May 26, 1970. By contrast, President Nixon and others credited or blamed Lindbergh for the U.S. Senate's decision late in 1970 to end government support for Boeing's SST because of environmental considerations. De Seversky, ever the cheerleader for aviation's progress, called the decision "ecological stupidity."[22]

As mentioned earlier, the U.S. Air Force awarded the Major its Exceptional Service Award in 1969 and continued to appoint him as advisor to the U.S. Air Force chief of staff. Moreover, the air force provided their Air University lecturer with two special treats. It arranged with NASA for de Seversky to witness in a special viewing area the launch of Apollo 9 on March 3, 1969. It was a ten-day mission in low Earth orbit to evaluate the performance of the spacecraft and lunar module. Even more fun was the invitation to watch liftoff of Apollo 11 on July 16, 1969, that put the first humans on the moon. The Major's itinerary also gave him two days of social functions to mingle with old friends as well as government and aerospace dignitaries such as Gen. Ira C. Eaker, Air Force Secretary Dr. Robert Seamans, and Vice President Spiro T. Agnew. In his subsequent thank-you letter to Dr. George E. Mueller, associate administrator for manned space flight, de Seversky admitted, "For me, who has been flying since the turn of the century, [the launch] was and forever will be an unforgettable experience." Almost as unforgettable was the state dinner for the Apollo 11 astronauts: Edwin E. Aldrin Jr., Michael Collins, and Neil A. Armstrong. Sponsored by NASA and the White House and held at the Century Plaza in Los Angeles on August 13,

1969, de Seversky joined a glittering array of 1,440 celebrity dinner-guests headed by President Nixon.[23]

Certainly, the Major enjoyed the occasion and was honored to be invited, but the dinner that became the true highlight of his life was held the following year in Dayton, Ohio. The Aviation Hall of Fame enshrined de Seversky on December 17, 1970. Chartered by the U.S. Congress, the organization housed awards and plaques of inductees in the U.S. Air Force Museum at Wright-Patterson AFB. Three other inductees shared the honor with the Major: the late Robert E. Gross, who had revived a bankrupt Lockheed Aircraft Company in 1932; Ira C. Eaker, who had organized and led the Eighth Air Force in World War II; and Juan T. Trippe, who had formed Pan American Airways in 1927. Golfing great Arnold Palmer served as master of ceremonies. An air force band performed martial music before and during dinner; after the enshrinement ceremony, the Paul Steele Orchestra provided the dance tunes for the Evening Ball. Following dinner, Palmer introduced individuals who read and presented the actual awards to the inductees. For de Seversky, this was done by former U.S. Air Force chief of staff Gen. John P. McConnell. Illustrator Milton Caniff, creator of the "Steve Canyon" comic strip, prepared portraits to accompany the awards.[24]

As if to complete the tribute of being a lasting part of the U.S. Air Force Museum, the Major lived long enough to see the same special treatment for his P-35 airplane. In fact, the one on display today is the last known P-35 in existence. (There are several surviving P-35As, but they were built by Republic Aviation.) Seversky Aircraft's P-35 went to the 94th Pursuit Squadron at Selfridge Field in Michigan in the late 1930s. Obsolete when the United States entered World War II, it served various training roles before being declared surplus at war's end. Airline pilot Charles P. (Chuck) Doyle eventually acquired the plane, which was in pieces. In 1971 he turned them over to the Minnesota Air National Guard, which restored the P-35 with help from students enrolled in the Minneapolis Vocational Institute. Once the restoration was completed in May 1974, de Seversky was invited to Minneapolis to celebrate the resurrection of "his" plane. De Seversky's picture was taken in front of the craft where he was flanked by Doyle and Brig. Gen. John R. Dolny, who had supervised the restoration. The laughing smile on the Major's face clearly showed his immense joy in seeing in mint condition the airplane that had added so much luster to his life and reputation. On June 1 de Seversky joined Doyle and Dolny and the restored

P-35 for the pursuit's official transfer to the U.S. Air Force Museum. After the accession ceremony and with help from Doyle and Dolny, the Major was eased into the plane's cockpit. As he sat in the plane, his life seemed to have come full circle as his mind was crowded with wonderful memories of his many test and record flights in the P-35, as well as the fame and glamour associated with the plane's victories in the national Bendix Trophy Races of 1937, 1938, and 1939.[25]

Certainly, de Seversky felt comforted near the end of his eighty years of life over the P-35's restoration and exhibition. Such comfort was matched by the friendship and solicitous care he received from a neighbor at 40 Central Park South. During the previous several years, the Major formed a warm relationship with Mary (Beebe) Bourne. She was the daughter of Saul Bourne, who founded, with Irving Berlin and Max Winslow, the Bourne Company Music Publishing in 1919. The firm controlled numerous classics, including "Unforgettable," "Me and My Shadow," and "When You Wish upon a Star." Along with her mother, Bonnie, who inherited the company upon Saul's death in 1957, Beebe helped manage the firm as well as the International Music Company and its prestigious catalog of classical music. Beebe had invested in Seversky Electronatom and, in fact, became the last CEO of the dying company. Because Beebe had become such an important part of his life, her importance continued after his death. De Seversky passed away in Manhattan's Memorial Hospital when his heart gave out at 6:25 p.m. on August 24, 1974. Beebe, executrix of his will, arranged for a Russian Orthodox service for her deceased friend at the funeral home of Frank E. Campbell. She also signed on September 17 the Woodlawn Cemetery orders to inter his ashes along with those of his wife's. The lots for Sasha and Evelyn had been bequeathed to the couple by Evelyn's mother.[26]

### Reflections

The discussion in chapter 17 about the Major's innovations, such as the Ionocraft and Hydro-Precipitrol, and foresight, such as space flights and environmental concerns, can be added to the summary comments about his accomplishments in the recognition he received from the Aviation Hall of Fame as revised with his passing in 1974:

AWARD

ALEXANDER P. de SEVERSKY

1894–1974

ACQUIRING AN AERONAUTICAL ENGINEERING DEGREE, de
SEVERSKY SERVED AS A RUSSIAN NAVAL COMBAT PILOT IN
WORLD WAR I. ALTHOUGH HE LOST A LEG IN HIS FIRST MIS-
SION, HE RETURNED TO DOWN 13 ENEMY AIRCRAFT IN 57
MISSIONS. IN 1918, HE CAME TO THE UNITED STATES AND
BECAME A CITIZEN.

FIRST APPOINTED AN AERONAUTICAL ENGINEER AND TEST
PILOT FOR THE WAR DEPARTMENT IN 1918, de SEVERSKY
BECAME A SPECIAL CONSULTANT IN 1921 AND AN ADVISOR IN
THE FAMOUS "AIRPLANES VERSUS WARSHIPS" BOMBING TESTS.
AFTER INVENTING THE IN-FLIGHT REFUELING METHOD, HE
DEVELOPED THE FIRST GYROSCOPICALLY STABILIZED BOMB
SIGHT IN 1921–23. HE BECAME A MAJOR IN THE ARMY AIR
CORPS IN 1928, AND ALSO FOUNDED THE SEVERSKY AIRCRAFT
CORPORATION. HE DEVELOPED AN ADVANCED DESIGN AMPHIB-
IAN, IN WHICH HE SET WORLD SPEED RECORDS IN 1933–35;
AND AN ALL-METAL MONOPLANE, WHICH SET SPEED RECORDS
IN THE 1933–39 NATIONAL AIR RACES AND IN WHICH HE SET
A TRANS-CONTINENTAL SPEED RECORD IN 1938. HE THEN
DEVELOPED THE P-35 FIGHTER AND THE P-47 "THUNDER-
BOLT" ESCORT FIGHTER, WHICH HELPED ESTABLISH ALLIED
AIR SUPERIORITY IN WORLD WAR II. IN 1942, HE WROTE THE
BOOK "VICTORY THROUGH AIR POWER." MADE INTO A MOVIE,
IT ALERTED THE ALLIES TO THE NEED FOR AIR POWER. FOR
THIS, AND FOR HIS INVALUABLE COUNSEL ON THE STRATEGIC
USE OF AIR POWER, HE WAS AWARDED THE MEDAL OF MERIT.
AFTER THE WAR HE SERVED AS A SPECIAL CONSULTANT TO
THE CHIEFS OF STAFF OF THE U.S. AIR FORCE, FOR WHICH HE
RECEIVED THE EXCEPTIONAL SERVICE MEDAL IN 1969.

TO ALEXANDER P. de SEVERSKY, FOR OUTSTANDING CONTRIBU-
TIONS TO AVIATION BY HIS ACHIEVEMENTS AS A PILOT, AERO-
NAUTICAL ENGINEER, INVENTOR, INDUSTRIALIST, AUTHOR,

STRATEGIST, CONSULTANT, AND SCIENTIFIC ADVANCES IN
AIRCRAFT DESIGN AND AEROSPACE TECHNOLOGY, THIS AWARD
IS MOST SOLEMENLY AND RESPECFULLY DEDICATED.

AWARDED DECEMBER 17, 1970, AT DAYTON, OHIO
THE AVIATION HALL OF FAME

As indicated earlier, Americans often confused de Seversky and Sikorsky
in print and broadcast media. And it is perfectly understandable. Both came
from Russia, where they attended the naval academy, studied engineering,
and gained fame for their accomplishments in aviation. Both fled Soviet
Russia and enjoyed successes and suffered failures in the United States. Each
gave the other employment at one point in their lives and each had careers
filled with twists and turns. The one gained fame for his huge reconnaissance
bomber while the other attracted attention as a combat pilot. In America,
Sikorsky taught math before designing and building commercial aircraft;
de Seversky invented aviation technologies before designing and building
military aircraft. Finally, Sikorsky lost his manufacturing company but then
bounced back with the helicopter; de Seversky also lost his manufacturing
company but received acclaim as a prophet and proponent of air power.
The helicopter, of course, has kept the name Sikorsky vibrant and alive;
by contrast, de Seversky did not have a prominent technology to carry his
name. He worked diligently and for decades to improve and strengthen
an institution. Nonetheless, his was one of the more important names of
those who helped create the powerful U.S. Air Force.

# Notes

## 1. INTRODUCTION

1. "Mr. Procofieff from the North," *The New Yorker* (October 5, 1940), 14; "De Seversky, Alexander P(rocofieff)," in *Current Biography: Who's News and Why 1941*, ed. Maxine Block (New York: H. W. Wilson Company, 1941), 222–23.

2. "Mr. Procofieff from the North," 14; press release from the Test Pilots Association, October 1959, Alexander P. de Seversky Papers, Cradle of Aviation Museum (hereafter CAM de Seversky Papers), Box 215.

3. For parental names, see "De Seversky, Alexander P(rocofieff)," 222. For confirmation of birth date, see "Aviators Certificate" issued by the Royal Aero Club of the United Kingdom in 1939, CAM de Seversky Papers, Box 1. De Seversky's birth date in the Julian calendar used by the Imperial Russian Empire was May 24, 1894. Draft material, "Special to the New York Mirror," December 31, 1941, CAM de Seversky Papers, Box 215, p. 4. The lengthy autobiographical statement by de Seversky became the basis for two articles prepared by Gerald R. Scott for the magazine section of the *New York Mirror*, January 25 and February 1, 1942.

4. Eugene Lyons, "Crusader," *Pageant* (August 1948), 140; Eugene Lyons, "Seversky—Aviation's Versatile Genius," *The American Legion Magazine* (December 1974), 18; "Mr. Procofieff from the North," 14.

5. Lyons, "Seversky—Aviation's Versatile Genius," 18; "Presenting Major Alexander P. de Seversky," *The Jeffersonian* (December 1945), 3; "Alexander P. de Seversky," *Pathfinder* (February 14, 1942), 16; Lynn Chilton, "Biographical Sketch: Alexander P. de Seversky" (undated, circa 1960), CAM de Seversky Papers, Box 215, p. 1.

6. Chilton, "Biographical Sketch," 1; United Artists, "Biography: Major Alexander P. de Seversky" (press release to coincide with the distribution of the Walt Disney film, *Victory through Air Power*, starring de Seversky, 1942), CAM de Seversky Papers, Box 215, p. 1; Alan Durkota, Thomas Darcy, and Victor Kulikov, *The Imperial Russian Air Service: Famous Pilots & Aircraft of World War One* (Mountain View, CA: Flying

Machine Press, 1995), 260; P(etr) D(mitrievich) Duz', *Istoriia vozdukhoplavaniia i aviatsii v Rossii: period do 1914g* [History of Aeronautics and Aviation in Russia: The Period Before 1914] (Moskva: Nauka, 1995), 297, 331, and 373–86; Frank J. De Lear, *Igor Sikorsky: His Three Careers in Aviation* (New York: Dodd, Mead & Company, 1976), 36; Igor I. Sikorsky, *The Story of the Winged-S: An Autobiography* (New York: Dodd, Mead & Company, 1944), 57.

7. Leonard E. Opdycke, *French Aeroplanes before the Great War* (Atglen, PA: Schiffer Publishing, 1999), 51–55 and 119–20; Christopher Chant, *Pioneers of Aviation* (New York: Barnes & Noble Books, 2001), 33–34.

8. John W. R. Taylor, ed., *The Lore of Flight* (New York: Barnes & Noble, 1996), 113; Tom Crouch, *The Bishop's Boys: A Life of Wilbur and Orville Wright* (New York: W. W. Norton & Company, 1989), 167–70.

9. Opdycke, *French Aeroplanes before the Great War*, 117–19; Taylor, *The Lore of Flight*, 116. For a brief discussion of the P-35, its evolution into the P-47, and its impact on military aviation, see Larry Davis, *P-35 Mini in Action* (Carrollton, TX: Squadron/Signal Publications, 1994), 1–50, and his *Thunderbolt in Action* (Carrollton, TX: Squadron/ Signal Publications, 1984), 4–6.

10. Durkota, *The Imperial Russian Air Service*, 336–37; Robin Higham, John T. Greenwood, and Von Hardesty, eds., *Russian Aviation and Air Power in the Twentieth Century* (London: Frank Cass, 1998), 25–26.

11. Higham, Greenwood, and Hardesty, *Russian Aviation and Air Power in the Twentieth Century*, 25–26; Bill Gunston, *The Development of Piston Aero Engines* (Newbury Park, CA: Haynes North America, 1999), 109.

12. In the military, Alexander did his preliminary flight training in a Farman Model IV. See Durkota, *The Imperial Russian Air Service*, 337; Higham, Greenwood, Hardesty, *Russian Aviation and Air Power in the Twentieth Century*, 32. The time mentioned in the narrative is confirmed by letter of de Seversky's secretary, M. P. Albert to P. Andrews, May 22, 1941, CAM Seversky Papers, Box 215.

13. "De Seversky, Alexander Prokofieff," 172; Michael Kort, *The Soviet Colossus: History and Aftermath* (Armonk, NY: M. E. Sharpe, 2001), 71–79.

14. Copy of letter from M. Nikita Procofieff (Alexander's first cousin) to Diane M. A. Procofieff de Seversky (Alexander's daughter), October 9, 2006; copy of letter from N. Procofieff to D. de Seversky, March 20, 2007; Felix Gilbert with David Clay Large, *The End of the European Era, 1890 to the Present* (New York: W. W. Norton & Company, 1991), 109.

15. Gilbert and Large, *The End of the European Era*, 110; Barbara W. Tuchman, *The Guns of August* (New York: Bantam Books, 1976), 91–157.

16. Thomas G. Paterson, J. Garry Clifford, and Kenneth J. Hagan, *American Foreign Relations*, vol. 1, *A History to 1920* (Boston: Houghton Mifflin Company, 2000), 274 and 282; Daniel M. Smith, *The Great Departure: The United States and World War I 1914–1920* (New York: John Wiley & Sons, 1965), 2 and 80; draft material, "Special to the New

York Mirror," 5; John H. Morrow Jr., *The Great War in the Air: Military Aviation from 1909 to 1921* (Washington: Smithsonian Institution Press, 1993), 35, 40, and 47–48.

17. M. C. Neshkin and V. M. Shabanov, comps., "PROKOF'EV (SEVERSKII), Alexander Nikolaevich," *Aviatori–kavaleri ordena Sv. Georgiia i Georgievskogo oruzhiia perioda Pervoi mirovoi voini 1914–1918 godov* [Aviators–Knights of the Order of St. George and the Golden Sword of St. George in the Period of the First World War 1914–1918] (Moskva: ROSSPEN, 2006), 238–40; press release, December 1940, Ligue Internationale des Aviateurs, Library of Congress, American Institute of Aeronautics and Astronautics Papers (hereafter, LC AIAA), Box 111, p. 1; René Greger, *The Russian Fleet 1914–1917* (Exeter, UK: Ian Allan, 1972), 27–28.

18. Greger, *The Russian Fleet 1914–1917*, 15; Evan Mawdsley, *The Russian Revolution and the Baltic Fleet: War and Politics, February 1917–April 1918* (New York: Harper & Row Publishers, 1978), 85.

19. Higham, Greenwood, and Hardesty, eds., *Russian Aviation and Air Power in the Twentieth Century*, 111; Durkota, *The Imperial Russian Air Service*, 22; David Kahn, "The Rise of Intelligence," *Foreign Affairs* 85 (September/October 2006): 131.

20. Block, "De Seversky, Alexander P(rokofieff)," 222; "Alexander P. de Seversky," *U.S. Air Services* (August 1937), 18; "Biographical Sketch," press release from Test Pilots Association, October 1959, CAM de Seversky, Box 215, p. 1.

21. Alexander Riaboff, *Gatchina Days* (Washington: Smithsonian Institution Press, 1986), 16; Russell Miller, *The Soviet Air Force at War* (Alexandria, VA: Time-Life Books, 1983), 17–19; V(alentin) P. Glushko, chief ed., "Zhukovskii, Nikolai Egorovich," *Kosmonavtika Entsiklopediia* ["Zhukovskii, Nicholas Egorovich," The Cosmonaut Encyclopedia] (Moskva: Sovietskaiia Entsiklopediia, 1985), 114.

22. W. Bruce Lincoln, *The Romanovs: Autocrats of All the Russias* (Garden City, NY: Anchor Books, 1981), 261–62.

23. Robert Wohl, *A Passion for Wings: Aviation and the Western Imagination 1908–1918* (New Haven, CT: Yale University Press, 1994), 146–47; Opdycke, *French Aeroplanes before the Great War*, 120; Viktor Kulikov, "Aeroplanes of Lebedev's Factory," *Air Power History* 48 (Winter 2001): 6–7.

24. Opdycke, *French Aeroplanes before the Great War*, 119–20; Chant, *Pioneers of Aviation*, 18; Taylor, *The Lore of Flight*, 50; James K. Libbey, "Flight Training and American Aviation Pioneers," *AAHS Journal* 49 (Spring 2004): 30.

25. Opdycke, *French Aeroplanes before the Great War*, 119–20; Chant, *Pioneers of Aviation*, 18; Riaboff, *Gatchina Days*, 38.

26. Durkota, *The Imperial Russian Air Service*, 102–03; telephone interview with D. de Seversky, September 21, 2005; Riaboff, *Gatchina Days*, 38–41; Chant, *Pioneers of Aviation*, 18.

27. Morrow, *Great War in the Air*, 12–13; Gunston, *Development of Piston Aero Engines*, 110–12; David Crocker, *Dictionary of Aeronautical English* (Teddington, UK: Peter Collin Publishing, 1999), 214.

28. Morrow, *Great War in the Air*, 12–13; Gunston, *Development of Piston Aero Engines*, 110–12; Crocker, *Dictionary of Aeronautical English*, 214; Riaboff, *Gatchina Days*, 41.

29. Draft material, "Special to the New York Mirror," 7; "Alexander P. de Seversky," *U.S. Air Service*, 18; press release, Ligue Internationale des Aviateurs, December 1940, LC AIAA, Box 111, de Seversky Folder, p. 1.

30. Durkota, *The Imperial Russian Air Service*, 102–3; Opdycke, *French Aeroplanes before the Great War*, 270–71; John W. R. Taylor, ed., *Combat Aircraft of the World: From 1909 to the Present* (New York: G. P. Putnam's Sons), 131–33.

31. Durkota, *The Imperial Russian Air Service*, 352 and 465; Chilton, "Biographical Sketch: Major Alexander P. de Seversky," 1; Taylor, *Combat Aircraft of the World*, 133 and 161.

### 2. THE RUSSIAN ACE IN THE GREAT WAR

1. Heinz J. Nowarra and G. R. Duval, *Russian Civil and Military Aircraft 1884–1969* (London: Fountain Press, 1971), 49; Bill Gunston, *The Osprey Encyclopedia of Russian Aircraft 1875–1995* (London: Osprey Aerospace, 1995), 6 and 8; Taylor, *Combat Aircraft of the World*, 582–83; Duz', *Istoriia vozdukhoplavaniia i aviatsii v Rossii*, 331–32; William Green and Gordon Swanborough, *The Complete Book of Fighters* (New York: Barnes & Noble, 1998), 202.

2. "Alexander P. de Seversky," 18; "One Legged Mercury," *Bill Barnes Air Adventurer* (February 1934), 110; Lyons, "Seversky—Aviation's Versatile Genius," 18; Robin Higham and Jacob W. Kipp, eds., *Soviet Aviation and Air Power* (Boulder, CO: Westview Press, 1977), 22; Durkota, *The Imperial Russian Air Service*, 29.

3. A. J. P. Taylor, *The First World War* (New York: Perigee Book, 1980), 38–41; Winston S. Churchill, *The Unknown War* (New York: Charles Scribner's Sons, 1931), 174–90; Norman Stone, *The Eastern Front 1914–1917* (London: Penguin Books, 1998), 70–91.

4. Stone, *The Eastern Front 1914–1917*, 122–36; Churchill, *The Unknown War*, 348; Mitchell B. Garrett and James L. Godfrey, *Europe Since 1815* (New York: Appleton-Century-Crofts, 1947), 529–36.

5. Stone, *The Eastern Front 1914–1917*, 171–72; Greger, *The Russian Fleet 1914–1917*; H(arold K.) Graf, *The Russian Navy in War and Revolution* (Honolulu: University Press of the Pacific, 2002), 42–49; Norman E. Saul, *Sailors in Revolt* (Lawrence: Regents Press of Kansas, 1978), 41.

6. Graf, *The Russian Navy in War and Revolution*, 49; Greger, *The Russian Fleet 1914–1917*, 18; "Excerpt from Paul Harvey News," February 13, 1955, CAM de Seversky Papers, Box 215, p. 1.

7. De Seversky quoted from Major Alexander P. de Seversky, "I Owe My Career to Losing a Leg," *Ladies' Home Journal* 61 (May 1944): 21; "Excerpt from Paul Harvey News," 1.

8. "Special to the New York Mirror," December 1941, CAM de Seversky Papers, Box 215, p. 7; Lyons, "Seversky—Aviation's Versatile Genius," 18; James Farber, "Major de Seversky—Engineer," *Popular Aviation* 17 (August 1935): 87.

9. A. D. McFadyen, "Major Alexander P. de Seversky," *Journal of the Patent Office Society* 19 (April 1937): 273; Swanee Taylor, "Seversky: An Ace's Place Is in the Air," *New York World Telegram Metropolitan Weekend Magazine* (December 12, 1936), 16.

10. De Seversky quoted from de Seversky, "I Owe My Career to Losing a Leg," 22; Graf, *The Russian Navy in War and Revolution*, 48–49.

11. De Seversky, "I Owe My Career to Losing a Leg," 22; Miller, *The Soviet Air Force at War*, 24–33; K(onstantin) N. Finne, *Igor Sikorsky* (Washington: Smithsonian Institution Press, 1987), 87.

12. "Russian Flyer with One Leg Seeks U.S. Job," *San Francisco Examiner*, April 22, 1918; Farber, "Major de Seversky—Engineer," 87; Saul, *Sailors in Revolt*, 7 and 19.

13. De Seversky quoted from de Seversky, "I Owe My Career to Losing a Leg," 22; letter to author from D. de Seversky, September 9, 2006.

14. Neshkin and Shabanov, *Aviatori*, 239; Farber, "Major de Seversky—Engineer," 87; "Excerpt from Paul Harvey News," 2; McFadyen, "Major Alexander p. de Seversky," 274; Lyons, "Seversky—Aviation's Versatile Genius," 19.

15. "Alexander P. de Seversky," 18; Gunston, *Osprey Encyclopedia of Russian Aircraft 1875–1995*, 82–85.

16. De Seversky, "Special to the New York Mirror," 8; McFadyen, "Major Alexander P. de Seversky," 274; "One Legged Mercury," 111.

17. De Seversky quoted from de Seversky, "I Owe My Career to Losing a Leg," 164; Lyons, "Seversky—Aviation's Versatile Genius," 19; "Alexander P. de Seversky," 18.

18. De Seversky, "I Owe My Career to Losing a Leg," 164; Chloe Arnold, "An Ace with One Leg and Nine Crosses," *The* (New York) *Sun*, October 20, 1918; Rear Admiral B(oris) Doudoroff, the Attaché, Russian Embassy, Tokyo, "Certificate," March 30, 1918, CAM de Seversky Papers, Box 1, p. 1.

19. De Seversky quoted from de Seversky, "I Owe My Career to Losing a Leg," 164; Arnold, "An Ace with One Leg and Nine Crosses," 9; "One Legged Mercury," 111.

20. Nicholas N. Golovine, *The Russian Army in the World War* (New Haven, CT: Yale University Press, 1931), 235; Graf, *The Russian Navy in War and Revolution*, 97; Saul, *Sailors in Revolt*, 47.

21. De Seversky, "Special to New York Mirror," 10; de Seversky, "I Owe My Career to Losing a Leg," 165; Robert A. Kilmarx, "The Russian Imperial Air Forces of World War I," *The Airpower Historian* 10 (January 1963): 93.

22. Doudoroff, "Certificate," 1; de Seversky, "Special to the New York Mirror," 13; Taylor, *Combat Aircraft of the World*, 135.

23. "Talk by Major Alexander P. de Seversky, Leonard S. Morange Post, American Legion, Hotel Gramatan, Bronxville, N.Y., November 10, 1933," CAM de Seversky Papers, Box 261, p. 1; Doudoroff, "Certificate," 1.

24. De Seversky quote from "Talk by Major Alexander P. de Seversky," 2; Gunston, *Encyclopedia of Russian Aircraft*, 82–85; Durkota, *The Imperial Russian Air Service*, 276–78.

25. "Talk by Major Alexander P. de Seversky," 2; Durkota, *The Imperial Russian Air Service*, 276–77; Major Alexander P. de Seversky, "Lest We Forget," *U.S. Air Services* (June 1937), 16.

26. Bruce Robertson, *Air Aces of the 1914–1918 War* (Fallbrook, CA: Aero Publishers, 1964), 155; Gunston, *Encyclopedia of Russian Aircraft*, 82–85; Taylor, *Combat Aircraft of the World*, 135.

27. Doudoroff, "Certificate," 1; Durkota, *The Russian Imperial Air Service*, 105.

28. De Seversky quoted from "Talk by Major Alexander P. de Seversky," 4; Taylor, ed., *Combat Aircraft of the World*, 135; Durkota, *The Imperial Russian Air Service*, 105–6.

29. De Seversky quoted in Arnold, "An Ace with One Leg and Nine Crosses."

30. Neshkin and Shabanov, *Aviatori*, 239; press release, December 1940, Ligue Internationale des Aviateurs, LC AIAA Papers, Box 111, p. 2; "de Seversky, Maj. Alexander P.," in *Who's Who in World Aviation and Astronautics*, ed. Marion E. Grambow, vol. 2 (Washington: American Aviation Publications, 1958), 116–17; "One-Legged Mercury," 7.

31. De Seversky quoted from de Seversky, "I Owe My Career to Losing a Leg," 166; Doudoroff, "Certificate," 1; Gunston, *Encyclopedia of Russian Aircraft*, 82–85.

32. Doudoroff, "Certificate," 2; Graf, *The Russian Navy in War and Revolution*, 96–99; Greger, *The Russian Fleet 1914–1917*, 24; McFadyen, "Major Alexander P. de Seversky," 274.

33. "Alexander P. de Seversky," 18; "Biographical Notes on Major Alexander P. de Seversky" (undated, circa 1950), CAM de Seversky Papers, Box 215, p. 3; letter to de Seversky from Ludmila Safanov, November 5, 1951, CAM de Seversky Papers, Box 217.

34. De Seversky, "Special to the New York Mirror," 17; United Artists, "Major Alexander p. de Seversky," 3; interoffice correspondence between Patent Attorney R. C. Rasche and Administrative Assistant M. P. Albert of Seversky Aircraft Corporation, September 27, 1938, CAM de Seversky Papers, Box 5, p.6.

35. Test Pilots Association, "Biographical Sketch," October 1959, CAM de Seversky Papers, Box 215, p. 1; Doudoroff, "Certificate," 2; Green and Swanborough, *The Complete Book of Fighters*, 256.

3. REVOLUTIONARY CHANGES

1. Doudoroff, "Certificate," 2; Arnold, "An Ace with One Leg and Nine Crosses."

2. Michael Kort, *The Soviet Colossus* (Armonk, NY: M. E. Sharpe, 2001), 87–91; Catherine Evtuhov et al., *A History of Russia* (Boston: Houghton Mifflin, 2004), 586–91; Doudoroff, "Certificate," 2.

3. Saul, *Sailors in Revolt,* 77; Graf, *The Russian Navy in War and Revolution,* 113–44.

4. Stone, *The Eastern Front 1914–1917,* 282–301; Saul, *Sailors in Revolt,* 50; Riaboff, *Gatchina Days,* 61–65; Higham, Greenwood, and Hardesty, *Russian Aviation and Air Power in the Twentieth Century,* 112.

5. Doudoroff, "Certificate," 2; Arnold, "Ace with One Leg and Nine Crosses"; Taylor, *Combat Aircraft of the World,* 138; Green and Swanborough, *The Complete Book of Fighters,* 13.

6. Test Pilots Association, "Biographical Sketch," 1; Ray Sanger, *Nieuport Aircraft of World War One* (Wiltshire, UK: Crowood Press, 2002), 117.

7. Sanger, *Nieuport Aircraft of World War One,* 117; Norman Franks, *Nieuport Aces of World War I* (Oxford, UK: Osprey Publishing, 2000), 8–9; Green and Swanborough, *The Complete Book of Fighters,* 430–33; Nowarra and Duval, *Russian Civil and Military Aircraft 1884–1969,* 4.

8. Doudoroff, "Certificate," 2; Arnold, "An Ace with One Leg and Nine Crosses"; Taylor, *Combat Aircraft of the World,* 114–15; Sanger, *Nieuport Aircraft of World War One,* 117.

9. Doudoroff, "Certificate," 2; Adam B. Ulam, *A History of Soviet Russia* (New York: Praeger Publishers, 1976), 8–9; Kort, *The Soviet Colossus,* 98–99.

10. Norman E. Saul, *War and Revolution: The United States and Russia, 1914–1921* (Lawrence: University Press of Kansas, 2002), 140–41; Evtuhov et al., *A History of Russia,* 598; Sanger, *Nieuport Aircraft of World War One,* 117.

11. Mawdsley, *The Russian Revolution and the Baltic Fleet,* 26–27, 38, 40, and 61; George F. Kennan, *Russia Leaves the War* (New York: Atheneum, 1967), 37; Saul, *Sailors in Revolt,* 96 and 123–25; appendix to the Aviation Hall of Fame's Enshrinement Ceremony, December 17, 1970, CAM de Seversky Papers, Box 265.

12. Height statistics are taken from de Seversky's "Certificate of Naturalization," November 26, 1927, CAM de Seversky Papers, Box 1.

13. De Seversky quote from Alexander P. de Seversky, "Welcoming in Response Speech" to a 1933 Dale Carnegie Speech Class, CAM de Seversky Papers, Box 261, pp. 2–3.

14. De Seversky, "Welcoming in Response Speech," 3; Sanger, *Nieuport Aircraft of World War One,* 118; Durkota, *The Imperial Russian Air Service,* 280; Morrow, *Great War in the Air,* 96–97.

15. Stone, *The Eastern Front 1914–1917,* 282; Sanger, *Nieuport Aircraft of World War One,* 118; Grambow, *Who's Who in World Aviation and Astronautics,* vol. 2, 117.

16. De Seversky quote from "Interview Alexander de Seversky, New York City, April 6, 1970" by Murray Green, Henry H. Arnold Collection, U.S. Air Force Historical Research Agency , Microfilm 4382; Sanger, *Nieuport Aircraft of World War One,* 118; Kilmarx, "The Russian Imperial Air Force of World War I," 94.

17. Durkota, *The Imperial Russian Air Service,* 107–8; Stone, *The Eastern Front 1914–1917,* 282; Greger, *The Russian Fleet 1914–1917,* 27.

18. Greger, *The Russian Fleet 1914–1917*, 27; Saul, *Sailors in Revolt*, 158.

19. Doudoroff, "Certificate," 2; Arnold, "Ace with One Leg and Nine Crosses"; Sanger, *Nieuport Aircraft of World War One*, 119.

20. Graf, *The Russian Navy in War and Revolution*, 46; Greger, *The Russian Fleet 1914–1917*, 27; Saul, *Sailors in Revolt*, 159.

21. Graf, *The Russian Navy in War and Revolution*, 151–52; Doudoroff, "Certificate," 2; Durkota, *The Imperial Russian Air Service*, 108.

22. Taylor, *Combat Aircraft of the World*, 114–15; Taylor, *The Lore of Flight*, 50.

23. Arnold, "Ace with One Leg and Nine Crosses"; Farber, "Major de Seversky—Engineer," 116.

24. Mawdsley, *The Russian Revolution and the Baltic Fleet*, 92; Green and Swansborough, *The Complete Book of Fighters*, 434–35; Doudoroff, "Certificate," 2; Farber, "Major Seversky—Engineer, 116.

25. Quote of Estonian from Taylor, "Seversky: An Ace's Place Is in the Air," 16.

26. Farber, "Major Seversky—Engineer," 116; Arnold, "An Ace with One Leg and Nine Crosses."

27. Graf, *The Russian Navy in War and Revolution*, 151–53; Saul, *Sailors in Revolt*, 159; Greger, *The Russian Fleet 1914–1917*, 29–30.

28. Toochkoff quoted in "Appendix" in Alexander P. de Seversky, *Air Power* (New York: Simon & Schuster, 1950), 359; "One Legged Mercury," 112; Neshkin and Shabanov, *Aviatori*, 239; Durkota, *The Imperial Russian Air Service*, 108; "Maj. Alexander P. de Seversky," in Biographies of Pioneer Aviators, Orvil A. Anderson Collection, U.S. Air Force Historical Research Agency, 168.7006-47, p. 2.

29. Press release, December 1940, Ligue Internationale des Aviateurs, 2; Saul, *War and Revolution*, 78; Sanger, *Nieuport Aircraft of World War One*, 119.

30. Kort, *Soviet Colossus*, 103–4; James K. Libbey, *Alexander Gumberg and Soviet-American Relations* (Lexington: University Press of Kentucky, 1977), 21–24.

31. De Seversky, "Special to the New York Mirror," 17; Doudoroff, "Certificate," 3; Taylor, *Combat Aircraft of the World*, 126–27; Green and Swanborough, *The Complete Book of Fighters*, 540–42.

32. Karl Marx, *Capital* (New York: The Modern Library, 1936), 648; Taylor, "Seversky: An Ace's Place Is in the Air," 16; letter from D. de Seversky to author, October 27, 2006.

33. Harold Goldberg, ed., *Documents of Soviet-American Relations*, vol. 1 (Gulf Breeze, FL: Academic International Press, 1993), 26–27; Adam B. Ulam, *Expansion and Coexistence* (New York: Frederick A. Praeger Publishers, 1968), 52–75.

34. Graf, *The Russian Navy in War and Revolution*, 173; Greger, *The Russian Fleet 1914–1917*, 30; Ulam, *Expansion and Coexistence*, 68–69.

35. John Lewis Gaddis, *Russia, the Soviet Union and the United States* (New York: McGraw-Hill, 1990), 71; George F. Kennan, *The Decision to Intervene* (New York: Atheneum, 1967), 43–46; Saul, *War and Revolution*, 240 and 247–48.

36. Saul, *Sailors in Revolt*, 210; Taylor, "Seversky: An Ace's Place Is in the Air," 16; Farber, "Major de Seversky—Engineer," 116.

37. Quote from summary of de Seversky speech published in "Report of the November 1940 Meeting," *The Adventurer* (December 1940), 8.

38. "Report of the November 1940 Meeting," 8; Taylor, "Seversky: An Ace's Place Is in the Air," 16.

39. Doudoroff, "Certificate," 1–3; "Russian Flyer with One Leg Seeks U.S. Job."

4. THE RUSSIAN TEST PILOT AND CONSULTANT IN AMERICA

1. "Russian Flyer with One Leg Seeks U.S. Job"; Kennan, *Russia Leaves the War*, 509–16; Evtuhov et al., *A History of Russia*, 609.

2. James M. Hurt, "Boris Bakhmetev and the Russian Embassy through Revolution and Civil War, 1917–1920," California State University, M.A. thesis, 1973, 28–30; "Presenting Major Alexander P. de Seversky," 3; Farber, "Major de Seversky—Engineer," 116.

3. Quotes from "Regulations of the Voluntary Association of Russian Army and Navy Officers in U.S.A.," CAM de Seversky Papers, Box 1, pp. 3–4. Box 1 also holds samples of certified documents.

4. Morrow, *Great War in the Air*, 341; Major Alexander P. de Seversky, "I Remember Billy Mitchell," *Vogue* (October 15, 1942), 91; memorandum, Subject: Alexander Procofieff Seversky, from Edward S. Moore, District Manager of Aircraft Production, Buffalo, NY, December 5, 1918, Long Island Studies Institute of Hofstra University (hereafter, LISI), de Seversky Family Papers, Folder 1.

5. Taylor, *Combat Aircraft of the World*, 406–7; Green and Swanborough, *The Complete Book of Fighters*, 507–8; Morrow, *Great War in the Air*, 312; Moore memorandum, December 5, 1918; letter from Jas. E. Kepperley to G. H. Curtiss, president, Curtiss Engineering Corporation, December 1, 1918, CAM de Seversky Papers, Box 1; Roger E. Bilstein, *Flight Patterns* (Athens: University of Georgia Press, 1983), 10.

6. Test Pilots Association, "Biographical Sketch," 3; de Seversky, "I Remember Billy Mitchell," 91; letter from de Seversky to Claim Department, American Express Company, February 13, 1919, CAM de Seversky Papers, Box 1; draft materials to Who's Who in World Aviation (undated, circa 1958), CAM de Seversky Papers, Box 215, p. 1; "Regulations of the Voluntary Association of Russian Army and Navy Officers in the U.S.A.," 3.

7. Kendrick A. Clements, *The Presidency of Woodrow Wilson* (Lawrence: University Press of Kansas, 1992), 149; "Christoffer Hannevig's Connections," *New York Times*, November 9, 1917; "Gift for National Portrait Gallery," *New York Times*, December 14, 1918; "Receivers Named for Hannevig & Co.," *New York Times*, February 12, 1921.

8. "Interview of Alexander P. de Seversky by Brigadier General George W. Goddard," (undated circa 1960), U.S. Air Force Historical Research Agency, Maxwell AFB, K168.051-17.

9. Finne, *Igor Sikorsky*, 161; Igor I. Sikorsky, *The Story of the Winged-S*, 146–47; Tom D. Crouch, *Wings* (Washington: Smithsonian National Air and Space Museum, 2003), 347; Morrow, *Great War in the Air*, 283; Test Pilots Association, "Biographical Sketch," 3; "New Incorporations," *New York Times*, May 28, 1919; A. Scott Berg, *Lindbergh* (New York: G. P. Putnam's Sons, 1998), 91.

10. "New Incorporations"; "Interview of Alexander P. de Seversky by Brig. Gen. George W. Goddard"; Maurice Allward, *Seaplanes and Flying Boats* (New York: Barnes & Noble, 1993), 37–39; "Receivers Named for Hannevig & Co."; Ted Wilbur, *The First Flight Across the Atlantic, May 1919* (Washington: National Air and Space Museum, 1969).

11. Sikorsky, *Story of the Winged-S*, 147; Crouch, *Wings*, 347; "Soviet's Railway Plans," *New York Times*, March 25, 1919; "American Capital in Deal with Reds?," *New York Times*, May 2, 1919.

12. "Soviet Railway Plans"; "American Capital in Deal with Reds?"; "Interview of Alexander P. de Seversky by Brig. Gen. George W. Goddard."

13. "Interview of Alexander P. de Seversky by Brig. Gen. George W. Goddard"; de Seversky, "I Remember Billy Mitchell," 91; Test Pilots Association, "Biographical Sketch," 3.

14. Test Pilots Association, "Biographical Sketch," 3; "Interview of Alexander P. de Seversky by Brig. Gen. George W. Goddard."

15. Taylor, *The Lore of Flight*, 78–79; Crouch, *Bishop's Boys*, 222–28.

16. De Witt S. Copp, *A Few Great Captains* (New York: Doubleday & Company, 1980), 241; "Interview of Alexander P. de Seversky by Brig. Gen. George W. Goddard"; William Wyatt Davenport, *Gyro!* (New York: Charles Scribner's Sons, 1978), 184–85.

17. "Interview of Alexander P. de Seversky by Brig. Gen. George W. Goddard"; "Fleet of Airplanes Auxiliary to Ships," *New York Times*, April 10, 1919; "Airplane Fall Kills Jolly," *New York Times*, April 28, 1919.

18. Test Pilots Association, "Biographical Sketch," 3; "Auto Money to Win War," *New York Times*, October 14, 1917; "New Aircraft Shown in Garden," *New York Times*, March 2, 1919; "Commercial Planes Making Big Strides," *New York Times*, March 9, 1919; Taylor, *Combat Aircraft of the World*, 362–64.

19. Test Pilots Association, "Biographical Sketch," 3; Roger E. Bilstein, *Flight in America* (Baltimore: Johns Hopkins University Press, 1994), 55–56; Bilstein, *Flight Patterns*, 48–49; Oliver E. Allen, *The Airline Builders* (Alexandria, VA: Time-Life Books, 1981), 52.

20. Quote from Alexander P. de Seversky, "Remember Billy Mitchell!," *The Air Power Historian* 3 (October 1956): 179; Dik Alan Daso, *Hap Arnold and the Evolution of American Airpower* (Washington: Smithsonian Institution Press, 2000), 140; Copp, *A Few Great Captains*, 255–57.

21. Bert Frandsen, "Mitchell, William 'Billy' (1879–1936)," in *Air Warfare*, ed. Walter J. Boyne (Santa Barbara, CA: ABC-CLIO, 2002), 430–31; William Mitchell, *Winged Defense* (New York: Dover Publications, 1988), iii–v; Ron Dick, *American*

*Eagles* (Charlottesville, VA: Howell Press, 1997), 45–46 and 50–52; Taylor, *First World War*, 232–34.

22. Mitchell, *Winged Defense*, xi–xix; Lt. Col. Stanley P. Latiolais, USAF, "The Re-evaluation of Douhet's, Mitchell's and de Seversky's Theories in the Light of Modern Weapons," thesis submitted to the faculty, Air Command and Staff School of Air University, Maxwell AFB Library (M-32.984-NCL357R), 16–18.

23. Theodore Roscoe, *On the Seas and in the Skies* (New York: Hawthorn Books, 1970), 148; Thomas G. Foxworth, *The Speed Seekers* (Newbury Park, CA: Haynes Publications, 1989), 13–14; "Airmen Challenge Test with Big Ships," *New York Times* (February 7, 1921); copy of memorandum from secretary of the navy to commander-in-chief of the Atlantic Fleet, "Destruction of Enemy Shipping in Custody of U.S. Navy," February 24, 1921, Library of Congress, William Mitchell Papers (hereafter LC Mitchell Papers), Box 9; memorandum from Major Walter G. Kilner, chief of U.S.A.A.S. Operations Division to chief of Training and Operations Group, "Plan of Operations for Bombardment by Airplane of Single Battleship," December 11, 1920, LC Mitchell Papers, Box 8, pp. 1–3.

24. Mitchell, *Winged Defense*, 43–46; Roscoe, *On the Seas and in the Skies*, 150; "Interview of Alexander P. de Seversky by Brig. Gen. George W. Goddard."

25. Taylor, *Combat Aircraft of the World*, 482–83 and 525–26; "Interview of Alexander P. de Seversky by Brig. Gen. George W. Goddard"; Alexander P. de Seversky, memo to editors, "Refueling in Flight," CAM de Seversky Papers, Box 208, pp. 1–3.

26. McFadyen, "Major Alexander P. de Seversky," 275; de Seversky, "I Remember Billy Mitchell," 92; U.S. Patent Office, Patent # 1728449, "Aerial Filling Device"; U.S. Patent Office, Patent # 1017348, "Sight Control for Aircraft" (latter not given public identification number until January 7, 1936); Isaac Don Levine, *Mitchell* (New York: Duell, Sloan and Pearce, 1943), 281; de Seversky "Remember Billy Mitchell!," 180; Roscoe, *On the Seas and in the Skies*, 154–55; Mitchell, *Winged Defense*, 56–66.

27. Foxworth, *Speed Seekers*, 13; Roscoe, *On the Seas and in the Skies*, 155–56; Mitchell, *Winged Defense*, 67–69; Taylor, *Combat Aircraft of the World*, 372–73 and 525–26; Bilstein, *Flight Patterns*, 12–13.

28. De Seversky quoted from de Seversky, "Remember Billy Mitchell!," 181.

29. "Interview of Alexander P. de Seversky by Brig. Gen. George W. Goddard"; Dr. Murray Green, interview of Alexander P. de Seversky on April 16, 1970, U.S. Air Force Historical Research Agency, General Henry H. Arnold Collection, Microfilm 43827, p. 2; Roscoe, *On the Seas and in the Skies*, 157.

30. Mitchell, *Winged Defense*, 71–73; "Report of Reconnaissance by Brigade Commander (Mitchell) of Operations by the 14th Heavy Bombardment Squadron, Langley Field, Against the Ex-German Battleship *Ostfriesland* with 2,000-lb. Bombs," LC Mitchell Papers, William Mitchell Journals, Box 4, pp. 1–3.

31. Levine, *Mitchell*, 263; Roscoe, *On the Seas and in the Skies*, 158.

5. THE RUSSIAN INVENTOR

1. Letter from director of Air Service to commanding officer of McCook Field, March 21, 1921, CAM de Seversky Papers, Box 1; "Russian Aviator at M'Cook with Novel Invention: 'Ace with Wooden Leg Claims He Can Fill Gas Tanks While Flying,'" *Dayton Evening Herald*, March 23, 1921; Mitchell, *Winged Defense*, 226–27; Ron Dick, *American Eagle* (Charlottesville, VA: Howell Press, 1997), 380–81; Crouch, *Wings*, 235; Copp, *A Few Great Captains*, 64.

2. Timothy Moy, *War Machines* (College Station: Texas A&M University Press, 2001), 34; Copp, *A Few Great Captains*, 278; Stephen L. McFarland, *America's Pursuit of Precision Bombing, 1910–1945* (Washington: Smithsonian Institution Press, 1995), 32–33; Test Pilots Association, "Biographical Sketch."

3. Moy, *War Machines*, 81; McFarland, *America's Pursuit of Precision Bombing*, 14–15.

4. McFarland, *America's Pursuit of Precision Bombing*, 14–15; Moy, *War Machines*, 81; de Seversky, "I Remember Billy Mitchell," 92.

5. De Seversky, "Remember Billy Mitchell!," 182; McFadyen, "Major Alexander P. de Seversky," 275; John F. Whiteley, "Alexander Seversky," *Aerospace Historian* 24 (Fall 1977): 155.

6. De Seversky, "Remember Billy Mitchell!," 182–83; de Seversky, "I Remember Billy Mitchell," 92; interview of Alexander de Seversky by Green; letter from Sperry to Major Bane, April 13, 1921, Hagley Museum & Library, Elmer Sperry Papers, Series V, Box 29, Seversky Bomb Sight Folder (hereafter Sperry Papers, Seversky Folder), pp. 1–2.

7. J. C. Hunsaker, *Biographical Memoir of Elmer Ambrose Sperry 1860–1930* (Washington: National Academy of Sciences, 1955), 3–12; Edna Yost, *Modern Americans in Science and Invention* (New York: Frederick A. Stokes Company, 1941), 134–42.

8. McFarland, *America's Pursuit of Precision Bombing*, 26–44; Moy, *War Machines*, 80–85; Thomas Parke Hughes, *Elmer Sperry* (Baltimore: Johns Hopkins University Press, 1974), 236–37.

9. Letter from Sperry to Bane, April 13, 1921; letters from Sperry to Captain Inglis, April 12 and 13, 1921; all in Sperry Papers, Seversky Folder.

10. Quote from letter from Sperry to Bane, April 21, 1921; letter reply from Bane to Sperry, April 23, 1921; both in Sperry Papers, Seversky Folder.

11. Letter from Sperry to Major Hobley, May 18, 1921, pp. 1–5; confirmation copy of telegram from Sperry to Hobley, May 18, 1921; telegram from Bane to Sperry, June 2, 1921, all in Sperry Papers, Seversky Folder.

12. Telegram from Bane to Sperry, June 2, 1921; letter from Major L. W. McIntosh, assistant division chief, Engineering Division, to Sperry, June 6, 1921; letter from Sperry to Bane, April 21, 1921, pp. 1–2, all in Sperry Papers, Seversky Folder.

13. Quote from Sperry's letter to Engineering Division, June 2, 1921; letter from Sperry to Bane, April 25, 1921; telegram from Sperry to Hobley, June 1, 1921, all in Sperry Papers, Seversky Folder.

14. General Mitchell quoted in de Seversky, "Remember Billy Mitchell!," 184; letter from Major Edward L. Hoffman to Sperry, September 6, 1921, Sperry Papers, Seversky Folder; "Interview of Alexander P. de Seversky by Brig. Gen. George W. Goddard"; Whiteley, "Alexander de Seversky," 155.

15. U.S. Patent Office, Alexander Procofieff-Seversky, "Sighting Control for Aircraft," filed April 10, 1922, Patent #2,027,348; letter from Bane to Sperry, January 24, 1922, and letter from Sperry to Bane, May 12, 1922, both in Sperry Papers, Seversky Folder. For discussion on how the bombsight could be operated by a single bombardier, see page 3 of the following: U.S. Patent Office, Alexander Procofieff-Seversky, "Range Finding and Flight Directing Apparatus for Use in Aircraft," filed June 18, 1923, Patent #2,027,349.

16. Letter from Sperry to Bane, May 12, 1922; letter from Captain R. H. Fleet, contracting officer, to Sperry, May 17, 1922; letter from Sperry to Fleet, May 22, 1922; Sperry Company interoffice memorandum, July 19, 1922, all in Sperry Papers, Seversky Folder; Maurer Maurer, *Aviation in the U.S. Army, 1919–1939* (Washington: Office of the Air Force History, 1987), 156–57.

17. Sperry Company interoffice memorandum, July 19, 1922; Maurer, *Aviation in the U.S. Army*, 161–63; U.S. Patent Office, Serial No. 708696, Alexander Procofieff-Seversky, "Aircraft Landing Gear," filed April 24, 1924; McFadyen, "Major Alexander P. de Seversky," 276; Farber, "Major de Seversky—Engineer," 132; Taylor, *The Lore of Flight*, 99–112.

18. Vernon B. Byrd, *Passing Gas* (Chico, CA: Byrd Publishing, 1994), 17; U.S. Patent Office, Alexander Procofieff-Seversky, "Aerial Filling Device," filed June 13, 1921, Patent #1,728,449; Alexander P. de Seversky, memo to editors, Subject: Refueling in Flight, March 3, 1949, CAM Seversky Papers, Box 208, pp. 1–3.

19. De Seversky quoted from his patent: "Aerial Filling Device," 1.

20. Edward Jablonsky, *America in the Air War* (Alexandria, VA: Time-Life Books, 1982), 72–79; Moy, *War Machines*, 62–63; Stephen Budiansky, *Air Power* (New York: Penguin Books, 2004), 184–86; James H. Willbanks, "Chennault, Claire L. (1890–1958)," in *Air Warfare*, ed. Boyne, 124; Taylor, *Combat Aircraft of the World*, 453–54; Ron Dick, *American Eagles: A History of the United States Air Force* (Charlottesville, VA: Howell Press, 1997), 171.

21. Bilstein, *Flight Patterns*, 11; Richard K. Smith, *Seventy-Five Years of Inflight Refueling* (Washington: U.S. Government Printing Office, 1998), 1; "Refueling Device Used by Army Endurance Plane Invented by Former Russian Ace," *New York Sun*, January 16, 1929; de Seversky, Refueling in Flight.

22. Sperry Company interoffice memorandum, July 19, 1922; letter from Hobley, acting chief of the Engineering Division to de Seversky, October 13, 1922, CAM de Seversky Papers, Box 1, pp. 1–2.

23. Hobley quoted from his letter to de Seversky, October 13, 1922; message to author from Marjorie McNinch, reference archivist, Manuscript & Archives Department, Hagley Museum & Library, July 14, 2007.

24. McFarland, *America's Pursuit of Precision Bombing*, 32; Taylor, "Seversky: An Ace's Place Is in the Air," 16; draft material sent to *Who's Who in World Aviation* undated (circa 1958), CAM de Seversky Papers, Box 215, pp. 1–2.

25. "Biographical Notes on Major Alexander P. de Seversky," CAM de Seversky Papers, Box 215 p. 4; Taylor, "Seversky: An Ace's Place Is in the Air," 16; Farber, "Major de Seversky—Engineer," 132; Seversky Aircraft Corporation interoffice correspondence from R. C. Rasche to M. P. Albert, Subject: Statement of All Patent Rights, etc., Appertaining to Seversky Aircraft Corporation, September 27, 1938, CAM de Seversky Papers, Box 5, pp. 1–6.

26. "Range Finding and Flight Directing Apparatus for Use in Aircraft"; de Seversky, "I Remember Billy Mitchell," 92; de Seversky, "Remember Billy Mitchell!," 183.

27. De Seversky quoted from de Seversky, "Remember Billy Mitchell!," 183.

28. Burke Davis, *The Billy Mitchell Story* (Philadelphia: Chilton Book Company, 1969), 73; Roscoe, *On the Seas and in the Skies*, 159; Crocker, *Dictionary of Aeronautical English*, 220–21; Taylor, *Combat Aircraft of the World*, 525.

29. "Range Finding and Flight Directing Apparatus for Use in Aircraft," figure 1; de Seversky, "I Remember Billy Mitchell," 92; Whiteley, "Alexander de Seversky," 155.

30. Whiteley, "Alexander de Seversky," 156.

31. U.S. Patent Office, Alexander Procofieff-Seversky, assigned to Seversky Aero Corporation, "Variable Speed Drive for Calculator Mechanism," filed September 23, 1923, Patent #2,026,912; "Airplanes to Bomb Old Battleships," *New York Times*, September 4, 1923; "Will Drop Bombs Two Miles in Air," *New York Times*, September 5, 1923; Davis, *Billy Mitchell Story*, 73.

32. Quote from Levine, *Mitchell*, 290; Roscoe, *On the Seas and in the Skies*, 159.

33. "Lone 1-Ton [*sic*] Bomb Sends U.S.S. Virginia to Bottom in Flash," *Washington Post*, September 6, 1923; Davis, *Billy Mitchell Story*, 73; "Importance of Air Control Shows."

34. General Pershing quoted from "Pershing Praises Air Bombers' Aim: But Tests Do Not Prove Modern Warships Can Be Sunk, He Says," *New York Times*, September 7, 1923; Davis, *Billy Mitchell Story*, 73; Levine, *Mitchell*, 291.

35. "Pershing quoted from "Pershing Praises Air Bombers' Aim"; Levine, *Mitchell*, 292; C. V. Glines, "The Long Road to an Independent Air Force," *Aviation History* 18 (September 2007): 30–31.

6. THE RUSSIAN INVENTOR BECOMES AN AMERICAN DESIGNER

1. Whiteley quoted from Whiteley, "Alexander de Seversky," 156; "Variable Speed Drive for Calculator Mechanism"; Sikorsky, *Story of the Winged-S*, 155–57; Frank J. Delear, *Igor Sikorsky* (New York: Dodd, Mead & Company, 1976), 102–5; Joseph Keogan, *The Igor I. Sikorsky Aircraft Legacy* (Stratford, CT: Igor I. Sikorsky Archives, 2003), 23.

2. Whiteley, "Alexander de Seversky," 156. Letter from Prince Obolensky, October 4, 2006; letters from N. Procofieff, October 9, 2006, and March 20, 2007, all to author from D. de Seversky.

3. "Variable Speed Drive for Calculator Mechanism"; "Professional Engineering License," February 4, 1924, CAM de Seversky Papers, Box 1.

4. Letter from Weeks to Davis, undated but circa November 25, 1923, CAM de Seversky Papers, Box 1, pp. 1–2.

5. Weeks quoted from letter to Davis, 1.

6. De Seversky, "Remember Billy Mitchell!," 184; passenger records and manifests pertaining to de Seversky's two voyages to Europe in 1924 are located in the American Family Immigration History Center of the Statue of Liberty–Ellis Island Foundation; application for pilot's license, Aeronautical Branch, U.S. Department of Commerce, June 3, 1927, CAM de Seversky Papers, Box 1, p. 1; letter from N. Procofieff, July 16, 2007, to author via D. de Seversky.

7. "Statement of All Patent Rights"; partial list of Maj. Alexander P. de Seversky's inventions, CAM de Seversky Papers, Box 8; letter from Sperry to Patrick, December 30, 1924, Sperry Papers, Seversky Folder; Hunsaker, *Elmer Ambrose Sperry*, 14; "Biographical Notes on Major Alexander P. de Seversky," 4.

8. Telegram from Patrick to Sperry, December 27, 1924; telegram from Sperry to Patrick, December 29, 1924, both in Sperry Papers, Seversky Folder; McFarland, *America's Pursuit of Precision Bombing*, 30; Moy, *War Machines*, 82; memorandum for chief, Materiel Division, from chief, U.S. Army Air Corps, January 5, 1928, National Archives, RG 342, Sarah Clark Collection, RD 3176, Box 5712, File 471.63 Bomb Sights (hereafter NA, Bomb Sights), 1–8.

9. Moy, *War Machines*, 82; memorandum from Gillmore to Fechet, "Bomb Sight Development," February 21, 1928, NA, Bomb Sights, 1; U.S. Patent Office, Alexander Procofieff-Seversky, "Apparatus for Use in Directing the Flight of Aircraft," filed July 20, 1925, assigned to Seversky Aero Corporation, Patent #2, 027,350.

10. Whiteley, "Alexander de Seversky," 156; "Interview of Alexander P. de Seversky by Brig. Gen. George W. Goddard."

11. News clipping from *Biloxi Herald*, CAM de Seversky Papers, Box 265; "Biographical Notes on Major Alexander P. de Seversky," 4; "Mrs. Alexander de Seversky, 60, Wife of Plane Designer Is Dead," *New York Times*, July 31, 1967. Online birth records for Orleans Parish reveal that Evelyn Olliphant was born in 1902, not 1907 as suggested by obituary.

12. De Seversky quoted from de Seversky, "I Owe My Career to Losing a Leg," 169.

13. *Biloxi Herald* news clipping, LC AIAA, Box 111; Woodlawn Cemetery, Lot #11964, Plot Brookside, Section 21, Vault #5; investment diary, CAM de Seversky Papers, Box 1; remittance advice to de Seversky, October 1, 1930, LISI de Seversky Family Folder.

14. Application for Pilot's License, 1–2; Crouch, *Wings*, 235; Bilstein, *Flight Patterns*, 140–41; Transport Pilot Certificate, No. 1769, from aeronautics director, U.S. Department of Commerce, to de Seversky, CAM de Seversky Papers, Box 1.

15. Letter from de Seversky to D. Scarritt, aeronautics director, U.S. Department of Commerce, February 20, 1928, CAM de Seversky Papers, Box 1; "Biographical

Notes on Major Alexander P. de Seversky," 4; "Russian Flying Ace Now American Citizen," *New York Times*, November 27, 1927.

16. Letter from Gillmore to Fechet, January 9, 1928, NA, Bomb Sights, 2; U.S. War Department, U.S. Army Air Corps Materiel Division, Contract No. 7 535 AC-648 between the U.S. Government and Seversky Aero Corporation, May 28, 1927, CAM de Seversky Papers, Box 7, pp. 1–9; Maurer, *Aviation in the U.S. Army*, 388.

17. Budiansky, *Air Power*, 172; Office of History, pamphlet, Pope AFB, "A Heritage Perspective of the 43D Airlift Wing and Pope AFB," September 2006, 20; James D. Perry, "Air Corps Experimentation in the Interwar Years—A Case Study," *Joint Force Quarterly* 22 (Summer 1999): 47.

18. Fechet quoted from memorandum for chief, Materiel Division, January 6, 1928, NA, Bomb Sights, 1; Moy, *War Machines*, 84–86.

19. Letter from Fechet to Gillmore, January 20, 1928; memorandum from Gillmore to Fechet, January 19, 1928; letter from Capt. O. S. Ferson, executive officer, Materiel Division, to Bombardment Board president, January 24, 1928; Maj. Hugh J. Knerr, Bombardment Board president, Bomb Sights Report to chief of Materiel Division, February 7, 1928, all in NA Bomb Sights.

20. Gillmore to Fechet, Bomb Sight Development, February 21, 1928, p. 3; Materiel Division Contract No. 7 535 AC-648; Maj. Delos C. Emmons, executive officer to Fechet, to Materiel Division chief, Subject: Bomb Sight Development, March 7, 1928; MacDill to de Seversky, Subject: Construction of Bomb Sights, March 16, 1928, pp. 1–2, all in NA, Bomb Sights.

21. Memorandum from MacDill to de Seversky, Subject: Bomb Sights, April 10, 1928; Inglis to Experimental Engineering chief, Subject: Report on Trip to Washington Conference, May 3, 1928; letter from de Seversky to Air Corps Chief, April 20, 1928, pp. 1–2, all in NA, Bomb Sights.

22. Letter from Maj. C. W. Howard, Experimental Engineering chief, to Fechet, December 5, 1928, NA, Bomb Sights; Maurer, *Aviation in the U.S. Army*, 389; McFarland, *America's Pursuit of Precision Bombing*, 34; Test Pilots Association press release, 4.

23. Mark Frezzo, "Great Depression," in *The American Economy*, ed. Cynthia Clark Northrup (Santa Barbara, CA: ABC-CLIO, 2003), 135–36.

24. Crouch, *Wings*, 287–88; Joshua Stoff, *Long Island Airports* (Charleston, SC: Arcadia Publishing, 2004), 83; "Hicksville Air Race Won by Eric Wood," *New York Times*, October 20, 1929.

25. Geoff Jones and Chuck Stewart, *Vintage Aircraft over America* (Shrewsbury, UK: Air Life Publishing, 2002), 9–10.

26. Quote from "Dances Plane to Waltz of Radio," *Cleveland Plain Dealer*, September 5, 1931; news clipping from *Cleveland News*, September 5, 1931, CAM de Seversky Papers, Box 2.

27. Stoff, *Long Island Airports*, 93–95 and 121–28; "Air Show Planes Swoop over City," *New York Times*, October 17, 1931; "Fliers to Aid Idle Today," *New York Times*,

October 23, 1931; "Russian Flier Stops Motor to Stunt," *New York Evening Journal*, November 12, 1931, news clipping, CAM de Seversky Papers, Box 2; "They'll Come, They'll Soar, They'll Conquer for Charity," *New York American*, November 20, 1931; and "Help for Jobless Falls from the Sky," *New York Evening Journal*, November 23, 1931, news clippings, CAM de Seversky Papers, Box 265.

28. Mrs. Alexander P. de Seversky's pilot log book, CAM de Seversky Papers, Box 1; picture news clipping of Mrs. Seversky, *The Sportsman Pilot* (September 1930), CAM de Seversky Papers, Box 265; "Women May Achieve Equality in Flying Says de Seversky, for Only Brain Counts," *New York World Telegram*, June 17, 1932, news clipping, CAM de Seversky Papers, Box 265; James H. Doolittle with Carroll V. Glines, *I Could Never Be So Lucky Again* (New York: Bantam Books, 1991), 230–88.

29. De Seversky quoted from interview transcript of WJZ's "If I Had a Chance," October 7, 1938, CAM de Seversky Papers, Box 261.

30. Quote from undated letter (circa January 1931) from Winkle to E. de Seversky and receipt to E. de Seversky from Winkle, February 9, 1931, both in LISI, de Seversky Family Folder; Bilstein, *Flight in America*, 85; Susan Butler, *East to the Dawn* (Reading, MA: Addison-Wesley, 1997), 232–33; "The Flying Ladies Have Their Day at Air Show," *Detroit News*, April 17, 1931; "In Benefit Air Show," *New York Daily News*, June 20, 1932; news clippings, CAM de Seversky Papers, Box 265.

31. Agreement between Sikorsky Aviation Corporation and Alexander P. de Seversky, January 2, 1930, CAM de Seversky Papers, Box 3, pp. 1–3; Delear, *Igor Sikorsky*, 131–35; James K. Libbey, "Sikorsky, Igor I. (1889–1972)," in *Air Warfare*, ed. Boyne, 567.

32. Sikorsky, *Story of the Winged-S*, 183; P. J. Capelotti, *Explorer's Air Yacht* (Missoula, MT: Pictorial Histories Publishing, 1995), 19–34.

33. Agreement between Sikorsky and de Seversky, 1; "E. R. A. Seligmans Reach Palm Beach," *New York Times*, February 25, 1930; letter from J. Castello Montenegro, Pan American Airways, to de Seversky, March 9, 1930, CAM de Seversky Papers, Box; Delear, *Igor Sikorsky*, 144–251.

34. "Lindbergh Tries Plane," *New York Times*, May 8, 1930; "Seversky Tries Out Plane," *New York Times*, May 11, 1930.

35. U.S. Patent Office, Alexander Procofieff-Seversky, "Testing Apparatus," filed April 3, 1926, Patent #1953045; "Amphibian Landing Gear for Aircraft," filed March 28, 1927, Patent #1963630; "Aircraft Landing Gear," filed April 25, 1928, Patent #2021876; "New Incorporations," *New York Times*, February 18, 1931.

## 7. THE INNOVATIVE DESIGNER

1. "Maj. Alexander P. de Seversky," *Aero Digest* 25 (July 1933): 28 and 72; Robert Hucker, "Seversky: Innovator and Prophet," National Air and Space Museum Archives, Seversky Biography Files, CS-415000-01 (hereafter NASM, Seversky Files).

2. Franks, *Nieuport Aces of World War I*, 86–87; "Pishvanov," *The Seversky News* (October 1936), p. 2. Latter made available to author by Pishvanov's son, Nicholas, October 4, 2006.

3. Telephone calls from Nick Pishvanov to author, October 8, 2006, and November 4, 2007; Jones and Stewart, *Vintage Aircraft over America*, 9–10; Seversky Aircraft Corporation Prospectus, July 11, 1936, LISI Seversky Family Papers, Folder 1; "P-47 Designer Retiring from Post at Republic," *New York Times*, May 15, 1962.

4. Nick Pishvanov to author, October 4, 2006; "New Incorporations"; Bilstein, *Flight Patterns*, 130; "Amphibian Racer Now," *New York Times*, May 21, 1933.

5. Quote from "The Founder Complains," *Time* (September 2, 1940), Time Archive Online; "Paul Moore, Lawyer, Dies at 74," *New York Times*, December 20, 1959; Seversky Aircraft Corporation Prospectus, 8.

6. Quote from "Amphibian of 220-Mile Speed and Novel Construction Now Being Built Here," *New York Times*, March 27, 1932; John Cummings, "Pioneers in Aviation," *Newsday*, March 14, 1987.

7. Quotes from "The Reminiscences of Alexander Kartveli," Columbia University Oral History Project, May 10, 1960, p. 10; Crouch, *Wings*, 337; WOR Radio Station transcript, January 27, 1933, CAM de Seversky Papers, Box 261, pp. 1–2.

8. "Amphibian of 220-Mile Speed and Novel Construction Now Being Built Here"; "A Novel Amphibian," *Scientific American* 149 (November 1933): 227; "Reminiscences of Alexander Kartveli," 10.

9. De Seversky quoted from WOR Radio transcript, 2; U.S. Patent Office, Alexander P. de Seversky, "Aircraft Anchor," filed December 22, 1931, assigned to Seversky Aircraft Corporation, Patent #2009356.

10. "One-Legged Mercury," 113; "Novel Amphibian," 227; U.S. Patent #1963630, "Amphibian Landing Gear for Aircraft"; U.S. Patent #2021876, "Aircraft Landing Gear"; Bill Gunston, *Development of Piston Aero Engines* (Newbury Park, CA: Haynes North America, 1999), 129–31; Michael H. Gorn, *Expanding the Envelope* (Lexington: University Press of Kentucky, 2001), 75 and 98–99.

11. "Stunt Fliers Thrill 7,500 at Air Show," *New York Times*, June 20, 1932; "Many Private Fliers to Make Air Tour from Roosevelt Field to Canadian Fete," *New York Times*, August 14, 1932; Doris L. Rich, *Jackie Cochran* (Gainesville: University Press of Florida, 2007), 30–31; "Army Fliers Thrill 25,000 at Air Races," *New York Times*, August 31, 1932; picture of de Seversky's plaque, CAM de Seversky Papers, Box 216.

12. Dale Carnegie, *Public Speaking and Influencing Men in Business* (New York: W. W. Norton, 1926); "Carnegie, Dale," in *Current Biography*, ed. Maxine Block (New York: H. W. Wilson Company, 1941), 138–41.

13. "Amphibian Racer Now," *New York Times*, May 21, 1933; "Fast Amphibian Nears Completion," *New York Times*, May 21, 1933; "Today on the Radio," *New York Times*, June 21, 1933.

14. Evelyn de Seversky quoted from "Mrs. Seversky's Talk over WMCA—6/21/33," CAM de Seversky Papers, Box 218, pp. 1–2.

15. "Dates for Air Races," *New York Times*, June 4, 1933; "Thaw Enters Air Derby," *New York Times*, June 25, 1933; "Noted Fliers Plan Charity Air Circus," *New York Times*, August 12, 1933.

16. "Noted Fliers Plan Charity Air Circus"; "Sky Knight to Aid Air Pageant Plans," *New York Times*, July 30, 1933; Donald Caldwell, "Udet, Ernst (1896–1941)," in *Air Warfare*, ed. Boyne, 641; "Amphibian Plane Sets World Mark," *New York Times*, October 9, 1933.

17. "Amphibian Plane Sets World Mark"; Davis, *P-47 Thunderbolt*, 4.

18. "De Seversky Again Sets Record in Amphibian," *New York Times*, October 10, 1933; FAI Diplôme de Record, 1933, CAM de Seversky Papers, Box 216; "De Seversky Breaks Amphibian Record," *New York Times*, September 16, 1935; FAI Diplôme de Record, 1935, LISI, de Seversky Family Papers, Folder 1.

19. "Reminiscences of Alexander Kartveli," 10; "De Seversky in Motor Post," *New York Times*, November 21, 1933.

20. Hucker, "Seversky: Innovator and Prophet," 56; Colombian contract discussed in "Agreement between Seversky Aircraft Corporation and Kirkham Engineering and Manufacturing Corporation," May 16, 1934, CAM de Seversky Papers, Box 3.

21. "Agreement between Seversky Aircraft Corporation and Kirkham Engineering and Manufacturing Corporation"; Crouch, *Wings*, 219–20 and 362–63; Stoff, *Long Island Airports*, 95–99.

22. "Agreement between Seversky Aircraft and Kirkham Engineering," 1–3.

23. "Agreement between Seversky Aircraft and Kirkham Engineering," 2; check #1708 from consulate general of Colombia to Seversky Aircraft Corporation, LISI, de Seversky Family Papers, Folder 1; letter from Kirkham to Seversky Aircraft Corporation, July 26, 1934, CAM de Seversky Papers, Box 3, pp. 1–3.

24. Letter from Kirkham to Frank L. North, secretary-treasurer of Seversky Aircraft, September 19, 1934, pp. 1–2; letter from Kirkham to North, September 24, 1934; letter from Kirkham to Seversky Aircraft Corporation, November 9, 1934, pp. 1–2; all in CAM de Seversky Papers, Box 3.

25. Letter from de Seversky to Kirkham Engineering, November 12, 1934; letter from Kirkham to Seversky Aircraft, November 16, 1934; letter from North to Kirkham Engineering, November 26, 1934; letter from P. E. Carroll, Legal and Claim Department, National Surety Corporation, to Kirkham, December 20, 1934; all in CAM de Seversky Papers, Box 3; Edward T. Maloney, *Sever the Sky* (Corona De Mar, CA: Planes of Fame Publishers, 1979), 15.

26. "Find Profits Fair on Navy Airplanes," *New York Times*, March 9, 1934; Copp, *A Few Great Captains*, 160.

27. "Alexander de Seversky, Whose Romantic Career Is Parallel to Fiction, 'Flying Stepson of Dayton,'" *The Dayton Journal*, January 13, 1935; Whiteley, "Alexander de Seversky," 156.

28. "Hull Challenges Arms Testimony," *New York Times*, September 11, 1934; Davis, *P-35*, 4; "35 Training Planes Ordered for Army," *New York Times*, January 3, 1935; "Seversky Basic Trainer," *Aviation* 24 (February 1935): 70.

29. "35 Training Planes Ordered for Army"; Hucker, "Seversky: Innovator and Prophet," 56.

30. Stoff, *Long Island Airports*, 95–96; "Airplane Maker Files Stock Issue," *New York Times*, June 23, 1936; "Aircraft Firm Buys Long Island Plants," *New York Times*, October 17, 1936.

31. "Interview Alexander de Seversky, New York City, April 16, 1970." Memorandum, Subject: Contract W 535 AC-7348 Production BT-8 Airplanes, To: Major de Seversky, From: Captain Gullet, March 16, 1936; letter from de Seversky to Gullet, March 13, 1936; statement for the files of Seversky Aircraft by S. P. Lyon, factory manager, December 21, 1935, all in CAM de Seversky Papers, Box 10.

32. "Alexander P. de Seversky," 20; Davis, *P-35*, 4; Maloney, *Sever the Sky*, 8.

8. THE P-35 MANUFACTURER

1. Mitchell, *Winged Defense*, 55; Giulio Douhet, *The Command of the Air*, trans. Dino Ferrari (Washington: Office of Air Force History, 1983—first rough translation available in the United States in 1923); Basil H. Liddell Hart, *Paris: Or, the Future of War* (New York: E. P. Dutton & Company, 1925).

2. Copp, *A Few Great Captains*, 103–6; Budiansky, *Air Power*, 184–86; Martha Byrd, *Chennault* (Tuscaloosa: University of Alabama Press, 1987), 38–64; Jack Samson, *Chennault* (New York: Doubleday, 1987), 87–102; Claire Lee Chennault, *Pursuit Aviation* (Maxwell Field, AL: Air Corps Tactical School, 1934).

3. De Seversky quoted from Alexander P. de Seversky, "How Can Pursuit Aviation Regain Its Tactical Freedom?," *U.S. Air Services* 19 (March 1934): 16.

4. Chennault quoted from Claire Lee Chennault, *Way of a Fighter* (New York: Putnam's Sons, 1949), 18; de Seversky, "I Remember Billy Mitchell," 93. Several telephone transcripts are in CAM de Seversky Papers, Box 10.

5. Hucker, "Seversky: Innovator and Prophet," 56 and 58; U.S. Patent Office, Alexander P. de Seversky, assigned to Seversky Aircraft Corporation, "Aircraft Structure" (gun mount), filed September 24, 1937, Patent #2,214,722.

6. Davis, *P-35*, 6; Hucker, "Seversky: Innovator and Prophet," 58; Green and Swanborough, *The Complete Book of Fighters*, 135–37, 455, and 522.

7. Crouch, *Wings*, 324; Green and Swanborough, *The Complete Book of Fighters*.

8. U.S. Patent Office, Alexander P. de Seversky, assigned to Seversky Aircraft Corporation, "Aircraft Structure" (retractable landing gear), filed December 16, 1937, Patent #2,180,462; Davis, *P-35*, 6; Maloney, *Sever the Sky*, 17; Murray Rubenstein and Richard M. Goldman, *To Join with the Eagles* (Garden City, NY: Doubleday & Company, 1974), 147.

9. U.S.A.A.C. telegram quoted from "COPY—December 31, 1935—Telephone conversation between Major Seversky and General William Mitchell," CAM de Seversky Papers, Box 10.

10. Ibid.; Rubenstein and Goldman, *To Join with the Eagles*, 146–47; Peter M. Bowers, *Curtiss Aircraft 1907–1947* (London: Putnam & Company, 1979), 348.

11. Hucker, "Seversky: Innovator and Prophet," 58; Davis, *P-35*, 6; "Army Tests New Planes," *New York Times*, May 17, 1936.

12. Green and Swanborough, *The Complete Book of Fighters*, 522–23 and 585; Maloney, *Sever the Sky*, 19; "Aviation," *Newsweek* (June 27, 1936), 31; "77 Tiny Fast Planes Ordered for Army," *New York Times*, June 17, 1936.

13. "Comparative Data between P-35 and P-36 Pursuit Airplanes," CAM de Seversky Papers, Box 10, pp. 1–17; Alexander P. de Seversky, "Lest We Forget," *U.S. Air Services* 25 (June 1937): 16–17 and 35.

14. "Comparative Data between P-35 and P-36 Pursuit Airplanes," 8–12 and 16–17.

15. Ibid., 9; Rubenstein and Goldman, *To Join with the Eagles*, 149; Doolittle, *I Could Never Be So Lucky Again*, 175–76.

16. "Seversky Aircraft Corporation Notice of Annual Meeting of Stockholders," from Secretary Frank L. North, May 6, 1936, CAM de Seversky Papers, Box 6; Seversky Aircraft Corporation Prospectus, July 11, 1936, p. 8; letter from Horace N. Taylor to de Seversky, June 25, 1936, CAM de Seversky Papers, Box 6.

17. "Airplane Maker Files Stock Issue," *New York Times*, June 23, 1936; "Financial Notes," *New York Times*, July 17, 1936; "Thirteen Listings Approved by Curb," *New York Times*, July 23, 1936; "Transactions on the New York Curb Exchange," *New York Times*, September 25, October 23, November 26, and December 31, 1936; "3 Nations to Test U.S. Planes," *New York Times*, July 4, 1936.

18. Seversky Aircraft Corporation Prospectus, July 11, 1936; George Brown Tindall, *America* (New York: W. W. Norton & Company, 1984), 1265; "Transactions on the New York Curb Exchange," *New York Times*, January 31, February 27, March 31, April 28, and May 22, 1937.

19. Message from Nick Pishvanov to author, October 17, 2006; "De Seversky, Alexander Procofieff," *Current Biography* 2 (February 1941): 14–15, copy in CAM de Seversky Papers, Box 215.

20. De Seversky, "I Owe My Career to Losing a Leg," 164–69; William D. Richardson, "First Lady a Fan in Throng Game," *New York Times*, November 29, 1936; "Society Present in Large Numbers," *New York Times*, October 13, 1936; "LeRoy G. Peed Weds Miss Anne Hardy," *New York Times*, January 11, 1935; "Plans Completed for Aviators' Ball," *New York Times*, February 17, 1935; "Mayor Ill, Leaves Desk," *New York Times*, June 12, 1936.

21. "Radio Programs Scheduled for Broadcast This Week," *New York Times*, January 31, 1937; "Events Today," *New York Times*, April 7, 1938; Gilbert and Large, *The End of the European Era*, 281–304.

22. Maj. Gen. H. H. Arnold and Col. Ira C. Eaker, *Winged Warfare* (New York: Harper & Brothers, 1941), 91–92; Copp, *A Few Great Captains*, 232; Daso, *Hap Arnold*, 142–44; Jablonski, *America in the Air War*, 19; Taylor, *Combat Aircraft of the World*, 454–55 and 485; David Lee, *Boeing* (Edison, NJ: Chartwell Books, 1999), 52–55.

23. Rubenstein and Goldman, *To Join with the Eagles*, 149; Bowers, *Curtiss Aircraft 1907–1947*, 358–59; "Interview Alexander de Seversky, New York City, April 16, 1970," 4–5.

24. "Interview Alexander de Seversky, New York City, April 16, 1970," 6; Davis, *P-35*, 8; letter from de Seversky to Kartveli, May 10, 1937, CAM de Seversky Papers, Box 10; letter from Oliver Gill to "Sev," January 15, 1938, CAM de Seversky Papers, Box 3.

25. Maloney, *Sever the Sky*, 60; Rubenstein and Goldman, *To Join with the Eagles*, 149.

26. Doolittle, *I Could Never Be So Lucky Again*, 158; Davis, *P-35*, 43; Maloney, *Sever the Sky*, 24–25; "Air Racers Are Ready," *New York Times*, August 1, 1937; "New Seversky Plane Is Tested for Race," *New York Times*, August 15, 1937.

27. "California Flier Shatters Mark in Bendix Race," *Washington Post*, September 4, 1937; "F W. Fuller Breaks Bendix Race Mark," *New York Times*, September 4, 1937; Stoff, *Long Island Airports*, 40–44.

28. Edward H. Phillips, *Beechcraft Pursuit of Perfection* (Eagan, MN: Flying Books, 1992), 12–18; Butler, *East to the Dawn*, 401–11; Rich, *Jackie Cochran*, 71; Jacqueline Cochran and Maryann Bucknum Brinley, *Jackie Cochran* (New York: Bantam Books, 1987), 144.

29. Rich, *Jackie Cochran*, 3 and 28–31; Frederick Graham, "First Lady of the Air Lanes," *New York Times*, September 25, 1938; Cochran and Brinley, *Jackie Cochran*, 7, 29 and 33; "Many Private Fliers to Make Air Tour from Roosevelt Field to Canadian Fete," *New York Times*, August 14, 1932.

30. Cochran and Brinley, *Jackie Cochran*, 146; Rich, *Jackie Cochran*, 71; Maloney, *Sever the Sky*, 134–39.

31. Cochran and Brinley, *Jackie Cochran*, 146–48; Rich, *Jackie Cochran*, 72–73; "De Seversky Breaks Cuba Flight Record," *New York Times*, December 4, 1937; "Seversky Sets East-West Record of 10 Hours, 3 Minutes in Bendix Race Plane," *New York Times*, August 30, 1938; Certificate of Record to de Seversky from the National Aeronautic Association, CAM de Seversky Papers, Box 216; "Miss Cochran Sets Women's Air Mark," *New York Times*, September 22, 1937; Robert S. Ball, "Record Set by Woman," *New York Times*, September 26, 1937; "Miss Cochran Sets New York–Miami Record at 278.13 M.P.H.," *New York Times*, December 4, 1937.

32. Letter contract, March 12, 1938, signed by de Seversky and Cochran, Jacqueline Cochran Papers, Annual File Subseries, Box 5, Dwight D. Eisenhower Presidential Library; Rich, *Jackie Cochran*, 79.

33. Ibid.; Cochran and Brinley, *Jackie Cochran*, 162–64; "Miss Cochran Wins Bendix Race," *New York Times*, September 4, 1938.

34. "Miss Cochran Wins Bendix Race"; Rich, *Jackie Cochran*, 86–89.

### 9. TROUBLED TIMES

1. Diane Tedeschi, "Bad Risk," *Air & Space* 13 (December 1994/January 1995): 20–21; NASM Seversky File, Mutual of New York Microfilm.

2. "Mrs. Samuel R. Olliphant," *New York Times*, March 21, 1937; investment diary, CAM de Seversky Papers, Box 1; Rubenstein and Goldman, *To Join with Eagles*, 149; Bowers, *Curtiss Aircraft*, 358–59; "Transactions on the New York Curb Exchange," *New York Times*, December 1 and 15, 1937.

3. Crouch, *Wings*, 183 and 362–63; Green and Swanborough, *The Complete Book of Fighters*, 90, 261, and 524–25.

4. De Seversky quoting General Arnold, "Interview Alexander de Seversky, New York City, April 16, 1970," 6; Green and Swanborough, *The Complete Book of Fighters*, 90–91 and 261–63.

5. Copp, *A Few Great Captains*, 431–32; Maurer, *Aviation in the U.S. Army*, 364–65; "Interview Alexander de Seversky, New York City, April 16, 1970," 7; Taylor, *Combat Aircraft of the World*, 182–84 and 386–88; Taylor, *The Lore of Flight*, 189–90.

6. De Seversky quoted from "Interview Alexander de Seversky, New York City, April 16, 1970," 7; Douglas G. Culy, "Engine Technology," in *Air Warfare*, ed. Boyne, 198 and 202; Taylor, *The Lore of Flight*, 186–99; Green and Swanborough, *The Complete Book of Fighters*, 586. For General Arnold's comments on de Seversky, see H. H. Arnold, *Global Mission* (New York: Harper and Brothers, 1949), 298.

7. Davis, *P-35*, 44; Maloney, *Sever the Sky*, 65–66.

8. Taylor, *Combat Aircraft of the World*, 481; Lloyd S. Jones, *U.S. Fighters* (Fallbrook, CA: Aero Publishers, 1975), 98–102; Culy, "Bell P-39 Airacobra and P-63 Kingcobra," in *Air Warfare*, ed. Boyne, 378; "Interview Alexander de Seversky, New York City, April 16, 1970," 15.

9. Secretary of War Woodring quoted from letter to Seversky Aircraft Corporation, October 15, 1937, CAM de Seversky Papers, Box 4.

10. De Seversky quoted from letter to Woodring, November 4, 1937, CAM de Seversky Papers, Box 10, p. 1; memorandum to de Seversky from F. William Zelcer, executive vice president of Seversky Aircraft, "Report of Telephone Conversation with Franklin K. Lane," October 16, 1937, CAM de Seversky Papers, Box 10; Maurer, *Aviation in the U.S. Army*, 364.

11. De Seversky to Woodring, November 3, 1937; Copp, *A Few Great Captains*, 379; letter from de Seversky to Kartveli, May 10, 1937, CAM de Seversky Papers, Box 10; "F. W. Fuller Breaks Bendix Race Mark," *New York Times*, September 4, 1937; "Miss Cochran Sets Women's Air Mark," *New York Times*, September 22, 1937.

12. Interoffice correspondence, Seversky Aircraft Corporation, "PRODUCTION REPORT #1—Week Ending Jan. 4, 1938," from George A. Meyerer, January 7, 1938, CAM de Seversky Papers, Box 6; letter from de Seversky to Maj. Gen. Oscar Westover, chief of the U.S. Army Air Corps, June 30, 1938, CAM de Seversky Papers, Box 7.

13. "Bids Sought on Airliner to Carry 100 Passengers," *New York Times*, December 11, 1937; letter from Gledhill to Zelcer, December 23, 1937, CAM de Seversky Papers, Box 10; Maurice Allward, *Seaplanes and Flying Boats* (New York: Barnes & Noble, 1981), 85–86 and 99; Lee, *Boeing*, 46–47; Crouch, *Wings*, 348–52.

14. U.S. Copyright, A. P. de Seversky Airplane, filed April 15, 1938, Design #112,834; "Huge Sea Airliner Designed for 120," *New York Times*, March 16, 1938, 12; "The Seversky Super-Clipper," *Model Airplane News* 19 (August 1938): 15, 42–43; letter from de Seversky to Lindbergh, March 14, 1938, CAM de Seversky Papers, Box 10, pp. 1–3.

15. "Huge Sea Airliner Designed for 120"; Maloney, *Sever the Sky*, 58; M. D. Klass, *Last of the Flying Clippers* (Atglen, PA: Schiffer Publishers, 1997), 72–81; James Trautman, *Pan American Clippers* (Erin, Canada: Boston Mills Press, 2007), 54–64; "Aircraft that Changed the World," *Air & Space* 23 (July 2008): 22–29.

16. Maloney, *Sever the Sky*, 25–29; "Aviation Records," CAM, Manufacturer's Collection: Seversky/Republic, 2–4; Doolittle, *I Could Never Be So Lucky Again*, 147–48 and 198.

17. Hucker, "Seversky: Innovator and Prophet," 56; author telephone interview with Nick Pishvanov about Alexander Toochkoff, February 15, 2008; "Russia Buys Planes Here," *New York Times*, May 26, 1937.

18. Libbey, *Russian-American Economic Relations*, 77; Glen Alden Smith, *Soviet Foreign Trade* (New York: Praeger, 1973), 58–59; Adolf Hitler, *Mein Kampf*, trans. Ralph Mannheim (Boston: Houghton Mifflin Company, 1962), 641–54.

19. Libbey, *Russian-American Economic Relations*, 110–11; Thomas R. Maddux, *Years of Estrangement* (Tallahassee: University Press of Florida, 1980), 85; Antony C. Sutton, *Western Technology and Soviet Economic Development, 1930–1945* (Stanford, CA: Hoover Institution Press, 1971), 161–63.

20. Libbey, *Russian-American Economic Relations*, 112; Crouch, *Wings*, 336; "Washington Voices Regret to Powers over Plane Deal," *New York Times*, December 31, 1936; "Fourth Quarter Gain Puts Douglas Aircraft Now above Estimates," *Wall Street Journal*, February 24, 1937; Charles E. Egan, "Position of Russia Held Secure Here," *New York Times*, June 27, 1937.

21. "Russia Buys Planes Here"; "Seversky Aircraft Awarded $780,000 Russian Contract," *Wall Street Journal*, May 26, 1937; Seversky Aircraft interoffice correspondence from Toochkoff to de Seversky, Subject: Russian Contracts, March 9, 1938, CAM de Seversky Papers, Box 10, pp. 1–3.

22. Arnold and Eaker quoted from *Winged Warfare*, 123; James Parton, *"Air Force Spoken Here"* (Bethesda, MD: Adler & Adler Publishers, 1986), 118. Arnold's biographer in discussing the general's views in *Winged Warfare* focuses on his quest for a balanced air force. See Daso, *Hap Arnold*, 172.

23. Arnold, *Global Mission*, 174; Maloney, *Sever the Sky*, 68–69; James S. Corum, "The Spanish Civil War Lessons Learned and Not Learned by the Great Powers," *Journal of Military History* 62 (April 1998): 313–34.

24. U.S. Patent Office, A. M. Pishvanov, "Aircraft Armament" (bomb racks), filed May 28, 1938, Patent #2,278,482; "The Reminiscences of Alexander Kartveli," 13–14; U.S. Patent Office, Alexander P. de Seversky, assigned to Seversky Aircraft Corporation, "Aircraft Structure" (gun mount), filed September 24, 1937, Patent #2,214,722; Maloney, *Sever the Sky*, 68–69 and 72–73; interoffice correspondence between Toochkoff and de Seversky, March 9, 1938.

25. Letter from "Iggy" J. Miranda to Zelcer, March 1, 1938, CAM de Seversky Papers, Box 10, pp. 1–2. The "Mr. Yamamoto" mentioned by Miranda was not Isoroku Yamamoto, who was then chief of Japan's Naval Aviation Department. Since the early

twentieth century, the U.S. Army had expected Japan to invade American-controlled Philippines. See Arnold, *Global Mission*, 11; Daso, *Hap Arnold*, 37.

26. Harry A. Gailey, *The War in the Pacific* (Novato, CA: Presidio Press, 1995), 15–23; letter from de Seversky to Westover, June 30, 1938, CAM de Seversky Papers, Box 7, p. 1.

27. "Our Latest Planes Aid Foreign Forces," *New York Times*, July 31, 1938; even the stockholder report mentions only an anonymous inquiry from a foreign source rather than listing the name of Japan. See "To the Stockholders of Seversky Aircraft Corporation," March 28, 1938, CAM de Seversky Papers, Box 5.

28. Green and Swanborough, *The Complete Book of Fighters*, 524; Taylor, *Combat Aircraft of the World*, 554; Davis, *P-35*, 27–33.

10. THE P-35 MANUFACTURER LOSES HIS COMPANY

1. George A. Meyerer quoted from interoffice correspondence, Seversky Aircraft Corporation, "Production Report #21," July 5, 1938, CAM de Seversky Papers, Box 6.

2. De Seversky quoted from letter to chief, Materiel Division, June 25, 1938, CAM de Seversky Papers, Box 7, pp. 1–2.

3. Ibid., 2–4; "The Following Proposals Seversky Aircraft Corporation Wish to Submit to Materiel Division for Consideration," CAM de Seversky Papers, Box 10.

4. Contract between de Seversky and Cochran, March 12, 1938; Rich, *Jackie Cochran*, 79; Maloney, *Sever the Sky*, 60; excerpts from minutes of Board of Directors, Seversky Aircraft Corporation, February 28, 1939, and May 23, 1939, CAM de Seversky Papers, Box 5.

5. Irving Brinton Holley, *Buying Aircraft* (Washington: Department of the Army, 1964), 93–103.

6. Ibid., 100–103. Letter from de Seversky to Westover, June 7, 1938; letter from de Seversky to the Honorable Louis Johnson, June 7, 1938; letter from de Seversky to Gen. Frank M. Andrews, June 16, 1938, all in CAM de Seversky Papers, Boxes 7 or 10.

7. Holley, *Buying Aircraft*, 96; letter from de Seversky to Arnold, July 1, 1938, CAM de Seversky Papers, Box 7; "Interview Alexander de Seversky, New York City, April 16, 1970," 6.

8. Arnold quoted from letter to de Seversky, July 13, 1938; Westover quoted from letter to de Seversky, July 11, 1938, both in CAM de Seversky Papers, Box 7.

9. Daso, *Hap Arnold*, 148; Arnold, *Global Mission*, 169; Meyerer, Production Report #19, August 31, 1938, CAM de Seversky Papers, Box 6, pp. 2–3; memo from de Seversky to Vice President W. Wallace Kellett, November 25, 1938, CAM de Seversky Papers, Box 3.

10. "Army Single Place Pursuit Proposal Seversky Model AP-4 General Description Report No. 60, Date: January 11, 1938," CAM de Seversky Papers, Box 10; Maloney, *Sever the Sky*, 61; Davis, *P-47 Thunderbolt*, 4–7; David Mondey, *American Aircraft of World War II* (Edison, NJ: Chartwell Books, 2001), 215–16.

11. Winston S. Churchill, *The Gathering Storm* (New York: Bantam Books, 1961), 250–66; Gerald Reitlinger, *The SS* (New York: Viking Press, 1957), 116.

12. Churchill, *The Gathering Storm*, 267–300; Gilbert with Large, *The End of the European Era*, 306–10.

13. "Seversky Single-Place Pursuit Model EP-1 Detail Specification Serial Report No. 68-1C Date: July 12, 1938," CAM de Seversky Papers, Box 10.

14. Excerpt from minutes of the Seversky Aircraft Corporation Board of Directors meeting, February 28, 1939, CAM de Seversky Papers, Box 5, p. 2; Seversky Aircraft Corporation Stockholder Report, March 21, 1939, CAM de Seversky Papers, Box 6, pp. 1 and 3; statement on AP-4 prepared for lawsuit of *de Seversky v. Republic Aircraft Corporation*, January 5, 1942, CAM de Seversky Papers, Box 10, pp. 1–4.

15. "Time Logged by Mrs. Seversky and Mr. George Seversky in Stinson NC 16116," August 1938, CAM de Seversky Papers, Box 262; 1938 Picnic Supplement, *The Sever / Sky News*, CAM de Seversky Papers, Box 4; "Export Price List—Seversky Airplanes," December 30, 1938, CAM de Seversky Papers, Box 7.

16. "Seversky Sets East–West Flight Record of 10 Hours 3 Minutes in Bendix Race Plane," *New York Times*, August 30, 1938; "Miss Cochran Wins Bendix Race," *New York Times*, September 4, 1938; telegram from G. de Seversky, European representative of Seversky Aircraft Corporation to SEVCO, Farmingdale, New York, October 13, 1938, CAM de Seversky Papers, Box 7; Seversky Aircraft Corporation Stockholder Report, March 21, 1939, pp. 5 and 8.

17. De Seversky quoted from telegram to Paul Moore, September 15, 1938, CAM de Seversky Papers, Box 5; Seversky Aircraft Corporation Stockholder Report, March 21, 1939, p. 4, Note 3.

18. Paul Moore quoted from letter to de Seversky, September 16, 1938, CAM de Seversky Papers, Box 5.

19. Ibid.; report on "Seversky Aircraft Corporation" prepared by Thomas P. Durrel of White, Weld & Co., September 15, CAM de Seversky Papers, Box 4.

20. Letter agreement between Moore and White, Weld & Co., October 27, 1938, CAM de Seversky Papers, Box 4, pp. 1–5; excerpt of Seversky Aircraft Corporation Board of Directors minutes, May 23, 1939, CAM de Seversky Papers, Box 5; Green and Swanborough, *The Complete Book of Fighters*, 491–92.

21. Seversky Aircraft Corporation Stockholder Report, March 21, 1939, p. 1; letter agreement between Moore and White, Weld & Co., October 27, 1938, p. 3; letter from Livingston Platt to Durrel, October 13, 1938, CAM de Seversky Papers, Box 4.

22. Letter agreement between Moore and White, Weld & Co., October 27, 1938, p. 3; Crouch, *Wings*, 465; Warren R. Young, *Helicopters* (Alexandria, VA: Time-Life Books), 61.

23. Quote of a summary of de Seversky's statement in an excerpt of the Seversky Aircraft Corporation Board of Directors minutes, November 11, 1938, CAM de Seversky Papers, Box 5; letter from de Seversky to Kellett, November 25, 1938, CAM de Seversky Papers, Box 3.

24. Letter from de Seversky to Kellett, November 25, 1938; interoffice correspondence Seversky Aircraft Corporation from J. J. Skelly (accountant) to de Seversky, Subject: "Statement of Your Account as of November 30, 1938, Balance Due Company per Memo Dated Nov. 9, 1938," December 6, 1938, CAM de Seversky Papers, Box 6.

25. "Myron C. Taylor Sails for Refugee Parley," *New York Times*, November 27, 1938.

26. Wattles quoted from his letter to de Seversky, November 26, 1938, CAM de Seversky Papers, Box 4.

27. Letter from F. J. G. Lynam to Major de Seversky, Hotel George V, Paris, France, January 23, 1939, CAM de Seversky Papers, Box 7; "Insider Trading," *New York Times*, January 6, 1939; "Insiders' Report Changed Holdings," *New York Times*, April 5, 1939; telegram from Kellett to de Seversky, February 16, 1939 and telegram from de Seversky to Kellett also on February 16, 1939, CAM de Seversky Papers, Box 7.

28. AVIATION RECORDS—Major Alexander P. de Seversky, CAM Manufacturers Collection, 1; "Hop by Seversky, Not Sikorsky," *New York Times*, January 14, 1939.

29. Letter from G. de Seversky to Commandant Labouchere, Attaché Militaire, Belgian Legation, January 24, 1939; letter from G. de Seversky to Albert Morel, March 24, 1939; letter from J. P. Ferreira dos Santos, Commercial Attaché, Portuguese Legation, to G. de Seversky, February 20, 1939, all in CAM de Seversky Papers, Box 7. Sample articles about de Seversky are located in Box 215.

30. Arnold, *Global Mission*, 177–78; Copp, *A Few Great Captains*, 456–57; Dick, *American Eagles*, 106; Holley, *Buying Aircraft*, 169–70.

31. Arnold quoted from "Reports Army Fund Largest since War," *New York Times*, March 2, 1939; Holley, *Buying Aircraft*, 179; *New York Times*, "Big Plane Output Mapped for Army," November 24, 1938, "Air Defense Needs Pressed on Nation," December 5, 1938, "Mobilization Master Plan Nearly Ready," December 25, 1938.

32. Kellett quoted from excerpt of Seversky Aircraft Corporation Board of Directors Meeting, December 29, 1938, CAM de Seversky Papers, Box 5; "Two Pursuit Planes Receive Army Tests," *New York Times*, April 16, 1939; Green and Swanborough, *The Complete Book of Fighters*, 55–56 and 525.

33. Copp, *A Few Great Captains*, 467; letter from de Seversky to Samuel H. Kaufman, re: *de Seversky v. Republic Aircraft*, January 6, 1942, CAM de Seversky Papers, Box 5; Taylor, *Combat Aircraft of the World*, 483 and 549.

34. Copp, *A Few Great Captains*, 467; letter from de Seversky to Alfons B. Landa re: *de Seversky v. Republic Aircraft*, May 21, 1941, CAM de Seversky Papers, Box 5; "Order $974,324 Pursuit Planes," *New York Times*, May 24, 1939; "Industry Notes," *New York Times*, June 11, 1939; excerpt from Seversky Aircraft Corporation Board of Directors minutes, May 23, 1939, CAM de Seversky Papers, Box 5.

35. Holley, *Buying Aircraft*, 578; "Army Planes Ordered," *New York Times*, September 14, 1939; James K. Libbey, "Lend-Lease Aircraft," in *Air Warfare*, ed. Boyne, 365–66; notes of James C. Dunn, Private Investigator, re: *de Seversky v. Republic Aircraft*,

October 31 and November 6, 1940, CAM de Seversky Papers, Box 5; "Heads Seversky Company," *New York Times*, April 19, 1939; "W. W. Kellett, 60, Autogiro Pioneer," *New York Times*, July 23, 1951.

36. Dunn's notes, November 6, 1940; cablegram from de Seversky to Kellett, February 16, 1939, and cablegram from de Seversky to Kellett, March 1, 1939, CAM de Seversky Papers, Box 7; "Seversky Shows Plane in Britain," *New York Times*, March 5, 1939; *So'ton Airport Notes & News*, clipping about de Seversky's *Spitfire* flight, LC, Seversky Papers, Box 1.

37. Cablegram from G. de Seversky to White, Weld & Co., April 14, 1939; letter from de Seversky to chief, Swedish Royal Air Force, April 17, 1939; cablegram from de Seversky to Kellett, May 3, 1939; "Export Price List—Seversky Airplanes"; cablegram from de Seversky to Kellett, May 6, 1939; letter from Kellett to Bleakley, Platt & Walker, May 15, 1939, all in CAM de Seversky Papers, Box 7. Green and Swanborough, *The Complete Book of Fighters*, 491–92.

38. Cablegram from G. de Seversky to White, Weld & Co., April 14, 1939; cablegram from de Seversky to Kellett, May 3, 1939; cablegram from By Order of Directors to de Seversky, May 9, 1939; cablegram from de Seversky to Kellett, May 15, 1939; cablegram from de Seversky to Platt, May 19, 1939; letter from G. de Seversky to F. Robbe, May 25, 1939, all in CAM de Seversky Papers, Box 7. "Seversky Ousted by Plane Company," *New York Times*, May 26, 1939.

11. THE MAKING OF AN AIR POWER PROPHET

1. De Seversky quoted from "Seversky Fears September War," *New York Post*, June 13, 1939; Eugene Lyons quoted from Lyons, "Seversky—Aviation's Versatile Genius," 41.

2. Rich, *Jackie Cochran*, 94; undated pamphlet, "Singers of Imperial Russia," vol. 5, Pavillion Records, Ltd. (Wadhurst, England), 5 and 7.

3. Notes from Dunn, October 31, 1940; "Seversky Ousted by Plane Company," 37; "Seversky to Vote on New Name," *New York Times*, September 2, 1939; Proxy Statement Special Meeting of Stockholders of Seversky Aircraft Corporation, October 13, 1939, CAM de Seversky Papers, Box 6; "Plane Company Changes Name," *New York Times*, October 14, 1939.

4. Draft biographical material sent and published in 1958 in *Who's Who in World Aviation*, CAM de Seversky Papers, Box 215; U.S. Patent Office, Alexander P. de Seversky, "Aircraft Structure" (gun turret), Patent #2,214,722, granted on September 10, 1940; Young, *Helicopters*, 78–81.

5. "Achievements of Major Alexander P. de Seversky," CAM de Seversky Papers, Box 1; letter from Albert to superintendent of documents, January 3, 1942, CAM de Seversky Papers, Box 8; author's telephone interview with Nick Pishvanov, October 1, 2008.

6. "Aircraft Designer Gets Office Space," *New York Times*, November 29, 1939; "Airplane Designer Rents Apartment," *New York Times*, January 23, 1942.

7. Bromo-Seltzer ad, *New York Times*, August 30, 1939; P.A.C. Newsletter (March 1940), CAM de Seversky Papers, Box 261, pp. 1 and 4.

8. De Seversky quoted from his P.A.C. speech, February 20, 1940, CAM de Seversky Papers, Box 261, p. 2.

9. Churchill, *Gathering Storm*, 417–30; J. E. Kaufmann and H. W. Kaufmann, *Hitler's Blitzkrieg Campaigns* (Conshohocken, PA: Combined Books, 1993), 105–39.

10. "Faster Take-Off, Slower Landing," *New York Times*, February 25, 1940; U.S. Patent Office, Alexander P. de Seversky, assigned to Seversky Aircraft, "Aircraft Wing," Patent #2,191,342, granted on February 20, 1940; "Sales by Insiders Revealed by SEC," *New York Times*, November 3, 1939.

11. "SEC Reports Shifts in Equity Earnings," *New York Times*, January 5, 1940; "SEC Reports Gift of $5,200,000 Stock," *New York Times*, February 7, 1940; "Shifts in Holdings Reported to SEC," *New York Times*, May 4, 1940.

12. "Shifts in Holdings Reported by SEC," *New York Times*, June 25 and July 10, 1940; "De Seversky Sues Republic Aviation," *New York Times*, August 22, 1940.

13. Letter to de Seversky from Earl J. Garey, June 13, 1940; letter from de Seversky to E. Garey, October 31, 1940; interviews conducted by Dunn, October 24, 1940, to January 22, 1941; press release, "Seversky Sues Republic Aircraft for $23,000.000," issued by H.A. Bruno & Associates, August 22, 1940, all in CAM de Seversky Papers, Box 5.

14. "Reports Seversky Suit Settled," *New York Times*, October 17, 1942; "R. S. Damon Heads Republic Aviation," *New York Times*, May 2, 1941; Sherwood S. Cordier, "Republic P-47 Thunderbolt," in *Air Warfare*, ed. Boyne, 524–25; "Reminiscences of Alexander Kartveli," 16–24.

15. Churchill, *Gathering Storm*, 581–87; Winston S. Churchill, *Their Finest Hour* (New York: Bantam Books, 1962), 24–102; Kaufmann and Kaufmann, *Hitler's Blitzkrieg Campaigns*, 141–304.

16. "Radio Programs This Week," *New York Times*, June 2, 1940; *We the People* radio transcript, June 4, 1940, CAM de Seversky Papers, Box 261.

17. De Seversky quoted from *We the People* transcript, June 4, 1940; Doolittle, *I Could Never Be So Lucky Again*, 197; Dick, *American Eagles*, 123.

18. *We the People* radio transcript for Major Seversky and Adm. William V. Platt, June 11, 1940; letter and polished transcript from Phillips H. Lord, Inc., to de Seversky, August 15, 1940; both in CAM de Seversky Papers, Box 261.

19. Later sample programs: WNBT interview on *Meet the Press*, *New York Times*, October 8, 1950; WABC Interview with Mike Wallace, *New York Times*, December 28, 1957; WMAC interview with Barry Gray, *New York Times*, April 25, 1961.

20. De Seversky, "Britain Cited for Aircraft," *Los Angeles Times*, June 4, 1940; de Seversky, "Seversky Doubts British Invasion," *New York Times*, July 22, 1940; Churchill, *Their Finest Hour*, 86–100.

21. De Seversky quoted from de Seversky, "Britain Cited for Aircraft."

22. Walter J. Boyne, *Clash of Wings* (New York: Simon & Schuster, 1994), 63–65; Kaufmann and Kaufmann, *Hitler's Blitzkrieg Campaigns*, 251–60; Paul Jacobs and Robert Lightsey, *Battle of Britain Illustrated* (New York: McGraw-Hill, 2003), 229–31.

23. Lyons quoted from Lyons, "Seversky—Aviation's Versatile Genius," 42; de Seversky, "Hard Facts on Air Power," *American Mercury* 59 (August 1940): 406–14.

24. De Seversky, "Hard Facts on Air Power," 406–9; Dennis R. Jenkins, "Consolidated Aircraft Corporation" and Alwyn T. Loyd, "Consolidated B-24 Liberator," both in *Air Warfare*, ed. Boyne, 147–49; de Seversky, "Expert Says War Planes Cannot Be 'Standardized,'" *Providence Journal*, February 3, 1941, clipping, LC, AIAA Papers Box 1.

25. De Seversky quoted from de Seversky, "Hard Facts on Air Power," 409 and 410.

26. De Seversky, "Hard Facts on Air Power," 411–12; Lee, *Boeing*, 59–61, 72–76, and 87–89; Procofieff Seversky, "Aerial Filling Device," Patent #1,728,449.

27. De Seversky, "Hard Facts on Air Power," 413–14; Crouch, *Wings*, 377; Michael S. Sherry, *Rise of American Air Power* (New Haven, CT: Yale University Press, 1987), 71–72.

28. Letter from de Seversky to Rita Potter, editorial assistant, *American Mercury*, July 9, 1940, CAM de Seversky Papers, Box 217; letter from Thomas D. Cooper to de Seversky, July 22, 1940, LC, Seversky Papers, Box 1.

29. De Seversky, "Nazi Air Siege Called 'Main Bout,'" *New York Times*, August 15, 1940.

30. Transcript of H. V. Kaltenborn's WEAF broadcast, August 14, 1940, LC, Seversky Papers, Box 1.

31. De Seversky, "Why Hitler's Planes Failed to Beat England . . . A Lesson," *Look* 4 (December 17, 1940): 8–11; Boyne, *Clash of Wings*, 72–75; Jacobs and Lightsey, *Battle of Britain Illustrated*, 331–32.

32. De Seversky quoted from de Seversky, "Why Hitler's Planes Failed to Beat England . . . A Lesson," 11; Boyne, *Clash of Wings*, 199 and 359; Lee, *Boeing*, 58.

33. De Seversky, "Why Hitler's Planes Failed to Beat England . . . A Lesson," 11; Boyne, *Clash of Wings*, 333–35; *The United States Strategic Bombing Surveys: European War/Pacific War* (Maxwell AFB, AL: Air University Press, 1987 reprint), 18–37; Budiansky, *Air Power*, 325–28; Sherry, *Rise of American Air Power*, 162–66.

34. Quote from Ligue Internationale des Aviateurs, circa December 19, 1940, LC, AIAA Papers, Box 111, p. 5; "De Seversky Honored for Plane Advances," *New York Times*, December 20, 1940.

## 12. PROPHET OF AIR POWER

1. Dick, *American Eagles*, 46; Frandsen, "Mitchell, William 'Billy' (1879–1936)," 430–31; Mitchell, *Skyways*, 235–88.

2. Mitchell quoted from Mitchell, *Skyways*, 235 (see 280–85 for air battle).

3. Ibid., 255 and 257; Hart quoted from Hart, *Paris*, 37; David Nevin, *Architects of Air Power* (Alexandria, VA: Time-Life Books, 1981), 17–33 and 54–71; Christopher H. Sterling, "Trenchard, Hugh (1873–1956)," in *Air Warfare*, ed. Boyne, 631; Douhet, *Command of the Air*, 103.

4. Selig Adler, *The Isolationist Impulse* (New York: Collier Books 1961), 219–49; Robert A. Divine, *The Reluctant Belligerent* (New York: John Wiley & Sons, 1965), 1–4.

5. Letters from General Andrews to de Seversky, January 3, 1941, February 7, 1941, April 18, 1941; letter from de Seversky to Andrews, June 17, 1941, all in Library of Congress, Frank M. Andrews Papers, Personal Correspondence, Box 6.

6. Daso, *Hap Arnold*, 142–43 and 240; Dick, *American Eagles*, 101–5; Parton, "*Air Force Spoken Here,*" 116; Lee, *Boeing*, 53–54; Arnold, *Global Mission*, 176–77.

7. Alexander P. de Seversky, "Why We *Must* Have a Separate Air Force," *Reader's Digest* 38 (March 1941): 107–13.

8. Ibid., 110–11.

9. Ibid., de Seversky quoted, 113.

10. Letter from de Seversky to Eugene Lyons, January 30, 1941, CAM de Seversky Papers, Box 217; letter from Senator Arthur Capper (Rep., Kansas) to *Reader's Digest,* March 4, 1941, LC, Seversky Papers, Box 1; "De Seversky Making Impact—1941," Henry H. Arnold Collection, USAF Historical Research Agency, Microfilm 43798; "On Radio This Week," *New York Times,* May 18, 1941; "Separate Air Arm Held Vital for Us," *New York Times,* May 19, 1941; "De Seversky Asks Air Arm Autonomy," *New York Times,* June 20, 1941.

11. Hedley Donovan, "Army Unifies Its Airforce with One Chief," *Washington Post,* June 22, 1941.

12. De Seversky quoted from *New York Post,* June 20, 1941; Andrews quoted from letter to de Seversky, June 27, 1941; letter from de Seversky to Andrews, July 1, 1941; all in LC, Andrews Papers, PC, Box 6.

13. Stephen E. Ambrose, *Rise to Globalism* (New York: Penguin Books, 1985), 5–7; George C. Herring, *From Colony to Superpower* (New York: Columbia University Press, 2008), 520.

14. Adler, *Isolationist Impulse,* 262–63 and 273–74; Berg, *Lindbergh,* 411–12; Wayne S. Cole, *Charles A. Lindbergh and the Battle against American Intervention in World War II* (New York: Harcourt Brace Jovanovich, 1974), 107–8 and 136–37.

15. Charles A. Lindbergh quoted from Lindbergh, "Letter to Americans," *Collier's* 107 (March 21, 1941): 14; de Seversky quoted from de Seversky, "Why Lindbergh Is Wrong," *American Mercury* 52 (May 1941): 520; letter to de Seversky from Thomas I. Power, National Headquarters, Committee to Defend America, July 30, 1941, CAM de Seversky Papers, Box 217.

16. De Seversky, "Why Lindbergh Is Wrong," 522–27; Lindbergh, "Letter to Americans," 75–77; "'Being Led to War' Lindbergh Warns," *New York Times,* March 21, 1941.

17. De Seversky quoted from de Seversky, "Why Lindbergh Is Wrong," 529; Lindbergh, "Letter to Americans," 75; Taylor, *Combat Aircraft of the World,* 152.

18. "Radio Today," *New York Times,* May 20, 1941; de Seversky, "Aviation vs. Isolationism: Our Safety Depends on Air Power," *Vital Speeches of the Day* 7 (July 1, 1941): 557–58; "Books–Authors," *New York Times,* May 24, 1941.

19. De Seversky quoted from de Seversky, "Air Power Ends Isolation," *Atlantic Monthly* 78 (October 1941): 416 and see also 408–15.

20. De Seversky quoted from de Seversky, "The Twilight of Sea Power," *American Mercury* 52 (June 1941): 647 and see also 648.

21. De Seversky, "The Twilight of Sea Power," 653–54; Green and Swanborough, *The Complete Book of Fighters*, 261–62, 376, and 559–60; James K. Libbey, "Vought Aircraft," in *Air Warfare*, ed. Boyne, 682–83.

22. De Seversky quoted from de Seversky, "The Twilight of Sea Power," 654, and see also 651–52.

23. De Seversky, "Is America Flying Blind?," *Coronet* (June 1941), Offprint, LC, Seversky Papers, Box 1.

24. Ibid., 4; quote is from "British Air Manual 'Insults' U.S. on Aid," *New York Times*, April 4, 1941; quote from Arthur Pearcy, *Lend-Lease Aircraft in World War II* (Osceola, WI: Motorbooks International, 1996), 156.

25. De Seversky quoted from de Seversky, "America Repeats Europe's Aviation Mistakes," *American Mercury* 53 (October 1941): 410, and see also 401–9; Green and Swanborough, *The Complete Book of Fighters*, 139 and 288; Culy, "Engine Technology," 197–98 and 201.

26. Letter from de Seversky to Andrews, October 27, 1941, LC, Andrews Papers, PC, Box 6; "Books–Authors," *New York Times*, January 8, 1942; letter from Albert to K. Chester, December 23, 1941, CAM de Seversky Papers, Box 215.

27. Gailey, *War in the Pacific*, 77–99; Donald J. Young, *First 24 Hours of War in the Pacific* (Shippensburg, PA: Burd Street Press, 1998), vii–ix and 35–36.

28. C. E. Black and E. C. Helmreich, *Twentieth Century Europe* (New York: Alfred A. Knopf, 1963), 552–53; Arnold, *Global Mission*, 275–83.

29. Herring, *From Colony to Superpower*, 533–34; de Seversky, *Victory through Air Power*, iii and vi.

### 13. VICTORY THROUGH AIR POWER

1. Boyne, *Clash of Wings*, 107–15; Crouch, *Wings*, 398–99.

2. Gailey, *War in the Pacific*, 104–9; Jablonski, *America in the Air War*, 53–54; Parton, "Air Force Spoken Here," 128–34 and 157; memo from Arnold to General Eaker, Subject: Initial Direction to Bomber Commander in England, January 31, 1942, Library of Congress, Ira C. Eaker Papers, Box 7.

3. De Seversky, *Victory through Air Power*, 330; de Seversky, "Is America Flying Blind?"

4. Boyne, *Clash of Wings*, 107–17; Mondey, *American Aircraft of World War II*, 172–73; Budiansky, *Air Power*, 330.

5. De Seversky quoted from Eugene Lyons, "Seversky Says: One Air Force for the U.S.A.," *Who: The Magazine about People* 2 (February 1942): 38, and see also 34–37.

6. Letter from de Seversky to Harry S. Truman, January 18, 1942; letter from Truman to de Seversky, December 21, 1943, both in CAM de Seversky Papers, Box 216;

Donald H. Riddle, *The Truman Committee* (New Brunswick, NJ: Rutgers University Press, 1964), 8–9 and 28; Donald R. McCoy, *The Presidency of Harry S. Truman* (Lawrence: University Press of Kansas, 1984), 7–8.

7. "Notes on Books and Authors," *New York Times*, April 4, 1942; de Seversky, "Why the Luftwaffe Failed," *Atlantic Monthly* 78 (March 1942): 293–302; de Seversky, "When Will America Be Bombed?," *American Mercury* 54 (April 1942): 412–20; de Seversky, "How We Must Bomb Japan," *American Magazine* 133 (April 1942): 14–15 and 102–4; de Seversky, "All Out Air Power—Key to Victory," *New York Times Sunday Magazine* (April 19, 1942), 6–7 and 34; "Tokyo Bombed!," *Los Angeles Times*, April 18, 1942; Doolittle, *I Could Never Be So Lucky Again*, 249–55.

8. Joseph Harrison quoted from "De Seversky's Armada," *New Republic* 106 (May 4, 1942): 609–10; Orville Prescott quoted from "Books of the Times," *New York Times*, April 20, 1942; quote from "Angry Sascha," *Time* 39 (April 27, 1942): 52–53; Maj. George F. Eliot, "Carriers Seen as Most Likely Source of Bombers of Tokyo," *Los Angeles Times*, April 19, 1942.

9. "Best Sellers of the Week," *New York Times*, April 27, 1942, May 25, 1942, and June 15, 1942; Book-of-the-Month Club ad, *New York Times*, September 6, 1942.

10. Simon & Schuster ad, *New York Times*, November 29, 1942; Arnold, *Global Mission*, 296.

11. Arnold quoted from Arnold, *Global Mission*, 297–98.

12. Green, "Interview Alexander de Seversky, New York City, April 16, 1970," 19–20; Arnold, *Global Mission*, 503 and 537; William Head, "George, Harold Lee (1893–1986)," in *Air Warfare*, ed. Boyne, 252.

13. Ibid.; de Seversky, "Remember Billy Mitchell!," 181; Roscoe, *On the Seas and in the Skies*, 157; Parton, "*Air Force Spoken Here*," 102 and 179.

14. Daso, *Hap Arnold*, 175; Head, "George, Harold Lee (1893–1986)," 252; Boyne, *Clash of Wings*, 128–38; Crouch, *Wings*, 406; Gailey, *War in the Pacific*, 156–71.

15. Arnold, *Global Mission*, 378–79; Boyne, *Clash of Wings*, 128–30.

16. De Seversky quoted from Green, "Interview Alexander de Seversky, New York City, April 16, 1970," 22, and see also 20–21.

17. Arnold quoted by de Seversky in ibid.; Russell E. Lee, "Impact of *Victory through Air Power* Part I: The Army Air Forces' Reaction," *Air Power History* 40 (Summer 1993): 6 and 11; Parton, "*Air Force Spoken Here*," 305–6.

18. William Bradford Huie, "What's Behind the Attacks on Seversky?," *American Mercury* 56 (February 1943): 155–65; Louis R. Eltscher and Edward M. Young, *Curtiss-Wright* (New York: Twayne Publishers, 1998), 77. "Aeronautical Engineer Discusses Writings of Alexander P. de Seversky," General Motors Press Release for August 23, 1942, pp. 1–3; letter from Felix Bruner to Anita Yale, September 8, 1942; both in CAM de Seversky Papers, Box 262.

19. Berlin quoted from "Aeronautical Engineer Discusses Writings of Alexander P. de Seversky," 2; de Seversky quoted from de Seversky, "Seversky, in Reply to Critic, Denounces 'Business as Usual,'" *New York Herald Tribune*, August 25, 1942.

20. De Seversky, quoted from de Seversky, "Seversky, in Reply to Critic Denounces 'Business as Usual'"; Eltscher and Young, *Curtiss-Wright*, 108.

21. Lee, "Impact of *Victory through Air Power* Part I: The Army Air Forces' Reaction," 9–10; David Brown, "Victory through Hot Air Power," "*Pic*," 15 Part I (January 12, 1943), 7–9 and Part II (January 19, 1943), 14–16; William S. Friedman, "Listen Major de Seversky—Wings of Victory," *Popular Science* 142 (January 1943): 69–83 and 224–27; Paul B. Malone, "Victory through Air Prophets?," *Skyways* 1 (November 1942): 6–9 and 74–75.

22. A. Toochkoff quoted from his letter, "Seversky's Military Career," *Skyways* 2 (February 1943): 8.

23. Roscoe Turner quoted from "An Open Letter to General Paul B. Malone from Colonel Roscoe Turner," *Skyways* 2 (January 1943): 50; Bob Thomas quoted from Thomas, *Walt Disney* (New York: Disney Editions, 1994), 183; Lee, "Impact of *Victory through Air Power* Part I: The Army Air Forces' Reaction," 11.

24. De Seversky Quoted from de Seversky, "Walt Disney: An Airman in His Heart," *Aerospace Historian* 14 (Spring 1967): 6; Stephen Joiner, "The Disney War Plan," *Air & Space* 24 (June/July 2009): 18; correspondence from Nick Pishvanov to author, November 4, 2008, and April 23, 2009.

25. De Seversky, "Walt Disney: An Airman in His Heart," 6; Thomas, *Walt Disney*, 183–85; "Screen News Here and in Hollywood," *New York Times*, September 5, 1942; credits, *Victory through Air Power*, Disc 2, © Disney.

26. "Screen News Here and in Hollywood," *New York Times*, October 14, 1942; Thomas F. Brady, "From Out of the West," *New York Times*, October 18, 1942; *Victory through Air Power*, Disc 2, © Disney.

27. *Victory through Air Power*, Disc 2, © Disney; de Seversky, "Walt Disney: An Airman in His Heart," 6; "Radio Today," *New York Times*, November 16, 1942, and December 17, 1942; "Screen News Here and in Hollywood," *New York Times*, November 5, 1942. Transcript, WNEW, February 6, 1943; letter from E. de Seversky to Cathryn Cragen, February 18, 1943; both in CAM de Seversky Papers, Box 218. De Seversky, "In the Lyons Den," *New York Post*, September 2, 1943.

28. Thomas, *Walt Disney*, 180–82; "Reception Honors Olav and Martha," *New York Times*, March 25, 1943.

29. De Seversky, "Walt Disney: An Airman in His Heart," 6; "Of Local Origin," *New York Times*, May 15, 1943; *Victory through Air Power*, Disc 2, © Disney; Hedda Hopper, "Looking at Hollywood," *Los Angeles Times*, June 8 and 21, 1943; "Pantellaria Victory Gives Seversky Talking Point," *Los Angeles Times*, June 14, 1943; "Purely Personal," *Los Angeles Times*, June 27, 1943.

30. "Of Local Origin," *New York Times*, June 29, 1943; *Victory through Air Power*, Disc 2, © Disney.

31. Green, "Interview Alexander de Seversky, New York City, April 16, 1970," 23; Thomas, *Walt Disney*, 185; printed script of the movie, CAM de Seversky Papers, Box 1.

32. Hopper quoted from Hopper, "Looking at Hollywood," *Los Angeles Times*, June 23, 1943; Thomas, *Walt Disney*, 185; Green, "Interview Alexander de Seversky, New York City, April 16, 1970," 23.

33. Quotes from "Air Power on the Screen," *New York Times*, July 26, 1943; Philip K. Scheuer, "Disney Picturizes de Seversky's Dream," *Los Angeles Times*, October 16, 1943; Marjorie Kelly, "'Victory Thru Air Power:' A Thrilling Documentary," *Washington Post*, August 11, 1943; "Sascha's Show," *Time* 41 (July 12, 1943): 63.

34. Sterling F. Green quoted from Green, "Army Getting Deadly New Super-bomber," *Washington Post*, October 15, 1943; "Give Air Power Its Wings," *Washington Post*, July 30, 1943; de Seversky, *Victory through Air Power*, 335; *Victory through Air Power*, Disc 2, © Disney.

35. Quote from *United States Strategic Bombing Survey*, 95, and see stats on 73 and 85–90; Crouch, *Wings*, 418–24; Jablonski, *America in the Air War*, 167–71; Dick, *American Eagles*, 230–37.

36. Arnold quoted from Arnold, *Global Mission*, 444, and see also 442–43.

37. Thomas, *Walt Disney*, 186; de Seversky, "Walt Disney: An Airman in His Heart," 7–8; Green, "Interview Alexander de Seversky, New York City, April 16, 1970," 24–25; Doolittle, *I Could Never Be So Lucky Again*, 384–85; Stephen E. Ambrose, *Eisenhower, Soldier and President* (New York: Simon & Schuster, 1990), 136–41; Jablonski, *America in the Air War*, 126–29; Arthur Bryant, *Triumph in the West* (New York: Doubleday & Company, 1959), 14.

### 14. THE PROPHET AT HOME AND ABROAD

1. Correspondence from Nick Pishvanov to author November 4, 2008, and April 23, 2009; clerk's Notice of Election to de Seversky, June 20, 1946, CAM de Seversky Papers, Box 218.

2. Correspondence from Nick Pishvanov to author, November 4, 2008.

3. Frederick R. Barkley, "Weekly Gas Ration Is 2 to 6 Gallons," *New York Times*, May 7, 1942; Thomas, *Walt Disney*, 120 and 145; correspondence from Nick Pishvanov to author, April 23, 2009.

4. Nick Pishvanov quoted from correspondence to author, December 29, 2006.

5. De Seversky wrote a touching obituary for Vodka, "Death of a Famous Dog," November 11, 1947, CAM de Seversky Papers, Box 218, pp. 1–2.

6. De Seversky, "Death of a Famous Dog," 2; *New York Times*: "Jet Plane Flies to Capital from N.Y. in 29 Min. 15 Sec.," April 22, 1946, "Navy Bomber Sets East–West Record," May 29, 1946, "Flier Sets New Records," November 28, 1947. For restrictions on civilian pilots, see Stephen G. Craft, *Embry-Riddle at War* (Gainesville: University Press of Florida, 2009), 133–34.

7. Letter contract from A. J. Naylor, Office of Military Director of Civil Aviation, to de Seversky, June 24, 1942, CAM de Seversky Papers, Box 218; correspondence

from Nick Pishvanov to author, December 7, 2008; Edward H. Phillips, *Beechcraft Pursuit of Perfection* (Eagan, MN: Flying Books, 1992), 12–18.

8. Mary Anderson, "Sees No Ceiling for Women in Aviation," *New York World Telegram*, October 6, 1943; Willa Martin, "Has Strong Yen to Join Civil Patrol," *Knoxville Tennessee Journal*, September 5, 1943; "Russian War Relief Will Gain by Party," *New York Times*, May 24, 1942.

9. *New York Times*: "Bond Drive Goals Told at Rally," September 2, 1943; Legion for American Unity ad, February 12, 1942; "Town Hall Program Stresses War Theme," November 1, 1942; "Victory Rally Tonight," May 1, 1942; "Davies Sees Guide to War's Duration," May 12, 1942.

10. De Seversky quoted from de Seversky, "I Owe My Career to Losing a Leg," 20; letters from Capt. Julian C. Blaustein, Signal Corps, to de Seversky, July 31 and August 5, 1944, CAM de Seversky Papers, Box 215.

11. De Seversky quoted from Anderson, "Sees No Ceiling for Women in Aviation." See correspondence between de Seversky and named individuals in paragraph, CAM de Seversky Papers, Boxes 7, 216, and 217.

12. "Radio Today," *New York Times*, August 8, 1942; "Plane Mad," *Hampshire Magazine* (September 1942), 23; NBC radio transcript: "Major Enjoys Having His Ears Burned," CAM de Seversky Papers, Box 215, p. 6; Anderson, "Sees No Ceiling for Women in Aviation."

13. "Radio Today," *New York Times*, August 24, 1943; "Disney's Salary $50,000," *New York Times*, February 2, 1944; Margo Tupper, "De Seversky Off on Vacation," *Orlando Morning Sentinel*, clipping listed for September 1943, CAM de Seversky Papers, Box 265; letter from de Seversky to Lord Brabazon, October 7, 1943, CAM de Seversky Papers, Box 216.

14. NBC radio transcript, August 27, 1942, CAM de Seversky Papers, Box 215; Anderson, "Sees No Ceiling for Women in Aviation," sample drafts of columns in CAM de Seversky Papers, Box 203.

15. De Seversky quoted from de Seversky, "United States Declared Remiss in the Development of Air Power," *New York Times*, October 4, 1943; Boyne, *Clash of Wings*, 183–86.

16. De Seversky quoted from de Seversky, "Air Power and the War," *New York Times*, September 29, 1944. See also de Seversky, "Air Power and the War" or de Seversky, "War and Air Power," *New York Times*, November 17, 1943, February 4, 1944, April 12, 1944, May 26, 1944, July 24, 1944.

17. De Seversky, "I Owe My Career to Losing a Leg," 20–23 and 164–69; de Seversky, *American Mercury*: "Myth of Fortress Europe" (October 1943), 417–21, "Bomb the Axis from America!" (December 1943), 675–83, and "Future of the Robot Plane" (September 1944), 322–25; letter from Amy Loveman of Book-of-the-Month Club to de Seversky, November 3, 1944, CAM de Seversky Papers, Box 261; de Seversky, "Air Power and the War," *New York Times*, December 17, 1943, December 29, 1943, and January 5, 1944.

18. Citation quoted from press release, February 21, 1944, CAM de Seversky Papers, Box 216; Kevin Gould, "Spaatz, Carl Andrew (1891–1974)," in *Air Warfare*, ed. Boyne, 586.

19. General Spaatz quoted from letter to de Seversky, June 29, 1945, CAM de Seversky Papers, Box 217.

20. Robert P. Patterson quoted from his memorandum to Arnold, August 3, 1944, Henry H. Arnold Collection, Microfilm #28132.

21. General White quoted from a memorandum for the chief of the air staff, August 6, 1944; White quoted from draft memorandum for General Echols; August 4, 1944; both in Henry H. Arnold Collection, Microfilm #28132.

22. De Seversky, "Role of the Engineer in This War," *The American Engineer* (January 1945), 14–18 and 28, USAF Historical Research Agency, Call #248.6252-12; "Olds Ask Policies for Higher Output," *New York Times*, December 6, 1944; letter from Arnold to de Seversky, December 23, 1944, Henry H. Arnold Collection, Microfilm #28058.

23. Arnold, *Global Mission*, 536–42; Daso, *Hap Arnold*, 198–203; Parton, *"Air Force Spoken Here,"* 432–35.

24. De Seversky quoted from "Report of Major Alexander P. de Seversky, to the Honorable Robert P. Patterson, Secretary of War, September 27, 1945," USAF Historical Research Agency, Call #170.332A, pp. 1–6; War Department appointment of de Seversky as Special Consultant, March 2, 1945, CAM de Seversky Papers, Box 265.

25. Sidney Shalett, "Planes Beat Reich, Seversky Asserts," *New York Times*, September 28, 1945; "Report of Major Alexander P. de Seversky . . . September 27, 1945," 1–2.

26. *United States Strategic Bombing Surveys*, 39; "Report of Major Alexander P. de Seversky . . . September 27, 1945," 2.

27. "Interrogation of Reich Marshal Hermann Goering," U.S. Strategic Air Forces Europe, USAF Historical Research Agency, Call #519.1612-2, pp. 1 and 3; Robert S. Hopkins, "Vandenberg, Hoyt S. (1899–1954)," in *Air Warfare*, ed. Boyne, 669.

28. Goering quoted from "Interrogation of Reich Marshal Hermann Goering," 6; Christopher H. Sterling, "V-1 Missile and V-2 Rocket," in *Air Warfare*, ed. Boyne, 199–201.

29. De Seversky and Goering quoted from "Interrogation of Reich Marshal Hermann Goering," 7.

30. Goering quoted from "Interview No. 56, Reichmarshal Hermann Goering, June 29, 1945," U.S. Strategic Bombing Survey, USAF Historical Research Agency, Call #520.056-265, p. 11; Goering quoted from Edward L. Homz and Horst Boog, cons., *The Luftwaffe* (Alexandria, VA: Time-Life Books, 1982), 19. See also Taylor, ed., *Combat Aircraft of the World*, 169–71.

31. U.S. Strategic Air Forces in Europe, General (Carl) Spaatz File, Call #519.1612-2; "Interview Alexander de Seversky, New York City, April 16, 1970," 29; Arnold, *Global Mission*, 502.

32. Daso, *Hap Arnold*, 203; Parton, *"Air Force Spoken Here,"* 434–35.

33. Arnold, *Global Mission*, 580–93; Daso, *Hap Arnold*, 208–9; Gailey, *War in the Pacific*, 482 and 489; McCoy, *Presidency of Harry S. Truman*, 35–38.

34. De Seversky quoted from "Interview Alexander de Seversky, New York City, April 16, 1970," 29, and see also 28; Arnold, *Global Mission*, 580.

35. "Interview Alexander de Seversky, New York City, April 16, 1970," 29; de Seversky, "Air Power and the War," *New York Times*, November 15, 1943, and June 2, 1944; Mark A. O'Neill, "Illyushin Il-2 Shturmovik," in *Air Warfare*, ed. Boyne, 316–17.

36. "Report of Major Alexander P. de Seversky . . . September 27, 1945," 1–4.

37. De Seversky quoted from ibid., 5 and 6.

38. *United States Strategic Bombing Surveys*, 3–42; "Alexander P. de Seversky 1894–1974," in *Enshrinee Album*, ed. James W. Jacobs (Dayton, OH: Aviation Hall of Fame, 1984), 50–51.

15. THE PROPHET CHALLENGED

1. Alexander P. de Seversky quoted from "Major de Seversky's Report on Pacific Air Power," press release, February 19, 1946, USAF Historical Research Agency, Call #170.332H, p. 1; Head, "George, Harold Lee (1893–1986)," 252.

2. "Major de Seversky's Report on Pacific Air Power," 1; "De Seversky in Tokyo," *New York Times*, October 14, 1945.

3. "Major de Seversky's Report on Pacific Air Power," 20. See also, Walter J. Boyne, *The Influence of Air Power upon History* (Gretna, LA: Pelican Publishing, 2003), 165–68.

4. De Seversky quoted from "Major de Seversky's Report on Pacific Air Power," 5; Dennis R. Jenkins, "Consolidated Aircraft Corporation" and "Consolidated B-36 Peacemaker," both in *Air Warfare*, ed. Boyne, 147 and 149.

5. De Seversky quoted from "Major de Seversky's Report on Pacific Air Power," 2; "Report of Major Alexander P. de Seversky . . . September 27, 1945," 2; Richard P. Hallion, *Strike for the Sky: The History of Battlefield Air Attack 1911–1945* (Washington: Smithsonian Institution Press, 1989), 217 and 227.

6. Jeffrey G. Barlow, *Revolt of the Admirals* (Washington: Brassey's, 1998), 33–44; Sahr Conway-Lanz, *Collateral Damage* (New York: Routledge, 2006), 23–58.

7. *United States Strategic Bombing Surveys*, 62–65 and 71–77; Ross, *Strategic Bombing by the United States in World War II*, 205; Mac Isaac, *Strategic Bombing in World War II*, 123–26.

8. Gailey, *War in the Pacific*, 488–89; "Supplementary Report on Atomic Bombings of Hiroshima and Nagasaki" to "Major de Seversky's Report on Pacific Air Power," 2.

9. Conway-Lanz, *Collateral Damage*, 12–22; "Supplementary Report on Atomic Bombings of Hiroshima and Nagasaki," 1–3.

10. "Supplementary Report on Atomic Bombings of Hiroshima and Nagasaki," 4–5; de Seversky, "Atomic Bomb Hysteria," *Reader's Digest* 48 (February 1946): 121–22.

11. De Seversky quoted from "Supplementary Report on Atomic Bombings of Hiroshima and Nagasaki," 5; de Seversky, "Atomic Bomb Hysteria," 122.

12. First de Seversky quote from "Supplementary Report on Atomic Bombings of Hiroshima and Nagasaki," 12; second de Seversky quote from "Interview: Bob Considine and Major de Seversky July 1947," CAM de Seversky Papers, Box 210, p. 1.

13. "Interview: Bob Considine and Major de Seversky July 1947," p. 1; de Seversky, "The Relative Effectiveness of Atomic and Conventional Bombs," Air University lecture, March 25 1947, CAM de Seversky Papers, Box 210, pp. 1–24.

14. De Seversky, "The Relative Effectiveness of Atomic and Conventional Bombs," 2–4 and 9–11.

15. De Seversky, "Supplementary Reports on Atomic Bombings of Hiroshima and Nagasaki," 6 and 9; de Seversky, "Atomic Bomb Hysteria," 124.

16. De Seversky quoted from de Seversky, "Supplementary Reports on Atomic Bombings of Hiroshima and Nagasaki," 1.

17. Boyne, Clash of Wings, 369–74; McFarland, America's Pursuit of Precision Bombing, 1910–1945, 202–5; Mac Isaac, Strategic Bombing in World War Two, 107–8; Sherry, The Rise of American Air Power, 273–82.

18. Gailey, War in the Pacific, 483–86; United States Strategic Bombing Surveys, 105–6.

19. De Seversky quotes from "Major de Seversky's Report on Pacific Air Power," 9 and 10.

20. Dr. Karl T. Compton quoted from "For Bomb Tests on 'City,'" New York Times, April 9, 1946; "Seversky Is Contradicted," New York Times, November 7, 1945; Sidney Shalett, "Pacific Won in Air, Seversky Asserts," New York Times, February 19, 1946.

21. Fletcher Pratt quoted from his article, "Seversky and the Bomb," New Republic 114 (March 11, 1946): 340; Fletcher Pratt, "Don't Look Now, But . . .," Sea Power (June 1946), 8–10 and 28; Alexander P. de Seversky, "Navies Are Finished," American Mercury 62 (February 1946): 135–43.

22. Senator Thomas Hart quoted from "Air Force Accused of Bikini Handicap," New York Times, July 26, 1946; Harold B. Hinton, "Atom Bomb Force in Big City Argued," New York Times, February 16, 1946; Eugene Lyons, draft of article (published in This Week, February 13, 1949), CAM de Seversky Papers, Box 215, pp. 1–15.

23. United States Strategic Bombing Surveys, 45–46 and 102–3; Budiansky, Air Power, 241.

24. Hinton, "Atom Bomb Force in Big City Argued," 15; Barlow, Revolt of the Admirals, 68 and 136–39; Crouch, Wings, 548–49.

25. Barlow, Revolt of the Admirals, 68–74; Don Whitehead, "Arguments Raging over Atomic Blast," Los Angeles Times, July 3, 1946; Ernest K. Lindley, "Big Let-Down," Washington Post, July 3, 1946; "The Second Atomic Bomb at Bikini," Los Angeles Times, July 26, 1946; "Bikini Trip Shows Jap Ship on Way Down," Washington Post, July 27, 1946.

26. Quotations from "Citation to Accompany the Award of the Medal of Merit to Alexander P. de Seversky," December 18, 1946, LC, AIAA Papers, Box 111; cover sheet for citation explaining the origins of the Medal of Merit signed by Truman and James Byrnes, December 18, 1946, LISI, de Seversky Family Papers, Folder 1; "Major Seversky Is Awarded Medal for Merit," American Mercury 64 (May 1947): 635.

27. Damon Runyon Jr., quoted from press release issued for publication on February 23, 1947, CAM, de Seversky Papers, Box 210, pp. 1–4; "Medal of Merit Given Seversky by War Dept.," *New York Daily Mirror*, February 7, 1947; "Democracy at Work," editorial, *New York Times*, February 8, 1947.

28. Citation quoted from Ligue Internationale des Aviateurs press release, "International Harmon Trophy Awarded to de Seversky," June 24, 1947, CAM, de Seversky Papers, Box 215; "Seversky War Aid Praised by Truman," *New York Times*, June 25, 1947.

29. James K. Libbey, ed., *Documents of Soviet-American Relations*, vol. 5, *The Cold War Begins 1946–1949* (Gulf Breeze, FL: Academic International Press, 2006), xvi–xix, 59–65, and 70–77.

30. President Truman quoted from "Special Message to Congress on Greece and Turkey: The Truman Doctrine. March 12, 1947," *Public Papers of the Presidents of the United States: Harry S. Truman* (Washington: USGPO, 1963), 176–80.

31. De Seversky, "A Lecture on Air Power," Part I and Part II, *Air University Quarterly Review* 1 (Fall 1947): 25–41 and (Winter 1947): 23–40; de Seversky speech, "Air Force of the Future," Armed Forces Staff College, May 26, 1947, Air University Library Documents, M-U 38043 D452a, pp. 1–10; letter from Lucy D. Costello to Air Marshal Sir Arthur Harris, March 4, 1946, CAM de Seversky Papers, Box 217; de Seversky, Draft #4, "Memorandum in Connection with the Formation of the Seversky Aviation Corporation," October 20, 1947, CAM de Seversky Papers, Box 4, pp. 1–6.

32. "Statement by Major Alexander P. de Seversky before the President's Air Policy Commission," December 1, 1947, CAM de Seversky Papers, Box 210, pp. 1–17; Charles Hurd, "Vast Air Strength Urged by Lovett and de Seversky," *New York Times*, December 2, 1947; de Seversky, "We're Preparing for the Wrong War," *Look* 11 (December 9, 1947): 21–25.

33. Barlow, *Revolt of the Admirals*, 182–88; Crouch, *Wings*, 548–49.

34. M. Robert Gallop of Kaufman, Gallop, Climenko, Gould & Lynton quoted from letter to de Seversky, June 17, 1948, CAM de Seversky Papers, Box 3; Herring, *From Colony to Superpower*, 623–24; "Creation of Trizonia," communiqué by United Kingdom, the United States, France, the Benelux Countries, March 6, 1948, and "Currency Reform in the Western Zones of Germany," U.S. State Department internal memorandum, June 4, 1948, both in Libbey, *Documents of Soviet-American Relations*, 349–51 and 352–54; Boyne, *Influence of Air Power upon History*, 290.

16. RETURN OF THE MEDIA PERSONALITY

1. Interview of Ann Hamilton Tunner by Dr. James Hasdorff, October 5, 1976, U.S. Air Force Historical Research Agency, Call # K239.0512-912C.1, pp. 20–21.

2. Dick, *American Eagles*, 260–63; James K. Libbey, "Berlin Blockade of 1948," in *Modern Encyclopedia of Russian and Soviet History*, ed. Wieczynski, 47, 75–80; Secretary of State for Foreign Affairs, *Selected Documents on Germany and the Question of Berlin* (London: H. M. Stationery Office, 1961), 61–63.

3. Lester H. Brune, *The Missile Crisis of October 1962* (Claremont, CA: Regina Books, 1985), 33–72; de Seversky, *Victory through Air Power*, vi.

4. "Subscribers to North American Newspaper Alliance," May 20, 1960; letters from John N. Wheeler, vice chairman, North American Newspaper Alliance, Inc., to de Seversky, January 31, 1958, February 11, 1958, and February 19, 1958, all in CAM de Seversky Papers, Box 209.

5. De Seversky, NANA press releases, October 8 and 11, 1948, CAM de Seversky Papers, Boxes 208 and 210.

6. "Testimony of General Carl Spaatz, chief of staff, United States Air Force before the House Appropriations Committee," April 1948, LC, Carl Spaatz Papers, Part I, Box 29, pp. 1–7; "Gen. Spaatz Is Retiring as Air Commander," *New York Times*, April 2, 1948.

7. NANA press release, October 9 and 11, 1948, both in CAM de Seversky Papers, Box 208.

8. De Seversky, *Air Power: Key to Survival* (New York: Simon & Schuster, 1950), 305–17, and see also 242–59; Herring, *From Colony to Superpower*, 617–21; Glenn J. Dorn, *Peronistas and New Dealers* (New Orleans: University Press of the South, 2005), 249–63.

9. Letter from Leon M. Pearson of NBC to de Seversky, July 7, 1949, CAM de Seversky Papers, Box 210, pp. 1–2; "Programs on the Air," *New York Times*, July 16, 1949; de Seversky, *Air Power*, 312–13.

10. De Seversky, "The U.S. Air Force in Power Politics," *Air Affairs* 2 (Winter 1949): 477–90; de Seversky, "Are We Headed for Military Dictatorship?, *Pageant* 4 (April 1949): 147–54.

11. De Seversky quoted from de Seversky, "Peace through Air Power," *Reader's Digest*, 54 (February 1949), 24, and see also 18–23 and 25–26.

12. De Seversky, "Peace through Air Power," 23; de Seversky, draft NANA press release, March 4, 1949, CAM de Seversky Papers, Box 208, pp. 1–4; "Air Force B-50 Circles Globe in Nonstop Flight of 94 Hours," *Los Angeles Times*, March 3, 1949.

13. De Seversky quotes from de Seversky, "The Only Way to Rearm Europe," *American Mercury* 68 (March 1949): 264 and 269, see also 263, 265–68, and 270–72.

14. De Seversky, "Our Antiquated Defense Policy," *American Mercury* 68 (April 1949): 389–99; de Seversky, "Are We Headed for Military Dictatorship?," *Pageant* 4 (April 1949): 147–54.

15. Ibid.; Barlow, *Revolt of the Admirals*, 173–74.

16. De Seversky, *Air Power*, 321–24; Crouch, *Wings*, 549; V. R. Montanari, "First Secretary of Defense Found with His Bathrobe Cord around Neck," *Washington Post*, May 23, 1949.

17. De Seversky, "Korea Proves Our Need for a Dominant Air Force," *Reader's Digest* 57 (October 1950): 7; "Mrs. Alexander de Seversky, 60, Wife of Plane Designer, Is Dead," *New York Times*, July 31, 1967; transcript, "Success Story," April 10, 1951, CAM

de Seversky Papers, Box 210, pp. 1–9; transcript, "Eloise Salutes the Stars," August 17, 1951, CAM de Seversky Papers, Box 211, pp. 1–7.

18. "Ten Year Summary of Thank You(s) for Lectures: Air University," CAM de Seversky Papers, Box 217, pp. 1–4; Howard A. Rusk, "New Goals for Handicapped to Be Cited by Disabled Folk," *New York Times*, November 6, 1949; letter from Nena W. Badenoch, NSCCA Convention coordinator, to de Seversky, December 6, 1949, CAM de Seversky Papers, Box 210; transcript, Nancy Craig Interview of de Seversky, WJZ Radio (November 9, 1949), CAM de Seversky Papers, Box 210, pp. 1–5.

19. "De Severskys Get Residence Here," *New York Times*, June 20, 1953; message from D. de Seversky to author, October 10, 2008; letter from Michail Ryl to author, April 11, 2006, p. 3.

20. Michail Ryl quoted from letter to author, April 11, 2006, 4; messages from D. de Seversky to author, November 15, 2007, October 10, 2008, and June 15, 2009; message from Nick Pishvanov to author, October 4, 2006; copy of letter from Florence Cummings to L. Levinson, April 6, 1951, CAM de Seversky Papers, Box 210.

21. Burton I. Kaufman, *The Korean Conflict* (Westport, CT: Greenwood Press, 1999), 3–4; McCoy, *Presidency of Harry S. Truman*, 221–24; David Dempsey, "In and Out of Books" (on title change), *New York Times*, October 15, 1950; Evtuhov et al., *A History of Russia*, 721–22; de Seversky, *Air Power*, xvii–xxiv, 39n, 74n, 299n, and 345n.

22. De Seversky quoted from de Seversky, *Air Power*, xxi.

23. Kaufman, *Korean Conflict*, 10–13; Boyne, *Influence of Air Power upon History*, 293–94; Herring, *From Colony to Superpower*, 639–41.

24. De Seversky quoted from de Seversky, "Korea Proves Our Need for a Dominant Air Force," 10, and see also 6–9; John Lewis Gaddis, *We Now Know* (New York: Oxford University Press, 1997), 108–10.

25. *New York Times*: "On Television This Week," *Meet the Press*, October 8, 1950, and *People's Platform*, March 11, 1951; transcripts: "American Forum" (November 12, 1950), 1–16, and "Town Meeting" (December 26, 1950), 1–13, and "American Forum" (February 25, 1951), 1–12, CAM de Seversky Papers, Box 210.

26. Ferdinand Kuhn (no title), *Washington Post*, February 22, 1951; McCoy, *Presidency of Harry S. Truman*, 258–61; Boyne, *Influence of Air Power upon History*, 298–99.

27. William S. White, "Le May Says Army Can't Hold Europe," *New York Times*, February 22, 1951; McCoy, *Presidency of Harry S. Truman*, 260; William Koenig and Peter Scofield, *Soviet Military Power* (New York: Bison Books, 1983), 77.

28. Stephen E. Ambrose, *Eisenhower: Soldier and President* (New York: Simon & Schuster, 1990), 268–70; "Taft Charges Backed: De Seversky Sees Plane Output Long Due Partly to Politics," *New York Times*, June 3, 1952; de Seversky, "De Seversky Assails Truman Air Force Figures," *Journal American*, June 11, 1952; de Seversky, "An Airman's Plea to All Republican Delegates," July 1952, CAM de Seversky Papers, Box 208, pp. 1–13.

29. Robert A. Divine, *Eisenhower and the Cold War* (Oxford, UK: Oxford University Press, 1981), 4–5; Ambrose, *Eisenhower*, 271–72; Lyons, "Seversky—Aviation's Versatile Genius," 43.

30. Lyons, "Seversky—Aviation's Versatile Genius," 43; de Seversky, *America: Too Young to Die!* (New York: McGraw-Hill, 1961), 66–70.

31. Letter from John N. Wheeler, NANA vice chairman, to de Seversky, January 31, 1958; "Contract for Purchase of Manuscript" from Ed McCarthy, managing editor of *This Week Magazine*, to de Seversky, February 21, 1958; copy of letter from de Seversky to Edward R. Murrow, CBS, March 19, 1958, all in CAM de Seversky Papers, Box 209.

32. For a sample of publications mentioned, see de Seversky, "World War III and How to Win It," *Coronet* 37 (January 1955): 116–21; de Seversky, "So That This Nation Shall Not Perish," *Pageant* 13 (March 1958): 60–67; de Seversky, "Air Power, Missiles, and National Survival," *Air Power Historian* 5 (January 1958): 20–29; de Seversky, "What Is Airpower?," *Air Force Magazine* 38 (August 1955): 21–22. Letter from Alfred Knopf Jr. to de Seversky, December 3, 1956; "Sample customary memorandum of agreement covering advisory and technical literary collaborative work" from Janet Mabie to de Seversky, undated, both in CAM de Seversky Papers, Box 215.

33. "Contract" between de Seversky and W. Colston Leigh for a lecture to be delivered before the Los Alamos Town Forum on November 2, 1951, CAM de Seversky Papers, Box 211; letter from William H. McDonnell to de Seversky, enclosing airline tickets and hotel reservations for his speech for the Chicago Automobile Show, December 18, 1957, CAM de Seversky Papers, Box 213; de Seversky, "Importance of Global Command of the Air," *Vital Speeches of the Day* 23 (November 1, 1956): 42–46; copy of de Seversky's Doctor of Science diploma from Southern Illinois University, June 16, 1957, CAM de Seversky Papers, Box 1; see, for example, sample annual appointments of de Seversky as advisor to the chief of staff of the U.S. Air Force, July 1, 1960, and June 24, 1972, both in CAM de Seversky Papers, Box 216 and Box 3, respectively; see also samples of de Seversky lectures: October 13, 1961, Institute of Technology, Wright-Patterson AFB; July 27, 1962, Squadron Officers School, Air University, Maxwell AFB; September 24, 1964, Ballistic Systems Division, Norton AFB; March 18, 1971, Squadron Officers School, Air University, Maxwell AFB; samples in CAM de Seversky Papers, Boxes 2 and 213. Twelve-page memoir given to author on July 9, 2006, by D. de Seversky; messages from D. de Seversky to author: April 20, 2010, June 5, 2010, June 10, 2010; U.S. Patent Office, Leonora Wingenroth, "Cleansing Device," filed March 26, 1956, received April 29, 1958, Patent #2,832,342.

34. Transcript of de Seversky's appearance on "The Mike Wallace Interview," August 3, 1958, CAM de Seversky Papers, Box 213, pp. 1–17; "On Television," *New York Times*, January 29, 1954; "Best TV Bets Today," *Los Angeles Times*, November 8, 1957; "On the Radio," *New York Times*, February 12, 1953; April 5, 1954; and June 5, 1957.

35. "De Seversky Stricken," *New York Times*, April 11, 1959; "Seversky's Condition Fair," *New York Times*, April 12, 1959; letter from Michail Ryl to author, December 23, 2009. To use appropriate medical terminology and secure information on DeBakey, the author interviewed Dudley A. Baringer, M.D., April 6, 2010.

17. THE FUTURIST

1. Maj. Gen. W. H. Hennig quoted from his letter to Alexander P. de Seversky, May 22, 1961, CAM de Seversky Papers, Box 262; "Books–Authors," *New York Times*, March 10, 1961; de Seversky, *America: Too Young to Die!*

2. Foster Rhea Dulles (John's brother), *America's Rise to World Power* (New York: Harper & Row, 1963), 273; Ambrose, *Eisenhower*, 356–57; Col. Alan J. Parrington, USAF, "Mutually Assured Destruction Revisited," *Airpower Journal* 11 (Winter 1997): 4–19.

3. McGraw-Hill ad quoted from *Los Angeles Times*, June 28, 1961; McGraw-Hill ad, *New York Times*, June 25, 1961; "Radio," *New York Times*, April 25, 1961; "Radio Programs," *New York Times*, July 16, 1961; "Television Preview," *Washington Post*, April 25, 1961; "Television," *New York Times*, July 18, 1961.

4. Henry A. Kissinger quoted from Kissinger, *Nuclear Weapons and Foreign Policy* (New York: Doubleday & Company, 1958), 14; de Seversky quoted from de Seversky, *America: Too Young To Die!*, 112; Spencer C. Tucker, *Vietnam* (Lexington: University Press of Kentucky, 1999), 98 and 176.

5. George P. Sutton, *Rocket Propulsion Elements: An Introduction to the Engineering of Rockets* (New York: John Wiley & Sons, 1992), 168–201; Joseph A. Angelo Jr., *Rockets* (New York: Facts on File, 2006), 131–44; de Seversky, speech for the Niagara Frontier Convocation, University of Buffalo, December 7, 1951, CAM, de Seversky Papers, Box 211, pp. 1–6.

6. De Seversky quoted from his speech for the Niagara Frontier Convocation, 1; de Seversky, "Artificial Gravity for Spaceships," *Science Digest* 20 (October 1946): 5–8; de Seversky, "Your Trip to Mars," *Pageant* 7 (August 1952): 4–15; de Seversky, "We'll Build Another Moon" (reprinted from *American Weekly*, February 24, 1952), *Science Digest* 31 (June 1952): 15–19; Wernher von Braun, "Crossing the Last Frontier," *Collier's* 129 (March 22, 1952): 24–29, 72, and 74.

7. Von Braun, "Man on the Moon: The Journey," *Collier's* 130 (October 18, 1952): 52–60; and "The Exploration of the Moon," *Collier's* 130 (October 25, 1952): 38–40; Dennis Piszkiewicz, *Wernher von Braun* (Westport, CT: Praeger, 1998), 73–91; Thomas, *Walt Disney*, 255.

8. De Seversky quoted from his "Biographical Sketch" (p. 3) that accompanied a copy of a letter from his secretary, Patricia Rittenhouse, to Joan Hanauer, United Press International, October 29, 1970, CAM, de Seversky Papers, Box 217; Angelo, *Rockets*, 145; Esther C. Goddard and G. Edward Pendray, eds., *The Papers of Robert H. Goddard*, vol. 1, *1898–1924* (New York: McGraw-Hill, 1970), 38–39 and 423–27.

9. "Rocket Ships to Moon Are Delayed," *New York Times*, December 23, 1951; U.S. Patent Office, Alexander P. de Seversky, "Ionocraft," filed August 31, 1959 / received April 28, 1964, Patent # 3,130,945; "De Seversky Stricken," *New York Times*, April 11, 1959.

10. Hans Fantel, "Major de Seversky's Ion-Propelled Aircraft," *Popular Mechanics* 22 (August 1964): 58–61, 194 and 196; "Ionocraft," Patent # 3,130,945, pp. 7–15; Stacy V. Jones, "De Seversky Receives a Patent for His Ionocraft," *New York Times*, May 2, 1964.

11. U.S. Patent Office, Alexander P. de Seversky, "Liquid Distributors for Wet Electrostatic Precipitators," filed July 25, 1972 / received July 3, 1973, Patent #3,742,681; U.S. Patent Office, Alexander P. de Seversky, "Self-Decontaminating Electrostatic Precipitator Structures," filed September 7, 1962 / received March 8, 1966, Patent #3,238,702; "A Mechanical Reader for Tolls Is Patented," *New York Times*, July 7, 1973; "Dust of Atomic Bomb Starts Cattle Cancer," *Los Angeles Times*, August 13, 1950; "Smog-Here-to-Stay Belief Draws Fire," *Los Angeles Times*, May 7, 1952; "Albany Aid Slated on Smoke Control," *New York Times*, February 19, 1952.

12. "Self-Decontaminating Electrostatic Precipitator Structures," Patent #3,238,702; Prospectus: Seversky Electronatom Corporation, May 23, 1968, CAM, de Seversky Papers, Box 4, pp. 10 and 16.

13. Prospectus: Seversky Electronatom Corporation, 5, 16, and 19.

14. Ibid., 11, 13–14, and 17.

15. Nick Pishvanov quoted from his message to the author, October 4, 2006; telephone call from Nick Pishvanov to author, April 10, 2006; "Death of Mrs. de Seversky Is Called Apparent Suicide," *New York Times*, August 1, 1967; "Mrs. Alexander de Seversky: Noted Pilot," *Los Angeles Times*, July 31, 1967.

16. Prospectus: Seversky Electronatom Corporation, 1 and 23–24.

17. Ibid., 1; "Seversky Electronatom Offer," *Wall Street Journal*, July 26, 1968. See also ad for Seversky Electronatom Corporation, *New York Times*, June 17, 1968.

18. Prospectus: Seversky Electronatom Corporation, 11; press release: "Fitzpatrick, Chicago Official, Named President of Seversky Electronatom Corporation," July 25, 1968, CAM de Seversky Papers, Box 215, pp. 5–8.

19. "Fitzpatrick, Chicago Official, Named President of Seversky Electronatom Corporation," 1–2; "Seversky Elects President," *New York Times*, July 26, 1968; Seversky Electronatom Corporation ad, *New York Times*, January 31, 1971.

20. Nick Pishvanov quoted from his message to author, November 4, 2008; Seversky Electronatom Corporation ad, *New York Times*, July 20, 1969.

21. "Over-the-Counter Quotations," *New York Times*, November 1, 1968; "Over-the-Counter Quotations," *New York Times*, February 23, 1973; letter from Clark H. Getts to de Seversky at his office at 630 Fifth Avenue, March 12, 1971, CAM de Seversky Papers, Box 213.

22. De Seversky quoted from "Notes on People," *New York Times*, August 12, 1971; "'Ecologists Ruin Us'—Seversky," *San Francisco Examiner*, August 11, 1971; Gene Smith, "De Seversky's New Role," *New York Times*, January 3, 1971; Gregory La Brache, "Preview: Life in 2000 AD," *Los Angeles Herald-Examiner*, August 5, 1971; Bob Lardine, "Dealing with a Major Subject," *New York News Coloroto Magazine* (June 20, 1971), 1–4; Berg, *Lindbergh*, 538, and see photos between 436 and 437.

23. De Seversky quoted from his letter to George E. Mueller, August 9, 1969; letter from Mueller to de Seversky, February 10, 1969; "Major's Itinerary July 13–18, 1969," all in CAM de Seversky Papers, Box 218. See also "Airman de Seversky Honored with

Award," *The* (Washington) *Evening Star,* December 17, 1969; Ted Thackrey Jr., "State Dinner for Astronauts," *Los Angeles Times,* August 14, 1969.

24. Letter from James W. Jacobs, Aviation Hall of Fame, to de Seversky (May 15, 1970); Aviation Hall of Fame Enshrinement Program, December 17, 1970; news clipping, "Air Pioneer: Major de Seversky Enters Hall of Fame," *Long Island Press,* December 17, 1970, all in CAM de Seversky Papers, Box 216. See also Aviation Hall of Fame Award for Alexander P. de Seversky, CAM de Seversky Papers, Box 1.

25. Whiteley, "Alexander de Seversky," 11; letter from Jacqueline Cochran to Gen. John R. Dolny, May 29, 1974, CAM de Seversky Papers, Box 217. Note: As displayed in the museum, the P-35 is given the markings of a P-35A that served in the Philippines in 1941. Krista Strider, curator at the USAF Museum, provided the author details about the restoration and accession of the P-35 in a phone call on June 2, 2010.

26. "Bourne–Beebe," *New York Times,* November 3, 2005; phone call from Nick Pishvanov to author, October 1, 2008; Certificate of Death for Alexander de Seversky, Memorial Hospital, August 24, 1974, signed by Paul D. Sabel, M.D., recorded for the Department of Health, Office of Vital Records, City of New York, Certificate #150 74-115265; "Alexander P. de Seversky Dies at 80; Early Strategic Air Power Proponent," *New York Times,* August 26, 1974; copy of Woodlawn Cemetery Order for Interment for Evelyn Olliphant de Seversky signed by Mary Bourne, September 17, 1974; copy of Woodlawn Cemetery Order for Interment for Alexander P. de Seversky signed by Mary Bourne, September 17, 1974. The latter two documents are courtesy of Diane de Seversky enclosed in her letter to the author, April 24, 2010.

# Selected Bibliography

MANUSCRIPTS AND ARCHIVAL MATERIAL

Columbia University, New York
   Oral History Research Office: Reminiscences of Alexander Kartveli
Cradle of Aviation Museum, Garden City, New York
   Papers of Alexander P. de Seversky
   Manufacturer's Collection: Seversky/Republic
Dwight D. Eisenhower Presidential Library, Abilene, Kansas
   Papers of Jacqueline Cochran
Hagley Museum & Library, Wilmington, Delaware
   Papers of Elmer A. Sperry
Library of Congress, Washington, D.C.
   Recording of Songs by N. G. Severskii
Library of Congress, Manuscript Division, Washington, D.C.
   Papers of the American Institute of Aeronautics and Astronautics: Seversky Folder
   Papers of Frank M. Andrews
   Papers of Ira C. Eaker
   Papers of William Mitchell
   Papers of Alexander de Seversky
   Papers of Carl Spaatz
Long Island Studies Institute, Hofstra University
   Papers of Alexander P. de Seversky Family
National Air and Space Museum Archives
   Seversky Biography Files
National Archives, College Park, Maryland
   Record Group 342 (Sarah Clark Collection): Bomb Sights File
Russian State Archive War-Naval Fleet, St. Petersburg
   World War I Military File for Aleksandr Nikolaevich Prokof'ev-Severskii

U.S. Air Force Historical Research Agency, Maxwell Air Force Base
Orvil A. Anderson Collection
Henry H. Arnold Collection
Marvin C. Demler Collection
George W. Goddard Interview of de Seversky
Murray Green Interview of de Seversky
Allen L. Patterson Collection
Sebie B. Smith Collection
Ann Hamilton Tunner Interview
U.S. Strategic Air Forces Europe: Interrogation of Reich Marshal Hermann Goering
U.S. Strategic Air Forces Europe: Carl Spaatz File
U.S. Strategic Bombing Survey: Interview No. 56, Reichmarshal Hermann Goering
War Department Bureau of Public Relations: Major Seversky's Report on Pacific Air Power February 19, 1946
War Department Bureau of Public Relations: Report (on Europe Air Power) of Major Alexander P. de Seversky to the Honorable Robert P. Patterson, Secretary of War, September 27, 1945

NEWSPAPERS
*Biloxi Herald*
*Cleveland News*
*Cleveland Plain Dealer*
*Dayton Journal*
*Detroit News*
*The* (Washington) *Evening Star*
(New York) *Journal American*
*Knoxville Tennessee Journal*
*Lexington Herald-Leader*
*Los Angeles Herald-Examiner*
*Los Angeles Times*
*Orlando Morning Sentinel*
*New York American*
*New York Daily News*
*New York Evening Journal*
*New York Herald Tribune*
*New York Mirror*
*New York Post*
*New York Times*
*New York World Telegram*
*San Francisco Examiner*

*The* (New York) *Sun*
*Wall Street Journal*
*Washington Post*

BOOKS BY ALEXANDER P. DE SEVERSKY
*Air Power: Key to Survival.* New York: Simon & Schuster, 1950.
*America: Too Young to Die!* New York: McGraw-Hill Book Company, 1961.
*Victory through Air Power.* New York: Simon & Schuster, 1942.

MAGAZINE/JOURNAL ARTICLES BY ALEXANDER P. DE SEVERSKY
"The Air Around Us." *This Week* (March 6, 1966), 2.
"Air Power Ends Isolation." *The Atlantic* 168 (October 1941): 408–16.
"Air Power, Missiles, and National Survival." *The Air Power Historian* 5 (January 1958):
   20–29.
"Air Power to Rule World." *Science Digest* 12 (October 1942): 33–36.
"The Airplane of Tomorrow." *Mechanix Illustrated* 28 (September 1942): 40–45, 156.
"America Repeats Europe's Aviation Mistakes." *American Mercury* 53 (October 1941):
   401–10.
"Are We Headed for Military Dictatorship?" *Pageant* 4 (April 1949): 147–54.
"Artificial Gravity for Spaceships." *Science Digest* 20 (October 1946): 5–8.
"Atomic Bomb Hysteria." *Reader's Digest* 48 (February 1946): 121–26.
"Aviation Ballyhoo vs. Aviation Facts." *American Mercury* 55 (September 1942): 263–74.
"Aviation vs. Isolation." *Vital Speeches of the Day* 7 (July 1, 1941): 557–58.
"Axis Blunders in Air Strategy." *Cosmopolitan* 112 (November 1942): 36.
"Bomb the Axis from America!" *American Mercury* 57 (December 1943): 675–83.
"Build an Invincible Air Force Now." *Vital Speeches of the Day* 17 (January 1, 1951): 173–78.
"Command of Space." *The Airpower Historian* 9 (October 1962): 253.
"De Seversky on Strategic Organization." *Air Force Magazine* 41 (June 1958): 83–84, 87–88.
"Don't Let Censorship Destroy Us!" *This Week* (September 18, 1955), 7, 34, 36–38.
"Future of the Robot Plane." *American Mercury* 59 (September 1944): 322–25.
"Hard Facts on Air Power." *American Mercury* 50 (August 1940): 406–14.
"How Can Pursuit Aviation Regain Its Tactical Freedom?" *U.S. Air Services* 22 (March
   1934): 16–17.
"How to Answer Neutralism." *The Freeman* (October 6, 1952), 17–19.
"How We Must Bomb Japan." *American Magazine* 133 (April 1942): 14–15, 102–4.
"I Owe My Career to Losing a Leg." *Ladies' Home Journal* 61 (May 1944): 20–23, 164–69.
"I Remember Billy Mitchell." *Vogue* 100 (October 15, 1942): 46, 91–93.
"Importance of Global Command of the Air." *Vital Speeches of the Day* 23 (November
   1, 1956): 42–46.
"Is German Air Power Finished?" *American Mercury* 57 (August 1943): 144–52.
"Is Our Army Too Large?" *American Mercury* 55 (November 1942): 519–28.
"Jet—Tomorrow's Plane." *Pageant* 1 (April 1946): 62–65.

"Korea Proves Our Need for a Dominant Air Force." *Reader's Digest* 57 (October 1950): 6–10.

"A Lecture on Air Power, Part I." *Air University Quarterly Review* 1 (Fall 1947): 25–41.

"A Lecture on Air Power, Part II." *Air University Quarterly Review* 1 (Winter 1947): 23–40.

"Lest We Forget." *U.S. Air Service* 25 (June 1937): 16–17, 35.

"Lindbergh Is Wrong Again." *General Training Continental Air Command* 11 (1956): 58–66.

"Military Key to Survival." *Reader's Digest* 57 (September 1950): 1–9, 163–80.

"Myth of Fortress Europe." *American Mercury* 57 (October 1943): 417–21.

"National Aims and Space Power." *Signal* 12, Part I (April 1958): 8–9, 11.

"National Aims and Space Power." *Signal* 12, Part II (May 1958): 17–19.

"Navies Are Finished." *American Mercury* 62 (February 1946): 135–43.

"Only Way to Rearm Europe." *American Mercury* 68 (March 1949): 263–72.

"Ordeal of American Air Power." *American Mercury* 53 (July 1941): 7–14 and 127.

"Our Antiquated Defense Policy." *American Mercury* 68 (April 1949): 389–99.

"Our Current Inferiority Is Not Scientific." *Vital Speeches of the Day* 24 (February 1, 1958): 238–42.

"Our Postwar Air World." *Scientist Digest* 14 (November 1943): 34–38.

"Peace through Air Power." *Reader's Digest* 54 (February 1949): 18–26.

"Remember Billy Mitchell!" *Air Power Historian* 3 (October 1956): 179–85.

"Scoring the Stunting Contest," *Sportsman Pilot* (May-June 1933), 10–12, 43, 45, 47.

"So That This Nation Shall Not Perish." *Pageant* 13 (March 1958): 60–67.

"State of Our National Defense." *Vital Speeches of the Day* 18 (June 15, 1952): 523–29.

"Twilight of Sea Power." *American Mercury* 52 (June 1941): 647–58.

"The U.S. Air Force in Power Politics," *Air Affairs* 2 (Winter 1949): 477–90.

"Victory through Air Power!" *American Mercury* 54 (February 1942): 135–54.

"Victory through Air Power." *Reader's Digest* 41 (July 1942): 119–37.

"Victory through Air Power?—'Yes.'" *Sea Power* 2 (June 1942): 7, 9, 25–26.

"Walt Disney: An Airman in His Heart," *Aerospace Historian* 14 (Spring 1967): 5–8.

"Wanted: True Air Strategy." *American Mercury* 56 (May 1943): 562–71.

"We Have No Air Power." *The Freeman* (June 16, 1952), 601–04.

"We Need Better Planes—Better Planning!" *Cosmopolitan* 112 (October 1942): 42–43, 118.

"We'll Build Another Moon." *American Weekly* (February 24, 1952), 4–5, 22 (condensed in *Science Digest* 31 [June 1952]: 15–19).

"We're Preparing for the Wrong War." *Look* 11 (December 9, 1947): 21–25.

"When Will America Be Bombed?" *American Mercury* 54 (April 1942): 412–20.

"Why the Luftwaffe Failed." *The Atlantic* 169 (March 1942): 293–302.

"What the Atom Bomb Would Do to Us." *Reader's Digest* 48 (May 1946): 125–28.

"What Is Air Power?" *Air Force Magazine* 38 (August 1955): 21–22.

"What Keeps a Man Young?" *This Week* (August 4, 1963), 2.

"Why Hitler's Airplanes Failed to Beat England . . . A Lesson." *Look* 4 (December 17, 1940): 8–11.

"Why Lindbergh Is Wrong." *American Mercury* 52 (May 1941): 519–32.

"Why We Must Have a Separate Air Force." *Reader's Digest* 38 (March 1941): 107–13.

"Why We Must Stop Wars." *This Week* (May 7, 1944), 2–3.
"World War III and How to Win It." *Coronet* 37 (January 1955): 116–21.
"Your Trip to Mars." *Pageant* 7 (August 1952): 4–15.

KEY SUPPORTING MATERIALS

Arnold, H. H. *Global Mission*. New York: Harper and Brothers, 1949.
Arnold, H. H., and Ira C. Eaker. *Winged Warfare*. New York: Harper & Brothers, 1941.
Berg, A. Scott. *Lindbergh*. New York: G. P. Putnam's Sons, 1998.
Block, Maxine, ed. "De Seversky, Alexander P(rokofieff)." In *Current Biography: Who's News and Why 1941*, 222–23. New York: H. W. Wilson Company, 1941.
Boyne, Walter J., ed. *Air Warfare: An International Encyclopedia*, 2 vols. Santa Barbara, CA: ABC-CLIO, 2002.
Boyne, Walter J. *The Influence of Air Power upon History*. Gretna, LA: Pelican Publishing, 2003.
Budiansky, Stephen. *Air Power: The Men, Machines, and Ideas That Revolutionized War, From Kitty Hawk to Iraq*. New York: Penguin Books, 2004.
Byrd, Martha. *Chennault: Giving Wings to the Tiger*. Tuscaloosa: University of Alabama Press, 1987.
Chant, Christopher. *Pioneers of Aviation*. New York: Barnes & Noble Books, 2001.
Chennault, Claire Lee. *Pursuit Aviation*. Maxwell Field: Air Corps Tactical School, 1934.
———. *Way of a Fighter*. New York: Putnam's Sons, 1949.
Cochran, Jacqueline, and Marryann Bucknum Brinley. *Jackie Cochran: An Autobiography*. New York: Bantam Books, 1987.
Cole, Wayne S. *Charles A. Lindbergh and the Battle against American Intervention in World War II*. New York: Harcourt Brace Jovanovich, 1974.
Copp, DeWitt S. *A Few Great Captains: The Men and Events That Shaped the Development of U.S. Air Power*. Garden City, NY: Doubleday & Company, 1980.
Crouch, Tom D. *Wings: A History of Aviation from Kites to the Space Age*. Washington: Smithsonian National Air and Space Museum, 2003.
Daso, Dik Alan. *Hap Arnold and the Evolution of American Airpower*. Washington: Smithsonian Institution Press, 2000.
Davis, Burke. *The Billy Mitchell Story*. Philadelphia: Chilton Book Company, 1969.
Davis, Larry. *P-35*. Carrollton, TX: Squadron/Signal Publications, 1994.
Delear, Frank J. *Igor Sikorsky: His Three Careers in Aviation*. New York: Dodd, Mead & Company, 1976.
Dick, Ron. *American Eagles: A History of the United States Air Force*. Charlottesville, VA: Howell Press, 1997.
Doolittle, James H., with Carrol V. Glines. *I Could Never Be So Lucky Again*. New York: Bantam Books, 1992.
Douhet, Giulio. *The Command of the Air*. Translated by Dino Ferrari. Washington: Office of Air Force History, 1983.

Durkota, Alan, with Thomas Darcey and Victor Kulikov. *The Imperial Russian Air Service: Famous Pilots and Aircraft of World War One.* Mountain View, CA: Flying Machines Press, 1995.

Duz', P(etr) D(mitrievich). *Istorriia vozdukhoplavaniia i aviatsii v Rossii: period do 1914 g* [History of Aeronautics and Aviation in Russia: The Period before 1914]. Moscow: Nauka, 1995.

Earle, Edward Mead, ed. *Makers of Modern Strategy: Military Thought from Machiavelli to Hitler.* Princeton, NJ: Princeton University Press, 1943.

Fantel, Hans. "Major de Seversky's Ion-Propelled Aircraft." *Popular Mechanics* 22 (August 1964): 58–61, 194, 196.

Farber, James. "Major de Seversky—Engineer." *Popular Aviation* 17 (August 1935): 87–88, 116, 132.

Finne, K(onstantin) N. *Igor Sikorsky: The Russian Years.* Washington: Smithsonian Institution Press, 1987.

Franks, Norman. *Nieuport Aces of World War I.* Oxford, UK: Osprey Publishing, 2000.

Goddard, Esther C., and G. Edward Pendray, eds. *The Papers of Robert H. Goddard,* 3 vols. New York: McGraw-Hill, 1970.

Graf, H(arold) K. *The Russian Navy in War and Revolution: From 1914 up to 1918.* Honolulu: University Press of the Pacific, 2002

Grambow, Marion E., ed. "De Seversky, Maj. Alexander P." *Who's Who in World Aviation and Astronautics,* vol. 2. Washington: American Aviation Publications, 1958, 116–17.

Green, William, and Gordon Swanborough. *The Complete Book of Fighters: An Illustrated Encyclopedia of Every Fighter Aircraft Built and Flown.* New York: Barnes & Noble, 1998.

Greger, René. *The Russian Fleet 1914–1917.* Exeter, UK: Ian Allan, 1972.

Hallion, Richard P. *Strike from the Sky: The History of Battlefield Air Attack 1911–1945.* Washington: Smithsonian Institution Press, 1989.

Hart, B. H. Liddell. *Paris: Or, The Future of War.* New York: E. P. Dutton & Company, 1925.

Hughes, Thomas Parke. *Elmer Sperry: Inventor and Engineer.* Baltimore: Johns Hopkins University Press, 1971.

Huie, William Bradford. "What's Behind the Attacks on Seversky?" *American Mercury* 56 (February 1943): 155–65.

Hunsaker, Jerome Clarke. *Biographical Memoir of Elmer Ambrose Sperry.* Washington: National Academy of Sciences, 1955.

Hurley, Alfred T. *Billy Mitchell: Crusader for Air Power.* Bloomington: Indiana University Press, 1975.

Keogan, Joseph. *The Igor I. Sikorsky Aircraft Legacy.* Stratford, CT: Igor I. Sikorsky Archives, 2003.

Latiolais, Stanley P. "The Re-Evaluation of Douhet's, Mitchell's and de Seversky's Theories in Light of Modern Weapons." Thesis, Air University, Maxwell AFB, 1948.

Lee, Russell E. "Impact of *Victory through Air Power,* Part I: The Army Air Forces Reaction." *Air Power History* 40 (Summer 1993): 3–13.

Lehman, Milton. *This High Man: The Life of Robert H. Goddard*. New York: Farrar, Straus, 1963.

Levine, Isaac Don. *Mitchell: Pioneer of Air Power*. New York: Duell, Sloan and Pearce, 1943.

Longyard, William H., ed. "de Seversky, Alexander Prokofieff." *Who's Who in Aviation History: 500 Biographies*. Novato, CA: Presidio Press, 1994.

Lyons, Eugene. "Crusader." *Pageant* 5 (August 1948): 138–42.

———. "Seversky—Aviation's Versatile Genius." *American Legion Magazine* (December 1974): 16–19, 40–44.

———. "Seversky Says: One Air Force for the U.S.A." *Who: The Magazine about People* 1 (February 1942): 34–38.

MacIsaac, David. *Strategic Bombing in World War Two: The Story of the United States Strategic Bombing Survey*. New York: Garland Publishing, 1976.

Maloney, Edward T. *Sever the Sky: Evolution of Seversky Aircraft*. Corona De Mar, CA: Planes of Fame Publishers, 1979.

Maurer, Maurer. *Aviation in the U.S. Army, 1919–1939*. Washington: Office of the Air Force History, 1987.

McFadyen, A. D. "Major Alexander P. de Seversky." *Journal of the Patent Office Society* 19 (April 1937): 273–76.

McFarland, Stephen L. *American Pursuit of Precision Bombing, 1910–1945*. Washington: Smithsonian Institution Press, 1995.

Mitchell, William. *Skyways: A Book on Modern Aeronautics*. Philadelphia: J. B. Lippincott Company, 1930.

Morrow, John H., Jr. *The Great War in the Air: Military Aviation from 1909 to 1921*. Washington: Smithsonian Institute Press, 1993.

Neshkin, M. S., and V. M. Shabanov, comps. *Aviatori–kavaleri ordema Cv. Georgiia I Georgievskogo oruzhiia perioda Pervoi mirovoi voini 1914–1918 godov* [Aviators–Knights of the Order of St. George and the Golden Sword of St. George in the Period of the First World War 1914–1918]. Moscow: ROSSPEN, 2006.

Nevin, David. *Architects of Air Power*. Alexandria, VA: Time-Life Books, 1981.

Opdycke, Leonard E. *French Aeroplanes before the Great War*. Atglen, PA: Schiffer Publishing, 1999.

Paret, Peter, ed. *Makers of Modern Strategy: From Machiavelli to the Nuclear Age*. Princeton, NJ: Princeton University Press, 1986.

Parton, James. *"Air Force Spoken Here": General Ira Eaker and the Command of the Air*. Bethesda, MD: Adler & Adler Publishers, 1986.

Piszkiewicz, Dennis. *Wernher von Braun: The Man Who Sold the Moon*. Westport, CT: Praeger, 1998.

Riaboff, Alexander. *Gatchina Days*. Washington: Smithsonian Institution Press, 1986.

Rich, Doris L. *Jackie Cochran: Pilot in the Fastest Lane*. Gainesville: University Press of Florida, 2007.

Robertson, Bruce, ed. *Air Aces of the 1914–1918 War*. Fallbrook, CA: Aero Publishers, 1964.

Ross, Stewart Halsey. *Strategic Bombing by the United States in World War II: The Myths and the Facts*. Jefferson, NC: McFarland & Company, 2003.

Samson, Jack. *Chennault*. New York: Doubleday, 1987.

Sanger, Ray. *Nieuport Aircraft of World War One*. Wiltshire, UK: Crowood Press, 2002.

Sherry, Michael S. *The Rise of American Air Power: The Creation of Armageddon*. New Haven, CT: Yale University Press, 1987.

Sikorsky, Igor I. *The Story of the Winged-S: An Autobiography*. New York: Dodd, Mead & Company, 1944.

Stoff, Joshua. *Long Island Airports*. Charleston, SC: Arcadia Publishing, 2004.

Taylor, John W. R., ed. *Combat Aircraft of the World: From 1909 to the Present*. New York: G. P. Putnam's Sons, 1969.

Thomas, Bob. *Walt Disney: An American Original*. New York: Disney Editions, 1994.

*The United States Strategic Bombing Surveys: European War / Pacific War*. Maxwell AFB: Air University Press, 1987 (reprint).

Whiteley, John F. "Alexander de Seversky." *Aerospace Historian* 24 (Fall 1977): 156–57.

# Index

Advertising Club, 182

Aero Club, Imperial All-Russian, 3–4, 9, 13–14, 42

Aeromarine Plane and Motor Company. *See* Uppercu, Inglis M.

Aeromarine West Indies Airways. *See* Uppercu, Inglis M.

Aeronautical Chamber of Commerce, 91, 165

Aeronautics Branch, U.S. Commerce Department, 85

Agnew, Spiro T., 278

Air Corps, U.S. Army, 2, 20, 71, 85, 91, 104, 116, 158; Air Corps Tactical School of, 113, 198; bombsight tests by, 86–87; Experimental Engineering Division of, 88; First Provisional Bombardment Squadron of, 87; formation of, 64; GHQ Air Force of, 122, 146, 165, 180; in-flight refueling tests by, 72; Materiel Division of, 86–88, 118, 110–11, 126, 134, 144–47; 94th Pursuit Squadron of, 279; Procurement Board of, 111, 123, 130, 146, 160; and renamed, 183. *See also* Air Forces, U.S. Army

aircraft: Albatros C.Ia, 23–25; Albatros W.4, 32, 39; Avro Lancaster, 206; Beechcraft Model 17, 125, 214–15; Bell P-39, 133, 157; Bleriot Model XI, 3–5; Boeing B-17, 71, 122, 128, 175, 181, 188–89, 193, 198–99, 206; Boeing B-29, 175, 208–9, 229, 233, 235–36, 241–42, 251, 254; Boeing B-50, 251, 254; Boeing B-52, 72, 173; Boeing KC-135, 173; Boeing Model 314, 136; Boeing P-26, 72, 115; Brewster F2A, 131; Brunner-Winkle *Bird*, 90–92, 98, 102, 126; Christmas *Bullet*, 54-56; Consolidated BT-7, 111; Consolidated PB-2A, 118; Consolidated-Vultee B-24, 175, 180; Consolidated-Vultee (Convair) B-36, 173, 233–34, 251; Curtiss NC-4, 53; Curtiss P-36, 119, 123–24, 131, 133–34, 157, 201; Curtiss P-40, 133, 157, 188–89, 193, 201, 249; Curtiss 75, 115–19; de Havilland DH-4, 59, 72; Douglas B-18, 122, 193; Douglas DC-2, 122; Douglas SBD, 199; Douglas XB-19, 175, 182; Farman Model III, 9; Farman Model IV, 3–5, 8–11; Felixstowe F-5-L, 56; Focke Wulf Model 200, 186, 225; Fokker Model D, 39; Franco-British FBA, 14, 17–18, 26; Grigorovich M-9, 20–27, 32, 36; Grigorovich M-11, 27–28, 30, 32; Grigorovich M-15, 36–37; Grumman F4F, 131, 187, 193; Handley Page V/1500, 61–62; Hannevig *Sunrise*, 52; Hawker *Typhoon*, 189; Heinkel He-177, 225–26; Ilyushin Il-2, 228; Keystone LB-5, 87; Lockheed P-2, 214; Lockheed P-38, 133, 194; Lockheed P-80, 214; Martin B-10, 111, 193; Martin MB-2, 59, 61–62, 69, 75; Martin Model 130, 135; Messerschmitt

Council of People's Commissars, 43, 45
Cradle of Aviation Museum, 63, 95
Cragen, Cathryn, 205
Craig, Nancy, 257
Cuban Missile Crisis, 250, 268
Cummings, Florence, 258
Curtis, Edward, 224
Curtiss, Glenn H., 10
Curtiss Aeroplane and Motor Company,
 50–51, 85
Curtiss-Wright Corporation, 109, 116–19,
 123–24, 131, 133, 157, 201

Daley, Richard, 276
Daly, John J., 152
Damon, Ralph S., 167
Daso, Dik Alan, 192
Davies, Joseph E., 216
Davis, Dwight F., 76
Davis, James J., 81
DeBakey, Michael E., 265
Democratic Party, 195, 261
Defense Department, U.S., 244, 251, 255
De Soto Motor Corporation of Chrysler
 Motors, 105
D. H. Blair & Company, 275–76
Disney, Diane (daughter), 212–13
Disney, Lillian (wife), 212–13
Disney, Sharon (daughter), 212–13
Disney, Walter E., 203–6, 212
D'Olier, Franklin. See Strategic Bombing
 Survey, U.S.
Dolny, John R., 279–80
Doolittle, James H. "Jimmy," 90–92, 137,
 196, 244
Doran, John, 83
Douglas, Melvyn, 264
Douglas Aircraft Company, 116, 122–23, 138
Douhet, Giulio, 113, 179, 195
Doyle, Charles P. "Chuck," 279–80
Dudorov/Doudoroff, Boris, 34, 47, 49
Dukh Company, 9, 33, 44
Dulles, John Foster, 268
Duma, 5, 30
Dunkirk, air battle of, 170–72
Dunn, Paul C., 167

Eaker, Ira C., 139, 193–94, 199, 226, 278–79

Earhart, Amelia, 90, 92, 125, 215
Eastern Championship Races and Con-
 tests, 91
eastern front, 16, 44–45
Echols, Oliver P., 108, 221
Edo Aircraft Corporation, 97, 99, 101
Edward G. Budd Manufacturing Com-
 pany, 136
Eisenhower, Dwight D., 210, 234, 257,
 261–62
Endo, Saburo, 233
Ennis, Arthur I., 200
Environmental Protection Agency, 277
Esnault-Peterie, Robert, 4, 70
Essen, Nicholas Otto von, 8
Estoppey, Georges, 67, 73, 83, 86
Eynart, William, 104

Fairchild Aviation Corporation, 106–7,
 109–10
Farman, Henry, 4, 7, 14
Farrell, Thomas F. See Manhattan Project
Fat Man. See atomic bombs
Fechet, James E., 87–89
Fédération Aéronautique Internationale,
 3, 85, 104
Findlayson, James G., 217
Firestone, Harvey S., Jr., 222
First Russian Aerostatics Company. See
 Shchetinin Works Factory
Fitzpatrick, James V., 276–77
Fleet, Robert H., 70
Fokine, Michel, 84
Ford Motor Company, 172
Forrestal, James V., 255
Foy, Byron C., 105
Francis, Arlene, 264
Franco-British Aviation Company, 14
Friedman, Melvin. See Manhattan Project
Friedman, William S., 202
Friends of New Germany. See Griebl,
 Ignatz T.
Fuller, Frank W. 124–25, 134, 136
Fuller Paint Company, 124
Fundamental Laws, 5
Furness, Betty, 256, 268

Gaddis, John Lewis, 259

# About the Author

James K. Libbey is professor emeritus at Embry-Riddle Aeronautical University, where he taught American aviation history and Russian-American relations. A lifelong modeler who took flying lessons as a teenager, he completed a graduate course in aerospace studies directed by NASA at Miami University. His numerous publications include articles in such magazines as *Aviation History* and *American Aviation Historical Society Journal* as well as aviation-related entries in such reference works as *Air Warfare* and *Modern Encyclopedia of Russian and Soviet History*. Earning a doctorate at the University of Kentucky, he studied Russian history and diplomacy under Dr. Robert D. Warth and specialized in the political ties shared by the United States and Russia; Dr. George C. Herring directed his dissertation. Many of Libbey's articles, entries, and two of his five earlier books focus on biography such as *Alexander Gumberg and Soviet-American Relations*. Along with this background in life-writing, his aviation avocation and formal studies merged seamlessly to produce the story of Russian-American aviator Alexander P. de Seversky. The author resides in St. Augustine, Florida.